THE BEST OF
THE
SIERRA
NEVADA

Also by Gerald W. Olmsted

The Morrow Guide to Backcountry Europe
Fielding's Lewis and Clark Trail
The Best of the Pacific Coast

THE BEST OF
THE
SIERRA
NEVADA

• Lake Tahoe • Reno •
• Sequoia • King's Canyon •
• Yosemite •
• The Gold Country •

GERALD W. OLMSTED

CROWN PUBLISHERS, INC
New York

Grateful acknowledgment is made to the following for permission to reprint published material:

The San Francisco Chronicle: "Big Plans for Public Lands" © San Francisco Chronicle.

The University of California Press: excerpts from UP AND DOWN IN CALIFORNIA IN 1860–1864 by William H. Brewer, translated/edited by Francis Farquhar. Copyright 1949 by The Regents of the University of California. Excerpts from BIGLER'S CHRONICLE OF THE WEST: THE CONQUEST OF CALIFORNIA, DISCOVERY OF GOLD, AND MORMAN SETTLEMENT by Edwin Gudde. Copyright © 1962 by The Regents of the University of California.

Published by Crown Publishers, Inc., 201 East 50th Street, New York, New York 10022. Member of the Crown Publishing Group

CROWN is a trademark of Crown Publishers, Inc.

Manufactured in the United States of America

Cartography by Meridian Mapping, Berkeley, California; Barbara Jackson

Library of Congress Cataloging-in-Publication Data

Olmsted, Gerald W.
    The best of the Sierra Nevada / Gerald W. Olmstead.
        p.   cm.
    Includes bibliographical references and index.
    1. Sierra Nevada Mountains (Calif. and Nev.)—Description and
travel—Guide-books.   I. Title.
    F868.S5046   1991
    917.94'40453—dc20   90-22102
                                                                    CIP

ISBN 0-517-57467-5

10 9 8 7 6 5 4 3 2 1

First Edition

To Daniel, Suzanne, and Richard

CONTENTS

MAPS

ACKNOWLEDGMENTS

Thanks to the Mariposa Historical Society for permission to use excerpts from Horace Snow's wonderful *Dear Charlie Letters*. Thanks also to the University of California Press for permission to use segments of Erwin Gudde's *Bigler's Chronicle of the West: The Conquest of California, Discovery of Gold, and Mormon Settlement,* and of William Brewers' insightful work, *Up and Down California.* Tom Baxter's quote is courtesy of *The San Francisco Chronicle.*

Special thanks to my brother Franklin H. Olmsted (who has logged a hundred times more miles of Sierra trails than I) for reviewing parts of the manuscript.

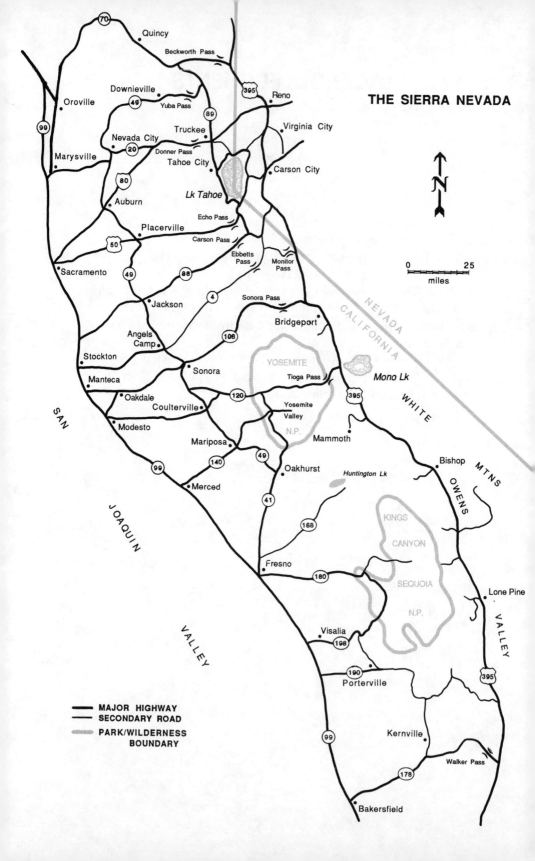

THE SIERRA NEVADA

N

0   25
miles

— MAJOR HIGHWAY
— SECONDARY ROAD
— PARK/WILDERNESS
    BOUNDARY

Quincy
Beckworth Pass
Downieville
Oroville
Yuba Pass
Reno
Virginia City
Truckee
Nevada City
Marysville
Donner Pass
Tahoe City
Carson City
Lk Tahoe
Auburn
Echo Pass
Placerville
Carson Pass
Ebbetts Pass
Monitor Pass
Sacramento
Jackson
Sonora Pass
Bridgeport
Angels Camp
Stockton
Sonora
Manteca
Tioga Pass
Mono Lk
Oakdale
Coulterville
Modesto
YOSEMITE
Yosemite Valley
N.P.
Mariposa
Mammoth
Oakhurst
Bishop
Merced
Huntington Lk
KINGS
CANYON
Fresno
SEQUOIA
N.P.
Lone Pine
Visalia
Porterville
Kernville
Walker Pass
Bakersfield

NEVADA
CALIFORNIA
WHITE
MTNS
OWENS
VALLEY
SAN
JOAQUIN
VALLEY

INTRODUCTION
The Range of Light

When viewed from the west, the Sierra Nevada hardly looks imposing. Motorists driving up and down the Central Valley barely give the range a second glance. But naturalist John Muir saw it differently. Plodding across the hot valley on his way to his first summer in the Sierra, Muir wrote:

> Along the eastern margin rises the mighty Sierra, miles in height, reposing like a smooth, cumulus cloud in the sunny sky, and so gloriously colored and so luminous, it seems to be not clothed with light, but whole composed of it, like the wall of some celestial city.

Muir had a premonition of the enchantment of the Sierra, and when he ventured into its bosom, he discovered the sublime:

> And after ten years spent in the heart of it, rejoicing and wondering, bathing in its glorious floods of light, seeing the sunbursts of morning among the icy peaks, the noonday radiance on the trees and rocks and snow, the flush of the alpenglow, and a thousand dashing waterfalls with their marvelous abundance of irised spray, it still seems to me above all others the Range of Light, the most divinely beautiful of all the mountain-chains I have ever seen.

Divinely beautiful indeed. The Sierra Nevada is the most massive mountain block in North America, an unbroken chain nearly as big as the Alps. It boasts the highest peak outside of Alaska, the largest (and perhaps the oldest) trees in the world, the highest and most spectacular waterfalls, the deepest valleys, the clearest lakes, even the greatest snow depths; yet at the same time the range has the finest mountain weather on earth. Ten million people a year find recreation here. As in the Alps, many resorts are high—sybarites come for the primary purpose of improving their suntan, golfers find that their drives go farther in the thin air. Boaters and fishermen bask on placid lakes, trout abound in unpolluted streams. Hikers and horse riders, and tourists too, find splendid scenery around every turn of the track. Deer, marmots, squirrels, even beaver are a common sight; birds abound.

But there is a ruggedness here too, which draws the active and the adventuresome. Clarence King, a geologist and one of the first to explore the range, wrote:

> I have never seen Nature when she seemed so little "Mother Nature" as in this place of rocks and snow, echoes and emptiness. It impresses me as the ruins of some bygone geological period, and no part of the present order, like a specimen of chaos which has defied the finishing hand of Time.

Today climbers search for vertical walls, skiers find runs as impressive as in Switzerland, kayakers and rafters challenge boisterous rivers. Wildness and solitude combine. I have hiked both the Sierra and the Alps and they are equally dazzling, but it is almost impossible to escape from people in the Alps and the summertime weather is often rotten. Here, it is a simple matter to lie in a sunlit meadow and be quite alone with your thoughts. The Rockies encompass a larger area and are almost as lofty, but they are essentially a conglomerate, each range separated by wide, often dry, wind-swept steppes. The Sierra Nevada, by contrast, is an unbroken monolith, the crest a series of ice-scoured peaks jabbing at the sky.

Except where the clouds coalesce around the highest peaks, the sun shines seven days out of ten and, at resorts such as Mammoth, summer rain is rare except for an occasional afternoon thundershower. Winter storms tend to come in bunches, with many sunny days in between. The air, as Mark Twain found, is terrific:

> Three months of camp life on Lake Tahoe would restore an Egyptian mummy to his pristine vigor, and give him an appetite like an alligator. [Having second thoughts, Twain added a qualifier.] I do not mean the oldest and driest mummies, of course, but the fresher ones.

Summer temperatures at Lake Tahoe fluctuate between a sleep-inducing fifty-degree morning low and a balmy seventy-five-degree afternoon high. Hillsides become an avalanche of flowers, as an early traveler observed:

> The Sierra spring is six or eights months long: one might almost say, indeed, in the words of the hymn, "There everlasting spring abides." Beginning in February or March, when the foothills blaze with the red gold of eschscholtzias, one might follow the spring upward, witnessing from week to week and meadow to meadow the perpetual miracle.

No wonder so many come to enjoy these splendors! But it was not always so. Sierra fauna watched silently while five phases of human history unfolded. The first was what I call the "time of indifference."

Juan Rodríguez Cabrillo, the fellow who gave us the name "Sierra Nevada," never saw these mountains. Given the times, of course, that wasn't surprising. Thirty years earlier his countryman, Garcí Ordóñez De Montalvo, had named a place he had never seen "California." Cabrillo at least had been in the neighborhood. In 1542, after pausing at San Diego Bay, he sailed north to the vicinity of Big Sur, where, spying some white-covered peaks, he entered in his journal the words "Sierra Nevada" ("Snowy Range"). Two hundred and thirty-four years elapsed, however, before a man of European stock actually saw that snowy range. Fray Pedro Font, standing near the foot of Mt. Diablo, looked across the San Joaquin Valley at some white peaks and assumed that, because the Coast Range seldom had snow, this must be what the navigator had had in mind. Cabrillo could not possibly have spied the Sierra from his tiny craft, of course, so—in a quirk of history—America's greatest mountain range was named sight unseen. Whatever the circumstances of its naming, however, there is only one "snowy range" so, at risk of being excised from the ranks of the Sierra Club, always use the singular, never the Sierras or Sierra Nevadas. And Sierra Nevada Mountains is, as wilderness activist David Brower pointed out, redundant: a bit like saying Saint San Francisco. Locals, incidentally, pronounce Nevada with a broad "a": Nev-ADD-a, not Nevadh-ah.

The existence of the Sierra was a matter of total indifference to the Californios (Spanish-Mexican settlers), who were busily establishing their vast cattle ranches and building their missions. For more than fifty years the few forays they made into the foothills were for the sole purpose of rounding up recalcitrant Indians, those who did not eagerly flock to the missions to receive the word of God. Jedidah Smith, the first American to visit what he called Mount Joseph (1827), trapped for a spell, then headed east. Joe Walker, a trapper in the employ of B. L. E. de Bonneville, crossed the Sierra in 1833, but his report was late in being published and Jed Smith's journals were not discovered for a hundred years. Thus, although Easterners knew about the Oregon-Washington Cascades from reading the journals of Lewis and Clark and about the Rockies from reading Zebulon Pike's, as the 1830s slipped into the 1840s, the Sierra Nevada remained *terra incognito.*

Then ensued the "time of annoyance," a twenty-five-year period when the Sierra was simply a "Chinese Wall" of mountain that got in people's way, what historian Oscar Lewis called "[A] bulky, awkward, and inconveniently high barrier shutting off [California] from the rest of the nation." Even today, between Lake Tahoe and the southern boundary at Walker Pass, a distance of two hundred and fifty miles, no road crosses the Sierra in winter. (Imagine what the Ohio Valley's commerce would be like if the Alleghenies were closed six months of the year.) Clarence King observed:

> For about three hundred miles it is a succession of sharp granite *aiguilles* and crags, rising cliff above cliff, precipice piled upon precipice, rock over rock, up against sky; the most gigantic moun-

tain-wall in America, culminating in a noble pile of Gothic-finished granite and enamel-like snow."

Adventurer John Charles Frémont learned the hard way what misery Sierra storms could bring. His party dallied; it was February before they started west across the range, and one member's diary is filled with comments like: "No longer any salt in the camp. This is awful," and "We had tonight an extraordinary dinner—pea soup, mule, and dog." Pioneers looked in horror as they faced mountains of unutterable age. After literally pulling and pushing their wagons nearly 8,000 feet into the sky, they found that nature had perversely thrust in their way the toughest barrier of all—snow. In this sense Cabrillo's name was well chosen; more snow has fallen here than almost any place else on earth—seventy-three *feet* in one winter. The tragedy of the Donner Party will be for all time a symbol of the harshness that can sometimes plague this country.

In the earliest white men's days, the Sierra wall stood in the way of those heading west, first settlers and then the hundred thousand or so '49ers who crossed over the Donner and Carson trails. But with the Bonanza discovery at Virginia City in 1859, the bulk of traffic—both people and supplies—went the other way, mostly over the Placerville Road. Wells Fargo's stages and the Pony Express followed the route, opening a chink in the barrier, but the Sierra was not truly tamed until the railroad tracks reached Truckee in 1868.

Meanwhile, a "time of exploitation" was in full swing. Both indifference and annoyance passed quite abruptly one January day in 1848 when an itinerant wheelwright, John Marshall, looked down into the gravel of the American River and saw gold. Within months, *terra incognito* became the most talked-about place on earth. With jackknife, pick, shovel, and pan, miners scoured a land that belonged to who knew whom. There were no laws—and no one to enforce them if there had been—and, of course, no land surveyor had ever driven a hub stake in the ground. It was finders, keepers: what historian Joseph Henry Jackson called "anybody's gold." These nineteenth-century Argonauts garnished the land with fanciful place names: Hottentot, Jawbone Ridge, Sawpit, Humbug Bar, Slumgullion, Shirttail

Canyon, Shorthair Creek. But they were exploitive of nature, as one observer wrote:

> The river, filled with flumes, dams, etc., and crowded with busy miners, was as much altered from its old appearance, as if an earthquake had frightened it from its propriety."

As the easy pickings became scarce, miners built flumes, whose waters washed away mountainsides, silting up farmlands in the valleys below. River bottoms were turned upside down, leaving mounds of debris and wounds on the land. Rapacious lumbermen began "mining" trees as old as the dinosaurs. The inventory seemed endless. Sheep herders took their flocks (John Muir called them "locusts on hoofs") to the high country, so denuding the grass that subsequent rains washed the soil away. Only now have the scars mostly healed. Later, great valleys were flooded by giant dams, the water sent to irrigate a parched Central Valley and to water city folk's lawns. But in time exploitation waned. Hydraulic mining was outlawed; controls on grazing were enacted. Lumbermen began replanting denuded forests and, after the rape of Hetch Hetchy (see Chapter 6), dam sites were chosen more carefully. By the 1870s, the Sierra was moving into the "time of conservation."

A common perception is that America's conservation movement began with the creation of Yellowstone Park in 1872, but the idea is much older. In 1815 Thomas Jefferson urged the federal government not to sell Virginia's Natural Bridge, writing:

> It is impossible for the emotions arising from the sublime to be felt beyond what they are here; so beautiful an arch. I view it in some degree as a public trust and would on no consideration permit the bridge to be injured, defaced or masked from public view.

Echoing the thought, Henry David Thoreau wrote, "A man is rich in proportion to the things he can afford to leave alone." Though gold was still on everyone's mind in California, men like Thomas Starr King, James Russell Lowell, and Frederick Law Olmsted began preaching the virtues of conservation. Olmsted, the noted landscape architect and designer of New York City's

Central Park, had come west to manage Frémont's Las Mariposas estate. Like everyone who had seen Yosemite, he was astonished by its beauty, and in 1864 he made a report to interested citizens that said in part:

> The first thing to be kept in mind is the preservation and maintenance as exactly as is possible of the natural scenery; the restriction, that is to say, with the narrowest limits consistent with the necessary accommodation of visitors, of all artificial constructions which would unnecessarily obscure, distort or distract from the dignity of the scenery.

California Senator John Conness carried the torch to Washington, introducing legislation ceding Yosemite Valley to the State of California but with an important caveat: "The premises shall be held for public use, resort, and recreation, and shall be inalienable for all time." Abraham Lincoln signed the bill on June 30, 1864, eight years before U.S. Grant established Yellowstone. A miracle it was. According to James Hutchings, who kept track of such things, exactly six hundred and fifty-three white men had been to Yosemite up to that time. Though many arguments followed about who should administer the park, and people have long debated what compromises should be made with Olmsted's "dignity of the scenery," the Yosemite legislation proved the harbinger. In time 10 million acres came under federal administration. Today, only a tiny fraction of Sierra land above 5,000 feet is under private ownership. For those of us who like to roam free, it is like being able to wander about an area the size of Massachusetts, Connecticut, and Rhode Island, confident of not having to worry about trespassing on someone's private property. The "time of recreation" had arrived.

But recreation got a rather inauspicious start. Historians George and Bliss Hinkle chronicled the adventures of the Sierra's favorite *demimondaine,* Lola Montez. In 1854 she and a party of ladies and gentlemen left Grass Valley for a pleasure jaunt near Donner Summit.

> Bedded down for the night on the bleak rocks, the countess had found their lumpy accommodations and the chilling gales of the pass too much for her hothouse sensibilities. She flew into a rage

and spent the night berating her "secretary" in assorted languages. By morning her outbursts were so threatening that [her host] took horse and fled hell-for-leather down the mountain toward home.

Others felt different: people began seeking out the invigorating climate of the high country. The first resort hotel was built, not in Yosemite Valley or at Tahoe, but on an obscure lake a dozen miles north of Truckee (Webber Lake). People came for the simple purpose of taking the air and enjoying the pleasures of what some called "strenuous discomfort." Mark Twain groused:

At the end of a week we adjourned to the Sierras on a fishing excursion, and spent several days in camp under snowy Castle Peak, and fished successfully for trout in a bright, miniature lake whose surface was between ten and eleven thousand feet above the level of the sea; cooling ourselves during the hot August noons by sitting on snowbanks ten feet deep, under whose sheltering edges *fine grass and dainty flowers flourished luxuriously;* and at night entertaining ourselves by almost freezing to death.

Multitudes followed. Today, 3½ million people a year visit Yosemite, 4 million Lake Tahoe. Winter is nearly as popular as summer—5 million lift tickets are sold at Sierra ski resorts, more than a million at Mammoth Mountain alone. Inyo National Forest, with virtually no timber, minerals, or grazing lands to administer, is almost entirely in the recreation business. Even the inaccessible spots that Muir and King found so tranquil have become so sought after that limits are now set on the number of people who can go there; a lottery is held to see who may climb Mount Whitney. Wilderness areas, stretching from Tahoe to Inyo, have been set aside. Access, even to backpackers, is controlled; pack stock is barred from some areas.

People of all ages and from all walks of life happily find that the Sierra is an egalitarian place. True, there is a perceived hierarchy of activities: fly-fishermen look aghast at "bait operators," sailors consider water-skiing rather gross, backpackers have no love for horsemen, and cross-country skiers believe that only they practice the "pure" sport. But people share lakes and streams and campgrounds too. Apparently they don't want things to be too primitive, as Tom Baxter of Sierra National Forest told a newspaper reporter:

The public wants more amenities. Demographics have changed. Instead of rural camp users who are happy staying two weeks and bathing in streams, we're getting more urban users. These are family groups in RVs who only stay a day or two and want to set up a TV dish and take showers while they're here.

Of course, not all share that value. Many of the wealthiest stay in crude cabins (or no cabins at all in one private estate at Lake Tahoe) for the chance to better enjoy this natural world.

For fifty years now, I have roamed these mountains, yet the list of places I hope to see someday keeps getting longer. I don't ever plan to scale El Capitan, but I find reading about the experiences of those who have fascinating. And the more early-day, first-hand accounts I find, the more I seek others. So, in part, the tour that follows is an in-place history lesson. Those pioneers who wrote of their adventure can lead us today. Enjoy what they saw, but go slowly, for as Muir said, "Life seems neither long nor short, and we take no more heed to save time or make haste than do the trees and stars."

THE ROUTE

We tour the Sierra following a zigzag route. Part One explores the emigrant passes (open all year) and Lake Tahoe. In Part Two we traverse the three trans-Sierra mining roads (closed in winter). Part Three covers Yosemite, Kings Canyon, and Sequoia National Parks and traverses the southern range over the Kern Plateau. The spectacular eastern escarpment to Reno and beyond is covered in Part Four. Finally, in Part Five we tour the gold fields of the western foothills.

RECREATIONAL FACILITIES

ACCOMMODATIONS

Which accommodations I have chosen to include needs explanation. In the large, popular areas and along the major highways, I have selected only the largest and/or best places to stay. In several of these areas I have included central booking offices. But even some rather trashy places are listed in the out-back areas, simply because that is all that is available. Accommodations in the cities, Reno, Carson City, and Bishop, of course, are open all year as are those at the resorts, Tahoe, Yosemite Valley, and Mammoth. Sequoia Park, however, has only limited accommodations during the winter. Hotels and motels near the ski resorts are almost always open both in winter and summer, but many shut down during the "shoulder" months. Many of the "rustic" resorts do not open until the Fourth of July and shut down shortly after Labor Day.

Accommodations are listed according to the character of the facility, which usually, but not always, reflects the price. These are:

✔✔✔ Luxury (and perceived luxury, such as Tahoe's casinos) accommodations.

✔✔ Historic hotels and bed-and-breakfast inns.

✔ Standard, motel-like accommodations and condominiums.

ΔΔ Rustic resorts, usually with housekeeping cottages. A few are so remote they have neither mail nor telephone service.

Δ Campgrounds. All but the most primitive charge a fee. The following generalities apply, but readers should consult any of the several excellent campground guides for more specific information.

State Parks Campgrounds have tables, piped water and usually flush toilets. Most have showers and can be reserved through Mistix, P.O. Box 85705, San Diego, CA 92138; (800) 446-7275.

National Parks Campgrounds have tables, piped water and usually flush toilets. Some campgrounds at Yosemite and Sequoia are reservable through Ticketron.

U.S. Forest Service Campgrounds vary widely. All have tables and at least vault toilets, but some do not have garbage pick up. Many have piped water and some have flush toilets. Sites at the more popular campgrounds can be reserved by calling (800) 283-CAMP.

County Campgrounds Facilities vary widely from primitive to those with RV hookups.

Pacific Gas & Electric (PG&E) Campgrounds All are first come, first served. Tables, firegrills, piped water, and vault toilets are provided. For specific information, call (415) 973-5552.

SCE Campground Camp Edison–Shaver Lake has tables, flush toilets, piped water, and electrical hookups. Sites can be reserved by writing P.O. Box 6, Shaver Lake, CA 93664 or by calling (209) 841-3444.

OTHER FACILITIES

• Restaurants, unless otherwise stated, are first-class, with an appropriate wine list.

§ Ski resorts ("snow-phone" numbers are listed), golf courses, and ranger stations are shown.

Ω Pack stations (summer phone numbers are listed) and commercial rafting outfitters are shown.

WILDERNESS PERMITS

Wilderness Permits can be obtained by mail by writing to the following locations:

U.S. Forest Service

Ansel Adams Wilderness West side entry, North Fork, CA 93643; (209) 877-2218. East side entry, P.O. Box 148, Mammoth Lakes, CA 93546.

Carson-Iceberg Wilderness 19777 Greenley Road, Sonora, CA 95370. (209) 532-3671.

Desolation Wilderness East side entry, 1052 Tata Lane, South Lake Tahoe, CA 95731. (916) 544-6420. West side entry, 100 Forni Road, Placerville, CA 95667. (916) 622-5061.

Dome Land Wilderness P.O. Box 6, Kernville, CA 93238. (619) 376-2294.

Emigrant Wilderness 19777 Greenley Road, Sonora, CA 95370. (209) 532-3671.

Golden Trout Wilderness East side entry, P.O. Box 8, Lone Pine, CA 93545. (619) 876-5542. West side entry, 32588 Highway 190, Porterville, CA 93257. (209) 539-2607.

Hoover Wilderness East side entry, Bridgeport, CA 93517. (619) 932-7070. South side entry, P.O. Box 10, Lee Vining, CA 93451. (619) 647-6525.

John Muir Wilderness West side entry, P.O. Box 300, Shaver Lake, CA 93664. (209) 841-3311. Northeast side entry, 798 North Main Street, Bishop, CA 93514. (619) 873-4207. Southeast side entry, P.O. Box 8, Lone Pine, CA 93545. (619) 876-5542.

Kaiser Wilderness P.O. Box 300, Shaver Lake, CA 93664. (209) 841-3311.

Mokelumne Wilderness North side entry, P.O. Box 1327, Jackson, CA 95642. (209) 223-1623. South side entry, P.O. Box 500, Hathaway Pines, CA 95223. (209) 795-1381.

Sequoia–Kings Canyon National Park

Three Rivers, CA 93271. (209) 565-3341.

Yosemite National Park

P.O. Box 577, Yosemite National Park, CA 95389. (209) 372-4461.

Part One

LAKE TAHOE
AND THE
EMIGRANT TRAILS

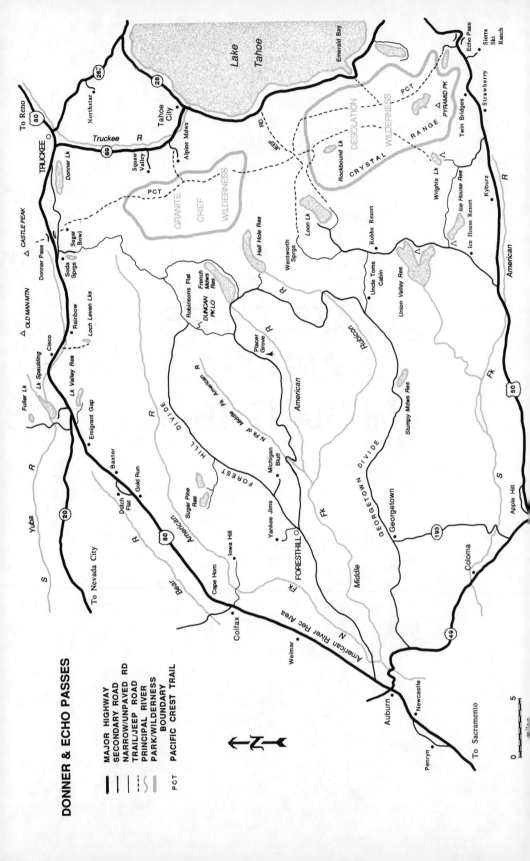

◀◀◀◀◀◆ 1 ◆▶▶▶▶▶

DONNER PASS

The Greatest Highway Yet Created for the March of Commerce and Civilization Around the Globe

Oh, California!
That's the place for me.
I'm off to Sacramento
With a washbowl on my knee.

The first wagon train to challenge the Sierra successfully came by way of the Truckee River and Donner Pass, so it seems fitting that we should begin our explorations by following their route. So, too, did the steel rails that forged the link between the Atlantic and Pacific come this way, as did America's first transcontinental motorway, the Lincoln Highway (U.S. 40). In an act of affirmation, the builders of Interstate 80, the only freeway to challenge the Sierra, chose the route as well, so we should perhaps excuse the hyperbole of a reporter for the *California Alta*, who, after riding the first train over the summit, waxed enthusiastic:

> John [the Chinese laborer] with his patient toil, directed by American energy and backed by American capital, has broken down the

great barrier at last and opened over it the greatest highway yet created for the march of commerce and civilization around the globe.

In the year of the great migration, 30,000 '49ers crossed Donner Pass. Now that many people do on a slow day. So much California history is entwined with this area that sagacious travelers will want to pause at numerous spots along the way to contemplate the monumental task of building the railroad, visit the sites of some emigrant travails, and also to examine some less heroic events associated with the growth of competitive skiing in the Far West. We'll go over "the Hill," as the railroaders call it, from the often scorchingly hot Sacramento Valley to the deserts of Nevada.

Theodore Judah, the fellow who deserves the most credit for the completion of the railroad, wrote:

> I have [discoved] of a practicable route from the city of Sacramento; upon the divide between the Bear River and the North Fork of the American, via Illinoistown, Dutch Flat and Summit Valley to the Truckee River which gives nearly a direct line to Washoe with maximum grades of 100 feet per mile—the elevation of the pass is 6,690 feet. It commands and will perform, the entire business of Nevada Territory, Washoe, and the silver mine region [and] reduces the time of passenger transit to and from the Washoe to 8½ hours.

Interestingly, it was the prospect of the lucrative freighting to the Washoe mines (Virginia City) that directed his energies, not the lofty idea of forging America's "Manifest Destiny."

THE FOOTHILLS

It is patently absurd, but the Sierra officially begins in the flatlands six miles northeast of Sacramento, where Interstates 80 and 880 merge. Skulduggery, of course. The Pacific Railroad Act appropriated $16,000 for each mile constructed in the flatlands and $48,000 for each mile in the mountains. The Big Four (see page 19) managed to move the mountains, employing no less a luminary than Professor J. D. Whitney (of Mt. Whitney fame) to do it. Improbably, looking at the rocks at nearby Arcade Creek, Whitney announced that they were the same color as those in the

Sierra. The coffers of the Central Pacific swelled by half a million dollars with that bit of chicanery. The foothills, as anyone can plainly see, start fifteen miles east at **Penryn,** where **Griffith's Quarry,** with its small **museum,** provides a nice picnic stop. Eighteen months elapsed before the railroad reached **Newcastle,** then construction ceased for nearly a year while the Big Four, beset by opposition from Wells Fargo Stage Line and the Pacific Mail Steamship Company, struggled to find money. **Auburn** high schoolers call their athletes the Hillmen (or Hillwomen), about the only link the town cares to make with the railroad (see Chapter 17). The little hamlet of **Weimar** was indeed named for the German republic but, unaccountably, is pronounced WEE-mar.

The Big Four

They seemed a perfect group to tackle one of the greatest construction feats in American history—four men with more or less common values, yet each with a special talent he could bring to the venture. Leland Stanford, the most well known, was a Sacramento grocer with a liking for politics, who had become modestly wealthy when a worthless mine he had acquired hit pay dirt. A large, deliberate person, he had a notably hesitant speech, unusual for a man who had helped to organize the Republican Party in California in 1862 and had served a two-year term as governor. Twenty years later (long before the Seventeenth Amendment changed the rules), he did what many rich men of that era did: he bought himself a seat in the U.S. Senate. Stanford was, in effect, the Big Four's front man, the one who turned the first spadefull of earth and who drove the last spike. He was once described as "having the ambition of an emperor and the spite of a peanut vendor."

Charles Crocker was the crudest of the four, a man historian Oscar Lewis described as "boastful, stubborn, tactless, vain, and completely lacking in the quality then described as low cunning." Charlie was the man to get things moving, the one who located the machinery and hired the men to build the railroad, and the one who wielded the whip that got it done. When asked what his epitaph should be, he unhesitating replied: "I built the Pacific Railroad." Mark Hopkins, at forty-eight, was the oldest. A thin, wiry man, he became the Scrooge-like accountant for the venture. "Uncle Mark," as he was called by the few who showed affection for him, had simple tastes and a miserly streak—traits his wife ignored shamelessly, building the most lavish mansion the West had ever seen. Colis Huntington was no doubt the shrewdest, a man variously described as "scrupulously dishonest" and "having no more soul than a shark." Setting up shop in New York, he purchased the equipment and managed affairs with Congress and the Eastern bankers. Shunning the limelight, he once growled at Stanford:

If you want to jubilate in driving the first spike go ahead and do it, I don't. These mountains look too ugly and I see too much work ahead. We may fail and I want to have as few people know it as we can. Any little nobody can drive the first spike, but there are many months of hard labor and unrest between the first and the last spike.

The railroad would make the four men enormously wealthy. When a proposed southern route threatened their transcontinental monopoly, they bought the company, merging the Central Pacific into the Southern Pacific, a firm that Californians came to call "The Octopus" because of its virtual stranglehold on the commerce of the state. Sacramento no longer seemed worthy of their presence—among other things, the streets were too dusty—so the four built mansions atop San Francisco's Nob Hill. None seemed fulfilled, however, as historians Watkins and Olmsted observed:

The corridors of their lives, like the halls and great rooms of the mansions they had erected—too ambitious to be called houses, too empty of meaning to be called homes—echoed with a certain hollowness; and the reverberations were the sound of irrelevance.

Their names are forever associated with great Western institutions, yet strangely, only Crocker left any sur-

viving offspring. Stanford's son died of typhoid at fifteen and got his name forever attached to a world-class university. But the Crocker Art Gallery in Sacramento was a gift of Charley's brother E. B. Crocker, and southern California's great Huntington Library and Art Gallery was built by Colis's nephew Henry (who married Colis's widow). The frugal Mark Hopkins would be appalled if he were to step into his legacy, the "Top of the Mark," a San Francisco watering hole that quite unabashedly charges dearly for the drinks they pour.

Shortly after the rails arrived at Illinoistown, Central Pacific officials felt obliged to change its name to **Colfax** (population 981; elevation 2,422 feet). Local residents might well wish they hadn't, since Schuyler Colfax turned out to be a scoundrel of the first order. As Speaker of the House and soon to be Ulysses Grant's Vice President, he taught the Big Four a bit about "creative railroad financing." His idea, as practiced at Crédit Mobilier, was to hire yourself to build the railroad, paying yourself handsomely with government money for the bother. Colfax got caught and was forced off Grant's reelection ticket; the Big Four didn't get caught and grew richer by $62 million. Today such dubious practices are confined mostly to the housing and defense contracting industries. Colfax has a pleasant, two-block-long commercial center, which boasts two saloons and a perfect example of an old-time general store, stocked with stationery, knitting yarn, magazines, toiletries, and inexpensive clothes. Amtrak's *California Zephyr* stops out front.

This a splendid place to gain an understanding of the dominate landform of the lower Sierra. The intrepid Frank Leslie came west on the Overland Train and wrote about the principal landmark here:

> Now comes Cape Horn, the jutting promontory that frowns at the head of the Great American River Canyon. The train swings round on a dizzily narrow grade, with a wall of rock towering above and the almost vertical side of the abyss sweeping down to the narrow bed of the river. Between its walls there seems just space enough for the narrow stream to slide and no more—not a trail wide enough for a jackrabbit on either side.

Though the train no longer stops at Cape Horn, you can get an idea of what Leslie saw by taking the twisty little Iowa Hill Road, which plunges three miles down to the **Auburn River Recreation Area.** Picnicking is especially nice in midwinter, because the North Fork canyon runs due north and south; the sun penetrates the gorge at midday. This is also a put-in for a fifteen-mile white-water adventure.

DUTCH FLAT • Population 250; elevation 3,114 feet

At **Gold Run,** Interstate 80 traverses the base of a red, gravelly bluff. Nature didn't make the bluff, men did—by washing away the hillside with giant streams of water. Prior to the uplifting of the Sierra, an ancient stream ran crosswise to the highway here, and its gravels were laced with gold. Not enough, apparently, for some years ago I came upon an abandoned mine building near here containing some soggy letters, penned in 1908 by an Englishman, Arthur Pease. "My dear Stewart," he wrote in impeccable script on stationery from the Waldorf-Astoria (two separate hotels in those days). Civilities over, he went on to castigate his partner for: (a) spending too much money; (b) providing wrong information which embarrassed him in meetings with San Francisco's moguls (L. G. Balfor was one); and (c) not finding enough gold. Old timers say there is still plenty by the side of the freeway, but it can't be mined because the railroad goes over the top of the gravel. A similar cliff graces the north side of the tracks.

Joseph Doranbach was from Holland, everyone thought, so they named the mining camp after his native land. He wasn't, but **Dutch Flat** endures. Downtown comprises a general store and a gorgeous, hundred-year-old hotel, now closed, which may become a museum. White, Gold-Rush-era houses are sprinkled about; in winter smoke curls from a couple of dozen chimneys. On a warm July day in 1860, Theodore Judah sat down with the town druggist, Dr. Daniel Strong, to lay out his plan. Strong was impressed, and the two set out to find subscribers for stock in the company they formed. San Francisco nabobs weren't interested, but the two found their way to Leland Stanford and the Pacific Railroad was born. All things considered, they should have found someone else, as we will see. Competitors called it the "Dutch Flat swindle," insisting that the Big Four had no intention of building beyond the point where the rails would connect with their hugely profitable Dutch Flat and Donner Lake Wagon Road. They did, and the swindle grew too big for this tiny town.

A rusty iron gate stands beside the old road at **Baxter** (elevation 3,886 feet). It seems incredible, considering today's traffic, but until 1931 that gate remained closed all winter. People going east took the train. Auburn Ski Club takes credit for getting it opened. Having plowed a single lane to a ski jump they had built five miles up the road, they loaded some influential state legislators into fifty-six automobiles and drove them to the competition. Another thousand followed. The wine flowed freely and everybody had good fun, but come time to go home there was no place to turn around. The lawmakers got the point, voting funds to keep Highway 40 open, a task that hasn't always been easy. Interstate 80, as it is now called, was touted as the Sierra's "all-weather" highway. It seemed fitting, therefore, to have a formal opening ceremony at Donner Summit, but on the appointed day nobody, not even Governor Pat Brown, showed up. The road was closed by a blizzard.

Even when heading east, there is a special reason to backtrack slightly to the **Emigrant Gap Viewpoint,** located along the westbound lanes of Interstate 80. Washington Ridge, which you see to the northwest, is a perfect illustration of the general character of the Sierra. Thomas Jefferson talked of a "Pacific Slope," but he had no idea how descriptive that phrase would be. That the Sierra is a tilted block, with the shallow gradient sloping west, is perfectly obvious here. This is the beginning of the high country, and the difference is dramatic. Glaciers goughed out the U-shaped canyon you see higher up. Relatively flat land borders the river, providing room for resorts and mountain homes. Throughout our Sierra explorations, we will find that most of the fun places are in the higher country, where the rocks and soil may be scaberous but the glaciers left us intriguing, more or less gentle places to linger in and enjoy. By contrast, as Frank Leslie said, there is scarcely room for a jackrabbit in the stream-cut Yuba River valley you see heading almost due north. Interestingly, over the eons, the Yuba kept eating its way back toward the valley of the Bear River directly below, eventually capturing its waters. Geologists call the act "stream piracy."

Pioneers found Emigrant Gap to be a memorable spot. After

using ropes to winch their wagons down to Bear Valley, they double-teamed them up to Washington Ridge, where the road, such as it was, struggled down to the promised land. Another interesting event occurred here in 1952 when passengers on the crack streamliner *City of San Francisco* found themselves in a bit of a fix. It had been snowing heavily and the engineer, emerging from a short tunnel, plowed into an avalanche. Backing up, he ran into another. Two rotary plows (steam in those days) were sent out. One went over the bank, killing the engineer. Fuel ran out, and passengers huddled in the cold for three days while skiers and dog sledders struggled to bring in supplies. Happily, all survived. A photo shows train number 101 dead in its tracks. Drifted snow rises to the top of the cab, a tiny hole reveals the windshield, and icicles dangle from the headlight cowling.

Shaped somewhat like Yosemite's Half Dome, Old Man Mountain rises nine miles due east of here, hiding one of the oddest places in the Sierra, a town called Summit City. In 1860 Henry Hartley found veins of quartz in the "old man's" eastern flank that yielded "color." Argonauts thronged the area; at one time there were several hundred houses, countless tents, a dozen hurdy-gurdys, two breweries, and a newspaper. Today, not a rusty nail marks the spot. Over the years, dozens of reservoirs have been built in this part of the Sierra, first by the mining and fluming companies, later by the utilities. All are popular recreation sites. Pacific Gas & Electric has camping at **Lake Spaulding** and **Lake Valley Reservoir.** The Forest Service has campsites at **Fuller** and **Carr Lakes** and atop **Grouse Ridge** (great view). **Grouse Lakes Basin** is laced with trails leading to a dozen or more natural lakes and ponds that make excellent overnight backpack destinations.

Recreational Facilities

△ **Forest Service Campgrounds** 3 campgrounds, 22 sites.

△ **PG&E Campgrounds** 2 campgrounds, 42 sites.

• **Monte Vista Inn** Restaurant and bar near Gold Run. (916) 389-2333.

§ **Eagle Mountain Lodge** Nordic skiing and mountain bicycling center. (916) 389-2254.

YUBA BOTTOMS

Old Highway 40, still extant from Cisco Grove to Truckee, wanders through an area the emigrants called Yuba Bottoms (elevation 5,800 feet), a perfectly respectable name. But it didn't stick. The collection of 1930s resort communities lining the Yuba's banks now go by their individual names: Cisco Grove, Big Bend, Rainbow, Plavada, and Kingvale. For nearly three years, **Cisco,** located on the hillside above the highway, was the most important place on "the Hill," the construction headquarters for the thousands of laborers who were struggling to push the tracks over the summit. From here, wagons (sleds in the winter) hauled tons of supplies and even a locomotive over the top so that construction could proceed from both sides. Today nothing remains of the town.

Though largely unheralded, this area was also important to early competitive skiing. Legendary jumpers from the "old country," Hans Halvorsen, Sig Vettestad, Roy Mikkelsen, and Otto Lirsch, came to compete on the Auburn Ski Club's hills, which had been removed here in 1932. I watched the competition in later years and found it thrilling, but for some reason, ski jumping never caught on in California. Alpine skiing did, of course. Most people credit the 1960 Olympics at Squaw Valley for popularizing the sport, but twenty-one years earlier, the world-championship F.I.S. *(Federation International de Ski)* giant slalom race was held on Mount McIntosh, just above the railroad tracks. Much of this lore is explained at the **Western America Ski Sport Museum,** located at the Boreal ski resort near Donner Summit.

Elizabeth Yuba Murphy came into the world at **Big Bend,** the first child of overland emigrants to be born in California. Her parents, who had come west with the Stevens party in 1844, managed to get their wagons this far before being trapped by a snowstorm. Not a trace of the hastily built cabin remains, nor is there a marker showing where Charley Stanton died two years later. Stanton, a bachelor traveling with the Donner Party, had gone ahead for help. He could well have stayed and lived the good life, but he returned with relief supplies just as the first snows hit. While leading some of the survivors to safety, another storm caught him here. Four days before Christmas, weary from fatigue and hunger, his spirits gave out. As his comrades struggled on, Charley sat by the fire, resignedly smoking his pipe, never to be seen again. A small **museum** is located at the Big Bend Ranger Station. Technical climbers enjoy the vertical granite across the road. Recently, runners and bicyclists have discovered the benefits of high-altitude training on this quiet paved road.

Backpackers and day hikers take the five-mile (round-trip) trail to **Loch Leven Lakes,** five rocky tarns on the ridge above the railroad. Although the basin is as pretty as any backcountry place in the Sierra, it is not designated as a "Wilderness Area" and thus there is no restriction on the number of people that are allowed to camp there at any one time. Does the area suffer from the dire consequences of overuse, as current thinking would have it? The campsites are clean as a whistle. Those who set wilderness policy might well study this phenomenon to see if perhaps access quotas elsewhere are too strict.

"Recommended by Duncan Hines" was a coveted honor in the 1930s when Rainbow Lodge was built. Before cake mix, the great man toured the country advising travelers where to eat, and he liked this place a lot. Years ago I happened to be at the bar when owner Herstle Jones asked if I would help with a chore. The sheriff, it seems, had called to say he was going to make an inspection, and Herstle needed help getting the slot machines down to the basement. Whether the sheriff was rewarded for his thoughtfulness in calling ahead, I do not know.

Recreational Facilities

✔✔ **Royal Gorge's Rainbow Lodge** Historic 30-room hotel, restaurant, and bar. Soda Springs, CA 95278. (916) 426-3871.

△ **Forest Service Campgrounds** 3 campgrounds along the Yuba River, 80 sites.

SUMMIT VALLEY

Soda Springs (elevation 6,780 feet) functions as the commercial center for several vacation-home communities and a number of ski resorts. Modern-day alpine skiing got started at Soda Springs, where a rope tow was built in the mid 1930s. Three chairs now service a small hill, used primarily on weekends.

Boreal, a huge complex along the interstate, is popular with beginning and intermediate skiers. Night skiing is offered. **Donner Ski Ranch,** located at the old highway summit, has a nice family atmosphere, a spectacular view of Donner Lake, and more challenging slopes.

But it is the venerable **Sugar Bowl,** California's first really first-class ski resort, that is the best in the area, and a longtime favorite of San Francisco's moneyed crowd. In 1939 almost no one knew how to build a chairlift. Sun Valley had the first; Sugar Bowl wanted the second. Moore Dry Dock Company in Oakland installed the contraption on Mount Disney (Walt Disney was an investor). It performed admirably for fifteen years, even though the bull-wheels, mounted on giant ramps, had to be relocated every time it snowed. For a dozen years this was *the* place to ski in California, but one spring day a moneyed New York man, Alexander Cushing, while sitting on the Bowl's sunny deck, chanced upon a man who had a mountain. Alex and Wayne Poulsen got together and started Squaw Valley, which quickly stole Sugar Bowl's glamor. Though the Bowl is no longer a stop for world-class racers, a lot of people like it just as it is. A fellow on a lift one day asked me if skiers still yodel from the tops of the peaks hereabouts. The answer is no, but the image lingers. It snows so much here that there never has been plowed road to the hotel; for years affluent guests rode in an army weasel, and the rest of us walked in on skis. Now everybody takes a gondola.

Royal Gorge claims to be the largest cross-country skiing resort in the United States, operating a new day lodge at the trailhead and a wilderness lodge (built in the 1930s as a Boy Scout camp) a couple of miles out in the snow. Guests ski in and enjoy a day or two of exercise coupled with fancy meals, French wine, and a relaxing trip to the hot tub. Guests help out with the chores at the Sierra Club's **Clair Tappaan Lodge,** but also ski on groomed trails. The club also owns four wilderness huts, located along the Pacific Crest Trail. **Peter Grubb Hut** is two miles north of the interstate in a bowl behind Castle Peak. **Benson Hut,** south of the Sugar Bowl, is a four-mile trek from the old summit. Skiers can continue along the Sierra spine, stopping at **Bradley Hut** behind Alpine Meadows and **Ludlow Hut** at the north end of the Desolation Wilderness. The unstaffed huts, which sleep about fifteen, are for winter use but are primitive—

you bring your own food and sleeping bag. The **Pacific Crest Trail** crosses Interstate 80 near the Boreal ski complex, where the Forest Service has built a trailhead parking area. Highly recommended is the half-mile **Glacier Meadow Loop Trail,** which gives those with little time a snapshot view of the high Sierra. Peakbaggers head for **Castle Peak** (elevation 9,103 feet), the most prominent landmark in the area.

Recreational Facilities

🗸🗸 **Sugar Bowl** Full-service winter hotel and downhill skiing resort. 7 lifts, 1,500 foot vertical. P.O. Box 5, Norden, CA 95724. (916) 426-3651. Snow phone (916) 426-3847.

ΔΔ **Serene Lakes Lodge** Restaurant, bar, and lakeside cabins. Baker Ranch Rd., Soda Springs, CA 95728. (916) 426-3397.

ΔΔ **Donner Spitz Hütte** *Bunk*-and-breakfast inn. Some private rooms. P.O. Box 8, Norden, CA 95724. (916) 426-9108.

ΔΔ **Clair Tappaan Lodge** Large, 140-bed, dormitory-style lodge, open to Sierra Club members and guests. Also operates the four wilderness huts. P.O. Box 36, Norden, CA 95724. (916) 426-3632.

§ **Alpine Skills Institute** Instruction in telemark and grand rondonnée skiing. Off-piste ski tours. P.O. Box 8, Norden, CA 95724. (916) 426-9108.

§ **Boreal** 10 lifts, 600 feet vertical. 36-room motel. P.O. Box 39, Truckee, CA 95734. (916) 426-3663.

§ **Donner Ski Ranch** 4 lifts, 720 foot vertical. Condo rentals. P.O. Box 66, Norden, CA 95724. (916) 426-3635.

§ **Royal Gorge** Nordic ski resort and wilderness lodge. P.O. Box 178, Soda Springs, CA 95728. (916) 426-3871.

§ **Soda Springs Ski Area** 4 lifts, 550 feet vertical. P.O. Box 39, Truckee, CA 95734 (916) 426-3663.

DONNER SUMMIT

Old Donner Pass (elevation 7,135 feet), located on Old Highway 40, marks the culminating event in the drama of the construction of the Transcontinental Railroad. For a sense of those times, drive (or ski in winter) a quarter mile past the summit to **Donner View Point,** one of the country's most famous belvederes. The tracks here cross a gully on what is now called the Chinese Wall, a massive structure as strong as the day the stones were laid down—a wonderful monument to the fortitude of those who built it (see below). Drilling the summit tunnel proved to be a Herculean task, made more difficult by the intransigence of the bosses. Charley Crocker boasted that he was directing the largest single force of workmen ever assembled in the country's history, but they had to make do with black powder; he was afraid to use nitroglycerine. The tunnel was finally holed through in September 1867, and the tracks were completed to Truckee in the following spring, less than five years after the first shovelful of earth was turned in Sacramento. (Interstate 80, by contrast, was twenty years abuilding.) As you gaze at the railroad tracks disappearing into the haze of Truckee, it is interesting to consider a rather startling fact, one that gives more meaning to the accomplishment. The railroad follows the Truckee River, which after a few dozen miles debauches into the Nevada desert, beyond which hardly a mountain blocks the way from there to the Missouri River (the connecting Union Pacific crosses the Rockies on a wide, level plain). Not a forest beautifies the tracks for the next sixteen hundred and five miles.

They Built the Wall of China

Originally they came to work the mines, perhaps 5,000 Asians who banded together to take gold from land that white people thought worthless. And for awhile they made a good living at it. Still, when labor was needed to build the railroad, Superintendent J. H. Strobridge was at best skeptical:

The weight of the average adult Chinese was probably less than a hundred and ten pounds; to attempt to build a railroad over the Sierra with these rice-eating weaklings was rank nonsense.

Whether he meant it as a joke, I don't know, but Strobridge went on to insist that they couldn't do rock work
because they weren't "Masons." Charles Crocker simply
retorted: "Well, they built the wall of China, didn't
they?" Charlie was right, of course, and at the height of
construction, 12,000 were engaged in the Herculean
task of pushing the tracks across these mountains. And
what a job they did. Mark Twain wrote:

They are quiet, peaceable, tractable, free from
drunkenness, and they are as industrious as the day is
long. A disorderly Chinaman is rare, and a lazy one
does not exist.

Chief Engineer Montague said of them:

When the Chinese came off the road, they filled their
little tubs made from powder kegs, took a hot sponge
bath, and changed clothes before their evening meal.
The menu included dried oysters, abalone and cuttle-
fish, dried bamboo sprouts and mushrooms, five kinds
of vegetables, port, poultry, vermicelli, rice, salted
cabbage, dried seaweed, sweet rice crackers, sugar,
four kinds of dried fruit, Chinese bacon, peanut oil,
and tea.

The fare of the Caucasian laborer consisted of beef,
beans, bread, butter, and potatoes.
    The famous photograph depicting the driving of the
last spike at Promontory Point, Utah, shows any number
of bankers, barons, and politicians, even Irish laborers—
but not a single Chinese.

Donner Peak, rising above the tracks, isn't that impressive and
sadly hides another, even less inspiring peak, Mount Judah,
about the only thing our hero got for his troubles. Judah, the man
who conceived the railroad, who surveyed the route, and who
lobbied Washington to get the money, never saw his dream
completed. The Big Four found it convenient to cut him out.
Judah headed for Washington to try to raise money to buy them
out, but bad luck haunted his corner. While crossing the Isthmus
of Panama he contracted the curse of that awful place, yellow
fever, and died, a few weeks shy of his thirty-eighth birthday.

Looking about, it seems impossible that anyone could have gotten wagons to the top of this pass. Moses Schallenberger, a member of the Stevens party of 1844, remembered the ordeal:

> After a tedious search they found a rift in the rock, just about wide enough to allow one ox to pass at a time. Removing the yokes from the cattle, they managed to get them one by one through this chasm to the top of the rock. There the yokes were replaced, chains were fastened to the tongues of the wagons, and carried to the top of the rock, where the cattle were hitched to them. Then the men lifted at the wagons, while the cattle pulled at the chains, and by this ingenious device the vehicles were all, one by one, got across the barrier.

Listen today and you might hear metallic clattering, clanking noises. No, not the sound of ox-team chains pulling covered wagons over the top. It's the rattle of a mountaineer's gear, chocks, pitons, and carabiniers dangling from his belt. The almost vertical rock face makes this one of the most popular climbing spots in the Sierra.

TRUCKEE/DONNER LAKE • Population 2,389—5,000 in summer; elevation 5,820 feet

Strangely, early diarists had little good to say about beautiful **Donner Lake,** perhaps because their minds were dulled by months on the trail and they felt a hollow feeling of foreboding at having to face the barrier looming up in the west. Long-time area residents George and Bliss Hinkle sensed this dichotomy:

> Seen from above, the long vale with its bright waters inevitably arouses anticipation and a sense of imminence. Seen from below, the lake's waters are often leaden and robbed of buoyance by the enclosing walls of the trough in which they lie. The overshadowing western crags bring an early dusk, and they present a cold gray face against the dawn.

Wakeman Bryarly, a 49er, felt otherwise:

> I went on to the lake & was fully repaid for my trouble, for it was beautiful, fresh, pure, clear water, with a gravelly bottom and

sandy beach. It was about 2 miles long, three-quarters wide &
confined between three mountains on three sides, which arose
immediately from its edge.

In 1887, *Frank Leslie's Illustrated Newspaper* waxed:

One of the most vivid pictures of all our journey is this of Donner
Lake, with its weird, tragic story clinging around it, lying white
and shining between the dark forests and the snow peaks under
the quiet stars.

Today, it is a scene of happiness: a slowly trolling fisherman, an
athletic-looking wind surfer, a water skier kicking up a spray. But
it is also the site of tragedy, and that adds the other dimension to
this curious place. **Donner Memorial State Park** has a fine
museum which explains a bit of what happened (see below).

The Star-Crossed Donner Party

They were not the first to come this way; 400 or 500
had preceded them this summer of 1846. But the fates
would make this loosely bound group of emigrants famous because they always seemed to be traveling under
a cloud: a hapless bunch who met bad luck at every turn
of the road. Most had planned to go to Oregon until
they chanced upon the villian of this story, Lansford
Hasting, who had published a book titled *The Emigrants' Guide to Oregon and California.* Describing California as a land of milk and honey, he advised:

Those who go to California travel from Fort Hall
w.s.w. about fifteen days to the northern pass in the
California mountains, thence three days to the Sacramento.

Hastings himself had spent four months in the effort,
traveling by horse with no wagons to slow him down.
The Donners must have known the folly of their decision
when they found themselves ensnared in a cottonwood-
choked canyon near the Great Salt Lake. In the desert,
two men got in a fight; one was killed, the other (James
Reed) ostracized. October found them at Truckee

Meadows (present-day Reno), barely able to go forward. They did—for thirty miles—but an early snow closed the trap. Better-led and better-equipped people would have survived the misfortune—two years earlier, seventeen-year-old Moses Schallenberger had spent the winter here, and he was all alone.

My life was more miserable than I can describe; the daily struggle for life and the uncertainty under which I labored, were very wearing. Fortunately, I had plenty of books. I used often to read aloud, for I longed for some sound to break the oppressive stillness.

But he had traps and knew how to use them:

To my great delight I found in one, a starved coyote. I soon had his hide off and his flesh roasted in a Dutch oven. I ate this meat, but it was horrible. I next tried boiling him, but it did not improve the flavor. I cooked him in every possible manner my imagination, spurred by hunger, could suggest, but could not get him into a condition where he could be eaten without revolting my stomach. [Afterward] I caught, on average, a fox in two days, (though entirely devoid of fat, delicious) and every now and then a coyote [which] I carefully hung up on the north side of the cabin, but I never got hungry enough to eat one of them again.

Members of the Donner party got hungry enough to eat each other.

Even in adversity, they couldn't seem to cooperate. The Breen family occupied Schallenberger's cabin and the Murphys built a lean-to against a nearby flat-sided granite boulder (the fire marks are still visible), but the Donners aloofly stayed at Alder Creek, seven miles northeast. The families refused to share what food they had, and on one occasion, when an ox died, a great haggle ensued over the price of the carcass. When day broke on December 4, the terrified travelers found seven feet of snow on the ground, prompting the organization of a party to snowshoe over the pass for help. Seventeen of what came to be known as the "Forlorn Hope" party started out; two turned back and the rest wished they had. Storms caught them bivouacked in the high country where ten perished; the others survived only by roasting and eating the livers and hearts of their comrades.

Those who stayed behind seldom left their cabins, preferring to boil the hides of oxen rather than try to hunt or fish (Donner Lake doesn't often freeze, but it might have that year). Patrick Breen's diary tells a pathetic story:

Weds 27th Began to snow yesterday & still continues to sleet thawing little. Mrs. Keyber here this morning Lewis Suitor she says died three days ago Keysburg sick & Lanthrom lyin in bed the whole of his time dont have fire enough to cook their hides.

One by one they died. A rescue party organized by Caleb Greenwood arrived in mid-February with enough food to encourage the stronger to push on to Sutter's Fort. Several perished en route. Breen's diary continues:

Frid 26th Mrs Murphy said here yesterday that thought she would commence on Milt. & eat him. I dont that she has done so yet, it is distressing. The Donnos told the California folks that they commenced to eat the dead people 4 days ago, if they did not succeed that day or next in finding their cattle then under ten or twelve feet of snow.

Another relief party, led by James Reed (the same James Reed who had been ostracized for the shooting incident in the desert), arrived on the first of March, only to discover a ghastly scene of rotting animals and excrement-covered hovels. Tamsen Donner sent her children on with Reed, but insisted that she would stay with her dying husband. A third relief party found survivors sitting in a stupor among half-eaten human remains. A few more were taken to safety. Finally, in mid-April a fourth party reached the Alder Creek camp only to discover that the sole survivor, Lewis Keseberg, had, they suspected, murdered Tamsen Donner. Two years later, Wakeman Bryarly said what we all feel today:

To look upon these sad monuments harrows up every sympathy of the heart & soul, & you almost hold your

breath to listen for some mournful sound from these blackened, dismal, funeral piles, telling you of their many sufferings & calling upon you for bread, bread.

The base of the emigrant statue at the state park is twenty-two feet above the ground, symbolizing the depth of the snow that awful winter. Yet that was unusual, for you have now moved into the Sierra's rain shadow. Normally, only a quarter as much snow falls here as at the Sugar Bowl, eight miles away. But the winter temperature here is ten degrees colder, on average (minus 45°F in 1937). The chamber of commerce, however, brags that the sun shines 300 days a year.

Truckee began life by serving three industries: railroading, logging, and ice harvesting. The sawmill is now slated to close, and mechanical refrigeration doomed the ice business (a wag blamed its demise on their having lost the formula), but railroading still plays a modest role. Before the skiing boom, all the local businesses were located on Commercial Row. Goodfellows and Brown's Cafe served down-home food. The barber was on the second floor; you had a wonderful mountain view while attending to tonsorial duties. Saloons were dark and smelled like stale beer. They still do, but all save the tourist-oriented merchants have fled to outlying shopping centers. Now Commercial Row is a string of boutiques. The downtown still has an Old West flavor with brick-sided, false-front buildings; covered sidewalks face the railroad tracks. Lace-windowed restaurants serving *California cuisine* beckon—zorie-shod vacationers in pedal-pushers wander along, eating ice cream cones or munching popcorn. Activity picks up when the Amtrak stops out front, for Truckee is a bit like Jasper or Banff, Alberta, a railroad town with a mountainy, let's-have-fun sort of exuberance.

Visitors interested in further tracing the route of the emigrants should drive three miles north on Highway 89 to the **Alder Creek** campsite of George and Tamsen Donner. To avoid the treacherous narrow canyon of the Truckee, most emigrants took a detour which you can follow by driving the backroads to Verdi, Nevada. This mostly gentle, sagebrushy country boasts three reservoirs, **Prosser, Stampede,** and **Boca.** Boat fisherman find these, together with **Martis Reservoir,** productive. The latter has been stocked with the threatened Lahontan cutthroat trout, so anglers use artificial barbless lures only, and the creel limit is zero.

Two vacation-home/resort developments are nearby. **Tahoe Donner** has a PGA-rated golf course, but the ski resort is of interest only to beginners. **Northstar at Tahoe** is a perfect example of a modern-day planned community. Though his comments are debatable, Bob Warren, manager of one of the area's ski resorts, told me, "Skiers don't want things rugged any more. They want to be entertained, amusement park style." If he is right, this is the place. Since the developers owned the mountain and the nearby meadow, they could do as they chose. (Most Sierra ski resorts are on Forest Service land.) So they built well-designed condos adjacent to the lower slopes (owners ski to their door) and along the golf links and around the tennis courts. Several restaurants and some fancy shops make up the community center. Tracked nordic skiing is offered in winter, swimming and horseback riding in summer. A gondola and several high-speed "detachables" serve Mount Pluto (elevation 8,618 feet), a mountain so easy to ski that until a lift was built on the more challenging back side, locals called the place "Flatstar."

Recreational Facilities

✔✔ **Richardson House** 7 room B&B. Spring and High Streets, Truckee, CA 95734. (916) 587-5388.

✔ **Best Western Truckee Tahoe Inn** 100-unit motel at Pondorosa golf course. 11331 Street, Route 267, Truckee, CA 95734. (916) 587-4525.

✔ **Donner Lake Village** 52-unit lakeside resort. Old Highway 40, Truckee, CA 95734. (916) 587-6081.

✔ **Northstar at Tahoe** 230-unit full-service condo resort. P.O. Box 2499, Truckee, CA 95734. (916) 562-1113.

Δ **State Park Campground** Donner Memorial. 157 sites.

● **Left Bank** Seafood restaurant. (916) 587-4694.

● **O'B's Pub & Restaurant**. (916) 587-4164.

§ **Northstar Ski Resort** 9 lifts, 1,800 foot vertical. (916) 562-1330.

§ **Tahoe Donner** 2 lifts, 600 foot vertical. (916) 587-9494.

§ **Tahoe Donner Golf Course** 18 holes. (916) 587-9440.

§ **Ponderosa** 9 hole golf course. (916) 587-3501.

Locals also ski and play at resorts near Lake Tahoe, a place we will visit in the next chapter.

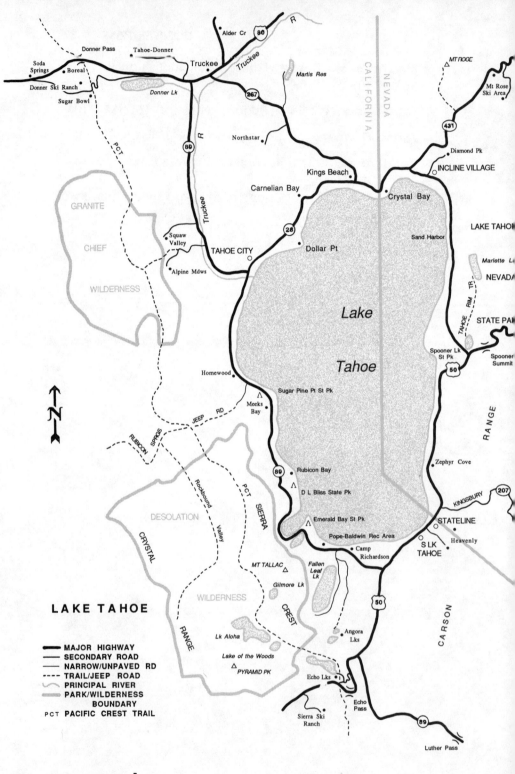

◀◀◀◀◀◆ **2** ◆▶▶▶▶▶

LAKE TAHOE

Here They Call It Pleasure

At the height of the Virginia City bonanza, a teamster paused at South Lake Tahoe and, puzzled by what he saw, had a short conversation with a bartender:

Teamster: A good many people here!
Bartender: Yes.
Teamster: What they all doing?
Bartender: Nothing.
Teamster: Nothing at all?
Bartender: Why, yes—in the city we would call it bumming, but here they call it pleasure.

A pleasuring ground then, and so it is now—a place to do whatever suits your fancy, even if it is absolutely nothing at all. Today, several million vacationers in a summer season try to do mostly that.

Seven roads lead into the Tahoe Basin, three from the north, two from the south, and two from the Carson Valley to the east. Of these, the Mount Rose Highway from Reno presents the most spectacular first view of the lake and is, for that reason, the one we will take. Ten miles south of downtown Reno, Nevada Highway 431 branches off from U.S. Highway 395 and climbs steeply, rising 2,500 feet in a little over twelve miles. After gaining a rather uninteresting summit, you traverse a flat plain, round a bend, and are suddenly presented with a spectacle. Spread out below is one of the most sublime scenes imaginable, a scene that inspired Mark Twain:

> At last the lake burst upon us—a noble sheet of blue water lifted six thousand three hundred feet above the level of the sea, and walled in by a rim of snow-clad mountain peaks that towered aloft a full three thousand feet higher still! As it lay there with the shadows of the mountains brilliantly photographed upon its still surface I thought it must surely be the fairest picture the whole earth affords.

Failing at several mining ventures, Twain and some pals had come here to make their fortune in the timber business. It came to naught: His campfire got a bit out of hand, setting the forest afire and destroying his raw material. The trees grew back, of course, and Americans have been flocking to these shores ever since.

What forest survived Twain's campfire was logged in the 1860s to provide timber and fuel for the Washoe mines, but that didn't seem to deter vacationers, who were quick to discover Tahoe's charms. Rich and famous Westerners, men like Stanley Dollar and Henry Kaiser, built mansions along the shore, but there was also a place for everyone. Tahoe was and still is a resort where people come and relax for a week or two (or a summer if they are lucky enough to have the time). Travel habits have changed, however. In 1915 my father found a summer job building a hydroelectric plant near Fallen Leaf Lake. He loved to relate how he took the Southern Pacific to Truckee, transferred to the little train that went up the Truckee River and out onto the pier at Tahoe Tavern, and then boarded *Nevada*, the diminutive steamship that circled the lake. At Tallac Lodge he was met by a horse and buggy, which took him the last five miles to Fallen Leaf. That way of traveling seems more European than Californian; it's the way you would go today if you were in, say, Paris, and planned to holiday at a resort along the shore of Lake Lucern. It beats driving. Judging by what people wrote, Tahoe was idyllic in those days. Great resort hotels were spotted around the shore, but there were few roads in between, so vacationers came and stayed put. The grandest was Tahoe Tavern, built by the Bliss family in 1901. A guidebook of the day reported:

> The railway deposits the traveler at Tahoe Tavern, prëeminently the chief resort for those who demand luxurious comfort in all its varied manifestations. Yet let it be clearly understood that it is not a fashionable resort in that every one must dress in fashionable garb. It is a place of common sense and rational freedom. If one comes in from a hunting or fishing trip at dinner time, he is expected to enter the dining room as he is. If one has taken a walk in his white flannels he is as welcome to a dance in the Casino as if he wore the most conventional evening dress.

Historian George James elaborated:

> For all the indoor sports a Casino has been erected, far enough away so that the music, dancing, the sharp clangor of bowling, the singing of extemporized glee-clubs, and the enthusiasm of audiences at amateur theatricals and the like do not disturb the peaceful slumbers of those who retire early. Tahoe Tavern is *sui generis* in that it is the most wonderful combination of primitive simplicity with twentieth century luxury.

Alas, the Rim of the Lake Road was completed in 1913, and some would argue that Tahoe has been in decline ever since. A national park was proposed in 1899 and again in 1912, but nothing was done. By 1935, William Penn Mott, who later became President Ronald Reagan's director of the National Park Service, bemoaned:

> Private enterprise and extensive development around the entire border of the lake has destroyed the possibility of conserving and preserving on a national scale the natural beauty, character, flora, and fauna of this area.

Speculators, bidding as much as $10 an acre, had simply pushed prices out of reach. Cottages and then motels began to spring up in the forests between the hotels. All but two of the great estates (the exceptions are now public parks) were subdivided into condo resorts. Still, Tahoe is a grand place to vaca-

tion at, and an even better place to live, as thousands have
learned. In 1863 the eminent theologian Thomas Starr King
suggested why:

> To a wearied frame and tired mind what refreshment there is in
> the neighborhood of this lake! The air is singularly searching and
> strengthening. The noble pines, not obstructed by underbrush,
> enrich the slightest breeze with aroma and music. Grand peaks rise
> around, on which the eye can admire the sternness of everlasting
> crags and the equal permanence of delicate and feathery snow.

Tahoe is rimmed by the Sierra on the west and the Carson
Range on the east. Geologists believe that during the epic events
of the Miocene and Pliocene ages, the Carson and Sierra ranges
were rising at the same time as the Tahoe Basin was dropping.
Much later, lava flows closed the gate along the Truckee River
and the jewel of the Sierra was born. If you're lucky enough to be
taking off from the Reno airport in a southerly direction, you are
presented with a quite unusual scene. The lake looks like a giant
cauldron, perched 1,700 feet above the Washoe Valley. If you
could drill a five-mile-long hole through the mountains, it would
drain in a trice—and cover the state of Nevada to a depth of
twenty inches. That feat very nearly happened, if you can believe
a story bandied about in Virginia City. It seems that the Savage
mine suddenly became flooded, and the ore could not be gotten
out. The stock price plummeted, of course. But an unscrupulous
San Francisco moneyman (certainly a redundancy) found that
the water had come from a hole in the bottom of Lake Tahoe.
After buying heavily into the Savage at bargain prices, he inserted
a plug (fashioned from a giant fir tree), which shut off the water,
allowing the mine shafts to drain. When the stock price soared he
sold short, pulled the plug, and ran.

For years people have argued about the name. Frémont called
it Lake Bonpland, which didn't stick, and then, in the mid-1860s
politicians decided to honor Democratic Governor John Bigler—
and so Lake Bigler appeared on official maps for almost a century.
Most Californians were outraged: Bigler was disliked, both for his
Southern sympathies and for his legendary intemperance. Historian Hubert Bancroft scoffed:

Nothing could have been in worse taste than in applying to a
liquid so beautifully clear and cool the name of one who so
detested water.

Debate has also raged over the meaning. "Tahoe," a Forest
Service sign says, "is Washoe for Big Water or Water in a High
Place," but I tend to agree with Mark Twain:

People say that Tahoe means "Silver Lake"—"Limpid Water"—
"Falling Leaf." Bosh! It means grasshopper soup, the favorite soup
of the Digger tribe—and of the Paiutes as well.

Whichever, this makes no matter to San Francisco's social set.
Just as "the City" means San Francisco, so "the Lake" means
Tahoe.

Most visitors don't "tour" Tahoe, but instead pick one spot, a
private home (theirs or a vacation rental), a condo, or a motel
room and settle down for a while. But we are on an exploring
venture, so we will circle the lake in a clockwise direction,
following what the Visitors Authority calls: "The Most Beautiful
Drive in America." The distance around is seventy-two miles.
We'll start by taking the Mt. Rose Highway from Reno.

MOUNT ROSE/INCLINE VILLAGE

"A rose is a rose, is a rose" may be true in Gertrude Stein's Paris
but not here, for the **Mount Rose Ski Resort** is located on Slide
Mountain. *The* Mount Rose is a mile northwest and soars to
10,800 feet, the highest point in the Tahoe area. This is a great
place to ski, with one of the most varied exposures anywhere. For
years, two separate resorts shared the mountain. Slide Mountain's lifts began on a spur road perched along the east side
overlooking the Washoe Valley, while Mount Rose's lifts started
from a pretty little basin on the northwest slope. Today they are
operated as one resort. Beginners and lower intermediates should
head for the latter, which has the only day lodge on the mountain. Beginner runs are long, and some nice intermediate runs
drop down from the Lake View chairlift (you have to climb to get
a view of the lake). Nearby, steep, but mostly groomed trails
plunge down from summit. The *base* elevation here is 8,250 feet

higher than the *top* of Diamond Peak at Incline (see below), so the snow is usually cold and dry. "The locals come to the Slide side," a lift operator told me. "Don't ask why, it's just traditional." The advanced runs aren't any steeper, but there are some dandy intermediate bowls, which, because they face the morning sun, tend to soften up early. With all these great runs (and moderate prices), I wondered why Mt. Rose isn't more popular. Todd Majoris, who works here, said, simply: "Sometimes the wind just kills us." The "Washoe zephyrs" (see Chapter 15) are as perverse as ever.

Nordic skiers and snowmobilers head for **Mount Rose Highway Summit** (elevation 8,900 feet), an area that is surprisingly flat, and almost treeless. A caution is in order. The lack of landmarks makes it easy to get lost in a fog, so carry a compass. A strenuous six-mile trail leads to the summit of Mount Rose, where the view is unsurpassed.

Incline Village's (population 6,225) uninspiring name comes from the days when a great incline railway, 4,000 feet long and powered by a forty-horsepower steam engine, was employed to transport logs to the ridgetop, where they were then flumed to Carson City. In the 1960s, developer Harold Tiller was determined to build a planned community that would be devoid of the honky-tonk that had sprung up at nearby Kings Beach and the awfulness of the strip development along the south shore. He was only partially successful. Street names like Caddy Court, Birdie Way, and Fairway Boulevard suggest that many homes overlook golf courses (there are two); tennis courts and playgrounds are scattered here and there. But the tightly clustered shopping area he sought was not to be. Tahoe Boulevard supports a string of gas stations, fast-food joints, and most of the other trappings found in a flatland suburban town. The forest is dense, however, and the buildings well done, so Incline is a nice place. The town supports a giant casino, several motels, a dozen restaurants, five churches, a library, a hospital, a high school, and a two-year college. The best attraction (or worst, depending on your point of view) is a modest theme park called Ponderosa Ranch, the setting for the TV series *Bonanza*.

Diamond Peak at Ski Incline was built as part of the planned community, so its location was chosen more for its proximity to where people lived than for having great ski fields.

With mostly beginner and intermediate runs, the resort acquired a reputation for being a place where you went primarily for the view (which is fantastic). Recently, an adjacent mountain has been developed, called Diamond Peak. Since resort maps use a black diamond to describe expert runs, the owners felt they could attract better skiers by changing the name to Diamond Peak. The new area does take the place out of the "family resort" category, but the slopes face almost due west, hardly the direction to guarantee good snow conditions. The proximity of the casino brings celebrities, and the patrons seem well dressed, but the better local skiers go to Mount Rose.

Recreational Facilities

✔✔✔ **Hyatt Lake Tahoe** 460-room full-service hotel and casino. P.O. Box 3239, Incline Village, NV 89450. (800) 228-9000.

§ **Diamond Peak at Ski Incline** 7 lifts, 2,200 foot vertical. Box AL. Incline Village NV 89540. (702) 832-3211.

§ **Incline Championship Golf Course** 18 holes. (702) 832-1144.

§ **Incline Executive Golf Course** 18-hole short course. (702) 832-1150.

§ **Mount Rose Ski Area** 5 lifts, 1,500 foot vertical. P.O. Box 2406, Reno, NV 89505. (702) 849-0706.

THE EAST SIDE • (lake elevation, 6,250 feet)

Tahoe's worldwide fame results from its setting, but it is the clarity of the water that astonishes most first-time visitors. Mark Twain gushed:

> So singularly clear was the water, that where it was only twenty or thirty feet deep the bottom was so perfectly distinct that the boat seemed floating in the air! Yes, where it was even *eighty* feet deep every little pebble was distinct, every speckled trout, every hand's-breadth of sand.

In places, the water has a turquoise hue, made more dramatic by its contrast with ivory-colored granitic boulders and the dark green foliage of the conifers. A hundred years ago a newspaper in San Francisco insisted that since the lake was so high, the water must be lighter, and therefore logs would sink and swimmers drown. Nonsense, of course, but it is cold, hardly ever rising above sixty-five degrees, and the lake is so deep (second to Oregon's Crater Lake in this country) that, with the exception of the Emerald Bay section, it never freezes.

Keeping the water clear hasn't been easy. Sewerage is now treated and piped over the mountains to the Washoe and Carson valleys, but erosion from land development has brought nutrients into the lake, producing a predictable deleterious effect. Building permits are now hard to come by. The best place on the entire lake to observe this clarity is at **Sand Harbor,** part of **Lake Tahoe Nevada State Park.** Picnic tables snuggle up to sandy beaches and rocky inlets. A beautiful cove has a boat ramp; concerts are held in an outdoor pavilion. This is one of the most popular beaches on the lake, with parking for 500 cars. On busy weekends, people are turned away after eleven in the morning.

Nevada Highway 28 leaves the lake shore and begins a climb toward Spooner Summit. Lovely views unfold, adding spice to the drive. People park alongside the road and scramble down to secluded coves. **Spooner Lake State Park** is a wonderful place to stop for a picnic. A nice day hike leads to **Marlette Lake,** following a portion of the **Tahoe Rim Trail.** This planned, 150-mile path, which will eventually girdle the lake, is being built entirely with volunteer labor. Judging from the newsletter I get, they are having a lot of fun.

Thanks primarily to the intransigence of the Forest Service, which now owns the land, two "old Tahoe" resorts still exist. **Zephyr Cove,** like Camp Richardson, which we'll visit in a bit, is by no means fancy; the cabins are run-down, the tent sites are too close together, and the place seems a bit hectic. *M.S. Dixie,* one of two paddle-wheelers cruising Tahoe's southern waters, is moored out front. Two or three times a day she sails over to Emerald Bay.

Recreational Facilities

ΔΔ **Zephyr Cove Resort** 4 lodge rooms and 26 rustic cottages in a pine forest along the lake. Grocery, cafe, bar, 165 tent and RV sites. P.O. Box 830, Zephyr Cove, NV 89448. (702) 888-6644.

Δ **Forest Service Campground** Nevada Beach, 56 sites.

§ *M.S. Dixie* (702) 588-3508.

§ **Glenbrook Golf Course** 9 holes. (702) 588-3566.

STATELINE/SOUTH LAKE TAHOE • Population 25,000

Voilà! Four twenty-story hotels, surrounded by a field of asphalt littered with 10,000 automobiles. Roof-top restaurants, theme restaurants, supper clubs; mirrored-ceiling casinos, carpeted in reds and golds. Statuesque waitresses, dressed as if they just left the movie set of *Ben Hur*, mill about; *croupiers* wearing tuxedoes pass dice and spin wheels. It's glamor, so they say. "Where did they get the money to build those hotels?" I asked Keith Justus, who clerked at a run-of-the-mill motel. "They weren't built by winners!" was his insightful reply (see below). There must be a goodly supply of gamblers willing to proffer their wallets, because these four garish hotels have rooms for 5,000. People come to **Stateline** for the extravagant dinner shows featuring star entertainers, for the glitz, for the chance to get rich, and, some will even admit, to see the lake. Many argue that these activities are better left to a less scenic area—Reno, for instance— but it is not to be. In 1944 Harvey and Llewellyn Gross opened Harvey's Wagon Wheel Saloon and Gambling Hall in a shack built with scrap lumber and $10 worth of nails. Harvey's is now the gaudiest. Bill Harrah, building on a Reno empire, arrived in 1956. Ceasar's Palace and Del Webb's High Sierra followed. They crowd the state line so closely that it looks like they might topple over into California, given a good wind from the east.

The Joy of Winning

About gambling, I find the pain of losing far greater than the joy of winning, so I'm terrible at it. My recent casino experience was therefore limited to a 6:00 A.M. breakfast at Caesar's. A high-stakes baccarat game was in progress in a glass-walled room. The half-dozen play-

ers, dressed as if they had just come off the range, were not the least bit sleepy-eyed. Nearby, a few middle-aged women were working some slots, but a thousand machines stood idle, their flashing orange and yellow lights beckoning no one. Several cashiers roamed the almost empty hall, each carrying a bus driver's change machine, with heavy suspenders to hold it up. The only blackjack player was a comely woman, dressed in a tight-fitting black lace dress, accented by elbow-length gloves and spiked heels. The vacant look in her eyes suggested a mind that was on something other than the spots on the cards. Half a dozen bench seats near the door were occupied by a group of Hispanic women, fighting hard to stay awake. After breakfast I spotted them traipsing toward their charter bus, one clutching a paper ice bucket filled with nickels.

In 1965, a string of hamlets along the south shore (Al Tahoe, Bijou, Tahoe Valley) were merged into the City of **South Lake Tahoe,** which stretches along Highway 50 for eight miles. A local bus system now alleviates the traffic, somewhat. The transition from Nevada to California is startling. The Chinese Wall of casino/hotels suddenly gives way to a string of motels, two miles long. Highway 50 becomes a four-lane road, lined with neon. Tom Hiscox at the Visitors Authority told me that there are 11,000 rental units (motel rooms and condos) on the south shore. They come in all varieties, from "auto court" to "adult motel," the latter featuring movies (guess what kind), heart-shaped waterbeds, mid-room spas, and mirrors everywhere. Few motels have lakeshore access. The city operates a nice picnic site along the beach, and a history **museum** is open during the summer. The stern-wheeler *Tahoe Queen* sails from a nearby pier. South Lake Tahoe has scheduled airline service from San Francisco and Los Angeles.

Thanks in no small part to its proximity to the casinos and their convention facilities, **Heavenly** is one of the most successful winter resorts in the country. Trade associations by the hundreds schedule meetings at Tahoe so that attenders can divide their time among business, gambling, and skiing. The slopes hardly compare with Sun Valley, Vail, or Aspen, but what other place in the world can boast *apré ski* with the likes of Bill Cosby, Englebert Humperdinck, or Tony Bennett? Heavenly is the Sierra's only skiing resort with a truly international clientele. When viewed from the lake, the slopes look like an impossible challenge, but the sinister Gunbarrel, with its yard-deep moguls, isn't typical. "We're an inverted mountain," Diana Arington told me. "Most of our slopes are intermediate, and they are out of sight up above." Hardly anyone skis back down to the lake, preferring instead the comfort of the tram. "I'm not ready to ski Gunbarrel in the morning and too pooped in the afternoon to try," a fellow who claimed to be an instructor told me. Heavenly (the resort has dropped "Valley" from its name) is two loosely connected resorts, one in Nevada, the other in California. The California side was built first, with a teleferic (the Sierra's first) leading to a knoll overlooking the lake. The view from the Top of the Tram Restaurant is magnificent. Gentle runs lead down from a higher mountain to the south. Resort literature lists the vertical drop as 3,600 feet, but you can't ski that far without stopping because you have to take a small lift out of a hollow about half way down. Although Nevada-side lifts, reached from the Kingsbury Grade Road, begin higher up on the mountain, they are longer. Skiers here are rewarded with a spectacular view of Carson Valley and—incredibly, given the depth of the snow—of the desert beyond. Three mid-mountain restaurants cater to a well-dressed crowd, and the California side has a large day-care center for toddlers. "We have the glitz," Diana told me, which I guess explains why Heavenly is the Sierra's highest-priced resort. But there is almost no place to stay within walking distance of the lifts. Most skiers take a shuttle bus.

Recreational Facilities

✔✔✔ **Caesar's Tahoe** 450-room full-service hotel and casino. P.O. Box 5800, Stateline, NV 98449. (800) 648-3353.

✔✔✔ **Del Webb's High Sierra Casino/Hotel** 540-room full-service hotel and casino. P.O. Box C, Stateline, NV 98449. (800) 648-3322.

✔✔✔ **Harrah's Tahoe Hotel/Casino** 540-room full-service hotel and casino. P.O. Box 8, Stateline, NV 98449. (800) 648-3733.

✔✔✔ **Harvey's Resort Hotel/Casino** 590-room full-service hotel and casino. P.O. Box 128, Stateline, NV 98449. (800) 648-3361.

✔ **South Lake Tahoe Visitors Authority** Central referral agency for motel and condo reservations. South Lake Tahoe, CA 95729. (800) AT TAHOE.

Δ **South Lake Tahoe Campground** 144-site city-owned campground.

● **Chez Villaret** French restaurant. (916) 541-7868.

● **Top of the Tram Restaurant** (916) 541-1330.

● **The Fresh Ketch** Marina-view restaurant. (916) 541-5683.

§ **Heavenly** 17 lifts, 2,000+ foot vertical. P.O. Box 2180, Stateline, NV 89449. (916) 541-SKII.

§ **M.S. Tahoe Queen** (916) 541-3364.

§ **Bijou Golf Course** 9 holes. (916) 544-5500.

§ **Edgewood Golf Course** (702) 588-3566.

§ **Lake Tahoe Country Club** 18-hole golf course. (916) 577-0788.

§ **Tahoe Paradise** 18-hole golf course. (916) 577-2121.

EMERALD BAY

Mount Tallac (elevation 9,785 feet) dominates the western skyline. Directly below is **Pope-Baldwin Recreation Area,** administered by the Forest Service. In 1879 E. L. Baldwin (see below) purchased several thousand acres of pine forest and built Tallac House, the most opulent pleasure palace of its day. Men wore neckties and sported bowlers while women toyed coyly with parasols. Diners enjoyed a string orchestra while feasting on such delicacies as Au Croquette Pomme de Terre, Westphalia Ham with Champagne Sauce, Stewed Terrapin à la Maryland, and Young Suckling Pig with Apple Sauce. The casino featured a ballroom, a ladies' billiard and pool room, and a gambling hall decorated with French plate mirrors. True or not, the story is told that prices were so high that when a highwayman on the Placerville Road learned that his victim was a guest there, he tossed the hapless fellow's purse back, announcing that he had already paid enough.

Lucky Baldwin

Elias Jackson Baldwin came to San Francisco in 1853, intent on going into the hotel business. Somehow he came into possession of some nearly worthless stock in Virginia City's Ophir mine. Intent on a Hawaiian holiday, he instructed his agent to sell; $2 a share seemed about the right price. Upon returning he learned two things: (1) he had neglected to sign the stock certificates so the agent was unable to effect the transaction; and (2) the stock was now worth $1800 dollars a share. From that day onward his sobriquet was not E. J., but "Lucky."

But Lady Luck, like the women in his life, did not hang around long. He built the Baldwin Hotel in San Francisco at the corner of Powell and Market, where the cable car turnaround now stands, and the Baldwin Theater nearby. Both burned to the ground, uninsured. After he moved to Southern California, his fancy turned to thoroughbreds, and to high-spirited ladies. The Santa Anita racetrack, which he founded, became synonymous with the sport of kings, while his *liaisons,* both marital and otherwise, made headlines. Alas, speculating in real estate was not his *tour de force,* and he died penniless, with little to show for his efforts save a name on a Southern California map. Fifty thousand people now live in Baldwin Park. Not a tear was shed at his funeral, according to reports of the day.

When Baldwin died in 1909, the hotel went into decline. A Tahoe newspaper reported that the halls were frequented by an Indian belle, who, they gleefully claimed, "chewed nigger-head [tobacco] and was capable of spitting through the keyhole of a door at three yards without splattering the edges." Aghast, Baldwin's widow had the place torn down. San Francisco nabobs George Pope, Lloyd Tevis, and Emanuel Heller bought most of the land and built magnificent summer "cottages," three of which still stand. In time, however, taxes and high maintenance took their toll: the heirs chose to donate the property to the federal government. Heller's Valhalla now serves as a **performing arts center;** Baldwin's mansion is a **museum,** displaying Washoe artifacts. Nearby **Baldwin Beach** is one of the best swimming spots on the lake. Picnic tables abound, and the area is very popular among bicyclists, who ride over from South Lake Tahoe on a paved path. The Forest Service has built an **interpretive center;** a pleasant nature trail leads to an area where you can observe what goes on at the bottom of a mountain stream. Sleigh rides are offered in the winter.

In 1911, some Stanford professors built summer homes at **Fallen Leaf Lake,** the hidden jewel of this part of the Sierra. The university connection has remained strong: the alumni association operates a large camp here. This is a popular gateway to the **Desolation Wilderness,** an area we'll explore more fully in the next chapter. The five-mile, 3,500-foot climb to the top of Mount Tallac, though strenuous, rewards the hiker with stupendous views. Along the way you pass Glen Alpine Springs, where cabins designed by Bernard Maybeck snuggle alongside a loquacious stream. Nearby a bumpy but quite passable dirt road leads to a fire lookout (great view) and continues on to within a half mile of **Angora Lakes,** where a rustic resort operates under permit from the Forest Service.

It's obvious to the motorist why the section of the Rim Highway skirting **Emerald Bay** was the last to be built: the countryside, to say the least, is precipitous. In 1915 George James wrote:

> Below us is the emerald-ringed bay, with its romantic little island at the west end, and nearby the joyously-shouting Eagle Creek as it plunges over the precipice and makes the foam-flecked Eagle Falls. Our road here was blasted through some fiercely solid and hostile rock. A new El Capitan now rises above us, though it lacks the smooth unbroken dignity of the great Yosemite cliff, yet it is sublime in its sudden rise and vast height.

Avalanches and rock slides frequently close the road, so Caltrans hoped in the 1960s to finesse the problem by building a bridge across the mouth of Emerald Bay. Mountain lovers stopped the project—better no road at all than one that would despoil such a scene. Most viewers rhapsodize about the beauty of Fannette Island, but author Barbara Lekisch disagrees. The name is a corruption of coquette and, Barbara insists,

> Though at the center of a brilliant circle of admirers attracted by her beauty, she still has a stony heart.

Vikingsholm, a castlelike structure built by Lora J. Knight in 1929, is open during the summer to those willing to negotiate the steep trail down to lake level. This handsome stone building has been described as the finest example of Scandinavian architecture in north America. Across the highway, a trail follows **Eagle Creek,** skirting around the foam-flecked falls before climbing into the Desolation Wilderness.

Duane LeRoy Bliss cut down most of the trees in the Tahoe Basin and thereby made a fortune. His heirs, perhaps in a gesture of atonement, donated some of his holdings to the state, which now operates **D. L. Bliss State Park.** Located on Rubicon Point, it has a lovely white-sand beach and a spectacular four-mile trail that leads to the mouth of Emerald Bay. I walked it one spring day when the elusive snow plants were about. This bright-red, short-lived plant has no green leaves, so is unable to use photosynthesis to manufacture food. Instead it gets its nourishment from the ground.

Recreational Facilities

ΔΔ **Richardson Bay Resort** "Old Tahoe" hotel, cabins, and 230-unit campground. Marina and waterfront restaurant. P.O. Box 89, South Lake Tahoe, CA 95731. (916) 541-1800.

ΔΔ **The Lodge at Fallen Leaf Lake** Store, 11 rooms and 4 cabins. 37-unit campground. P.O. Box 8879, South Lake Tahoe, CA 95731. (916) 541-6330.

Δ **State Park Campgrounds** Emerald Bay, 100 drive-in and 20 boat-in sites; D. L. Bliss, 168 sites. All reservable through Mistix, (800) 444-7275.

Δ **Forest Service Campground** Fallen Leaf Lake, 208 sites.

Ω **Camp Richardson Pack Station** Day rides and packing into Desolation Wilderness. P.O. Box 8335, South Lake Tahoe, CA 95731. (916) 541-3113.

THE WEST SHORE

Half a dozen hamlets make up the West Shore, the most affluent part of the lake. A series of summer-home tracts stretches along fifteen miles of shoreline from Rubicon Bay to Tahoe City. Modest homes dot the forest west of the highway, but those along the lake shore have long been the summer retreat of the wealthy. Rustic homes, best described as gracious, dot the shoreline, most with a pier out front, a Criss Craft or Gar Wood speedboat tied up alongside. Oriental rugs grace oiled fir floors, the kitchen likely has a sugar pine drainboard and perhaps a fifty-year-old Wedgewood range. Fleur du Lac, Henry Kaiser's lavish estate, is now a condo development, hidden by a rock wall and guarded by iron gates, but the most opulent, the **Ehrman Mansion,** is now a state park. Built at the turn of the century by San Francisco banker I. W. Hellman (Sidney Ehrman was his lawyer son-in-law), the grounds are open most of the year and house tours are given in the summer. The three-story, 12,000-square-foot Queen Anne-style building sits on a knoll overlooking the water. Two thousand acres of forest land stretching along the lake for a mile and a half now comprise **Sugar Pine Point State Park.** Picnicking here is splendid, but the beach is a bit rocky.

Meeks Bay was, and I guess still is, a family resort: the place where, as a teenager, I came for some summer courting. The old pavilion is gone, but the beach (and the girls) are as pretty as ever. Several picnic areas are located along the shore, but the "in" crowd heads for **Sunnyside,** a once funky resort that has been remodeled into one of the more popular eating places around. The affluent motor over in their classic, high-powered inboards, wooden boats that more than anything symbolize the life-style of this summer paradise. (The Wooden Boat Festival is held in mid-summer at Tahoe City.) Sailboats, too, are popular, in spite of the fluky winds.

Homewood Ski Area is a modest resort with two base areas, the result of having absorbed the old Tahoe Ski Bowl. Four chairlifts service a single mountain. From the parking lot the runs look a bit steep, but there are easy ways down. Most skiers head for the upper slopes, where the snow is better and the view is terrific. Homewood has a fine ski school, but the resort would be much better if it were a thousand feet higher. The earliest skiing at Tahoe was at nearby Olympic Hill, where a jumping meet was held in 1930. A famous photograph shows the Engen brothers, Alf and Sverre, jumping together, their hands clasped in midflight. **Granlibakken,** a condo resort that now occupies the site, has a beginner slope but is known primarily for Nordic skiing.

Recreational Facilities

✔✔✔ **Sunnyside Lodge** 22-room hotel, waterfront restaurant and bar. P.O. Box 5969, Tahoe City, CA 95730. (916) 583-7200.

✔✔ **Alpenhaus** 9-room country inn and restaurant. P.O. Box 262, Tahoma, CA 95733. (916) 525-5000.

ΔΔ **Meeks Bay Resort** 20 cottages and condo units. Snack bar. 150-unit campground. Summer only. P.O. Box 7979, Tahoe City, CA 95730. (916) 525-7242.

Δ **State Park Campground** Sugar Pine Point, 175 sites. Reservable by calling Mistix at (800) 444-7275.

Δ **Forest Service Campground** Wm. Kent, 95 sites.

• **Swiss Lakewood Restaurant** Seventy-year-old Swiss/French restaurant. (916) 525-5211.

• **Chambers Landing** Dockside bar and nearby restaurant overlooking the lake. Summer only. (916) 525-7672.

§ **Granlibakken Ski Area** P.O. Box 6329, Tahoe City, CA 95730. (916) 583-9896.

§ **Homewood Ski Area** 5 lifts, 1,600 foot vertical. P.O. Box 65, Homewood, CA 95718. (916) 525-7256.

TAHOE CITY, ALPINE MEADOWS, AND SQUAW VALLEY

In 1942, the last train steamed out onto the half-mile-long pier at Tahoe Tavern, putting an end to an era. Then, in 1964, the *grande dame* herself felt the wrecker's ball. But thanks to its location at the outlet of the lake, **Tahoe City** (population 1,300–6,000 in summer) remains the commercial hub of the north shore. The two-block-long main street has changed little over the years, but most people now shop at fancy indoor malls such as the Cobblestone, Boatworks, and Roundhouse. A small dam, built around the turn of the century, allows the lake level to be adjusted a few feet. The Gatekeeper's House is now a **museum.** A nice picnic area abuts the lake. Rafting on the Truckee River has become so popular that at times traffic jams develop along the quieter stretches of water. Boaters (most use inflatable three- to eight-person rafts) either arrange for a shuttle car or return on a commercial bus. A very popular paved bicycle path stretches south to Sugar Pine Point; another follows the Truckee River along the old railroad right-of-way.

Two of Tahoe's most famous ski resorts are located in side canyons of the Truckee River. The name of **Alpine Meadows** (elevation 6,835 feet) is redundant (an alp is a sloping meadow), but no one seems to mind because the skiing here is excellent. The resort opened in the 1960–1961 season with a single, mile-long lift (since replaced with a high-speed detachable) to the top of Ward Peak (terrific view). The developers eschewed the glitzy image of nearby Squaw Valley, preferring instead to focus on the ski fields, a policy that has earned them a loyal following, despite a terrible avalanche in 1982 that left several dead and entombed Anna Conrad for five days. Other chairs were added, opening up slopes facing in all directions with a variety of snow conditions. Experts found shoots and gullies and gave them fanciful names: Promised Land, Chute That Seldom Slides, and the infamous Our Father. With an uphill capacity of 16,000, there is a place for skiers of all skills. The resort prides itself on having the longest season, one year opening before Thanksgiving and not closing until the Fourth of July. Alpine, however is strictly a day ski area; there are no overnight public accommodations within easy walking distance of the lifts. Adventurers in the summer take the trail to the tiny, but nice, **Granite Chief Wilderness.**

Squaw Valley, by contrast, is the closest thing in California to a compact Alpine-like village, boasting accommodations for several thousand within walking distance of the lifts. For that blessing we can, in part, thank the State of California, which, having found itself suddenly saddled with an international ski competition, frantically scurried about to build a semblance of a resort. The state put up $8 million, the federal government another $4 million. Though much has changed since the VIIIth Olympiad, it brought much-needed facilities to the valley. It was a bit of a miracle that the event even ocurred. When the Olympic Committee chose the site in 1954, Squaw Valley had only one chair (the world's first double), plus a rickety "jig-back" contraption where two dozen skiers sat sideways as they rode up the hill. Owner Alex Cushing later admitted that he had submitted the bid simply to get publicity. Squaw Peak was high enough, but since the lower slopes are shallow, the downhill course had to terminate some distance up the mountain. And the bobsled events had to be canceled—there was not enough money to build a course. Given today's hype, and all the television coverage, the games were definitely low-key, but Walt Disney choreographed the opening ceremonies (Vice President Richard Nixon presiding), and CBS sent Walter Cronkite out to anchor the TV coverage. The highlight was the U.S. hockey team's defeat of the Soviets. I watched the jumping (Helmut Recknagle won the gold) on hills that haven't been used since. Squaw Valley, more than any other resort in the West, changed downhill skiing away from a rustic, yodeling sort of mountain activity, into the modish, go-for-it, loud and aggressive sport we know today. The architecture for the original lodge was in the traditional chalet style, but when it burned the replacement was painted in colors of purple, pink, and mauve, and the fireplaces—done in stainless steel— were anything but old-world. *Haute couture* fashion shows set the *apré ski* mood, and at a time when guests at other resorts were dancing the schottische, Squaw Valley hired a band to play the twist.

The Olympics pushed Squaw Valley into world-class status, which it retains to this day. The fantastically steep Red Dog and KT 22 lifts (the owner's wife made twenty-two kick turns getting down, thus the name) were built for the GS and slalom events, and the downhill required the installation of the Siberia lift. Today, chairlifts go seemingly everywhere, scaling five peaks with the most varied and the most challenging ski runs in the Sierra. In a way, Squaw Valley is two resorts, the second based at Gold Coast, 2,000 feet above the valley floor, where the easier slopes are found. A gondola and a cable car (teleferic) ferry skiers up and bring many of them down. But over the years people began to grumble. "Sure Squaw has the slopes," they would say, "but they don't give a damn," a reputation brought on by the perceived aloofness of the owner, the surly employees ("Shut up and ski!"), and the widespread belief that lifts were poorly maintained. (Several people died when a hauling cable slashed through the top of the cable car, a catastrophe for which Squaw was subsequently absolved of fault.) Today the logo "We Care" is used on resort literature, but a recent experience made me wonder. An unusual cold storm had dropped a foot of dry powder; hundreds of skiers were anxious to get going. But it was late spring and the lower slopes were bare, so the gondola was merely an access lift to the day lodge at Gold Coast, a twenty-minute ride away. Nevertheless it was not opened until 9:00 A.M., and by the time we got to the ski fields the famous Sierra sun had turned the powder to hasty pudding.

Recreational Facilities

✔✔✔ **Olympic Village Inn** Condo resort. P.O. Box 2648, Olympic Valley, CA 95730. (916) 583-1501.

✔✔✔ **The Resort at Squaw Creek** 405-room full-service conference hotel. P.O. Box 3333 Olympic Valley, CA 95730. (800) 3CREEK3.

✔✔✔ **Squaw Valley Lodge** 95-unit condo resort at the base of the ski lifts. P.O. Box 22364, Olympic Valley, CA 95730. (916) 583-5500.

✔✔✔ **Squaw Valley Inn** 60-room hotel at the base of the ski lifts. P.O. Box 2407, Olympic Valley, CA 95730. (800) 323-ROOM.

✔ **North Lake Tahoe Visitors & Convention Bureau** Central referral agency for motel and condo reservations. P.O. Box 5578, Tahoe City, CA 95730. (800) 824-6348.

✔ **River Ranch** Full-service hotel alongside the Truckee River. P.O. Box 197, Tahoe City, CA 95730. (916) 583-4264.

ΔΔ **The Cottage Inn** 1930s-style resort with 15 knotty-pine cottages and studios. P.O. Box 66, Tahoe City, CA 95730. (916) 581-4073.

ΔΔ **Mayfield House B&B** 6-room B&B. P.O. Box 5999, Tahoe City, CA 95730. (916) 583-1001.

Δ **Lake Forest Campground** 20-site municipal campground.

• **Pfeifer House** Continental restaurant. (916) 583-3102.

§ **Alpine Meadows Ski Area** 11 lifts, 1,550 foot vertical. P.O. Box 5279, Tahoe City, CA 95730. (916) 583-6914.

§ **Tahoe City Golf Course** 9 holes. (916) 583-1516.

§ **Squaw Valley Nordic** (916) 583-8951.

§ **Squaw Valley USA** 29 lifts, 2,500 foot vertical. Olympic Valley, CA 95730. (800) 545-4350.

Ω **Mountain Air Sports** Truckee River float trips and shuttle bus. (916) 583-5606.

THE NORTH SHORE

Six communities line the north shore: Dollar Point, Carnelian Bay, Tahoe Vista, Kings Beach, Brockway, and Crystal Bay. Kings Beach, in spite of its name, never had a regal feel; most of the area is run-down, but the old spa resort at nearby Brockway is now a fashionable condo development. Frank Sinatra once owned Cal-Neva. The state line runs through the middle of the building, with the glitzy side in Nevada and the old, charming side in California.

Recreational Facilities

✓✓✓ **Tahoe Vista Inn & Marina** 7 luxury lakeview suites. P.O. Box 236, Tahoe Vista, CA 95732. (916) 546-4819.

✓✓✓ **Cal-Neva Lodge** P.O. Box 368, Crystal Bay, NV 89402. (800) CAL-NEVA.

• **Jakes at the Lake** Lakeside bar and restaurant. (916) 583-0188.

• **Gar Wodds Grill & Pier** Lakeside dining. (916) 546-3366.

• **La Playa** Seafood restaurant. (916) 546-5903.

§ **Woodvista Golf Course** 9 holes. (916) 546-9909.

Near the end of his famous High Sierra trip in 1870, Joseph LeConte, a fellow we will meet often on this sojourn, camped along the north shore and wrote:

> Of all the places I have yet seen, this is the one which I could longest enjoy and love the most. Reclining thus in the shade, on the clean white sand, the waves rippling at my feet, with thoughts of Lake Tahoe and of my loved ones mingling in my mind, I fell in to a delicious doze.

Considering that he had also been in Yosemite Valley, that was quite a compliment.

◄◄◄◄◄◆ 3 ◆►►►►►

ECHO PASS

The Great Bonanza Road

A teamster, apparently feeling unloved, his efforts unappreciated, lamented:

> Ox teams and mules and freight wagons is just as important openin' up a new country as what gold is. And we was haulin' freight, and feedin' folks, and bringin' in tools and things to make life comfortable and all. And while some of the rich ones was soberin' up from their champagne wine jags, and feelin' mean, and figurin' out how they could open up another bonanza or bilk somebody out of a claim or somethin', I was feelin' good out under the stars, and what you might call possessin' my soul in peace.

He may have not received the glory, but historians speculate that more Comstock silver went to pay the teamsters who brought in the supplies and equipment than went to the miners who mucked it out of the ground. Until the railroad was opened in 1868, everything needed to sustain Virginia City, which had a population of upwards of 40,000, came via the Placerville Road, now U.S. Highway 50. A fellow with the unlikely name of Colonel John Calhoun (Cock-Eye) Johnson built it, and according to William Brewer he was well rewarded for his trouble:

A portion of the road, which is *assessed* as worth $14,000, last year collected over $75,000 in tolls. With such strong inducements men could afford to "lobby" in the legislature and get the franchises.

One user grumbled: "The road from Placerville to Washoe is five feet deep by a hundred and thirty miles long and composed mostly of mountains, snow and mud," but nevertheless, for a time "Johnson's Cut Off" became the most highly used in the Sierra. Eye witnesses reported seeing as many as 350 wagons struggling up the grade on a single day. Even today (winter plowing commenced in 1945), if one includes "Gambler's Specials" (buses), it carries nearly as many people as Interstate 80. Things become an awful mess when it snows too much.

ECHO PASS

Once past the village of Meyers, Highway 50 almost immediately starts a grand assault on the Sierra's spine, slabbing upward along a steep granite wall (see map, Chapter 1). Great vistas begin to unfold, but since the highway is crowded and there are few turnouts, it's better to be patient. At Echo Pass (elevation 7,382 feet) the granite gives way; you suddenly find yourself in a dense conifer forest. Now is the time to go for the view. Turn north on the road to Echo Lakes and follow the old highway a mile or so to Johnson's Pass, where a grand old two-story building (owned by a ski club) sits on a precipice overlooking Lake Tahoe. Numerous turn-of-the-century vacation cabins sidle up to the far end of **Echo Lake** (elevation 7,480 feet). Over the years, avalanches have taken their toll (over a dozen have been lost), but home owners in the more protected areas still boat out to their isolated retreats. The lovely meadow beyond the lake has produced hay since the days of the Bonanza Road.

Sierra Ski Ranch is one of Tahoe's nicer winter resorts. It's very much the creation of Vern Strock, an old-timer who seems to march to his own drummer. "Grooming is what makes the sport," Vern told me, "so early on I invested heavily in equipment. And big lifts too. I've got more horsepower on this slope than Heavenly! You know, before the grooming, teenagers would ski a lot but they would give it up when they married and had kids. It was just too hard to get proficient at skiing the crud (called "Sierra cement" locally). Now I have a large daycare center and they're coming back in droves. I don't serve booze, though, or even beer. We have no lodging here, so everyone has to drive somewhere and I don't want my customers heading down the highway half snockered." (Judging from the bottles and cans left in the parking lot, his scheme isn't always successful.) I asked Vern if his proximity to Tahoe's south shore helped. "Sure. There are so many motels it pays to run free shuttle buses. Skiers gamble, of course, but gamblers don't ski." Half a dozen major chairlifts (including detachables) serve two separate mountains. The vertical drop is not great, but several runs are steep enough to challenge experts, and numerous cruising slopes are just plain fun.

Desolation Wilderness

As far back as the 1930s, a portion of El Dorado National Forest was set aside as a "Primitive Area," meaning no new roads would be constructed, and logging would be curtailed. Then, in 1966, the area was included in the Wilderness Act, which among other things, banned the use of all vehicles (including bicycles). Existing roads were allowed to deteriorate, and trails were constructed in their place. The wilderness is named for Desolation Valley, one of two principal watersheds (the other is Rockbound Valley) that lie between two subsidiary mountain ranges. The peaks bordering Lake Tahoe, capped by **Mount Tallac** (elevation 9,735 feet), form the actual Sierra Crest, while the parallel, twelve-mile-long Crystal Range, with its landmark **Pyramid Peak** (9,983 feet), make up the western boundary. In between is typical "High Sierra" granite country, lightly forested and puncuated by a hundred lakes—a mountain lover's paradise.

By Sierra standards, Desolation Wilderness is small (100 square miles), low (8,000 feet on average), and accessible—three factors that have made it almost loved to death. This area was the first to feel the impact of the boom in backpacking that began in the mid 1960s. Suddenly, granite basins, slatey tarns, and pool-and-drop creeks were overrun with people (3,000 or 4,000 on a typical summer weekend) who had not yet been educated in wilderness ethics. Trash accumulated, water supplies were fouled. Newspapers began referring to it as "Desecration Valley" or worse, "Devastation Valley." The Forest Service reacted by shifting gears; instead of encouraging human use, the Service began a policy of trying to play down the area's charms, proposing that fish not be planted in the lakes and streams, an idea that was, fortunately, shelved. A wilderness permit program was established, California's first, and daily quotas were set. Today, you have to fill out a form, even if you're just going for a day hike.

Echo Lakes is the most popular access point for two reasons: the trailhead is high, and for a modest fee you can take a water taxi, thereby shortening the trek by three miles. An easy day hike is to explore the Desolation Valley area including the inappropriately named **Lake of the Woods** (how many of those are there in this country?) and **Lake Aloha** (elevation 8,100 feet), which, not surprisingly, is particularly devoid of palm trees. Both are planted with eastern brook trout released from low-flying airplanes. Other trails lead to higher lakes where the catch is primarily rainbow trout. The more remote areas of the wilderness, however, are best visited from the west side, which we will visit soon.

Recreational Facilities

△△ **Echo Chalet** Grocery and housekeeping cabins. Echo Lake, CA 95712. (916) 659-7207.

§ **Sierra Ski Ranch** 9 lifts, 1,500 foot vertical. Twin Bridges, CA 95735. (916) 659-7475.

§ **Lake Tahoe Ranger District** (U.S.F.S.) Information and wilderness permits. 1052 Tata Lane, South Lake Tahoe, CA 95731. (916) 544-6420.

Strawberry

Present-day Highway 50 drops steeply into the canyon of the American River on a precipitous slope that teamsters used to call Slippery Ford Hill. Lover's leap, a great granite monolith, soars a thousand feet above the river bottom. The drivers who put their lives (and their passengers) in peril negotiating grades like this elicited no small amount of comment from early travelers and so, each June, the Highway 50 Association celebrates that brother-hood of Jehu by staging a ten-day wagon-train ride from Virginia City to Placerville. There were heroes aplenty in that ancient fraternity—Newt Spencer, Curly Bill Gearhardt, and Baldy Green, for instance. But it was Hank Monk, "King of the Whips," who commanded the most attention.

Keep Your Seat, Horace!

Hank Monk, legend has it, could drive when he was so drunk he couldn't walk; a man who could turn a six-horse coach at full gallop with every line loose. He is once reported to have fed whiskey to the horses and watered himself, thus becoming accidentally sober enough to handle the inebriated team. But it was his ride with Horace Greeley that made him famous—as re-lated here by Artemus Ward, Abraham Lincoln's favorite humorist:

Mr. Greeley was to be fêted at 7 o'clock that eve-ning by the citizens of Placerville, so the Stage Com-pany said to Henry Monk, "Henry, this great man must be there by 7 to-night." And Henry answered, "The great man shall be there." The roads were in an awful state, and during the first few miles slow progress was made.

"Sir," said Mr. Greeley, "are you aware that I *must* be at Placerville at 7 o-clock to-night."

"I've got my orders!" laconically returned Henry Monk. Still the coach dragged slowly forward.

"Sir," said Mr. Greeley, "this is not a trifling matter."

Again came the answer: "I've got my orders!"

But the speed was not increased, and Mr. Greeley chafed away another half hour when suddenly the horses started into a furious run, and all sorts of encouraging yells filled the air from the throat of Hen-ry Monk.

And on they tore over stones and ruts, up hill and down, at a rate of speed never before achieved by stage horses. Mr. Greeley, who had been bouncing from one end of the coach to the other like an india-rubber ball, managed to get his head out the window when he said:

"Do—on't you—u—u—think we—e—shall get there by seven if we do—on't go—go so fast?"

"I've got my orders!"

And on tore the coach. Another frightful jolt, and Mr. Greeley's bald head suddenly found its way through the roof of the coach, amidst the crash of small timbers and the ripping of strong canvas.

"Stop, you—maniac!" he roared.

Again answered Henry Monk:

"I've got my orders! *Keep your seat, Horace!*"

Roaring into Mud springs, a few miles from Placerville, the stage was met by a committee of prominent citizens who had come out to welcome the editor.

"Is Mr. Greeley on board?" asked the chairman. . . .

"He was a few miles back," said Mr. Monk; "Yes," he added, after looking down through the hole which the fearful jolting had made in the coach roof—"yes, I can see him! *He is there!*'

In *Roughing It,* Mark Twain told the story three times, verbatim, and then explained why he felt such repetition necessary:

Within a period of six years I crossed and recrossed the Sierras between Nevada and California thirteen times by stage and listened to that deathless incident four hundred and eighty-one or eighty-two times. I have the list somewhere. Bayard Taylor has written about this hoary anecdote, Richardson has published it: so have Jones, Smith, Johnson, Ross Browne, and every other correspondence-inditing being that ever set his foot upon the great overland road anywhere between Julesburg and San Francisco; and I have heard that it is in the Talmud. I have seen it in print in nine different foreign languages; I have been told that it is employed in the inquisition in Rome; and I now learn with regret that it is going to be set to music. I do not think that such things are right.

Neither did Horace Greeley. Ward's story achieved wide circulation during Greeley's Presidential campaign and contributed to his loss to Ulysses Grant. A splendid painting of the event by R. T. Sheridan now hangs in the Wells Fargo Museum in San Francisco. Henry Monk died in 1883 and is buried in Carson City.

Hank Monk insisted it was Irad Fuller Berry's parsimonious habits that inspired the name **Strawberry** (elevation 5,800 feet):

> That son of a b_____ used to steal the oats and barley from the horses of the teamsters, and put straw in place of the grain, so we all called him "Straw" Berry.

It's been called that ever since, even though many confuse it with another Strawberry, located thirty-five miles south on Highway 108. The old hotel, the last remaining stagecoach stop on the Bonanza Road, has a somewhat worn look, but is a nice place to stop for a meal or to spend the night. Trout fishermen and swimmers enjoy the river out back, and the Forest Service has built a number of picnic places nearby. Another granite outcropping near the village of **Kyburz** is called the Sugar Loaf.

Recreational Facilities

✓✓ **Strawberry Lodge** Restaurant, bar, and 35-room historic hotel. Kyburz, CA 95720. (916) 659-7200.

△ **Forest Service Campgrounds** Two riverside campgrounds (one on Silver Fork), 65 sites.

WRIGHT'S LAKE WILDERNESS ACCESS

A well-graded, paved road climbs the canyon wall to the lovely and isolated **Wrights Lake** (elevation 6,941 feet), one of the Sierra's more pristine vacation retreats. A hundred cabins circle the lake, but because there is no running water, no electricity, and no telephones, the place retains a backwoods feel. Motor boats are not allowed. The campground has become so popular that reservations are recommended. The rocky-shored, naturally occurring lake sits on the flank of the Crystal Range, adjacent to the wilderness area. Nice day hikes lead to **Island Lakes** (8,150 feet) and the **Lyons Lake** (8,400 feet). Those with strong legs head for **Pyramid Peak,** a landmark that can be seen from the Sacramento Valley. The six-and-a-half-mile hike requires climbing 3,000 feet. **Rockbound Valley** in the untamed headwaters of the Rubicon River is reached by a six-mile trail that crosses Rockbound Pass (8,500 feet). Those able to effect a car shuttle can make a nice three- or four-day loop, coming out at Loon Lake.

Recreational Facilities

△ **Forest Service Campground** Wrights Lake, 71 reservable sites.

CRYSTAL BASIN RECREATION AREA

Highway 50 follows the American River for another dozen miles, but is then forced up onto a ridge by a gradually steepening canyon. The drive is pretty, but once past Pollock Pines the scene is more akin to the Gold Country (see Chapter 18). So we shall turn north to explore the backroads of the West-of-Tahoe Sierra.

There is little granite here. The area is (or was) heavily forested, but clearcutting has been practiced in recent years. When I asked Ranger Art Allen why this was, he seemed a bit defensive; he muttered something about "sustained yield harvesting" and gave me a handout reading:

> Clearcutting is the most used logging method because it's been shown to increase timber yields, is more practical and re-establishes healthy trees quicker. Clearcutting's openings let foresters replant genetically superior seedlings.

Maybe, but a fellow I met at Robbs Resort who drove a log truck didn't like the practice any more than the rest of us. Readers wishing to get a better understanding of modern silviculture should tour the **Forest Service nursery** at Apple Hill near Placerville. Seed cones are brought here from each of California's twenty forest districts. White fir and ponderosa are the principal crops, but experimental plantings of Port Orford cedar, Bishop pine, and redwood are also being studied. Sugar pine is in disfavor because of problems with blister rust. I was surprised to learn that the best seed cones are often found at the very tops of trees, so helicopters are used in the harvest. Millions of trees are planted each year.

Much of the timber around **Ice House Reservoir** (elevation 5,500 feet) still stands, so it is a nice vacation spot. **Union Valley Reservoir,** although lower (4,900 feet), has an equally nice woodsy feel. Both lakes are great for fishing and water skiing, as long as the utility keeps them reasonably full. **Loon Lake** (6,378 feet), a granite-ringed reservoir, provides our final access to the

Desolation Wilderness. An almost level trail skirts around the north end of the Crystal Range, joining the Rubicon River near Rockbound Lake. Those able to bum a ride on someone's motor boat can cut the six-mile walk to the wilderness boundary in half.

Wentworth Springs, located down in a hole, is the starting point for the infamous **Rubicon Springs Jeep Road,** which crosses the Sierra crest and drops into Lake Tahoe via McKinney Creek. Most adventurers allow two days for the drive, and only the foolish go alone. (Photos on the wall of the Miner's Club saloon in Georgetown illustrate the hazards.) Hal Sowers, an enthusiast, told me that he (and his Jeep) survived the infamous "Sluice Box," but he says he'll never try it again.

A washboardy, but quite passable dirt road goes down the divide, connecting with the paved road from Georgetown. Historic **Uncle Toms Cabin,** a tiny log shack, has served as a roadhouse for a century. Host Jim Berry keeps a cheery fire going in winter. A sign on the front door sternly admonishes: "Tractors Prohibited Beyond This Sign."

Recreational Facilities

△ **Ice House Resort** Cafe, bar, grocery store, and RV camp. P.O. Box 839, Pollock Pines, CA 95726. (916) 293-3321.

△ **Robbs Valley Resort** Cafe, bar, grocery store, and RV camp. P.O. Box 69, Pacific House, CA 95725.

△ **Forest Service Campgrounds** Ice House Reservoir, 2 campgrounds, 94 sites; Union Valley Reservoir, 3 campgrounds, 275 sites; Loon Lake, 34 sites plus a boat-in campground with 10 sites; Wentworth Springs, 10 sites; Stumpy Meadows, 40 sites.

§ **El Dorado National Forest** Information and wilderness permits. 100 Forni Road, Placerville, CA 95667. (916) 622-5061. Crystal Basin Information Center. (916) 293-3450.

FOREST HILL DIVIDE

You have to, as it were, cross the Rubicon to continue exploring the West-of-Tahoe Sierra. The road, paved now, drops into the valley of the Rubicon River (nice fishing) and then skirts around the hillside, climbing into the headwaters of the middle fork of the American River. **Hell Hole Reservoir** (elevation 4,580 feet) snuggles in a rather steep-sided canyon. Placer County Water Agency, builder of the dam, has provided a boat-launching ramp, so fishing is popular. **French Meadows Reservoir** (5,200 feet) has the better camping because the countryside is not quite as steep. Its waters inundated an absolutely lovely, almost level valley, filled with stands of giant red fir and stately ponderosa. The campground, a ranger told me, is often full on weekends, even though it is seventy-five miles out into the woods. This is a game refuge, which no doubt contributes to its popularity. I saw a bear cub glomping awkwardly down the road. A dirt road, slow for the most part, continues north, first dropping into the North Fork of the American and then climbing up onto the ridge to join Interstate 80 near Soda Springs (see Chapter 1).

A treasure of this part of the Sierra is the **Placer County Grove** of giant sequoias. Though only half a dozen redwoods are still extant (not counting the ones the local Lions Club planted), they stand here as a last remnant of a species that once covered much of North America. Today, their nearest brethren lie sixty miles south in the Calaveras Grove (Chapter 5).

The road from here to Foresthill is paved all the way, but it is slow going and very twisty where it drops into the North Fork of the Middle Fork of the American River. Backtracking to the Robinsons Flat Road is more pleasant, even though the first five miles are dirt. A reasonable side road leads to the **Duncan Peak Lookout** (elevation 7,200 feet), where you get a fine view of the area. From Robinsons Flat, the county road leading down the Forest Hill Divide is wide and reasonably fast. Two long-distance races held each summer traverse this area: the Western States Endurance Run, in which competitors must run from Squaw Valley to Auburn, a distance of a hundred miles, in less than twenty-four hours; and the Tevis Cup, a similar ordeal for those on horseback.

Recreational Facilities

△ **Forest Service Campgrounds** Hell Hole Reservoir, 10 sites; French Meadows Reservoir, 3 campgrounds, 125 sites; Robinsons Flat, 6 sites.

FORESTHILL

The countryside near **Sugar Pine Reservoir** (elevation 4,000 feet) is laced with off-road-vehicle trails. Kids (and adults too) go careening about on three- and four-wheel motorcycle-like vehicles. Foresthill (population 1,304; elevation 3,225 feet), an old sawmill town, is growing, thanks to a new, high-level bridge spanning the American River, which cuts the driving time to Interstate 80 in half. Built because the Auburn dam was to flood the canyon, it cost more than the assessed value of all the land it serves. So far, earthquake concerns have stopped the dam, so Foresthill property owners are the primary beneficiaries. The town has a small **museum** and a couple of pretty cemeteries. **Michigan Bluff,** the gold town where Leland Stanford got his start in the grocery business, is now pretty much falling down. Alas, so is **Yankee Jims,** a town named for a fellow described by locals as: "somewhat given to banditry." Of the several accounts of the scoundrel's fate, the most probable is:

> He was hung by orders of an irregular court at Los Angeles in 1852 for an attempt to steal the pilot boat *Plutus* with the intention of putting to sea [with] the likely intent of engaging in piratical acts.

Recreational Facilities

Δ **Morning Star Lake Resort** Boat rentals, RV camping. P.O. Box 119, Foresthill, CA 95631.

Δ **Forest Service Campgrounds** Sugar Pine Reservoir, 2 campgrounds, 60 sites.

To continue your Sierra adventure, meet us in Placerville.

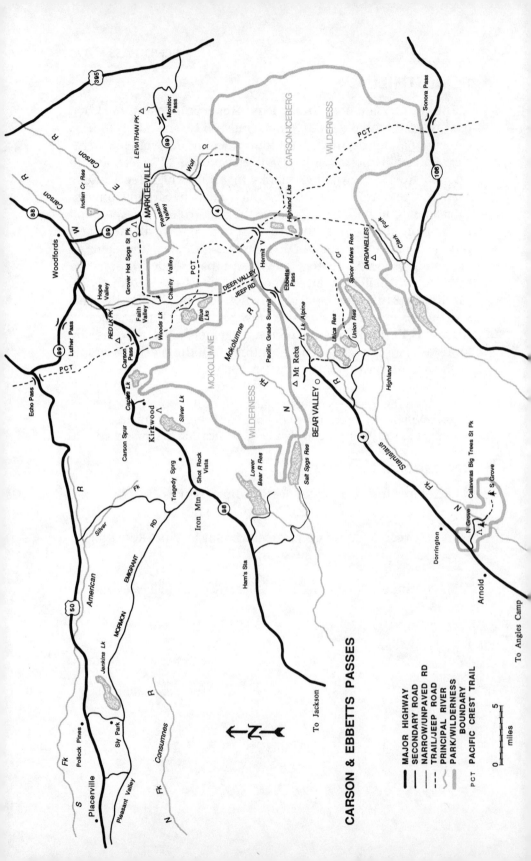

CARSON & EBBETTS PASSES

MAJOR HIGHWAY
SECONDARY ROAD
NARROW/UNPAVED RD
TRAIL/JEEP ROAD
PRINCIPAL RIVER
PARK/WILDERNESS
BOUNDARY
PCT PACIFIC CREST TRAIL

0   5
miles

◄◄◄◄◄◄◆ 4 ◆►►►►►►

THE CARSON EMIGRANT ROAD

Tracks of the Elephant

Merril Mattes, in his book, *The Great Platte River Road*, commented:

> To read the diaries of the Gold Rush, one might suppose that elephants flourished in 1849, but the emigrants weren't talking about woolly mammoths or genuine circus-type elephants. They were talking about one particular elephant, *the* Elephant, an imaginary beast of fearsome dimensions which, according to Niles Searls, was "but another name for going to California."

We will find several references to that beast as we follow what was one of the most popular routes to the gold fields. Through their diaries, we will meet some of the explorers and pioneers who struggled west, but we will make the journey in the other direction. Curiously, this was the way the first wagon train went. Brigham Young, anxious to get on James K. Polk's good side, had organized what became known as the Mormon Battalion, sending them south to fight in the Mexican War. With the treaty of Guadalupe Hidalgo, California was ceded to the United States and the battalion found themselves out of a job. Moving north, the men found employment helping to build John Sutter's sawmill at Coloma. Henry William Bigler, a member of the battalion, is of special interest because his account provides us with a marvelous guide to follow. Bigler had the good fortune to be in the right place at the right time (his diary provides the only eyewitness account of James Marshall's discovery of gold on the American River), but he seemed little interested in the yellow metal. He and his band of "boys" continued to build the sawmill, amusing themselves on the Sabbath by digging chunks of gold out of cracks with a jack knife. But Brigham Young called the flock home and so, as spring turned into summer that fateful year of 1848, the Mormon Battalion packed their wagons and headed east. The trip across the Sierra took a month. The road they built went up the divide that separates the American and Consumnes rivers and thence over Carson Pass, more or less following what is now State Highway 88 (see map, Chapter 5). We will follow their route as closely as possible.

MORMON EMIGRANT ROAD

From Placerville, take Newton road to **Pleasant Valley.** Looking about, it's easy to imagine how the first settlers, those who came before the gold rush, must have felt when they arrived here. Gone were the endless prairies, the sage brush of the Rockies, the alkali deserts, and the snows of the Sierra. Here they found that the stories they had heard were true, stories like one which appeared in the St. Louis *Saturday Evening Gazette:*

> The climate is salubrious and delightful—the soil rich—the natural productions various—and all the means of a pleasant and comfortable subsistence afforded in abundance. A glorious era is, no doubt, dawning in those regions so favored by nature.

Favored it was: water was plentiful, the sun seemed to shine every day and the grass was as high as the bellies of their half-starved cows. Today, encina oak and digger pine crowd the hilltops, and pastures, nourished by spring-fed streams, cover the gentle valley floor. Fields of California poppies (the state flower) reflect the color of the mineral that once laced the ground. A few barns, some run-down houses, several country stores, and a

Pentecostal church dot the landscape. Sly Park Road climbs a bit, but the grade is not noticeable until you top a hogback, where surprisingly deep canyons suddenly appear on both sides.

> [Bigler] July 4th. We rolled out after the camp, taking the divide between the American River and the Consumnes.

Soon, the Mormons began to worry about three men who had gone ahead to "pioneer" the route.

> July 5th. We sent out ten men to look for them, while the rest of us took the stock down into the little valley, which we called Sly's Park after one of our men.

Today the former community of Sly Park is drowned by **Jenkins Lake.** Picnicking and boating are popular. The **Mormon Emigrant Road,** which crosses the dam, doesn't exactly retrace Bigler's route, but by following it you get an idea of what they were up against.

> July 15th. This morning, myself and three others went ahead with axes to cut brush and roll rocks out of the way for our wagons and packs. A wagon never had been here before since these mountains were made and for aught I know, not even a white man.
> July 16th. Cutting our way as yesterday, the road very bad; broke a coupling pole to one of the wagons.

This is a Forest Service road, not maintained by the state, so snow is not removed. Between October and April you travel at your own risk; often it is closed. Highway maps relegate the route to country-lane status (if they show it at all), so there is seldom traffic, save for the log trucks that are its *raison d'être.* Wide shoulders and sparse traffic make this one of the best trans-Sierra bicycle routes.

The highway climbs steadily, with only the changing foliage hinting that you're approaching the high country. The digger pines of the upper Sonoran zone surrender their turf to ponderosa pines in the transition zone. Mariposa lilies, cow parsnip, larkspur, and the white-flowered, prickly leafed, mountain misery prevail. The air becomes cooler, four degrees on average for every thousand feet of climb. Above 5,500 feet you enter the snow belt, the so-called Canadian zone, where the increased moisture allows white fir and incense cedar to flourish. Sugar pine, which John Muir called "the nobelist pine yet discovered," once flourished here, but because of its large size and resistance to warping, it became the loggers' tree of choice. Modern logging operations are easily spotted by simply looking at the road. Log trucks, coming out of the woods, leave a telltale splattering of mud or dirt on the pavement. I stopped when I spotted a crew working a hundred yards off the road. The buzz of the chainsaw was replaced by the metallic sound of hammer against wedge as they muscled the tree in the direction they wanted it to fall. Then, as the crew boss let out an ear-piercing "ye-ouw-ee," the monster fell with a snapping of branches and a ground shaking crash.

At the 6,000-foot level a twisty, but paved road drops steeply into the **Silver Fork** of the American River, where a campground sidles up to the rocky stream. The fishing, I'm told, is great.

Our road joins State Highway 88 at the parking lot of the **Iron Mountain Ski Area** (elevation 7,200 feet). This "family" resort is a bit unusual in that the lodge is at the top of the slopes. Chairlifts bring skiers up from runs that lead down toward Silver Fork. It's a nice place to ski when there is enough snow. **Lower Bear River Reservoir** and **Salt Springs Reservoir** both have summer-time boating. The latter, reached by a nineteen-mile paved road, occupies a spectacular site, with the dam framed by the lovely Calaveras Dome. The road in parallels the Mokelumne River for four miles, providing access to this fine fishing stream.

Recreational Facilities

- ✔ **Iron Mountain Inn** Cafeteria, bar, 36-room motel. Highway 88, Pioneer, CA 95666. (209) 258-4672.

- △ **Bear River Lake Resort** Store, marina, snack bar, and 125-site RV resort. Snowmobiling. 40800 Highway 88 Pioneer, CA 95666. (209) 295-4868.

- △ **Forest Service Campground** South Shore campground on Lower Bear River reservoir, 22 sites. Three unimproved campgrounds about the Mokelumne River near Salt Springs Reservoir.

- **Ham's Station** Hundred-year-old roadhouse, restaurant, and bar. (209) 295-4810.

§ **Iron Mountain Ski Resort** 4 lifts, 1,200 foot vertical. Highway 88 Pioneer, CA 95666. (209) 295-3685

SILVER LAKE

Highway 88, which has been hugging the ridge between the Consumnes and Mokelumne rivers, suddenly takes on a "High Sierra" feel. You're almost as high as the summits of Interstate 80 and Highway 50, but unlike those quick-up, quick-down roads, here you traverse this lofty country for another twenty miles. **Shot Rock Vista Point** has lovely views out over the granite wastes of the Mokelumne (pronounced Mo-kél-um-ne) Wilderness. A more sorrowful spot is **Tragedy Spring**.

> [Bigler] July 18th. As we were returning to camp we found the place where we supposed our three pioneers had camped by a large spring. Near where they had their fire, was the appearance of a fresh grave. Some of us thought it might be an Indian grave, as near it was an old wickey up, but the more we looked at it, the more we felt there lay the three men. Determining to satisfy ourselves, it was soon opened. We were shocked at the sight. There lay the three murdered men robbed of every stitch of clothing, lying promiscuously in one hole about two feet deep. Allen was lying on his back and had the appearance that an ax had been sunk into his face and that he had been shot in the eye. We cut the following inscription on a balsam fir that stood near the grave: "To the memory of Daniel Browett, Ezrah H. Allen, and Henderson Cox, who were supposed to have been murdered and buried by Indians on the night of the twenty-seventh of June, A.D. 1848." We called this place Tragedy Spring.

Browett was forty years old, Cox, the youngest, barely out of his teens. The tree blew down some years ago, but the portion with the markings was salvaged and now rests proudly at the museum in Coloma. A bronze replica is affixed to a granite boulder here. The spring is as pure as ever.

Bigler's road turned due east here, skirted around the south side of Silver Lake, and climbed over Squaw Ridge (elevation 9,640 feet), eventually joining our highway near Caples Lake.

Highway 88 takes a much more direct route. The country has a rocky, sub-alpine appearance. Granite predominates, punctuated by thick forests of lodgepole, mountain hemlock, and an occasional juniper. Jeffery pines replace the ponderosa. Corn lilies, tiger lilies, and camass grow in the sunnier spots. **Silver Lake** (7,209 feet), which occupies a wide, almost flat basin, is a popular camping and boating resort.

Recreational Facilities

ΔΔ **Kit Carson Lodge** Restaurant, grocery, 8 rooms and 19 housekeeping cottages. Kit Carson, CA 95644. (209) 258-8500.

ΔΔ **Kay's Silver Lake Resort** Store, cafe, and housekeeping cabins. P.O. Box 77, Kirkwood, CA 95646. (209) 258-8864.

Δ **Plasse's Resort** Restaurant, bar, store, and R.V. park. 30001 Plasse Road, Silver Lake, CA 95666. (209) 223-1540.

Δ **Forest Service Campgrounds** Silver Lake 97 sites.

Ω **Albiani Pack Trains** Plasse Road, Silver Lake, CA 95666. (209) 258-8814.

KIRKWOOD MEADOWS • Population 300; elevation 7,800 feet

The "new" road, built in 1863, circles around a volcanic outcropping that caught early explorer William Brewer's attention:

We crossed the Carson Spur, a high ridge of stratified volcanic ashes and breccia, capped by hard lava. Here we had the most picturesque scenery of the route. Below us, a thousand feet, dashed the river over granite rocks, the cliffs worn into very fantastic shapes—old castles, towers, pillars, pinnacles—all were there; while above, rugged rocky peaks, volcanic, of fantastic shapes, rose a thousand feet more, fearfully steep, the snow lying in patches here and there.

Aptly named Pyramid Peak is the prominent landmark on the far side of the American River canyon. On Washington's birthday, 1844, German-born cartographer Charles Preuss was among the first to look out over this rock-bound scene, and he did not think the country at all picturesque:

> The lower mountains, through which and over which we must wind our way, look confoundedly rocky. If we were not tied to the miserable beasts, without which we cannot transport our baggage, I believe we could reach the valley on foot in two days. But as it is—only a few miles—God knows when.

Preuss was on Frémont's second expedition and the party was on the verge of disaster. Despite being guided by two trail-wise mountain men [Kit Carson and Thomas (Broken Hand) Fitzpatrick], they had been forced to abandon their wagons back in the desert and now their mules were being sacrificed to their appetites. Preuss' forboding proved propitious: several animals fell off cliffs, carrying the botanical samples (a major reason for funding the trip) to the icy bottom of the American River. Today a rugged jeep road is all that penetrates that confoundedly rocky canyon.

Kirkwood Meadows holds the beauty: a mile-long sea of green surrounded by wildflower-covered slopes and soaring, snow-clad peaks.

> [Bigler] July 22nd. I passed over snow more than two feet deep and saw banks ten and perhaps fifteen feet deep. This day I gathered flowers with one hand and snow with the other.

People have marveled ever since that snow and wildflowers can coexist; Mark Twain wrote about the experience in *Roughing It*. The nearby rustic log-cabin roadhouse, built by Zack Kirkwood in 1864, has served its intended function ever since. Kirkwood Meadows is primarily a place for winter fun, despite management's efforts to boost the summer trade. Occupying an isolated valley, it has the potential for becoming one of the nicest ski areas in California. The planners are trying to create an "Alpine village," where people shop, dine, play, and sleep within walking distance of the ski slopes. A noble idea, but Vail (Colorado) it is not. The resort boasts a couple of day lodges and a sit-down restaurant, but overnight guests stay in condos strung out along the access road. Nearby lifts serve beginners and shuttle skiers to the main slopes. Kirkwood boasts the highest base elevation in the Tahoe area (7,800 feet) and therefore claims to have the driest and best snow, but I'm not sure that is meaningful. Heavenly's base (Chapter 2), for all intent and purposes, is the top of the tram at 8,200 feet. The resort is almost as big as Alpine Meadows (prices too are similar) and has some magnificent and challenging slopes, especially the bowls west of the Cornice lift. But it suffers from a dearth of intermediate runs, and when I was there the grooming was spotty and the lifts kept breaking down. Lift lines were bothersome.

The area has fine Nordic ski facilities, served by a day lodge near Kirkwood Inn. **Caples Lake,** located a few miles up the highway, is a nice rock-bound reservoir with a character similar to Silver Lake.

The most used part of the **Mokolumne Wilderness** is the area near Carson Pass, popular because the countryside is not overly steep and is punctuated by a number of lakes. The **Pacific Crest Trail** crosses the highway here, giving backpackers access to the entire Sierra range. Most, however, prefer shorter weekend overnight trips to **Emigrant Lake** (trailhead at Capels Lake) or **Round Top, Fourth of July,** and **Winemucca** lakes, which have access from **Woods Lake** (elevation 8,500 feet). Picnickers will enjoy the short walk from the summit to **Frog Lake.**

Recreational Facilities

  ✔✔ **Kirkwood** Full service ski resort. 10 lifts, 2,000 foot vertical. Groomed cross-country skiing with warming hut.
P.O. Box 1, Kirkwood, CA 95646. Snow phone (209)
258-3000. Central reservations for summer and winter
condo rentals (209) 258-7000.

  ✔ **Caples Lake Resort** 6 lodge rooms and 7 housekeeping
cabins. Cafe and marina. P.O. Box 8, Kirkwood, CA,
95646 (209) 258-8888.

  △ **Forest Service Campground** Woods Lake, 14 sites; Kirkwood Lake, 13 sites.

  ● **Kirkwood Inn** Old stage coach stop, now a bar and cafe.

§ **El Dorado National Forest** Information and wilderness permits. P.O. Box 1327, Jackson, CA 95642. (209) 223-1623.

CARSON PASS

Rock upon rock—rock upon rock!
Snow upon snow—snow upon snow!
Even if you get over the snow you will not
be able to get down from the mountain.

With those words the old Washoe warned John Charles Frémont not to attempt a Sierra crossing in the dead of winter. Charles Preuss was even more gloomy about their prospects:

[January 26] We still do not know where we really are. Yesterday we passed through the mountains with deep, deep snow; for tomorrow there are even higher ones ahead of us. [February 6] Today the "field marshal" [Frémont] marched out with a party on snowshoes to open a way to the summit. [February 14] No longer any salt in the camp. This is awful.

Preuss's foul mood was understandable: he had refused to partake of his mule Jack, who had been slaughtered that day for the dining table. That perhaps explains why he neglected to mention a remarkable event that he and Frémont shared:

With Mr. Preuss I ascended to-day the highest peak to the right; from which we had a beautiful view of a mountain lake at our feet, about fifteen miles in length, and so entirely surrounded by mountains that we could not discover an outlet.

Standing atop Red Lake Peak, the two were the first Whites to lay eyes on Lake Tahoe. Today the walk takes a couple of hours. That same day Kit Carson carved his name on a tree at the summit, the only two words he ever learned to write. Frémont was lucky, a warm rain had melted much of the snow and he was impressed:

Scenery and weather combined must render these mountains beautiful in summer; the purity and deep-blue color of the sky are singularly beautiful.

Carson's thoughts were less sanguine:

> We returned to the place from which we had sent back our animals, and with nothing to eat but mule meat commenced the work of making the road. Driven by hunger, they had eaten one another's tails and the leather of the pack saddles, in fact everything they could lay hold of.

The '49ers too, felt a sense of exaltation when they at last topped the mighty Sierra. Sarah Royce stood here on October 19 in that eventful year:

> I had purposely hastened, that morning, to start ahead of the rest; and not far from noon, I was rewarded by coming out on a rocky height whence I looked, *down,* far over constantly descending hills, to where a soft haze sent up a warm, rosy glow that seemed to me a smile of welcome. California, land of sunny skies—that was my first look into your smiling face.

Carson Pass (elevation 8,573 feet) is a beehive of activity during the summer, the parking lot filled with hikers' cars. A Forest Service information hut is staffed during working hours. Plaques have been placed about to honor Kit Carson and some pioneering "Odd Fellows," but the most moving memorial is a granite obelisk, broken off at the top, erected to the memory of Snowshoe Thompson (see below).

Snowshoe Thompson

In his native Norway, he was christened Jon Torsteinson Rui. Friends at his farm near Sacramento, where he had emigrated in the mid-1850s called him John A. Thomson, but the world would soon know him as "Snowshoe" (and add a "p" to his new last name). To him, mountains were a challenge, not a barrier, and so, when learning of the closing of mail service to the Washoe mines during the winter, he offered to help. Fashioning a pair of "Norwegian snowshoes" (what we now call skis) twelve feet long and weighing twenty-five pounds, he set off from Placerville in January of 1856 with an eighty-pound knapsack filled with mail. It took three days to cross the Sierra, two to return. With no room for blankets, or even a coat, he kept warm when he stopped by building a fire or, failing that because of storm, by standing on a rock and jumping up and down all night. For twenty winters he repeated the trek, furnishing the only connection the miners had with the outside world. His fee: fifty cents a pound. For two of those years he had a contract with the U.S. Mail but never got paid.

Tales of his heroism abound. Once, stumbling upon a supposedly deserted cabin, he found James Sesson on the verge of chopping off his frozen legs with an axe. Thompson raced to Genoa, rounded up some aides, and returned with a sled. After they got the poor fellow to safety, the doctor refused to operate without chloroform, so Thompson immediately started out for Placerville, returning with the vital fluid after almost no sleep. Sesson survived.

Thompson moved to the Carson Valley but, perhaps because of overwork, died an untimely death on May 15, 1876, at the age of 49 years. His gravestone in the lovely cemetery near Genoa (Chapter 15) is marked with a pair of crossed skis. Dan De Quille, Mark Twain's friend at the *Territorial Enterprise,* interviewed Thompson. On learning of his death, he was moved to write:

There ought to be a shaft raised to Snowshoe Thompson, not of marble, not carved and not planted in the valley, but a rough shaft of basalt or granite, massive and tall, with the top ending roughly, as if broken short to represent a life which is strong and true to the last, and this should be upreared on the summit of the mountains over which the strong man wandered so many years, as an emblem of that life that was worn out.

And so there is.

HOPE VALLEY/WOODFORDS

Bigler's party now had to face a steep descent to Red Lake, which comes into view just over the summit.

July 24th. Moved about six miles and camped just over the summit. Two wagons broke down and two were upset.
[July 26] As usual we broke down again; an axle tree snapped in two.

The following year Carson Pass became one of the Argonauts' favorite routes to the gold fields, but apparently the road wasn't much better, as '49er Jasper Morris Hixon recalled:

Just ahead was a wall several thousand feet high. Had we not seen by the dust arising from those ahead that others were going that way, we would have come to the conclusion that this was the end of the road, but as others had gone up this hill, we could do the same. It was called the "Devil's Ladder."

A short side road leads to Red Lake, where you can park and climb the Devil's Ladder on a foot path. Locals say that on some trees you can still see marks cut by the chains that were used to winch the wagons up the hill.

Highway 88 now descends into one of the prettiest valleys in the Sierra (elevation 7,000 feet).

[Bigler] July 29th. Moved across about one mile and half and camped at the head of what we called Hope Valley, as we began to have hope.

Later emigrants learned that there was not one, but three valleys (meadows, actually), strung out along tributaries of the Carson River. Logically enough, they named the other two Faith and Charity. These mountain meadows, unfortunately, are a transitory element on this earth, a way station for a place that was once a lake and will, in time, become a forest. A pity, for they hold a special place in the hearts of mountain lovers. John Muir said of them:

With inexpressible delight you wade out into the grassy sun-lake, feeling yourself contained in one of Nature's most sacred chambers, withdrawn from the sterner influences of the mountains, secure from all intrusion, secure from yourself, free in the universal beauty. And notwithstanding the scene is so impressively spiritual, and you seem dissolved in it, yet everything about you is beating with warm, terrestrial, human love and life delightfully substantial and familiar.

Sacred chambers indeed! Muir might well have chosen other words to describe their character: pastoral, solemn, bucolic, sublime—all seem fitting, especially for Faith, Hope, and Charity valleys. The meadows are gentle, but looming darkly on the western skyline is the **Elephant's Back,** a peak that seems the embodiment of the barrier that stood in the way of the emigrants' path.

For decades developers have cast covetous eyes on this area (South Lake Tahoe is only a twenty-minute drive away), and for almost as many years a group called Friends of Hope Valley have kept them out. A back-country road, some barbed-wire fences, and a single tumbled-down barn in Charity Valley are about the only indication that people ever set foot into this unsullied paradise. The only hint of commercialism is an outfitter who takes people on dog-sled rides in the winter. A trail from Charity Valley goes east toward **Grover Hot Springs** (Chapter 5), more or less following the route that Carson and Frémont took in 1844. Cross-country skiers find the area ideal.

Beyond the uppermost meadow, the back road crosses the Sierra crest at the unexciting Border Ruffian Pass and then dips into the surprisingly gentle headwaters of the Mokolumne. **Blue Lakes** (elevation 8,100 feet), two reservoirs built by PG&E, provide an agreeable recreation area for fishermen and campers. Numerous trails lead to a half dozen other nearby lakes. **Deer Valley Jeep Road,** maintained by four-wheel-drive clubs, pierces the Mokolumne Wilderness, eventually joining the Ebbetts Pass Highway at Hermit Valley. The route follows a road built in 1856 to service some silver mines.

Bigler's hopes must have been dashed when he encountered **Woodfords Canyon,** the steep, narrow, and rocky gulch that separates Hope Valley from the Nevada basin.

July 30th. Worked and made a road for about two miles. Here we expect to lay by for several days in order to work a road through the canyon about four miles and very bad. (July 31st) A general turnout to work on the road. Considerable digging to do and rolling rocks out of the way. (August 3rd) Road working. In the afternoon fell a little rain and snow. (August 4th) We finished our road. Moved through the canyon all safe. Four Indians came into camp. We were overtaken today by thirteen of our boys with pack animals. They had left the mines five days ago.

Hixon's party, coming the other way, fared hardly better:

The rocks we had to pass over ranged in size from a nail keg to a whiskey barrel. Finally we encountered one as large as a sugar hogshead and that proved too much for one of our wagons. [When] the hind axle broke, we cut the bed and put the hind wheels on the forward axle and made a cart.

Diaries of other emigrants spoke of equally dire mishaps. Wakeman Bryerly, struggling on the Bear River, wrote:

Everyone is liable to mistakes & everyone has a right to call a road *very* bad until he sees a worse. My mistake was that I had said I had seen "The Elephant" when getting over the first mountain. I had only seen the tail. This evening I think I saw him in toto.

Upon emerging from that awful gorge, you figuratively, at least, find yourself in Nevada. The canyon debauches into the wide Carson Valley at the hamlet of **Woodfords** (population 300; elevation 5,800 feet), now little more than a store and a gas station, The new motel could well have chosen a more historic name, for Daniel Woodford opened a hotel here in 1849. He called it Sign of the Elephant.

Recreational Facilities

- ✔ **Woodfords Inn** 20-room motel. P.O. Box 426, Markleeville, CA 96120. (916) 694-2410.

- ∆∆ **Sorensen's** Outdoor cafe and 23 housekeeping cabins. One unit is a handsome replica of a Norwegian farm house. Hope Valley, CA 96120. (916) 694-2203.

- ∆ **Hope Valley Resort** Store, restaurant, and RV park. P.O. Box 600, Hope Valley, CA 96120. (916) 694-2292.

- ∆ **Forest Service Campgrounds** Four campgrounds in and about Hope Valley, 60 sites.

△ **PG&E Campgrounds** Three campgrounds at Blue Lakes, 46 sites.

● **Woodfords Station** Cafe & Grocery. (916) 694-2930.

Highway 88 continues on to Minden/Gardnerville (Chapter 15). The Mormon Battalion went this way, eventually crossing the infamous Forty-Mile Desert, which led them to the Humboldt River. We'll take leave of Bigler and his band of "boys" here, noting only that he found himself encountering emigrants with a more frenzied agenda.

August 12th. Traveled rather a north-west course for twenty-five miles, when we struck the old Truckee road. August 15th. Toward evening eighteen emigrant wagons rolled in and camped by us. They had traveled about one hundred miles without water. [August 16th] Today we met twenty-five wagons, emigrants for California.

The rush to the gold fields was on.

Part Two

TRANS-SIERRA MINING ROADS

◀◀◀◀◀◀◆ 5 ◆▶▶▶▶▶▶

EBBETTS PASS

The Big Trees Road

On a hot July day in 1827, Jedediah Smith sat in camp on Utah's Little Lake of the Bear River and penned a short letter to the great explorer William Clark, then Superintendent of Indian Affairs in Saint Louis. His terse sentences chronicle the first-ever crossing of the Sierra by a white man.

> I started with two men, seven horses and two mules, which I loaded with hay for horses and provisions for ourselves, and started on the 20th of May, and succeeded in crossing it in Eight days, having lost only two horses and one mule. I found the snow on the top of this mountain from 4 to 8 feet deep, but it was so consolidated by the heat of the sun that my horses only sunk from half a foot to one foot deep.

Historians believe that he worked his way up the ridge separating the Mokelumne and Stanislaus rivers and then more or less followed the route of what is now State Highway 4. The pass over the summit would carry his name if there were justice in the world (see below). Instead, it honors Major John Ebbett, who, after conducting a survey in 1853, proclaimed this to be the perfect route for the transcontinental railroad. The famous cartographer G. G. Goddard agreed, but both were wrong. Not only is the pass 1,500 feet higher than the route the railroaders eventually chose, but it would have required a steep, 1,000 foot dip into Hermit Valley before climbing again to a suitable summit. Most of the '49ers opted for nearby Carson Pass, and it is doubtful that a road would ever have been built here were it not for a silver strike on the East Carson River. According to an 1864 edition of the *Alta California:*

The Immigrant Road from Murphy's to Carson Valley is complete. The workmen came in several days ago, and all who have passed over the road speak of it in the highest terms of praise. Travelers from Sacramento to Carson can accomplish the journey easily in two days, and without wearying unnecessarily either horses or riders.

Jedediah Smith: Mountain Man

In 1822, General William H. Ashley placed a famous ad in the St. Louis *Gazette and Public Advertiser:*

Enterprising Young Men . . . to ascend the Missouri to its source, there to be employed for one, two, or three years.

The Americans had, at last, decided to challenge the Hudson's Bay Company's monopoly on the fur trade. One of those to answer the call was twenty-four-year-old Jed Smith, an explorer who deserves to rank with Lewis and Clark. It took little time for the young man to receive his baptism into the ways of the West. In South Dakota Ashley's men found themselves under attack by the Arikaras, the Missouri River pirates of the time. Twelve voyagers and trappers were killed; Smith survived only by swimming for his life. The following year he led a party into Wyoming's Wind River Range and in the process discovered South Pass, the gentle gap in the Rockies that became the emigrants' "Gateway to the West." Our hero's wilderness smarts grew, and a couple of years later he joined two other trappers to form Smith, Jackson and Sublette, one of the most profitable firms in the fur trade.

Jed Smith, though, had an insatiable wanderlust. In

**1826 he became the first American to brave the deserts
between the Great Salt Lake and southern California,
and the following spring he made his epic Sierra crossing. Replenishing his supplies and recruiting more men
at the annual rendezvous in Utah, he again headed
west. While crossing the Colorado River, his party was
attacked by a band of Mojaves. Ten trappers and two
Indian women were slain—Jed and nine men survived.
After being expelled by the Mexican governor at Los
Angeles, he and his party headed north toward Oregon.
While crossing the Umpqua River, their party of nineteen was attacked by a tribe of Kelawatsets. Smith and
three others lived to tell the tale. Three years later
Smith's luck finally ran out. Rivers, apparently, were his
nemesis, for he stopped a Comanche arrow while crossing the Cimarron on a trade mission to Santa Fé. His
death at thirty-one delayed publication of his maps and
journals, and it wasn't until the 1930s that he finally
gained his rightful place in the history books.**

Highway 4 is paved now, as befits a state highway, but in many
places it is no wider than a stagecoach road, and its steepness
discourages truck use. Yet much of the country it traverses is
spectacular, and it is certainly the least traveled of the trans-Sierra
roads.

Begin by taking combined Highways 4 and 89 south from
Woodfords. This is Alpine County, established at a time when it
seemed like the silver mines would last forever. They didn't, and
the reason for having a separate county disappeared. Nevertheless, Alpine County struggles along, basking in the distinction of
having America's smallest population (for some years voter regis-
tration hovered around two hundred and six). In the 1970s,
members of Los Angeles' gay community looked at those numbers and saw an opportunity. Here was a place they could move to
and take charge—a municipality they could govern, erasing laws
they felt were discriminatory. It didn't happen, apparently for
two reasons: state laws were enacted mandating fairer treatment,
and the locals were reluctant to set out the welcome mat. The
county has since grown in population to over a thousand, largely
because of two new ski resorts, Kirkwood and Bear Valley. Bear

Valleyians must feel a bit left out. Since Highway 4 is closed in winter, the only way they can get to their county seat is to drive all the way to the foothills and come back through Jackson. What is a nice 35-mile jaunt in summer becomes a 160-mile ordeal in winter.

A side road climbs the ridge separating the East and West Carson rivers, eventually terminating at **Indian Creek Reservoir.** The water here is the effluent from South Lake Tahoe's sewage treatment plant, a fact that doesn't seem to bother either the fish or the fishermen. Along the way you pass the interesting **Crutz Lake Environmental Study Area.** A brochure for one trail explains things geologic (mostly about volcanic rocks), another how a lake eventually becomes a meadow, and a third discusses vegetation; the third is especially informative, because the trees and plants here are quite different from those on the western slopes. Here piñon pine and juniper replace the lodgepole and the incense cedar. A sign explains how these Jeffery pines differ from their cousins the ponderosa (the stickers on the cones turn inward; the bark has a wonderful smell of vanilla), and how bitter brush can be distinguished from the ubiquitous sage.

MARKLEEVILLE • Population 100; elevation 5,501 feet

When the mines played out at Silver Mountain City in 1875, the county seat was relocated to this beautiful spot on the verge between the lushness of the Sierra and the dryness of Nevada. Markleeville's most prominent landmark, the Alpine Hotel (now bar and restaurant), was moved here at that time. So were the iron cells of the jail, now part of **Alpine County Historical Complex,** which includes a small museum. In 1861 residents saw a curious sight. Bactrain camels from the Gobi Desert of Mongolia were being driven to Nevada for use as pack stock in the deserts. The experiment didn't work out. Today, though, Markleeville's citizens look to Nevada for their commerce and entertainment; students go to Douglas County High School in Gardnerville, Nevada.

I visited **Grover Hot Springs** in the 1940s when it was a funky spa with a board fence about to fall down. The grizzled owner boasted that you could make instant coffee from the water, which came out of the ground at 140 degrees. Now a state park, it is a modern plunge, bathing suits are required, and it often gets so crowded (a ranger told me more than half the visitors come from Nevada) that they shut the gate. The park is open all year. Because state campgrounds have hot showers (except in winter), this is one of the most popular camping spots on the east side of the Sierra. Fly fishing only is the rule for nearby **Pleasant Valley,** a place of uncommon beauty reached by a short dirt road. John Frémont's party spent a week hereabouts while they struggled to pack down a road over the summit. Charles Preuss grumbled:

> We are faced with a very definite, but damned unpleasant pro-spect. Two old, tall, thick fir trunks were set afire, and the eight-foot-deep snow soon melted all around. Two snow-free holes are now our living quarters and our kitchen. Several horses were slaughtered so that the men might preserve their strength.

A diarist with another party wrote:

> We had been out of meat for some time and gophers were very numerous—my husband being an excellent shot killed ten and I made them into a stew which was delicious.

Twenty-five years later the wilds had been tamed. After a supper of mutton chops, Joseph LeConte sat under a tree and wrote:

> This indeed is a most delightful place. In such a secluded, beautiful dell, deep sunk in the mountaintop, might a Rasselas dream away his early life.

Our route follows the East Carson for a few miles, crossing the river on the interestingly named Hangman's Bridge. It seems that during the silver rush, a local fellow was charged with murder. The judge, believing a fair trial impossible, ordered the case re-moved to Mono County. But Mono's citizens insisted that Alpine County pay the costs. Having a chronic shortage of cash, the locals thought they had a better idea. Catching up with the hapless fellow as he was being escorted over the mountains, they hanged him on the spot, thus giving justice a dubious name but preserving the solvency of the county treasury. In spring, Hangman's Bridge is a favorite put-in for rafters, most of whom take two days for the twenty-mile run to Highway 395.

For reasons only a bureaucrat would understand, the powers-that-be decided that all county seats in California would be connected by state highways. So in 1954 Caltrans extended Highway 89 south over **Monitor Pass** (elevation 8,314 feet). The torturous road goes up 3,000 feet and then promptly drops 3,000 feet. At the summit a dirt road climbs to **Leviathan Peak,** where a fire lookout occupies a dynamic setting. The view of the Sierra to the west and the desert to the east is dazzling. A road down the East Carson River would have been a few miles longer, but virtually flat, much faster, and would not have been closed by snow half the year. But drivers would have had to use a dozen miles of Nevada's highways.

A short spur road leads to trailheads at **Wolf Creek Meadow. Bull Lake,** seven miles from the roadhead, makes a nice overnight destination. Fishermen enjoy both the **East Carson** (a two-and-a-half-mile walk) and **Wolf Creek** itself, which meanders through a lovely valley. Those with more time head for **Soda Springs,** in the isolated upper reaches of the East Carson River.

Recreational Facilities

△△ **East Fork Resort** 7 housekeeping cabins. P.O. Box 457, Markleeville, CA 961220. (916) 694-2229.

△ **State Park Campground** 76 units, reservable through Mistix. (800) 444-PARK.

△ **Alpine County Campground** Turtle Rock, 28 sites.

△ **BLM Campground** Indian Creek, 29 sites.

△ **Forest Service Campgrounds** Markleeville and Silver Creek campgrounds together have 32 sites.

§ **Carson Ranger District** Information and wilderness permits. 1536 South Carson Street, Carson City, NV 89701. (702) 882-2766.

Ω **Wolf Creek Pack Station** P.O. Box 362, Markleeville, CA 96120. (702) 345-6104.

A sign near the Wolf Creek turnoff states, rather ominously,

VERY STEEP, WINDING, NARROW ROAD
VEHICLES OVER 25 FEET LONG NOT ADVISABLE

Like all the trans-Sierra highways, it was built to serve mining interests, and its steepness reminded me of something John Muir wrote:

A trail was made through it [Bloody Canyon] by adventurous miners and prospectors—men who would build a trail down the throat of darkest Erebus on the way to gold.

Almost nothing is left of **Silver Mountain City** save the rock walls of the old jail. It was a bustling place, as William Brewer observed:

Perhaps half a dozen women and children complete that article of population, but there are hundreds of men, all active and busy, scampering like a nest of disturbed ants. One hears nothing but "feet," "lode," "indications," "rich rock," and similar mining terms. [A] log shanty has a sign up, "Variety Store"; the next, a board shanty the size of a hogpen, is a "Wholesale & Retail Grocery"; the shanty without a window [has] a canvas door [with a] large sign, "Law Office"; and so on to the end of the street. The best hotel has not yet got up its sign, and the "Restaurant and Lodgings" are without a roof as yet, but shingles are fast being made.

EBBETTS PASS

Highway 4 makes several switchbacks as it struggles upward. The countryside is heavily forested; unlike the approach to other Sierra summits, there is little granite and no grand vistas unfold. At the summit (elevation 8,730 feet), an easy trail (ideal for a day hike) leads to the **Kinney Lakes** in the **Mokelumne Wilderness.** To visit the **Carson-Iceberg Wilderness** (the name reflects the Carson River and a prominent peak called the Iceberg), take the dirt road (slow but suitable for sedans) that heads south to **Highland Lakes** (elevation 8,600 feet). The area here is lightly forested, with an occasional meadow surrounded by mod-estly steep metamorphic peaks. A number of trails lead south and west into the upper reaches of the Stanislaus River.

The highway drops steeply into **Hermit Valley** (elevation 7,060 feet), drained by the north fork of the Mokelumne. A popular Jeep trail follows the old wagon road to Blue Lakes (Chapter 4). We then climb again, entering a land of granite where the countryside starts to become really pretty. Tiny but popular Mosquito Lake almost straddles **Pacific Grade Summit** (elevation 8,050 feet). Mike Orr, who works at the Forest Service information office near Bear Valley, told me that the two most popular overnight hikes are to **Heiser** and **Bull Run** lakes, both located a few miles south of the highway. "We don't have quotas yet," he said, "but overuse is beginning to be a problem." (Yose-mite Park mitigates this threat by banning backcountry camping within three miles of a road.)

Recreational Facilities

△ **Forest Service Campgrounds** Small, partially developed campgrounds at Bloomfield, Highland Lakes, Hermit Val-ley, and Pacific Valley, 32 sites in all.

§ **El Dorado National Forest** Information and wilderness permits. P.O. Box 1327, Jackson, CA 95642. (209) 223-1623.

LAKE ALPINE

Built by PG&E, Lake Alpine (elevation 7,350 feet) has long been a favorite family resort, popular for sailing, fishing, and swimming. A number of rustic cabins, dating from the 1930s, occupy sites leased from the Forest Service. Pleasant trails abound, three of which deserve special mention. **Duck Lake** is an easy, one-mile walk from the Silver Valley Campground. On nights near a full moon, trail riders have a romantic dinner here; your horse finds his way home by Luna's soft light. A great sunset walk is to take the moderately steep trail to **Inspiration Point,** which looks out over the Stanislaus River canyon. A nine-mile (round-trip) trail leads to **Rock Lake** (elevation 7,350 feet), and the popular **Slick Rock Jeep Road** goes to the dam at Utica Reservoir. Snowmobiling is popular at Lake Alpine because Highway 4 is plowed to within a mile of the resort. The highway stub becomes a "Sno-Park" (fee) where RV camping is allowed.

Recreational Facilities

ΔΔ **Lake Alpine Lodge** Store, marina, restaurant, bar, and 19 housekeeping cabins. P.O. Box 5051, Bear Valley, CA 95223. (209) 753-6358.

Δ **Forest Service Campgrounds** Silver Tip, Silver Valley, and Pine Marten together have 86 sites.

BEAR VALLEY • Population 450 winter, 1,000 summer; elevation 7,120 feet

Bear Valley is a first-class development; the 500 or so house and condo units are tastefully designed and well sited. Home owners elected not to plow the roads, preferring instead to come in on snowmobiles (rentals available). The large parking lot near the highway serves as a winter staging area and in summer a place to erect a large circus tent, the setting for the popular Music from Bear Valley Festival. Nordic skiers enjoy the meadow and surrounding hills, which are open and sunny.

Harvey Blood opened a toll station here in 1864, bequeathing his name to the little creek that runs through the lovely meadow. He named nearby Mount Reba for his daughter. When the ski resort first opened it passed out bumper stickers reading "Ski Bear." Wags promptly cut them apart, rearranging the letters and augmenting their message by adding a picture of comely lass, backside to camera, wearing only skis boots and gloves. Now the resort is called **Mt. Reba Ski Area,** even though the lifts are on Bloods Ridge (elevation 8,500 feet), which, it seems to me, would have been a better name, more—well, Western sounding. The downward-sloping parking lot more or less parallels one of the easier chairlifts, so you can ski to your car. Bloods Ridge has a vertical of only 700 feet, but there is more to the place than first meets the eye. Two back-side lifts offer fine intermediate runs, and two others drop steeply into the canyon of the Mokelumne.

Though the bottom elevation here is at a snow-robbing 6,400 feet, the runs are steep and challenging. The views are terrific: north into the great granite basin of the Mokelumne, south to the volcanic plug called the Dardanelles. Despite what appeared to me to be a penchant for knocking down all the bumps, Mt. Reba is a great skier's mountain. The inside of the day lodge, however, looks like a well-lit mine shaft. Home owners (shuttle bus service is offered) can ski back to their doorsteps at Bear Valley.

Nearby **Tamarack,** now just a wide spot in the road, has a place in the record books because a total of 884 inches (seventy-three and a half feet) of snow fell one winter, the heaviest snowfall ever recorded in the United States. Tamarack, lying due east of Vallejo, gets the brunt of Pacific storms, which, after being sucked in through the Golden Gate, make a jog through the Carquiniz Strait and head east. The storms are forced higher when they hit the Sierra, the air temperature drops, and the clouds can no longer hold their moisture. The foothills get perhaps twenty inches of precipitation a year, virtually all falling as rain. At 7,000 feet the number soars to a hundred inches, ninety percent of which falls as snow. In the terrible winter of 1906–1907 almost nine feet dropped in a single storm; and in March, when it piled up the highest, snowshoers found themselves walking thirty-seven feet off the ground. Try to imagine what it would be like to come across, say, a New England village where only the tip of the church spire was standing above the snow.

A new paved road leads into tributaries of the North Fork of the Stanislaus, an area being developed as a major recreation area. **Utica and Union Reservoirs** sit side by side on a rocky ledge at an elevation of about 7,000 feet. Though few campsites have yet been built, a road suitable for sedans leads to a place where you can launch small boats. The surrounding lodgepole pine forest is especially pretty. Nearby **Spicer Reservoir** fills the not-too-steep canyon of Highland Creek. Most of the seven-mile-long lake is closed to motorized boating; canoeists can paddle into the Carson-Iceberg Wilderness.

Recreational Facilities

✔✔✔ **Bear Valley Lodge** Full-service resort hotel, restaurants, bar, grocery. 54 rooms. Central reservation service for vacation rentals. P.O. Box 5038, Bear Valley, CA 95223. (209) 753-2327.

✔ **Red Dog Lodge** Hotel (share bath), restaurant, and bar. P.O. Box 5034, Bear Valley, CA 95223. (209) 753-2344.

△ **Forest Service Campgrounds** Big Meadow, 68 sites; Sand Flat, 4 sites.

§ **Bear Valley Cross Country** P.O. Box 5207, Bear Valley, CA 95223. (209) 753-2834.

§ **Mount Reba** 9 lifts; 2,100 foot vertical. P.O. Box 5038, Bear Valley, CA 95223. (209) 753-2308.

§ **Calaveras Ranger District** Information and wilderness permits. P.O. Box 500, Hathaway Pines, CA 95232. (209) 795-1381.

Ω **Ebbetts Pass Pack Station** Trail rides and pack trips. P.O. Box 2539, Arnold, CA 95223. (209) 795-3397.

CALAVERAS BIG TREES STATE PARK

In the 1850s and 1860s the Calaveras Grove (elevation 4,700 feet) was *the* sight to see in California; nobody believed trees could be so big (see below). Innkeepers James Sperry and John Perry built a magnificent hotel here, complete with a fenced greensward, ornamented with a marble fountain. The great and famous made it a tourist attraction of the first order, a reputation that lasted into the 1940s when the hotel was destroyed by fire.

The California Hoax

In the spring of 1852 one Augustus Dowd went chasing after a bear. The beast led him into a grove of trees of such giant proportions that he quickly forgot about his quarry and set about trying to take stock of their dimensions. Using a string, he measured the circumference of the biggest sequoia he could find. Nobody believed him when he got back to town; the string had stretched out a hundred feet. Several days later Dowd led the doubters to the real thing, and it was not long before the "Discovery Tree," as it was dubbed, became the talk of the world. The Miwoks, of course, had known about it for centuries.

The Californians of the day decided to try and cut it down: the ultimate proof that man could dominate nature. James Hutchings described the process:

This tree employed five men for twenty-five days in falling it—not by chopping it down, but by boring it off with pump augers. After the stem was fairly severed from the stump, the uprightness of the tree, and breadth of its base, sustained it from falling over. To accomplish this, about two and a half days of the twenty-five were spent in inserting wedges, and then driving them in with the butts of trees, until, at last, the noble monarch of the forest was forced to tremble and then to fall, after braving "the battle and the breeze" of nearly three thousand winters.

In later years, loggers discovered they could ease the task by the simple expedient of using dynamite. A section from the log (about the size of a New England saltbox house) was shipped to New York for exhibit in the Crystal Palace. Easterners considered it just another "California hoax." The stump, however, was evened off and fashioned into a dance floor, prompting Hutchings to continue:

Incredible it may seem, on the 4th of July, 32 persons were engaged in dancing four sets of cotillions at one time, without suffering any inconvenience whatever; and, besides these, there were musicians and lookers on too.

Later, two parallel alleys for tenpins were fashioned on the log and a gazebo-like pavilion was built atop the stump, presumably so revelers wouldn't be inconvenienced by a chance thundershower. But back then, what might be called a "Nagasaki" mentality seemed to prevail. (Truman, believing that the Japanese didn't think the Hiroshima bomb real, showed them another.) So a crew worked most of the following summer, removing 116 feet of bark from a tree known as the "Mother-of-the-Forest." Each piece was numbered and, this time, reassembled in London. When both specimens

**burned in separate fires, people's attention, fortunate-
ly, began to focus on live trees rather than dead bark.**

Today, a walk through the **North Grove** is a solemn experience. Once I had the good fortune to do it at six-thirty in the
morning when soft light filtered through the branches creating a
million dancing shadows. The sounds were as pronounced as in
John Muir's day:

> In the midst of this glad plant world the birds are busy nesting,
> some singing at their work, some silent, others, especially the big
> pileated woodpeckers, about as noisy as backwoodsmen building
> their cabins.

It's the bark, I think, that gives these trees their specialness.
Unlike the coast redwood, it changes with age. The young tree's
bark is dark, deeply serrated, and not particularly handsome.
Then, Mother Nature does a curious and wonderful thing. As if to
bestow a two-thousandth birthday present, she drapes the sequoia in a mink coat, soft to the touch, with delicate fibers that
catch the light and reflect it in a brilliant glow. The sun must
sense this change too, for, in an equally wonderful way, it ignores
the rest of the forest, leaving it a dusty gray, while at the same
time concentrating all of its energy on the sequoia's bark. At
special times of the day, early morning or late evening, the forest
takes on a Rembrandt-like quality; golden pillars frame a scene
more inspiring than the holiest of temples.

A stairway allows you to stand on the stump of the Discovery
Tree. What's left of the log lies nearby on the ground. Its diameter
has shrunk a bit in a century and a half and the bark is gone, but
you still can't climb on its top without a twenty-five-foot ladder.
Incredibly, a sugar pine now stands in the gap between log and
stump, one which would have been destroyed had it been there
when the tree was felled. It's nearly eight feet around. Scientists
had long been thwarted in their efforts to measure the age of live
sequoias because the augers they used to collect core samples
measured only four feet—hardly long enough to penetrate the
bark of some giants. But by studying the width of the annual
growth rings of this downed tree, they came to a startling conclu-

sion. It was growing at a furious pace. Had it lived, they speculate, it would now be the largest living thing on this planet.

Park trails lead past named trees such as "Pioneer Cabin," the dead "Mother-of-the-Forest" (which stalwartly refuses to topple over), and the "Old Bachelor." A particularly lovely group is called the "Three Graces." You're left to speculate which is Aglia (Brilliance), Thalia (Bloom), and Euphrosyne (Joy). The **Visitors Center** has displays of the flora and fauna of the area. Picnicking and swimming spots are located along the Stanislaus River, a few miles from the park entrance on the new road that leads to the **South Grove.**

In the 1950s I had the good fortune to tour the South Grove (sometimes called the Stanislaus Grove) before it was absorbed into the state park. The walking was rough, and my more pleasant thoughts were being constantly interrupted by having to cope with elbowing through the underbrush and climbing over fallen snags. But I got a sense of how Augustus Dowd must have felt when he suddenly found himself amidst such splendors. Returning to our pickup, my friend Dick Pland, a forester for the lumber company that owned the land, asked if I had seen any young sequoias. The answer was no. "It takes sunlight and sometimes fire to get the seeds to germinate," he said. "We said we would give this grove to the state if they would let us take the sugar pine first. That way sun could get in. But they said no, so we sold it to them for $2.8 million. Now the only young trees you see are along the right-of-away of our old railroad." But the state got its money's worth. The sugar pine is also a majestic tree, and its removal would have been tragic. When the lumber company called them "overripe," State Forester Frederick A. Meyer responded:

> If we were engaged in forest management, these trees would be an economic liability; they are over-ripe. But our parks must be neither woodlots nor tree farms. We are preserving primeval forests, because they are primeval, and because the primeval is inspiring.

As to the dearth of seedlings, in those places where the state has conducted a controlled burn, future giants are sprouting up like mushrooms.

A tour of the South Grove is, in many ways, more inspiring than one of the North Grove. The new road makes access easier, but the planners purposefully stopped it a mile short of the grove. To see the giants you have to walk, five miles or more (round trip) on a reasonably level trail. A selection process occurs; those who go there do so in part because they don't like crowds. They want time to prime their minds for the experience, and it works. I came upon a mountain lion cub along the trail. We stared at each other for perhaps thirty seconds, then we each went our own way. The trail goes through only half the forest; to see it all you still must climb over the snags and elbow your way through the brush, much as Augustus Dowd did in 1852.

The once sleepy town of **Arnold** (population 2,385–4,000 in summer; elevation 4,000 feet) is fast becoming a major retirement center, thanks to the beauty of its forests and its favorable elevation (above the heat and below the snow). Residents play golf or work out in a large fitness center. Tourists, however, will find nearby Murphys (Chapter 18) more interesting.

Recreational Facilities

Δ **California State Park** Visitors Center and 129 campsites, reservable through Mistix. (800) 444-PARK.

• **Dorington Hotel** 1860s road house restaurant. (209) 795-5800.

§ **Sequoia Woods Country Club** Restaurant, bar, and 18-hole golf course. (209) 795-1378.

Logical chapter organization would suggest that we continue our Sierra adventure by next exploring Sonora Pass and then returning by the Tioga Road. But the experience is better if you do it the other way around. Chapter 6, therefore, begins in the gold town of Sonorra and heads toward Yosemite National Park.

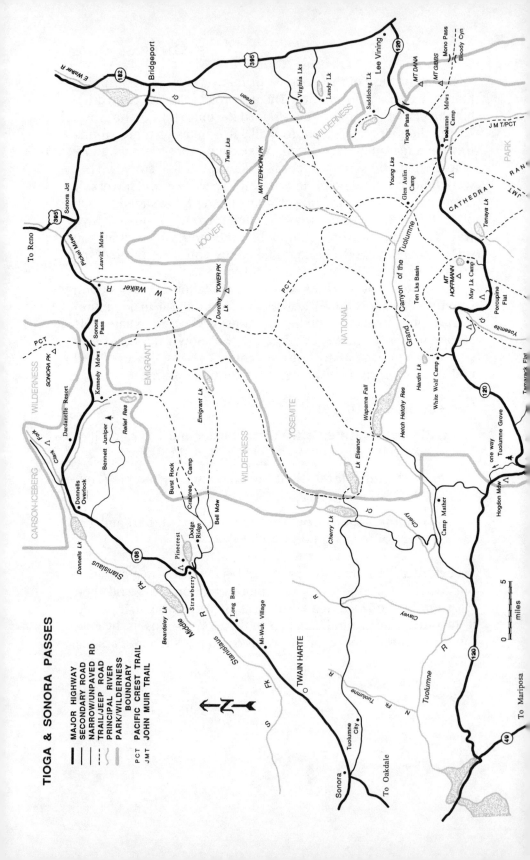

TIOGA & SONORA PASSES

MAJOR HIGHWAY
SECONDARY ROAD
NARROW/UNPAVED RD
TRAIL/JEEP ROAD
PRINCIPAL RIVER
PARK/WILDERNESS
BOUNDARY
PCT PACIFIC CREST TRAIL
JMT JOHN MUIR TRAIL

◄◄◄◄◄◆ 6 ◆►►►►►

THE TIOGA ROAD

Up Here All the World's Prizes
Seem Nothing

John Muir was enthralled:

> From garden to garden, ridge to ridge, I drifted enchanted, now on
> my knees gazing into the face of a daisy, now climbing again and
> again among the purple and azure flowers of the hemlocks, now
> down into the treasuries of the snow, or gazing far over domes and
> peaks, lakes and woods, and the billowy glaciated fields of the
> upper Tuolumne. In the midst of such beauty, pierced with its
> rays, one's body is all one tingling palate. Who wouldn't be a
> mountaineer! Up here all the world's prizes seem nothing.

Yosemite Valley may have the fame, but many Sierra lovers
would much rather be in the National Park's backcountry; the
scenery is nearly as grand and the experience far more serene. It is
accessible too. The *crème de la crème* of the trans-Sierra highways,
the Tioga Road boasts unparalleled scenery, numerous oppor-
tunities for outdoor activities, and, best of all, a complete absence
of commercial traffic. Driving, you get the sense that everyone is
having a good time, stopping to read the interpretive signs,
picnicking at sunny meadows, climbing rocks, or just enjoying
superb Alpine air.

The Great Sierra Wagon Road, a grand moniker for what was, by all accounts, a miserable excuse for a highway, was built to serve mining interests and abandoned when the lodes petered out in the 1890s. But Stephen T. Mather, who in 1915 was Assistant Secretary of the Interior, felt so strongly about public access to the high country that he organized a group to purchase this relic of adventurous engineering and donate it to the National Park. The Sierra Club raised $6,000, other individuals a couple of thousand, and Mather put up $7,000 of his own money, a gesture that perhaps explains why he is so highly esteemed in park circles. When I first traveled the road in the 1940s, it was a tortuous route in many places and in others downright scary. And that was after many improvements—at least it was paved all the way. (My father delighted in telling of how his sister kept her eyes closed all the way up the Lee Vining grade, such was her terror of tumbling off into the abyss below.) In the 1960s the road was realigned, straightened, and widened, and the speed limit in most places increased. So (at least in the summertime) it is now the fastest route between the Bay Area and the east-side resorts of Mammoth and Bishop, a fact that contributes more traffic than perhaps the Park Service intended. Were it not a de-facto toll road (the park entrance fee), usage would no doubt be much higher. You can drive it in a couple of hours, but please don't. The country is too lovely to hurry through.

CHERRY VALLEY/HETCH HETCHY SIDE LOOP

The obvious way to begin is to take Highway 49 south from Sonora and then simply follow Highway 120 to Tioga Pass. But there is a back road to follow, one that is more fun, which takes you to the fringe of the seldom-visited northern part of Yosemite National Park. The road is twisty (twenty miles an hour is tops), but it is paved throughout and wiggles through some intriguing backcountry. Begin by first taking the county road to Tuolumne City (an old sawmill town) and then follow the signs to Cherry Valley.

Almost immediately you plunge into the steep-sided canyon of the Tuolumne River's north fork; the hot, dry slopes of the Sonoran zone are covered with scrub oak, mountain mahogany, toyon, manzanita (Spanish for "little apple"), and chaparral. Digger pines, with their enormous cones and long, gray needles, dot the hilltops. But soon the road starts climbing; you enter the transition zone where ponderosa and sugar pine begin to dominate, interspersed with incense cedar and white fir. Big-leaf maple and dogwood (wonderful springtime bloom) occupy the wetter spots. The road then dips into the Clavey, a classic "pool-and-drop" river—a fly fisherman's delight. Logging operations are evident; much of the land between the Clavey and Cherry Creek is privately owned and has been clear-cut. Replanted ponderosa are beginning to achieve a respectable height; range cattle have been imported to feed on the undesirable plants.

Cherry Valley Reservoir (elevation 4,700 feet) marks the boundary of the granite country. When I came here in mid-July the lake was only half full and not very pretty (the canyon sides are too steep), but water skiers seemed to be having a good time and dozens of bait fishermen were out in their aluminum boats. Nearby **Lake Eleanor** (4,657 feet), which is inside the National Park, is far more enticing. First-time backpackers love it here because the swimming is great, numerous granite domes (the exfoliated rocks, often hundreds of feet high, that give the central Sierra so much character) are especially pretty, and you get a nice hint of the high country. Yet it's only a short walk to the first campsite. The relatively low elevation makes this a popular spot in the early season (the road is plowed from Highway 120 to the Cherry Creek dam), but a ranger told me the mosquitoes can be annoying. Several long-distance trails (part of a Yosemite National Park network that is 750 miles long) lead into the tortured canyons of the Tuolumne.

Our road becomes 1N03 as it drops steeply into the Tuolumne, crossing the river near Early Intake Powerhouse, a put-in for more experienced white-water enthusiasts (Chapter 19). Penstocks and power lines seem to go everywhere, for you are now in the heart of San Francisco's Hetch Hetchy system. Creek beds that are virtually dry above generating plants carry a torrent below. The canyon here is not pretty; the gorge is too steep and too dry. But not so twenty miles upstream. Few people had seen **Hetch Hetchy Valley** (elevation 3,796 feet) when the City of San Francisco proposed building a dam. John Muir had, and he was outraged:

Dam Hetch Hetchy! As well dam for water tanks the people's cathedrals and churches, for no holier temple has ever been consecrated by the heart of man.

A "Little Yosemite Valley," people said; flat-bottomed and sprinkled with luxuriant meadows of an edible grass that the Miwoks called "Hatchatchie." But in 1915, in spite of desperate efforts by Muir and the Sierra Club, the project was approved. Seven years later the dam gates were closed and the world lost a precious jewel. (In the 1980s, President Reagan's interior secretary, Walter Hodel, suggested the lake be drained and the land returned to nature. The thought of walking through a bathtub-ringed, barren gorge left mountain lovers notably unimpressed.) Out of the debacle came the seeds of today's conservation movement, though, so in that sense, maybe Yosemite's loss became the nation's gain.

Camp Mather, now a summer recreation area for citizens of San Francisco, was the headquarters during construction of the dam. From there, a narrow but paved eight-mile road leads down to the reservoir. Along the way impressive views unfold of the dam and the granite domes beyond. The lake too is quite pretty, at least when it is full. Trails to the backcountry leave from the north abutment of the dam. A wonderful six-mile (round-trip) day hike is to walk along the almost-level trail to **Wapama Falls.** You pass beneath the equally spectacular but ephemeral **Tueelulala Falls.** (Note: There are no places to camp near the reservoir, and boating is not allowed.)

Recreational Facilities

ΔΔ **Evergreen Lodge** 22 rustic housekeeping cabins near Camp Mather. Store and cafe. Star Route 160, Groveland, CA 95321. (209) 379-2606.

Δ **Forest Service Campgrounds** Cherry Valley, 46 sites, Carlon, 16 sites, and Middlefork, 25 sites, are located on the county road to Hetch Hetchy. Three other campgrounds with a total of 28 sites are along Highway 120.

§ **Groveland Ranger District** (U.S.F.S.) Information and wilderness permits. P.O. Box 709, Groveland, CA 95321. (209) 962-7825.

Ω **Cherry Valley Pack Station** Groveland, CA 95321. (209) 962-5671.

HOGDON MEADOW/CRANE FLAT

When it became obvious that Yosemite Valley would become a major tourist attraction, two companies built competing, nearly parallel toll roads. The first wagons reached the valley floor via the Coulterville Road on July 17, 1874, thereby beating those on the Big Oak Flat Road by a couple of months. The Coulterville Road is mostly gone, but the Big Oak Flat Road endures, though over the years it has been rerouted, straightened, and widened to the point that if a teamster magically came back, he would have absolutely no idea where he was. The park entrance is at **Hodgdon Meadows** (elevation 4,800 feet), site of the original toll station for the Great Sierra Wagon Road (Jeremiah Hodgdon was the builder). A campground reservation office is staffed during the summer. Yosemite Valley has over a thousand campsites, but most are spoken for months in advance. If you arrive *sans* reservation, stop here for information.

In 1833 Joseph Redford Walker, in the employ of B. L. E. de Bonneville, led a party of trappers across the Sierra somewhere between Tioga and Sonora passes. The trek, the first to cross from east to west, took a month. Historians believe that they followed this ridge down to the San Joaquin Valley, for on October 30, Zenas Leonard, a member of the group, wrote:

> In the last two days travelling we have found some trees of the Redwood species, incredibly large—some of which would measure from 16 to 18 fathoms around the trunk at the height of a man's head from the ground.

Historians differ, but it seems likely that the Walker party passed through one or both of the redwood groves near **Crane Flat** (elevation 6,200 feet) and so became the first whites to see the giant sequoia. The original Big Oak Flat Road, which has been converted to one-way, west-bound traffic, leads back toward Hodgdon Meadow, dropping down a fairly steep canyon to the **Tuolumne Grove,** a modest collection of sequoias that can be viewed from a short nature trail. Watch for a road branching to the right, which leads to the Sierra's only still-standing "drive-thru" tree, a dead giant whose trunk has been hollowed out to allow passenger cars to pass. The nearby **Merced Grove** is more special, however, because you have to walk (three miles round trip). Here, the lack of people and cars makes it easy to imagine the sense of astonishment those jaded mountain men must have felt when they suddenly found themselves surrounded by giants whose branches were bigger around than any trees they had ever seen.

Recreational Facilities

△ **Park Service Campgrounds** Hodgdon Meadows, 105 sites, and Crane Flat, 166 sites, are reservable through Ticketron. Tamarack Flat, located three miles off Highway 120, has 53 sites and is first-come, first-served.

WHITE WOLF/TENAYA LAKE

Crane Flat is the present-day beginning of the Tioga Road, the point where the gates are closed in winter because too much snow at the higher elevations makes plowing impractical. But come spring, when the snow melts, the streams overflow, and Mariposa lilies, cow parsnip, and larkspur come out, the gates are swung open to reveal a mountain paradise. Fifty-five highway miles separate Crane Flat and the east-side town of Lee Vining. It is arguably the most scenic road in America. Hiking trails are everywhere, many of which lead down to Yosemite Valley. A quite useful but little publicized **hikers bus** makes this country accessible to one-way travel; you can plan a walk so that it is mostly downhill.

At first, little seems different from other trans-Sierra highways. The road works its way up the ridge separating the Tuolumne and Merced rivers, but the forest is so dense you can't see very far. There is no hint that the rock-bound splendor of the Grand Canyon of the Tuolumne lies to the north, the mighty Yosemite Valley to the south. This is the transition zone where white fir and ponderosa dominate. **White Wolf High Sierra Camp** (elevation 7,750 feet) is a wonderful place to stop and take stock of things because it lies on the verge of the high country; granite boulders stud the landscape, but granite is not yet ubiquitous. Lodgepole pine has become the dominant tree, signifying the beginning of the Canadian zone. Tiny meadows abound, used in the early days for summer pasturage. (A sheepherder claimed he spotted a white wolf in the vicinity, thus the name.) A roadhouse was built here in the 1930s and taken over by the Park Service in 1960. It's not that there is much to do here; no nearby lake or stream adds charm to the area, but the tent cabins, with their wood stoves made of tin are cozy (linen is provided), and the place has a homey, Depression-era feel. I had no trouble at all imagining a Hudson or a Packard motor car gassing up at a glass-tanked hand pump in front of the little grocery store. The trail to **Hardin Lake** is the most popular day hike; overnighters can walk into the **Ten Lakes Basin** area perched on the south rim of the Grand Canyon of the Tuolumne.

Highway 120 now dips into the shallow draw of **Yosemite Creek,** which, because it is not very long and has little soil to gradually release rainfall, dries up in mid-summer. Geologists call this a "hanging valley"; the glacier that carved out the Merced River canyon left it stranded in space. When there is water, the creek tumbles along for a couple dozen miles, bubbling and gurgling and being quite content with itself, filling trout-spawning pools and making a home for beaver and quail. But then these waters confront an alarming precipice. This modest creek suddenly has to cope with the highest and most precipitous fall in North America, a 2,425-foot drop into the canyon of the Yosemite. John Muir was enraptured by the sight:

> To gain a perfect view one must go farther, over a curving brow to a slight shelf on the extreme brink. This shelf is formed just wide enough for one's heels. To me, it seemed nerve-trying to slip down to this narrow foothold and poise on the edge of such a precipice so close to the confusing whirl of waters. After casting longing glances over the shining brow of the fall and listening to its sublime psalm, I concluded not to attempt to go nearer, but nevertheless, against reasonable judgement, I did. In spite of myself, I reached the little ledge, got my heels well set, and worked sidewise twenty or thirty feet to a point close to the out-plunging current. Here the view is perfectly free down into the heart of the bright irised throng of comet-like streamers into which the whole ponderous volume of the fall separates.

Repeating Muir's stunt is not recommended, but a reasonably level trail leads to the top of the falls. It's a long walk, sixteen miles round trip from the Tioga Road (twelve from the Yosemite Creek campground), but certainly worth the effort. The trail continues on to the valley floor, steeply descending the canyon wall in a series of breathtaking switchbacks.

About here, the countryside starts to get really interesting. You round a bend and the Clark Range comes into view, the obelisk of Mt. Galen Clark rising majestically across the canyon of the Merced. A mile or so beyond the Porcupine Flat campground, a rather strenuous seven-mile (round-trip) trail leads to **North Dome,** perhaps the spot where members of the Walker party stood, mouths agape, as they stared into the abyss of Yosemite Valley, the first whites to do so. Zenas Leonard later recalled:

> Here we began to encounter in our path, many small streams which would shoot out from under these high snow-banks, and after running a short distance in deep chasms which they have through ages cut in the rocks, precipitate themselves from one lofty precipice to another, until they are exhausted in rain below. Some of these precipices appeared to us to be more than a mile high. Some of the men thought that if we could succeed in descending one of these precipices to the bottom, we might thus work our way into the valley below—but on making several attempts we found it utterly impossible to descend, to say nothing of our horses.

Leonard's estimate of the height of the precipices wasn't too far off the mark. Glacier Point, which dominates the southern scarp, soars two-thirds of a mile above the valley floor.

A portion of the old Tioga Road leads to the trailhead for May Lake, the most accessible of Yosemite's five High Sierra camps. The walk takes about an hour and a half. Soaring above the lake is **Mount Hoffman** (elevation 10,850 feet), the geographic center of both Yosemite Park and the entire Sierra range. (Charles Hoffman was the principal topographer with the Whitney survey. Much of the mapping of Yosemite was done from this summit.) The climb is relatively easy and the view spectacular. Half Dome looms up to the south, the Cathedral Range and the Sierra spine to the east, and the Grand Canyon of the Tuolumne to the north.

It is **Lake Tenaya** (elevation 8,141 feet), however, that is the crown jewel of the mid-Sierra, the quintessential mountain tarn, surrounded on all sides by extraordinary slabs of granite. The scene seems too glorious to be a place of sadness, but the lake marks the spot where the Mariposa Battalion, bent on rounding up the last Yosemites (Chapter 8), caught up with their half-starved quarry. Chief Tenaya, making a little speech (echoed a quarter century later by Chief Joseph when the Nez Perce were cornered in Montana), said: "Where can we go that the Americans will not follow us? Where can we make our homes, that you will not find us?" The Indians, appropriately, called this place *Pywiak,* meaning "shining rock," but Lafayette Bunnell, discoverer of Yosemite, chose another name.

> Looking back to the lovely little lake, where we had been encamped during the night, and watching Ten-ie-ya as he ascended to our group, I suggested that we name the lake after the old chief. [But] upon telling him that, his countenance fell [and] as he left us, indicated that he thought the naming of the lake no equivalent for the loss of his territory.

The survivors of the once-free Yosemite tribe were herded off to a reservation near Fresno. The lake is best viewed from **Olmsted Point.** Clouds Rest and its neighbor, Half Dome, dominate the southern skyline; outstanding granite domes frame the lake, while the flat-topped Mount Conness punctures the Sierra Crest. It is an especially beautiful peak because the afternoon light on its barren summit seems always changing, shadows come and go, and at sunset the alpenglow seems to show brighter than any gold hidden in Sierra veins. Tenaya Lake is fine for swimming, if you don't mind freezing to death. Better to sit by its shores and dream, as Joseph LeConte did with his friend John Muir:

> The deep stillness of the night; the silvery light and deep shadows of the mountains; the reflections on the water, broken into thousands of glittering points by the ruffled surface; the gentle lapping of the wavelets upon the rocky shore—all these seemed exquisitely harmonized with one another and the grand harmony made answering music in our hearts. Gradually the lake surface became quiet and mirror-like, and the exquisite surrounding scen-

ery was seen double. For an hour we remained sitting in silent enjoyment of this scene, which we reluctantly left to go to bed.

A popular walk-in campground occupies the west end; numerous picnic spots line the northern and eastern shores. First-time rock climbers practice on the gently sloping granite. Several trails lead down into Yosemite Valley and one goes to the Sunrise High Sierra Camp, but the most rewarding is the climb to the top of **Clouds Rest** (elevation 9,926 feet). It is a strenuous fourteen-mile walk (round trip), but the view, I'm told, is better than from the top of Half Dome.

Recreational Facilities

ΔΔ **White Wolf High Sierra Camp** Cabins (with facilities) and tent cabins (without). Cafe and grocery. Yosemite Reservations—High Sierra Desk. 5410 East Home, Fresno, CA 93727. (209) 454-2002.

Δ **Park Service Campgrounds** White Wolf, 88 sites; Yosemite Creek, 75 sites reached by a narrow, twisty, five-mile access road; Porcupine Flat, 55 primitive sites; Tenaya Lake, 50 walk-in sites (all first-come, first-served).

Ω **Hikers Bus** During summer, a bus leaves Yosemite Lodge daily at 8:00 A.M., arriving at Tuolumne Meadows at mid-morning. Hikers can get off wherever they choose. The bus then continues on to Lee Vining where it turns around, leaving about 1:30 P.M. and returning by the same route.

Ω **White Wolf Stables** Yosemite Park, CA 95389. (209) 372-1248.

TUOLUMNE MEADOWS

The Tioga Road now threads its way through, not a forest, but a series of incredible pieces of sculptured granite: Pywiak Dome, Polly Dome, Medlicott Dome, Daft Dome, Pothole Dome, Fairview Dome. Smeaton Chase looked out over the scene and remarked:

One has a vision of Nature in the rôle of housemaid, scouring away through patient centuries at these granite blisters with a glacier in her hand, polishing and finishing them to perfection.

Each rock you pass seems more fanciful than the last. Then, suddenly, you burst out onto Tuolumne Meadows (elevation 8,575 feet), the fairest sight in all the Sierra. To get a sense of this rhapsodical land, park near the point where the Dana Fork combines with the Lyell Fork to form the Tuolumne River and walk across the valley to **Soda Springs.** Or climb **Lembert Dome,** or better still, the dome just behind Lembert, where you get the same grand view without the distraction of having a highway of cars directly below. Great mountains come into view— Mammoth, Donohue, Amelia Earhart, Johnson Peak, and the Cockscomb. Cathedral Peak and Unicorn Peak are the stars of the show: great slabs of metamorphic rock, sculptured into finely carved masonry, crumbling to decay. The round trip to Lembert Dome takes a couple of hours.

During the summer a sizable community gathers here—the huge campground is always full (backwoods camping is prohibited within three miles of the road). A grand, rough-hewn building, built by the Civilian Conservation Corps for their mess hall, now serves as a **museum and interpretive center.** The Yosemite School of Mountaineering has its summer offices nearby. In early spring the building serves as a hut for skiers making a guided trans-Sierra trek under the auspices of the Yosemite cross-country ski school. Across the meadow, **Parsons Lodge,** a handsome rock building designed for the Sierra Club by the firm of famed Berkeley architect Bernard Maybeck, serves as a reading room (Edward Whymper, first to climb Switzerland's Matterhorn, contributed money to the project). The grocery store and fast-food outlet are appropriately housed in tents. So are most of the structures at the **Tuolumne Meadows High Sierra Camp.** Built in 1916, it has a wonderful mountainy feel. Guests, who sleep on cots and dine at giant round tables illuminated by Coleman lanterns, spend the day hiking, fishing, botanizing, birding, and otherwise enjoying the simpler life. College students do the chores. One evening after dinner I sauntered up to a cascade on the Dana Fork. The moon had just risen and spume from the fall wafted in the air, catching the light in such a way that it looked like a million fireflies were flitting about in the blackened sky.

Hiking and Backpacking

One has only to look around the grocery store to get an idea of why this area is so popular. An entire aisle is devoted to "gorp," that mixed nut-and-dried fruit concoction that keeps hikers going, even on the most tiring of days. If any place can make the claim, this is the backpacking center of the world. Today, freeze-dried foods make life simpler, but early trekkers had the better diet—"chops on the hoof," for example. Joseph LeConte, on his celebrated trip to Tuolumne Meadows with John Muir in 1870, noted that the meadow shuddered under a juggernaut of 12,000 sheep—his party of ten ate one a day. And a Sierra Clubber wrote:

> Of course, we despised the sheep and the sheepmen, but we learned not to scorn the advent of a "stray sheep," which it was our bounded duty to shoot, in order to save it from a hungry bear. Thus did we prey upon the beasts of the wilderness, and send some poor bruin supperless to his lair.

Early explorers lacked goose-down sleeping bags and Gor-Tex parkas, but there was plenty of wood around. After a thunder-shower, the LeConte party built a fire that roared twenty feet into the air—their wool blankets dried out soon enough. Today, wood fires are not even allowed in many parts of the wilderness; meals are prepared on propane stoves. (Rangers, however, still maintain the tradition of nightly campfires here in the Meadows.) The John Muir Trail (see below) joins the Pacific Crest Trail here, so hikers can head out in all directions. **Cathedral Lakes** is the most popular day hike (eight miles round trip), but other trails go north to **Young Lakes** (ten miles) or south to **Budd** (five and a half miles) and **Elizabeth Lakes** (five miles). The principal climbing challenge is **Cathedral Peak** (elevation 10,940 feet).

The John Muir Trail

Shortly after its founding in 1892, the Sierra Club set about campaigning for the construction of a trail along

the crest of the Sierra to connect Yosemite Valley with Mount Whitney, thereby helping to fulfill one of the club's original objectives of making the mountains more accessible. It became the harbinger of other trails with a national interest, including the much longer Appalachian and Continental Divide trails. Theodore Solomons conceived the idea, and Joseph N. ("Little Joe") LeConte carried the torch; by 1915 he had inveigled $10,000 out of the state legislature and construction began. Twenty-four years were spent in the effort, the work shared by the Park Service and the National Forest Service (Sierra Club work parties help with the maintenance). The last sections to open were Forester Pass, dividing the Kings and Kern watersheds (1932), and Mather Pass, straddling the middle and south forks of the Kings (1938). When John Muir, the president of the Sierra Club, died, people felt it fitting that it should carry his name. Today, it forms a key link in the 2,500-mile *Pacific Crest Trail,* a ridgeline path that also traverses the Cascade Mountains of the Pacific Northwest.

A comparison with other national trails is not appropriate, however, for the initial purposes were quite different. Benton MacKaye, "father" of the Appalachian Trail, sought a linear park, a means whereby the inexorable westward march of urbanization could be interrupted, severed in a way that would return at least a part of the land to wilderness. In the Sierra the wilderness was all around. The problem was getting people there. The Muir Trail served that purpose almost too well. In 1951, some friends and I walked from Tuolumne Meadows to the Devil's Postpile and saw only one other group, three Stanford coeds leading burros. With the onset of the "back-to-nature" ethic of the 1960s, however, the trail became too much of a success; so many people began using it that the land was beginning to suffer, and quotas had to be instituted. Although back-country usage has since declined, by forty percent between 1984 and 1989, the phrase "and render accessible the mountain regions of the Pacific Coast" has been dropped from the Sierra Club's stated objectives.

The John Muir Trail officially begins at Happy Isles in Yosemite Valley and ends 212 miles south at the top of

Mount Whitney. No one knows who was the first to make the entire trek in one shot, but many have over the years, setting out caches beforehand or arranging for food drops along the way. Most follow the route by referring to _Starr's Guide to the John Muir Trail_ (published in 1943), the first of many excellent High Sierra trail guides. A mountain is named for Pete Starr, who died in a climbing accident on Mt. Ritter. He joins the ranks of other Sierra Clubbers who left their imprimatur on this landscape: Joseph LeConte, Will Colby, Francis Farquahr, Clair Tappaan, Ansel Adams, Cedric Wright, François Matthes, and many, many more. The first to make the trek in winter was Orland Bartholomew, who started out alone on Christmas Day in 1928 and arrived in Yosemite Valley fourteen weeks later.

High Sierra Camps

Donald and Mary (Curry) Tresidder (he was head of the Yosemite Park and Curry Company and later became president of Stanford University) long dreamed of establishing a European-style _La Haute Route_, which would loop around Yosemite Valley much as Mount Blanc is girdled by trails. _Burghuttes_, spaced an easy day's walk apart, would make the high country accessible year around. The idea died aborning; only one winter structure was built (Ostrander Hut on the south side of the valley), but five camps were eventually set up for summer use. All supplies are packed in by mule. Guests sleep in four-person tents and are treated to meals served in a large commissary tent. Best of all, hot showers await trail-weary hikers. In my view, this is absolutely the nicest way to tour the Sierra backcountry. All camps are within a day's walk of a road and therefore can be visited individually, but the best way to capture their magic is to make a week-long tour, especially if accompanied by a naturalist ranger.

The loop trail, which begins in Tuolumne Meadows, drops moderately to **Glen Aulin Camp** (elevation 7,800 feet), snuggled in a forest along the Tuolumne River. It's an easy walk, so many hikers spend the afternoon visiting Waterwheel Falls, a long, rolling cascade located a few miles downstream. The second day is spent climbing to **May Lake** (9,200 feet), where trekkers get a chance to strengthen leg muscles for the more rigorous climb the third day. After dropping to Tenaya Lake, the trail climbs steeply to **Sunrise Camp** (elevation 9,400 feet), the last camp to be built and, I'm told, Mary Tresidder's favorite. The tents stand alongside a high, boulder-studded meadow. The view of the Matthes Crest at sunset is especially enchanting. The fourth day is mostly a downhill walk to **Merced Lake Camp** (7,150 feet), the largest of the five. Here, you enjoy a layover day to rest, read a book, or fish the usually productive Merced River. The sixth day is the toughest, a 3,000-foot, eight-mile climb to **Vogelsang,** but by then your legs are in shape. Vogelsang, almost at treeline (elevation 10,300 feet), has the most Alpine feel; several nearby tarns reflect the slaty peaks that surround the camp. From there it is downhill all the way back to Tuolumne Meadows. A six-day saddle trip leaving from the Tuolumne Meadows stable is also offered, but a caution is in order. These camps are open only in July and August and are always booked solid. Check locally for cancellations at individual camps.

Recreational Facilities

ΔΔ **Tuolumne Meadows Lodge** and **High Sierra Camps** Written reservations accepted starting the first Monday in December of the preceding year (list as many alternate dates as possible). A grocery, cafe, gas station, and post office are nearby. Yosemite Reservations—High Sierra Desk. 5410 East Home, Fresno, CA 93727. (209) 454-2002.

Δ **Park Service Campground** Tuolumne Meadows, 330 sites. Half the sites are reservable through Ticketron, half the new vacancies are available on the day of arrival. Reservation offices are at Hogdon Meadows and Tuolumne Meadows.

Ω **Tuolumne Meadows Stables** Yosemite Park, CA 95389. (209) 372-1248.

TIOGA PASS

The Tioga Road makes it's final assault on the Sierra crest by working its way up the Dana Fork. We leave the predominantly granite country here; the brooding twins, mounts **Dana** (elevation 13,053 feet) on the left and **Gibbs** (12,764) on the right, are composed of metamorphic slates, variegated remnants of volcanic plugs (James Dana was a geology professor at Yale, Wolcott Gibbs a Harvard chemist). To the right is **Mono Pass,** where the mule trail went before the Tioga Road was built. After passing some restored mining shacks, the trail drops down the other side through the infamous Bloody Canyon. Historians are divided about the name. It either refers to the color of the rocks, which are quite red, or to the condition of the mules' legs when they got to the bottom. The countryside has a wild, yet gentle feel; Dana Fork reminded J. Smeaton Chase of Scotland:

> If I had not known that I was in California, I could easily have believed that it was a Highland burn that came shouldering down between bossy, over-curving banks of rough mountain grass, pouring steadily over ledges and boulders, swirling in elbows, draining and sucking through matted roots of heather, and tossing crisp, hissing drops a yard into the air.

This is the Hudsonian or sub-Alpine zone, where whitebark pine (a cousin of the bristlecone), juniper, and mountain hemlock (the tree with the drooping top) carry forth the flag of the tree kingdom. Indian paintbrush abounds. Above lies the Arctic-Alpine zone, where no trees at all exist, only dwarf and matted flowering plants with delicate flowers, grasses, and sedges. The summit entrance station lies atop the Sierra's highest highway pass (9,941 feet). A mile-long trail climbs steeply to **Middle Gaylor Lake,** where adventurers can scramble on to view the reason why the Tioga Road was built, the site of the derelict Great Sierra Consolidated Silver Company mine.

The change to an east-side environment is almost immediate. The canyon walls become brown and dry, seemingly inhospitable, but they are not. Big-horn sheep graze in this country. Two small lakes line the highway, but the more interesting spot is **Saddlebag Lake** (elevation 10,051 feet), reached by a bladed dirt road. Adventurers can hire a boat to take them to the far end of the lake, where an easy mile-and-a-half trail leads to an Alpine wonderland, almost level, with twenty rock-bound, trout-filled lakes, the perfect place to see the High Sierra backcountry without expending a lot of effort.

Recreational Facilities

ΔΔ **Tioga Pass Resort** Store, cafe, and housekeeping cabins. Also open in the winter for adventurers who ski up from the gate six miles down the highway. P.O. Box 330, Lee Vining, CA 93541. (209) 379-2420.

Δ **Forest Service Campgrounds** 5 small campgrounds have 60 sites.

§ **Saddlebag Lake Resort** Cafe, store, boat rentals. P.O. Box 440, Lee Vining, CA 93541.

You leave the high country at Ellery Lake, where the Tioga Road begins its long, swooping descent to Mono Lake, a place we will visit in Chapter 14.

◀◀◀◀◀◆ 7 ◆▶▶▶▶▶

SONORA PASS

You Who Have Walked Otherwise Through All the Earth, Walk Gently Here

Even in the best of weather, you feel a sense of foreboding as you look west from the junction of State Highway 108 and U.S. 395. The mountains look much too steep to harbor a trans-Sierra road. It is easy to imagine what John Bidwell and his travel-mates must have thought when they looked at this sight in 1841. The party, the first settlers to come overland to California, had long since abandoned their wagons in the deserts of Nevada.

> Leaving the Sink of the Humboldt, we crossed a consider-able stream which must have been Carson River, and came to ano-ther stream which must have been Walker River, and followed it up to where it came out of the mountains, which proved to be the Sierra Nevada. We did not know the name of the mountains. Neither had these rivers then been named; nor had they been seen by Kit Carson or Joe Walker, for whom they were named.

Bidwell was wrong about Joe Walker, who had been here in 1833, but nevertheless, his recollections, together with fellow traveler Josiah Beldon's diary, provide an appropriate guide that we can follow. They were a stalwart bunch (see The First California Emigrants below). Though the route they blazed saw no more emigrant or '49er traffic, in 1865 it become the principal road to the Mono mines, despite the fact that it took three weeks for a six-mule team to make the trip from Sonora to Bridgeport and return. Today you can do it in a few hours, at least in summer when the road is open. But its steepness (fifteen percent in places) makes it unsuitable for large vehicles, and it is unlikely that the road will ever be plowed in winter.

The First California Emigrants

Jedediah Smith was the first Anglo to cross the Sierra, having traveled from west to east in the spring of 1827. Five years later Joe Walker crossed going the other way. (Both referred to the range as Mount Joseph.) But they were trappers, and neither had any intention of staying in California. Another eight years would elapse before the first would-be settlers discovered to their dismay that, after braving the deprivations of prairie and desert, they had to come to terms with the Sierra before reaching the promised land. The loosely bound outfit was called the Bartleson party, for reasons John Bidwell explained:

> We organized by electing as captain of the company a man named Bartleson from Jackson County, Missouri. He was not the best man for the position, but we were given to understand that if he was not elected he would not go; and he had seven or eight men with him, and we did not want the party diminished, so he was chosen.

Bartleson had a "take for yourself and let the Devil have the hindmost" attitude, and can well be forgotten, but the fates of history were to endow this group with four other men of amazing character, pioneers who deserve much of the credit for forging America's "Manifest Destiny."

Arriving safely in California, Charles Weber started a shoe manufactory in San Jose, led a cavalry company during the Mexican War, and later donated much of his land grant to form a city, which he named after his

commanding officer, Commodore Robert F. Stockton. Josiah Belden was appointed *acalde* of Monterey and was elected the first mayor of San Jose. Talbot Green, for whom Green Street in San Francisco is named, amassed a great fortune, but he had a darker side too, as it later came out. Having defaulted his employer, an eastern bank, he deserted his wife and children to come west. And his real name was Paul Geddes. Nevertheless, when he sailed east with the avowed purpose of clearing his reputation, San Francisco's most prominent citizens came to the pier to see him off. He never returned. John Bidwell lived another sixty years, founded the city of Chico, became a delegate to the convention that nominated Abraham Lincoln for President, and served for many years in Congress. Historians now refer to the adventurers as the Bidwell-Bartleson Party.

The Sonora Road is a wonderful way to cross the Sierra, traversing the boundaries of three wilderness areas that embrace some fine Sierra country. Those who leave the road find themselves in a pleasant world of volcanic peaks and rock-bound lakes, of stunted trees and perennial snowfields. In places, particularly in the Emigrant Basin Wilderness, the hand of man hardly seems to have touched the land and, with any luck, never will. Phoebe Anne Sumner, writing in the *Sierra Club Bulletin*, said:

> Here is a different wealth from that which most men understand. It may not be gained by blasting these rocks, felling these trees, damming this stream; it could be lost forever in an hour. To try to take this treasure is to lose it. Leave it unchanged; the gain will not be yours alone, but every man's.

She concludes with an unattributed, but quite appropriate quote:

> You who have walked otherwise through all the earth, walk gently here.

WEST WALKER RIVER/HOOVER WILDERNESS AREA

The adventure begins with a drive along the West Walker, a typical east-side stream that alternatively meanders through lush meadows and then tumbles, pool-and-drop fashion, over sage-brushy steps. Pickel Meadow is the site of the huge Marine Corps High Altitude Training Center. Camouflage-clad trainees march about, learning whatever mountain soldiers are supposed to know. At the end of the day most head for the store at Leavitt Meadows to fill up on corn chips and soda pop.

All sense of things military disappears when you stroll up the river into two-mile-long **Leavitt Meadows** (elevation 7,200 feet), one of the most serene spots in the Sierra. Well-named Tower Peak, with perennial snowfields clinging to its fluted sides, dominates the southern skyline. Much of this canyon is scheduled to become part of the **Hoover Wilderness,** an extraordinary place dotted with granite-ringed tarns and more placid meadows. Backpackers head for **Fremont Lake** (elevation 8,400 feet) or **Long Lakes** or continue on along the Pacific Crest National Scenic Trail, crossing into Yosemite National Park at **Dorothy Lake Pass** (elevation 9,600 feet). Toyabe (pronounced Toy AH bee) National Forest has an outpost at **Upper Piute Meadows** (elevation 8,400 feet).

Recreational Facilities

ΔΔ **Leavitt Meadows Lodge** Cabins, grocery, cafe. Highway 108, Bridgeport, CA 93517. (No phone).

Δ **Forest Service Campgrounds** Sonora Bridge, 23 sites (some reservable); Leavitt meadows, 16 sites.

§ **Bridgeport Ranger District** Information and wilderness permits. P.O. Box 595, Bridgeport, CA 93517. (619) 932-7070.

Ω **Leavitt Meadows Pack Station** P.O. Box 1244, Bridgeport, CA 93517. (619) 495-2257.

Hopes of an easy Sierra crossing disappear at Leavitt Meadows, for the road begins an alarmingly steep, 2,500-foot climb to the summit at **Sonora Pass** (elevation 9,628 feet). Josiah Belden reminisced:

The way was very rough, and one day, in winding round the side of a mountain, we lost four of our animals, who missed their footing, and rolled down the mountain. We finally reached the summit with great labor and difficulty, and after getting a little beyond the summit on the other side, we struck a little stream of water that seemed to run westward and by following the stream as well as we could, it would lead us down the westerly slope of the mountain.

The date was October 18th, 1841. A monument erected by E. Clampus Vitus honors the event. A small picnic area, surrounded by stunted foxtail pine, sits on a bluff above the pass. The view, especially to the east, is stunning. **Sonora Peak** (elevation 11,459 feet) is the highest thing around, but across the road, **Mount Finiski,** an unimpressive volcanic plug, is more famous in some circles, being the venue for "Ski Finis," the last slalom race of the season. Competitors make remarkable time in getting to the wine flask at the finish line. The Bidwell party went slightly northwest, crossing **St. Mary's Pass** (elevation 10,400 feet) and then descending into the Clark Fork of the Stanislaus. Those able to effect a car shuttle can follow the eight-mile route, but the Forest Service warns that the trail is for experienced hikers only. Our road follows a little stream, which begins to plunge down Deadman Canyon in a bewildering way, dropping more than 3,000 feet in less than ten miles. By the time you reach the Kennedy Meadows turnoff, you feel like you've been on a roller-coaster.

KENNEDY MEADOWS/EMIGRANT WILDERNESS AREA

Highway 108 ceases to be a "High Sierra" road when it joins the middle fork of the Stanislaus. (Place names seem to be ecumenical here; the Spanish named an Indian chief Estanislao after a Polish saint.) **Kennedy Meadows** (elevation 6,500 feet) is an old-time resort with a very "Out West" feel. The present lodge was built in 1945 to replace one inadvertently burned by the Marines during World War II. Guests ride horseback, fish the river, or just enjoy the sunny meadow. Nearby granite walls challenge rock climbers. This is the northern gateway to the **Emigrant Wilderness,** an area that has a High Sierra feel (lots of granite), yet is relatively low—the sort of country Smeaton Chase had in mind when he wrote:

Lakes by scores and hundreds lay before us; strung like beads along every cañon; sunk like secrets in every dark belt of forest; smiling frankly open on high granite plateaus and under eaves of perpetual snow.

The land is not particularly steep—it has been described as a granite ocean—so it has become quite popular for horseback riders and backpackers. The trail from Kennedy Meadow passes **Relief Valley Reservoir** (elevation 7,800 feet) and then enters the wilderness at more or less the 8,000-foot level. Those able to effect a car shuttle can make a marvelous twenty-five-mile circuit, coming out near Pinecrest.

Recreational Facilities

ΔΔ **Kennedy Meadows Resort** 20 cabins, rooms, store, bar, cafe and pack station. Star Rt. Box 1490, Sonora, CA 95370

Δ **Forest Service Campgrounds** 2 campgrounds, 61 sites.

CLARK FORK/CARSON-ICEBERG WILDERNESS AREA

For the next ten miles the road closely follows one of the Sierra's most popular fishing streams as it tumbles through a glacier-carved, U-shaped canyon. Both the **Douglas Picnic Ground** and the nearby **Columns of the Giants,** a miniature Devils Postpile (Chapter 13), are nice places to stop. Near Brightman Flat, a pretty, one-mile, level trail leads to the world's largest Jeffery pine. Someone thought that the most prominent landmark north of the highway, a large volcanic plug, looked like the **Dardenelles** in Turkey, thus the name. It doesn't. The old Dardanelle Resort (elevation 5,900 feet) has recently been staying open in winter. Guests come in on snowmobiles, in good weather making day excursions as far away as Sonora summit. At times it seems like everyone with an RV has come to **Clark Fork** to try his luck in this renowned rainbow-trout stream. The campgrounds are often full. Scout and church camps are nearby; families pedal about on bicycles or swim in the many tiny pools. The river, although not especially steep, is quite rocky, as the Bidwell Party found out:

After passing the summit, and striking this stream, we worked our way along down for some distance, occasionally having to leave the track and go on to the ridges, to avoid getting into deep cañons, blocked with immense boulders.

The nine-mile paved road ends at **Iceberg Meadow** (6,600 feet), another nice place for a picnic (the volcanic monolith north of the meadow is called the Iceberg). This is the principal southern gateway to the **Carson-Iceberg Wilderness,** an area quite different from the country to the south. Few lakes grace this land. Instead, lava peaks guard steep canyons, so although the fishing is good, the wilderness lacks the gentleness of the granite country and therefore is much less used. Day hikers can make an eight-mile (round-trip) excursion to **Boulder Lake** (elevation 8,000 feet). Peakbaggers head for **Disaster Peak** (10,046 feet) on the Sierra crest, a strenuous all-day climb, or scale the **Dardenelles** (8,875 feet).

Recreational Facilities

ΔΔ **Dardanelle Resort** 14 cabins, cafe, grocery, RV park. Highway 108, Dardanelle, CA 95314. (209) 965-4355.

Δ **Forest Service Campgrounds** 4 campgrounds near the Dardanelles, 100 sites; 1 walk-in campground. 3 campgrounds along the Clark Fork, 140 sites. 3 campgrounds along Highway 108, 26 sites.

The highway leaves the river and begins contouring around toward the south fork of the Stanislaus, staying more or less at the same elevation for the next fifteen miles. **Donnells Overlook** (elevation 6,400 feet) is a wonderful place to stop, not only for its spectacular beauty, but to get an idea of what the by-now starving Bidwell-Bartleson Party had to cope with. The overlook, reached by a short trail, is perched on the edge of a 1,600-foot vertical wall of granite: You feel like you're standing atop Half Dome. The lake below, built by several irrigation districts, flooded a canyon that, to say the least, proved troublesome.

I explained and warned them that they could not get down; but they went on as far as they could go, and then were obliged to stay all day and night to rest the animals, and had to go about among the rocks and pick a little grass for them, and go down to the stream through a terrible place in the cañons, to bring water up in cups and camp-kettles, and some of the men in their boots, to pour down the animal's throats in order to keep them from perishing.

This band of emigrants had, unfortunately, discovered the perverseness of the Sierra—the deep, V-shaped gorges of the lower mountains. Though the high-country weather might be miserable, the canyons, carved by glaciers, were at least passable. Not so for the stream-cut canyons below. They quickly learned that they must stick to the ridges, which, in a maddening way, all too often ended when two subsidiary canyons joined. It was like working down a feather backwards. If they had started from the west, they could have taken a ridge between two rivers and avoided the problem, but they didn't, so they suffered.

The next morning we were off as usual, but soon found that we were "in a fix"—great granite precipices descended ahead of us. We turned back, and after much trouble found a very steep, rocky place where we could get down.

Almost miraculously, on October 30, the party arrived on the lower Stanislaus, shot twenty-six deer, and feasted.

We finally succeeded in working down to the north side of the river, and finding difficulty there, got on to the south side of the river. We went a little ways from the river, working down on that side, and passed I suppose the neighborhood of where Sonora is now.

The Sierra had been challenged—California had been opened to overland immigration. Not all felt it was worth it, as William Swain reported:

Tell all whom you know that are thinking of coming that they have to sacrifice everything and face danger in all its forms, for George, thousands have laid and will lay their bones along the routes to and in this county. Tell all that "death is in the pot."

Nevertheless, that band of two dozen pioneers would grow to hundreds in a few years and to thousands in eight, and eventually would swell to the tens of millions who have, over the years, chosen to pick up stakes and make a new life in the Golden State.

A perfectly passible ten-mile dirt road leads to the lovely gnarled hulk of the **Bennett Juniper,** the world's largest of that species and, some think, perhaps as old as the bristlecones (Chapter 12). A paved side road leads to **Beardsley Lake** (elevation 3,400 feet), the second of three reservoirs built in the 1960s as part of the Tri-dam project. No camping is allowed here, but the lake is popular for all kinds of boating, and the low elevation means nice swimming.

PINECREST/DODGE RIDGE AREA

In winter, Highway 108 is plowed only as far as **Strawberry** (elevation 5,320 feet), an old resort community located along the south fork of the Stanislaus. Nearby **Pinecrest Lake** (5,600 feet), originally built to supply water to the southern mines, has been enlarged several times and has long been the principal summer resort for this part of the Sierra. A hundred and fifty thousand fish are planted each year. Fifty-year-old cabins nestle in the dense forest; several campgrounds are often filled to capacity. There is a nice sense of nostalgia here. Smoke from a hundred campfires fills the evening air, and in the morning the smell of cookstove bacon competes with the fragrance of the pines.

Good old **Dodge Ridge** (elevation 6,600 feet), the place where a generation of Californians learned to ski, is having a bit of a renaissance. "It's a matter of demographics," marketing manager Dave Blank told me. "The 'baby boomers' came here with their parents. But when they got out on their own, they headed for the more challenging slopes at Squaw and Alpine. Now they've got their own kids so they are coming back. We've responded by expanding our ski school and adding a child care center." The resort has added lifts too, and hopes to expand into the back side of the ridge, but the place hasn't lost its "family" character. Dodge Ridge is the closest resort to the San Jose area and to the booming cities of the San Joaquin Valley, so its success is assured. The management does a good job—parking is handy and the lodge pleasant, but although the hill has a respectable vertical drop, the runs offer little challenge for skiers with advanced skills.

Three trailheads serve as the western gateway to the **Emigrant**

Wilderness, all very popular because the gradients are easy for the most part, and the countryside is beautiful. **Burnt Rock** trailhead (elevation 8,400 feet) provides access to the northern area, including popular Long Lake. Other hikers enter from **Crabtree Camp** (7,200 feet), though the lowest trailhead, **Bell Meadows** (6,400 feet), is an easy walk to the Bucks Lakes area. I was fortunate to explore this area with Helen and Ed Bodington, who have led Sierra Club backpack trips for many years. I understand that lately the epicurean delights of the trips have improved greatly because Canelo, a plucky llama, totes in food that we otherwise might consider too burdensome.

Recreational Facilities

🗸🗸 **Strawberry Inn** Rooms, restaurant, and bar. P.O. Box 68, Strawberry, CA 95375. (209) 965-3662.

ΔΔ **Pinecrest Lake Resorts** 7 cabins, 14 condo rentals, and 6 motel units. Boat rentals. P.O. Box 1216, Pinecrest, CA 95364. (209) 965-3411.

ΔΔ **Sparow's Resort** Cabins. Strawberry, CA 95375. (209) 965-3278.

Δ **Forest Service Campgrounds** Pinecrest, 200 sites reservable through Ticketron. Meadowview, 100 sites.

§ **Dodge Ridge Ski Area** 7 lifts; 1,600 foot vertical. (209) 965-4444.

§ **Leland Meadow Resort** Snow play area, snowmobile rentals. (209) 965-4389. P.O. Box 1273, Pinecrest, CA 95364.

§ **Summit Ranger District** (U.S.F.S.) Information and wilderness permits. Star Route Box 1295, Sonora, CA 95370. (209) 965-3434.

Ω **Reno Sardella's Pack Station** P.O. Box 1435, Pinecrest, CA 95364. (209) 965-3402.

MI-WUK VILLAGE/TWAIN HARTE

Several vacation and retirement communities straddle the lower section of Highway 108. Oldest is Twain Harte (population

1,639; elevation 3,650 feet), named for the Gold Country's two most famous authors.

Recreational Facilities

✔✔ **Twain Harte's B&B Inn** 6 rooms. P.O. Box, 1718, Twain Harte, CA 95383. (209) 586-3311.

✔ **Christmas Tree Inn** 16-unit motel. P.O. Box 186, Mi-Wuk Village, CA 95346. (209) 586-1005.

✔ **Eldorado Motel** 11 units. P.O. Box 368, Twain Harte, CA 95383. (209) 586-4479.

✔ **Mi-Wuk Motor Lodge** 17 units. P.O. Box 70, Mi-Wuk Village, CA 95346. (209) 586-3031.

✔ **Wildwood Inn Motor Lodge** 21 units. P.O. Box, 457, Twain Harte, CA 95383. (209) 586-2900.

✔ **Long Barn Lodge** Rooms, restaurant, and bar. P.O. Box 100, Long Barn, CA 95335. (209) 586-3533.

● **Eproson House Restaurant.** (209) 586-5600.

● **Vila d'Oro Restaurant.** (209) 586-2182.

§ **Stanislaus National Forest** Information and wilderness permits. 19777 Greenly Road, Sonora, CA 95370. (209) 532-3671.

We now turn our attention to the grandest spectacle in the Sierra, the incomparable Yosemite Valley.

Part Three

YOSEMITE, KINGS CANYON, AND SEQUOIA NATIONAL PARKS, AND THE KERN RIVER COUNTRY

YOSEMITE VALLEY

MAJOR HIGHWAY
SECONDARY ROAD
NARROW/UNPAVED RD
TRAIL/JEEP ROAD
PRINCIPAL RIVER
JMT JOHN MUIR TRAIL

0   miles   3

To Tuolumne Meadows

120

To Oakdale

Crane Flat

Tamarack Flat

White Wolf Camp

Yosemite Cr

May Lk Camp

MT. HOFFMANN

Porcupine Flat

Olmsted Pt

Tenaya Lk

Sunrise Camp

Vogelsang Camp

Washburn Lk

Merced Lk Camp

JMT

Merced R

CLARK   RANGE

Ostrander Hut

Westfall Mdws

Badger Pass

Chinquapin Jct

WAWONA RD

To Wawona

140

Merced

El Portal

To Mariposa

120

Big Oak FLT RD

Bridalveil Fall

Bridalveil

Inspiration Pt

Dewey Pt

Taft Pt

Sentinel Dome

Glacier Pt

El Capitan

Curry Village

Yosemite Village

Yosemite Falls

NORTH DOME

Yosemite Cr

Happy Isles

Vernal Fall

Nevada Fall

Illilouette Fall

Illilouette Cr

HALF DOME

CLOUDS REST

Tenaya Cr

Little Yosemite V

Merced

JMT

◀◀◀◀◀◀◆ 8 ◆▶▶▶▶▶▶

YOSEMITE

Incomparable Valley

Twenty-seven year old Lafayette Bunnell, a recruit in the hastily formed Mariposa Battalion, found himself among the first party of whites to set foot in Yosemite Valley. The date was March 27, 1851. Reflecting on the experience, he wrote:

> The grandeur of the scene was softened by the haze that hung over the valley—light as gossamer—and by the clouds which partially dimmed the higher cliffs and mountains. This obscurity of vision but increased the awe with which I beheld it, and as I looked, a peculiar exalted sensation seemed to fill my whole being, and I found my eyes in tears with emotion.

That night, while sitting around a campfire, he proposed that they name the valley after the tribe of recalcitrant Yosemites they were chasing. And they did, even though the Indian name Ahwah'nee, meaning deep valley, was more appropriate and certainly just as pretty. Bunnell was the first to write about these splendors, but hardly the last. James Hutchings, a man no one accused of lacking verbosity, was dumfounded when he first looked out over the scene:

The truth is, the first view of this convulsion-rent valley, with its perpendicular mountain cliffs, deep gorges, and awful chasms, spread out before us like a mysterious scroll, took away the power of thinking, much less of clothing thoughts with suitable language.

Writers have been looking for suitable language ever since. "Incomparable" is a word that seems to have stuck in many people's minds. Not everyone, however, was as impressed. In 1870 Olive Logan endured an uncomfortable night on a steamboat to Stockton followed by two days bouncing in a dusty stagecoach and then another on horseback. Arriving in Yosemite, she reportedly had to be lifted off her mount and revived by alcohol rubs. Writing in the magazine *Galaxy*, she grumbled:

As a reward for all this hardship, what is there to be seen? Tall rocks, a few tall trees, a high and narrow waterfall which looks like a fireman's hose playing over the top of Stewart's store. The travelers one meets are "poor candlemoth tourists"; the only people who really seem to enjoy themselves are the clergymen.

Not many agreed with the poor lady. Hutchings, who was to spend the rest of his life catering to valley tourists, prophesied:

Before many years shall have passed, Yo-ham-i-te Valley will become as a place of resort where, in the calm solitude of mountain life, the excitements of business may be forgotten; and in the unbroken stillness of this magnificent spot men shall, with deep reverence, commune with the sublime and beautiful.

Today the scenery is still "sublime and beautiful," but it is hard to find a place of "calm solitude and unbroken stillness" (see Yosemite's Fatal Beauty, page 139). Yosemite, unfortunately, suffers from an abundance of riches. Not only is the scenery unsurpassed, but the climate is superb. People just want to be here. And for very good reasons, many want to linger. When legendary naturalist Carl Sharsmith was asked what he would do if he had only one day to spend in the Valley, he said simply: "I'd go sit by the Merced River and cry!"

Yosemite's Fatal Beauty

Frederick Law Olmsted sensed that there would be problems. In 1865 he wrote a report which among other things suggested:

In addition to the more immediate and obvious arrangements are two considerations which should not escape attention. First: the value of the district in its present condition as a museum of natural science. Second: that in permitting the sacrifice of anything that would be of the slightest value to future visitors to the convenience, bad taste, playfulness, careless-ness, or wanton destructiveness of present visitors, we probably yield in each case the interest of the uncounted millions to the selfishness of a few in-dividuals.

Over the years, few heeded his warning. Today, 3 mil-lion people a year visit an area of barely three square miles. It is not at all clear whether the powers-that-be think of it as a place of nature or an amusement park. Shortly after the turn of the century, James Bryce coun-seled: "If you were to realize what the result of the automobile will be in that incomparable valley, you will keep it out." In 1913 a Locomobile came to the valley on the Coulterville Road—rangers prudently chained it to a tree. But the cat was out of the bag. Seven years later the number had swelled to 13,000 cars: visitation, which, in 1914 had been 15,000, soared to nearly 70,000. Incredibly, park superintendent W. B. Lewis pro-posed to ease overcrowding through encouraging more high-country use by building a highway up the Merced Canyon to Little Yosemite Valley, where it would then turn north, cross Forsyth Pass, and connect with the Tioga Road, an idea that fortunately died aborning. To-day traffic is so severe on three-day weekends that visi-tors may be required to drive loops around the lower valley, like jets in a holding pattern at O'Hare. (In 1984, Memorial Day drivers faced gridlock for four hours.)

Summertime population (which turns over every few days) hovers around 25,000. Weekend campsites are snapped up eight weeks in advance, the earliest they can be reserved. Sprinkled about under the cedar, Kellogg oak, and Jeffery pine is a pizza parlor, a one-hour film-processing center, a beauty salon, a bank with an automatic teller machine, a supermarket, video rental shop, three bars, fourteen other liquor outlets, two hamburger stands, two ice cream parlors, a delicatessen, six gift shops, six restaurants, a dentist's office, a twenty-bed jail, and a federal courthouse. The Lions Club and Rotary hold weekly meetings at one of the restaurants. Author Richard Reinhardt, writing in *Wilderness* magazine, reflected:

> The trouble was, too many people like me had assumed that Yosemite was indestructible. We had taken for granted the privilege not only to go to the Valley, but also to do whatever we wanted when we got there: to eat and drink and spend the night, to play golf, swim, ride horseback, gas up our cars, kennel our pets, convene conventions, stage pageants, put on wine-tastings, weddings, beer-busts, weenie roasts—anything. Wasn't that what a national park was for?

The answer, of course has to be no. The National Park Service and the Yosemite Park and Curry Co. (the concessionaire) are slowly removing the more excessive assaults on Olmsted's museum of natural science. Sideshows like the Glacier Point firefall have been eliminated, and bears are no longer fed under spotlights at 8:00 P.M. The dance hall and golf course are gone, but tennis courts, two swimming pools, and an ice skating rink remain. Free shuttle busses roam about the east end of the valley, easing daytime traffic. And the video store now rents tapes only to employees. Proposals surface from time to time to replace Camp Curry's tent cabins with motel units—an idea the Park Service seems to be ambivalent about—and the master plan, which called for the elimination of day-use automobiles, has been shamelessly ignored. (Eighty percent of the Park Service's $100 million capital improvement budget is earmarked for road improvements. Apparently the thinking is that the way to solve the overcrowding is to make it faster and easier to get here.) Both park and concessionaire employees, quite naturally, are balking at

being asked to live outside the valley. Solomon-like decisions will be required to determine what the Sundance Institute called "the fate of heaven."

For years, debate raged about how such an incredible valley had formed. Some insisted that glaciers had scoured the land, a belief the eminent state geologist Professor Josiah Dwight Whitney dismissed out of hand, writing: "A more absurd theory was never advanced than that by which it was sought to ascribe to glaciers the sawing out of these vertical walls and the rounding of the domes." The cleft, he insisted, was rent by land upheavals— great earthquakes shook the earth. But he was wrong, and who proved him wrong was a part-time shepherd with a keen, inquisitive mind, a fellow largely unschooled in geology but a man with the patience to look carefully at what lay about. His name was John Muir.

> It is hard without long and loving study to realize the magnitude of the work done on these mountains during the last glacial period by glaciers. Careful study of the phenomena presented goes to show that the pre-glacial condition of the range was comparatively simple: one vast wave of stone in which a thousand mountains, domes, cañons, ridges, etc., lay concealed. And in the development of these Nature chose for a tool not the earthquake or lightning to rend and split asunder, not the stormy torrent or eroding rain, but the tender snowflowers noiselessly falling through unnumbered centuries, the offspring of the sun and sea.

Those noiseless snowflowers did a mighty thing indeed.

Three gates guard the way into the valley, two of them tunnels blasted into the granite and the third a narrow slot carved by the Merced River, called, appropriately enough, El Portal. Of the three, the southwest entrance via Wawona is the most dramatic, for when you emerge from the tunnel at **Inspiration Point,** you are presented with almost exactly the same sight as brought tears to Bunnell's eyes, a place of such beauty that Ralph Waldo Emerson was forced to admit that it was "the only spot that came up to the brag." Moody El Capitan is on your left, Bridalveil Fall on the right, the top of Half Dome barely poking up above Sentinel Rock. But those entering from the north on the **Big Oak**

Flat Road should not feel cheated. A small turnout just beyond the first tunnel provides almost as nice a view.

For many years, most people entered the valley through **El Portal** (population 850; elevation 2,100 feet), because that is where the steam train went. The "short line to Paradise," people called it. What an improvement over the automobile that ride must have been! Author Christopher Swan, in his book, *YV 88*, urged that the system be rebuilt. He envisioned single-car trams, open to the sky and powered by electric wires (buried in the ground) gliding silently into the valley itself. Now the old station at El Portal is gone; the only reminder of that slower age is a small outdoor **museum** displaying a Shay locomotive, some old stagecoaches, and the buses that replaced them.

THE VALLEY

First-time visitors are surprised to find that after negotiating miles of roads alongside V-shaped canyons and over knife-edge ridges, they emerge into a valley (elevation 4,000 feet) whose floor is virtually flat. Credit the glacier, which left a terminal moraine near El Capitan, creating a lake that gradually filled with stream-borne sediment and detrius from the cliffs all around. Bunnell wrote:

> The whole valley had the appearance of park-like grounds, with trees, shrubbery, flowers and lawns. The balm of gilead, alder, dogwood, willow and buckthorn lend an agreeable variety to the scenery along the river. The black oak is quite abundant in the valley and upon the slopes below.

John Muir found meadows where forests now exist.

> Sheer precipices three thousand feet high are fringed with tall trees growing close like grass on the brow of a lowland hill, and extending along the feet of these precipices a ribbon of meadow a mile wide and seven or eight long, that seems like a strip a farmer might mow in less than a day.

These meadows would eventually have become forests—that's the nature of things—but the process was hastened when cattlemen dynamited the moraine so that their pastures would be less swampy. Today, "Keep off the grass" signs warn people away from those that are left.

A curious thing about Yosemite history is that some of the best geology was done by a poet, John Muir, and that a geologist, Joseph LeConte, penned some of the most poetical prose. In camp near **Bridalveil Fall,** he wrote:

> There is considerable breeze to-day; and now, while I write, the Bride's veil is wafted from side to side, and sometimes lifted until I can almost see the blushing face of the Bride herself—the beautiful spirit of the fall. But whose bride? Is it old El Capitan? Strength and grandeur united with grace and beauty! Fitting union!

El Capitan, of course, is the principal landmark in the lower valley, as much a symbol of Yosemite as is Half Dome. Two thousand eight hundred and fifty feet of granite, it is the largest vertical wall on this planet, four times as big as Gibraltar, three times as high as the Empire State Building. A joke among park rangers is that a skier schussed El Cap. "Only fell once," he boasted. (One person did in fact ski off the top, deploying a parachute when he was airborne. That time, the rangers were not amused.) Sun-up or sun-down is the best time to view the precipice; the slanting light reflects off cracks and fissures, etching faint lines in the alabaster-colored rock. It was first conquered in 1958 by a team led by fabled mountaineer Warren Harding, who spent a good part of the summer in the effort. During the final assault the climbers were on the wall for thirteen days straight.

A great drama was unfolding on one of my trips here. Mark Wellman, a paraplegic injured in a climbing accident, and his partner, Mike Corbett, were nearing the top—they had spent the last eight days inching their way up, literally climbing hand over hand. TV reporters in helicopters were about, shooting pictures that were beamed around the world. The event seemed to capture both man's indomitable spirit and the intrepidness of the rock itself.

Day visitors are directed to a large parking area near the center of the valley, where shuttle buses provide access to the other attractions. Most head for **Yosemite Falls,** with a total drop of 2,425 feet, the third highest in the world [after Angel Falls in Venezuela (3,212 feet) and Tugela in South Africa (2,810 feet)].

Only in winter and spring does it really show off for tourists: in winter when a giant ice cone builds up at its base, and in the spring when the water is high. Late spring produces magic too. One morning, when the light was low and the creek hardly flowing, I watched as the water seemed to coalesce into a heavenly assembly of a million shooting stars. But by mid-summer there is no water at all to hide the brown-stained rocks. Yet there is an even better attraction a few hundred yards to the east, a rock spire called the **Lost Arrow.** For a height equivalent to a twenty-story building, this needle of granite soars upward, separated from the adjacent cliff by fifty feet of nothingness. Climbing it looks to be an impossible feat, but of course it has been conquered. Early in 1947, two men stood on the crown. They had pulled themselves up using a rope, thrown over the top by their partners standing on the cliff. The mountain-climbing fraternity thought that rather gauche. So the true glory belongs to Ax Nelson and John Salathé, who, on the following Labor Day weekend, climbed it straight up in five days. (They did use a rope thrown over from the cliff to make their return, executing a hair-raising maneuver called a "Tyrolean traverse.") The feat was conceded to be the classic climb of the Sierra. Today, modern equipment allows climbers to do it in one day, "free" (ropes and pitons are used only for safety).

Most day-use tourist facilities are located at **Yosemite Village,** where the rather ugly **Information Center** has some well-done geologic and ecological exhibits. A theater is used for stage performances and the screening of nature films. The **Pioneer Graveyard** and reconstructed **Indian Village** are also here. Nearby, people shop for hand-made crafts and signed Ansel Adams photographs. Scheduled activities are numerous, including interpretive talks, guided walks, and free art and photography classes. Bicycling (rentals available) is very popular. Elephant trains roam the valley so that less active people can get a sense of its splendors. This is also the place where the boys hang out, hoping to meet the girls. Leidig Meadow is the perfect place to go for a stroll.

The **Ahwahnee** is the most well-loved man-made attraction in the valley. Built of stone and concrete by the W.P.A. in 1927, this elegant hotel has, except for a war-time stint as a naval convalescent hospital, welcomed the rich and famous ever since. The pseudo "Navajo" motif seems at first glance to be incompatible with this Alpine scenery, but the place endures. The dining room, with its twenty-four-foot-high ceiling, full-length windows, and grand chandeliers, has been called the most beautiful restaurant in America. Reservations are almost impossible to come by for the Bracebridge Dinner, a Christmas musical extravaganza done in the Elizabethan manner.

Truncated **Half Dome** (elevation 8,842 feet), its near side emasculated by the Tenaya Glacier, stands guard over the upper valley. Professor Whitney announced:

[It is] perfectly inaccessible, being probably the only one of all the prominent points about the Yosemite which never has been, and never will be, trodden by human foot.

In 1875 George Anderson did exactly that, and today, climbers by the thousands claim its summit each year, aided by a system of cables that the Park Service installs on the back side each summer. The front side is another matter, however. Not until 1956 was it conquered—a feat that took Jerry Gallwas, Mike Sherrick, and Royal Robbins five days to accomplish. Chris Jones described the final assault:

Not far above their bivouac rose the dread summit overhangs. Fortune was with them; a fifty-foot "Thank God" ledge led off to the left. Leaving a relatively secure stance, the leader worked out over one of the most appalling voids in climbing. It was like stepping out of a skyscraper onto a one-foot ledge.

Across the canyon, the **Royal Arches** and **Washington Column** flank Tenaya Creek; **Glacier Point** hovers over the Merced. Alas, an old favorite, **Mirror Lake,** is now Mirror sandpile, someday to become Mirror meadow. The valley floor abruptly terminates at **Happy Isles,** where the John Muir Trail starts off toward Mount Whitney. A former fish hatchery now houses another **interpretive center,** this one geared to the youngsters. Nearby, the handsome **LeConte Memorial Lodge** houses a library maintained by the Sierra Club.

Camp Curry's semipermanent tents snuggle up to the cliff below Glacier Point. Nearby are campgrounds, five of them, standing athwart the Merced River. For a hundred years now, people have been coming here, not only to enjoy the scenery, but to experience the joy of camping out.

Although we tend to presume that it is the popularity of RVs that has exacerbated the overcrowding, this is not true. Ranger John Bingaman reported that in 1935 he had to impose a thirty-day limit, despite the fact that they had room for 8,000 campers. Today the limit is seven days. The Park Service has wisely resisted the temptation to provide hookups and showers. Curiously, before the days of RVs, campers would erect canvas walls around their sites, a gesture that seems to reflect our uneasiness at being entirely exposed to the outdoors. Now we use tents for the same reason, because there is seldom a wind, there are few bothersome insects, and summer rains are rare. Sleeping *al fresco* is simply not *de rigeur*.

Hiking Trails

Yosemite plays hosts to an enormous number of foreign visitors each summer and so, I suppose, I should not have been surprised to find that those from the Alpine regions of Europe love to take long walks. Nevertheless, just for fun of it, I decided on an experiment. Rather than just nod to those I met on the trail, I said *Groose Gott*, the standard greeting in the German-speaking Alps. Nearly half responded in kind.

It seems unbelievable, but five trails scale the almost vertical walls of the valley, dizzily switching back and forth while hugging stupendous cliffs. Of these, the trail to the top of **Yosemite Falls** and the **Four Mile Trail** to (or more likely from) **Glacier Point** are well used. But the most exciting day trek is the **Giant Stairway** to the **Mist Trail,** which leads to close-up views of the valley's most boisterous cataracts, **Vernal** and **Nevada** falls. Lafayette Bunnell named them "spring" and "snow," as he later explained:

> The cool, moist air, and newly-springing grass, with the sun shining through the spray as in an April shower, suggested the *sensation* of spring; while the white, foaming water, as it dashed down from the snowy mountains, represented to my mind a vast avalanche of snow.

Thousands start the walk on a typical summer day, many taking the paved trail only far enough to view Vernal Fall. Serious hikers intermingle with sandal-shod, Bermuda shorts-clad city folk, a few incomprehensibly carrying portable stereos. Parents push toddlers along in strollers, and I once saw a kid's wagon with bright red wheels lying upside down next to a boulder, abandoned like a prairie schooner on the Forty-Mile Desert. But above the Merced River bridge things take on a more mountain-like feel. Shortly, Vernal Fall's whirling spume fills the air. The trail is forced almost under the water itself; stone and iron stair-ways, with sodden handrails, switch back and forth up the nearly vertical, 300-foot cliff. Those forewarned wear foul-weather gear and Wellingtons. One spring morning, with the sun low on my back, I stood on a tread halfway up and looked upon a memorable scene, one that Albert Richardson had described a hundred years before in *Beyond the Mississippi:*

> I saw what to a Hebrew prophet had been a vision of heaven, or the visible presence of the Almighty. It was the round rainbow— the complete circle. There were two brilliant rainbows of usual form, the crescent, the bow proper. But while I looked the two horns suddenly lengthened, extending on each side to my feet, an entire circle, perfect as a finger ring. I stood for an hour and saw fully twenty times that dazzling circle of violet and gold on a ground-work of wet, dark rocks, gay dripping flowers and vivid grasses. I never looked upon any other scene in nature so beautiful and impressive.

John Muir echoed the thought:

> This divine light may be seen whenever water is falling, dancing, singing; telling the heart; peace of Nature amid the wildest displays of her power.

While Vernal Fall evokes thoughts of peace, nature, and the Almighty, Nevada suggests the aggressive:

> No other of the Yosemite waterfalls conveys so sublime an expression of dynamic power and irresistible energy as does Nevada. Seen from below, the water seems to be hurled in masses of the polished brink, to burst wildly on the ledges and fly out in whirling water-smoke, like storm-waves crashing upon a rocky coast. In the berserk fury of its rush it might embody some stalwart young god of Norse mythology, and its voice might be the death-song of a Jötun.

The mist trail scales the north flank of Nevada Fall, emerging at the foot of a noble granite bulwark that early explorers unaccountably called Miss Liberty's Cap (it looks more like a fez than a cap). This is the gateway to **Little Yosemite Valley** and the Merced Lake High Sierra Camp (Chapter 6). Day hikers can return to the valley by the less dramatic John Muir Trail.

Recreational Facilities

Yosemite Reservations Hotel, motel, and tent cabin reservations can be made up to a year and a day in advance. 5410 E. Home, Fresno, CA 93727. (209) 252-4848. Facilities Include:

✔✔✔ **Ahwanee Hotel** Full-service luxury hotel.

✔ **Yosemite Lodge** Restaurant, cafe, bar, motel, and cabins.

ΔΔ **Curry Village** Cafe, bar, rooms, cabins, and tent cabins (no cooking).

ΔΔ **Housekeeping Cabins**

Δ **Campgrounds** Five campgrounds; 1,200 sites, reservable up to eight weeks in advance. Those arriving without a confirmed campsite should check at the reservation office located at the day-use parking lot. P.O. Box 577, Yosemite National Park, CA 95389, and local Ticketron outlets. No phone reservations.

§ **Yosemite Mountaineering School** (209) 372-1244.

Ω **Yosemite Stables** Yosemite Park, CA 95389. (209) 372-1248.

GLACIER POINT ROAD

On a map, Glacier Point appears to be about a quarter mile from Curry Village, but it is really somewhat more than a mile away, mostly straight up. The view from the top is the Sierra's most glorious. By car it is an hour-and-a-quarter drive of thirty miles through wonderful country with all kinds of things to see and do—an ideal place for an all-day adventure. Two buses a day make the trip during the summer, allowing the more adventuresome to ride up and walk back. During winter the road is plowed only to **Badger Pass** (elevation 7,200 feet), site of California's oldest ski resort. The runs here are not especially challenging, but the chalet-style lodge, built in 1935, gives the place a nice Alpine feel. Donald and Mary Tresidder had the foresight to bring in a Swiss, Ernst Des Baillets, who in turn recruited a cadre of instructors who became legends in Western skiing: Jules Fritsch, Rolph de Pfyffer, Hannes Schroll (the "wild man from Austria"), Sig Engl, Luggi Foeger, and Charley Proctor. Skiers rode up the hill in two cable-pulled sleds, the *Queen Mary* and *Big Bertha.* They were replaced by a T-bar in 1948 and then by chairs in 1964. Shuttle buses stop at valley hotels, so skiers have a wonderful time of it: a nice day on the slopes followed by lodging in a beautiful spot, all without having to use an automobile.

Nordic skiing is even more popular; a great day trek leads to **Dewey Point,** with its great views of the Valley. Guided overnight trips are made to **Glacier Point** (twenty miles round trip) on weekends. Skiers stay in what is the gift shop during the summer. A popular, but strenuous and somewhat tricky, excursion is the nine-mile trek into **Ostrander Lake** (elevation 8,500 feet), where a hut (*matratzenlager* if this were the Alps), built in the 1930s, is kept open during the winter. Managed by the nonprofit Yosemite Association, skiers carry in their own food and sleeping bags, with mattresses and cooking equipment provided. A wood stove and Coleman lanterns keep the place cozy. Unfortunately, there are beds for only twenty-five, far less than the weekend demand, so the lucky ones are chosen by lottery.

Beyond Badger Pass, the road dips slightly into the valley of Bridalveil Creek, where a nice trail heads south to **Westfall Meadows,** which Ranger Jana Walker told me is the prettiest on the south rim. From Pothole Meadows, two short (less than a mile) trails lead to lovely belvederes. **Taft Point** (elevation 7,400 feet) looks down the valley toward El Capitan, while a more popular trail leads to **Sentinel Dome** (elevation 8,122 feet), which looks out on just about everything. Many a love-struck couple has said their wedding vows on this spectacular site. Smeaton Chase came here in 1910 and reported:

> On the precise summit of the round a Jeffery pine has established itself, the trunk a shapeless, rooty mass and the limbs blown away

horizontally to the east. Its branches are like iron, its twigs like whipcord, and its needles like steel.

A wonderful Ansel Adams photograph made the pine one of the most famous trees in the country, but, alas, it is now dead. Try to resist the temptation to rush immediately to Glacier Point, because there is another spot that deserves your attention. The view from **Washburn Point** looks directly east toward the Sierra Crest with the elusive **Illilouette Falls** directly below. This is the only spot you can drive to where it can be seen. Beginning as a cylindrical spout, the water breaks up a hundred feet below the lip and spreads filmlike over the face of the cliff, plunging another 200 feet to the rocks below. During the spring runoff, the film is twice as wide but hardly thicker.

Glacier Point (elevation 7,214 feet), of course is the *crème de la crème*, a tableau of the world's greatest collection of sculptured granite. Joseph LeConte arrived at dawn and enthused:

> Rosy-fingered Aurora revealed herself to us, her votaries, more bright and charming and rosy than ever before. But the great charm was the view of the valley and the surrounding peaks. . . . The shadow of the grand Half Dome stretches clear across the valley, while its own "bald, awful head" glitters in the early sunlight. To the right, Vernal and Nevada falls, while directly across, see the ever-rippling, ever-swaying gauzy veil of the Yosemite Falls, reaching from top to bottom of the opposite cliff, 2,600 feet. Below, and a depth of 3,200 feet, the bottom of the valley lies like a garden. There, right under our noses, are the hotels, the orchards, the fields, the meadows, the forests, and through all the Merced River winds its apparently lazy serpentine way.

Unaccountably, LeConte failed to mention that you can clearly hear the pounding roar of Nevada Fall, more than two miles away. John Muir and Teddy Roosevelt camped out here in a snowstorm and apparently had a fine time. A ranger reported that the President was given forty blankets to do with as he chose, on top to keep warm or underneath to cushion his substantial bulk. Later, a hotel occupied perhaps the most dramatic site anywhere. It burned in 1969, replaced by a junky hotdog stand and gift shop. Over the years daredevils have walked out on the rock that juts out over the cliff and done handstands, three quarters of a mile above the valley floor. A famous photograph shows a 1920s Studebaker perched on the same rock. Fortunately, the Park Service has erected barriers to keep people from such foolishness.

Two trails lead back to the valley. The **Glacier Four Mile Trail** drops directly to the Middle Valley, while the more popular **Panorama Trail** goes east, dropping first into the Illilouette Valley (great view of the fall) and then climbing over a spur to the top of Nevada Fall. The nine-mile trek back to the valley takes about five hours.

Recreational Facilities

ΔΔ **Ostrander Hut** Yosemite Association. P.O. Box 230, El Portal, CA 95318. (209) 379-2317.

Δ **Park Service Campground** Bridalveil Creek; 110 nonreservable sites.

§ **Badger Pass Ski Area and Cross-Country Ski School** 4 lifts. Yosemite Park, CA 95389. Winter reservations (209) 454-2000. Snow phone (209) 372-1338.

I found it difficult to leave this place, preferring to reflect on Smeaton Chase's thoughts:

Those who may wish to commune with Nature's God alone while in the Yosemite, will be in the very innermost sanctuary of all that is Divine in material creation, for the valley is a holy Temple, and if their hearts are attuned to the harmony surrounding them, "the testimony of the Rocks" will bring conviction to their souls.

But there is more Yosemite to command our attention, a sea of huge granite waves, which we will now explore.

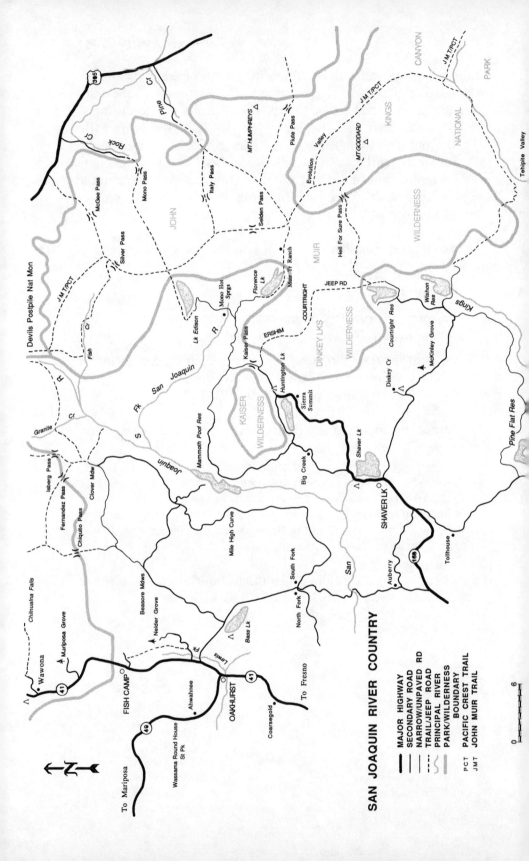

SAN JOAQUIN RIVER COUNTRY

MAJOR HIGHWAY
SECONDARY ROAD
NARROW/UNPAVED RD
TRAIL/JEEP ROAD
PRINCIPAL RIVER
PARK/WILDERNESS
BOUNDARY
PCT   PACIFIC CREST TRAIL
JMT   JOHN MUIR TRAIL

0   6

◀◀◀◀◀◆ 9 ◆▶▶▶▶▶

SOUTHERN YOSEMITE AND THE SAN JOAQUIN RIVER COUNTRY

A Sea of Huge Gray Granite Waves

Some of the prettiest high country lies south of Yosemite Valley, but it is not well known and, not surprisingly, is less crowded. The principal topographic feature of the area is San Joaquin River Canyon. With its headwaters due east of Half Dome, the river slabs diagonally southwest, carving a several-thousand-foot-deep, forty-mile-long trench before turning west to debouch into the San Joaquin Valley. Looking out over this country from Mount Ritter, John Muir wrote:

> Westward, the general flank of the range is seen flowing sublimely away from the sharp summits, in smooth undulations; a sea of huge gray granite waves dotted with lakes and meadows, and fluted with stupendous canyons that grow steadily deeper as they recede in the distance.

Two road networks make this country accessible, one north of the river, the other south. Our exploration begins at the Chinquipin Junction, where the road to Glacier Point turns off.

WAWONA

If Yosemite has the greater glory, Wawona has the deeper charm. Tucked away along a gentle section of the Merced's south fork, it struck me as the Sleepy Hollow of the West, for if Ichabod Crane were to gaze upon the Wawona Hotel, he might well think he had returned to upstate New York. Green lawns, perfect for a game of croquet, and a nine-hole golf course surround a complex of century-old, white-painted, two-story buildings. Guests enjoy a good book or a game of checkers while relaxing on wisteria-draped verandas furnished with wicker tables and chairs. A pianist plays cocktail music in the sofa-filled lobby with its twelve-foot-high ceiling. Many of the rooms were built at a time when the toilet was not even in the building let alone in the room—guests walk outside, to an outbuilding. Inconvenient, but wonderfully nostalgic—for those who mourn the loss of Tahoe Tavern (Chapter 2) and the Feather River Inn (Chapter 16), this is the place.

Wawona (elevation 4,012 feet) began life as Clark's Station, named for Galen Clark, who, on the advice of doctors (they gave him only a few months to live), came here in 1857. The climate apparently did wonders for Clark's health: he discovered the Mariposa Grove, became its guardian, a post he held for fifty years, and published his first book, *Indians of the Yosemite*, at the age of ninety. The Clark Range honors his memory. Clark's Station was, for many years, the "gateway to Yosemite," the place where stagecoach passengers paused to recruit before continuing on to the Valley. This "stagecoach" atmosphere has been preserved at the **Pioneer Yosemite History Center,** an attractive complex focusing on a rather horse-oriented part of Sierra history. A number of old buildings have been removed here—docents dressed in period garb demonstrate domestic arts and crafts and answer tourists' questions. Stagecoach rides are offered in the summer.

The Miwoks called this place Chilnualna, meaning "leaping water," because there is a wonderful waterfall, reached by an eight-mile (round-trip) trail. Smeaton Chase was taken by its magic:

> The wayward water every moment changes its mood, now plunging in bursts of hissing spray, now circling in pools where you

wonder whether some slender naiad has not slipped under the rocking water at your approach, and fancy that it is the lifting and spreading of her hair that makes that misty gloom in the emerald depths.

Plan on five hours for the walk. One of the few in-holdings in Yosemite National Park has taken the name Chilnualna. Several hundred summer homes and a modest resort nestle among the trees. I asked Norman May, who had lived here for fifty-six years, if there was a lot of pressure to sell out to the Park Service. "They were a bit heavy-handed for awhile," he replied, "but now they make it attractive to sell, tax-wise. But otherwise, they leave us alone." The area is ideal for cross-country skiing.

At the **Mariposa Grove** (elevation 5,620 feet), in 1881 the Washburn brothers, who built the Wawona Hotel, enlarged a fire-hollowed core of a giant sequoia so that a stagecoach could drive through. The 2,000-year-old **Wawona Tunnel Tree** quickly became one of the wonders of the world. The idea of a "drive-thru" tree was apparently so appealing that the concept was expanded to a "drive-thru forest"; people could visit the redwoods without having to get out of their cars. Just what caused the catastrophe is uncertain, but the tree fell in 1969, prompting the Park Service to take a second look at the practice. Today, visitors ride in open-air elephant trains (fee) while drivers point out sights such as the Telescope Tree (you can look up through the trunk at the sky), the Clothes Pin tree (it looks like one), and the Fallen Monarch, a tree of such dimensions that a famous photograph shows twelve mounted riders of C Troop, United States Cavalry, standing atop the trunk, nineteen more posed below. People from all over the world ride the trams— Chinese, Indians, Turks, Eastern Europeans, South Americans, Africans—many carrying video cameras to record the event. They seem to enjoy the experience but, to me, walking is more appropriate, especially early in the morning before the smelly and noisy trams have started. Or even better in winter, a perfect time to reflect on something John Muir said about sequoias:

> When the storm roars loudest, they never lose their god-like composure, never toss their arms or bow or wave like the pines, but only slowly, solemnly nod and sway, standing erect, making no sign of strife, none of rest, neither in alliance nor at war with

the winds, too calmly, unconsciously noble and strong to strive with or bid defiance to anything.

Two groves are spaced a mile apart. The upper, where the tunnel tree stood, is 500 feet higher in elevation, so allow three hours to visit them both. In the lower forest, an easy twenty-minute walk leads to a tree of special interest, as Joseph LeConte pointed out a century ago:

> The Grizzly Giant impressed me most profoundly; not, indeed, by its tallness or its symmetry, but by the hugeness of its cylindrical trunk, and by a certain gnarled grandeur, a fibrous, sinewy strength, which seems to defy time itself. With its large, rough, knobbed, battered trunk, more than thirty feet in diameter—with its great limbs, six to eight feet in diameter, twisted and broken— [it] seemed to me the type of a great life, decaying, but still strong and self-reliant. Perhaps my own bald head and grizzled locks— my own top, with its decaying foliage—made me sympathize with this grizzled giant.

Recreational Facilities

✓✓ **Wawona Hotel** Full-service historic hotel. Pool and golf course. Yosemite Park and Curry Co., 5410 E. Home, Fresno, CA 93727. (209) 252-4848.

✓ **The Redwoods** Chilnualna vacation rentals. P.O. Box, 2085 Wawona Station, CA 95389. (209) 375-6666.

✓ **Yosemite West Cottages** Vacation rentals near Chin-quapin. P.O. Box 36, Yosemite, CA 95389. (209) 642-2211.

✓ **Yosemite West Condominiums** Rental condos near Chin-quapin. 6061 North Fresno St., Fresno, CA 93710. (209) 454-2033.

△△ **Camp Chilnualna** 35 housekeeping cabins. P.O. Box 2095, Wawona Station, CA 95389. (209) 375-6295.

△ **Park Service Campground** 100 nonreservable sites.

Ω **Wawona Stables** Yosemite Park, CA 95389. (209) 372-1248.

FISH CAMP • Population 60–200 summer; elevation 4,990 feet

Madera means "timber" in Spanish, and before the logging commenced there was plenty of that around. Now a ride on the **Sugar Pine Railroad** provides a more appropriate link to the word. The pride of the fleet is a diamond-stacked, three-truck Shay, manufactured in Ohio in 1928 by the Lima Locomotive Works. Weighing thirty-five tons, it is the largest geared locomotive ever built for narrow-gauge logging operations. Passengers sit in open cars as they wiggle down a four-percent grade into Lewis Creek Canyon. The round trip takes forty-five minutes. Model A-powered "jennys" substitute on slow days. The Forest Service maintains a wonderful picnic spot here, nestled in a second-growth forest. Nearby **Goat Meadow** has cross-country skiing; in spring, hikers enjoy the four-mile **Lewis Creek Trail,** which branches off from the road into Sugar Pine, following the route of an abandoned log flume.

Because Muir found a friend, what used to be called the Fresno Grove is now named for John Nelder, a worn-out gold miner who made his home in the sequoias.

> Then, health and gold gone, the game played and lost, like a wounded deer creeping into this forest solitude, he awaits the sundown call. A fine kind man, who in going into the woods has at last gone home; for he loves nature truly, and realizes that these last shadowy days with scarce a glint of gold in them are the best of all.

Muir was wrong; Nelder lived here for many years. A back road, variously called Sky Ranch Road, Gooseberry Flat Road, or just plain Road 632, leads to **Nelder Grove** (elevation 5,300 feet). The last few miles are unpaved. The **Shadow of the Giants Trail** leads through the partly logged forest, passing a dozen or so giants.

Recreational Facilities

✔✔✔ **Mariott's Tenaya Lodge** 242-room, full-service hotel and conference center. 1122 Highway 4, Fish Camp, CA 93623. (209) 683-6555.

✔ **Narrow Gauge Inn** 26-unit motel. 48571 Highway 41, Fish Camp, CA 93623. (209) 683-7720.

△ **Forest Service Campground** Nelder Grove, 10 primitive sites.

§ **Mariposa Ranger District** P.O. Box 366, Oakhurst, CA 93644. (209) 683-4665.

§ **Yosemite Mountain-Sugar Pine Railroad** Steam excursions. (209) 683-7273.

OAKHURST • Population 1,952—13,500 in area; elevation 2,290 feet

Fresno Flats was more descriptive, but the citizens of this lovely valley changed the name to something that seemed more respectable, Oakhurst. Once a mill town, it is fast becoming a retirement center of some repute. (Fresno is an hour's drive away.) Dan Long, at the Chamber of Commerce, boasted that nearly 30,000 people live in the vicinity, and that the number may well double within the next twenty years. The reasons: the fine climate (above the fog, below the snow); pleasant, oak-studded scenery; and cheap land. The town boasts the best (and most expensive) restaurant on this entire sojourn, but otherwise there is little to interest the tourist here except **Fresno Flats Historical Park,** a museum complex with a couple of old homes, a jail, a blacksmith shop, and a barn full of old wagons. A more serene spot is **Wassama Round House State Historic Park.** Maintained by members of local Miwok tribes, the ceremonial house is one of only three surviving in California—a wonderful place to have a picnic and reflect on the lot of the first Californians. (See The First Californians, below.) Recommended reading is *Ishi in Two Worlds*, Theodora Krober's fine account of the life of the last "wild" California Indian.

The First Californians

As many as 300,000 people lived in what is now California at the time Cabrillo dropped anchor in San Diego Bay (1542), fifteen percent of the Native American population of the entire country. For the most part they

were a pacific people, prone to combat only when exposed to some outrageous indignity. Their religion, practiced in roundhouses, was simple and totemistic; ceremonies centered around the rites of puberty and of death and in appeasing the gods of disaster. The pioneers had little good to say of their hygiene:

These poor creatures were entirely naked with the exception of a quantity of grass bound round the waist and covering the thighs midway to the knees perhaps. [So filthy], if one of them should venture out into the rain, grass would grow on her neck and arms.

Even John Muir, who normally reserved his vitriolics for sheepherders, reported:

The dirt on their faces was fairly stratified, and seemed so ancient and so undisturbed it might almost possess a geological significance.

Almost everyone, however, was impressed with their basketry:

Each one carried two brown baskets woven with a neatness which is absolutely marvellous, when one considers that they are the handiwork of such degraded wretches. . . . These they fill half full of water, which is made to boil by placing in it hot stones. When the water boils, they stir into it, until it is about as thick as hasty-pudding, the powdered acorns, delicately flavored with dried grasshoppers, and lo! dinner is ready.

And they seem to have had the same free spirit that later Californians would espouse. John Bidwell observed:

The harvest of weeks was piled up in the straw in the form of a huge mound in the middle of a high, strong, round corral; then three or four hundred wild horses were turned in to thrash it, the Indians whooping to make them run faster. In an hour the grain would be thoroughly threshed and the dry straw broken almost into chaff.

The mission system was designed to help the Indian, but had the opposite effect. By 1848, white men's diseases had reduced their numbers by half. The luckless survivors, living in small bands and speaking a hundred mutually unintelligible languages, were ill-equipped to handle the onslaught of miners, intent on genocide. But they didn't take long to learn the white man's ways, as a woman who had come to California before the gold strike discovered:

Afore these here *emigrants* ['49ers] come the Injuns were as well-behaved and bidable as could be; I liked 'em more'n the whites. When we begun to find gold on the Yuber, we could git 'em to work for us day in and day out, fur next to nothin'. We told 'em the gold was stuff to whitewash houses with, and we give 'em a hankecher for a tin cup full' but after the *emigrants* begun to come along and put all sorts of notions into their heads, there was no gettin' them to do nothin.

In 1850 the trading post owned by Major James D. Savage (who by some accounts had thirty-three Indian wives) was destroyed, prompting the organization of the Mariposa Battalion, the discoverers of Yosemite. Few deaths were recorded in the so-called Mariposa Indian War, but by 1880 fewer than 20,000 native Californians were left. Ishi was the last to live in the wild. When he died, his friend Dr. Saxton Pope wrote:

He looked upon us as sophisticated children—smart, but not wise. We knew many things, and much that is false. He knew nature, which is always true. He was kind; he had courage and self-restraint, and though all had been taken from him, there was no bitterness in his heart. His soul was that of a child, his mind that of a philosopher.

Recreational Facilities

- ✔ **Best Western Gateway Inn** 92-unit motel. 40530 Highway 41, Oakhurst, CA 93644. (209) 683-2378.

- ✔ **Oakhurst Lodge** 60-unit motel. P.O. Box 24, Oakhurst, CA 93644. (209) 683-4417.

✔ **Shilo Inn** 80-unit motel. 40644 Highway 41, Oakhurst, CA 93644. (209) 683-3555.

✔ **Sierra Sky Ranch** Restaurant, bar, 28-unit guest ranch, and nine-hole golf course. P.O. Box 1076, Oakhurst, CA 93644. (209) 683-4433.

● **Erna's Elderberry House** Country-French restaurant. (209) 683-6800.

§ **Ahwahnee Country Club** Nine-hole golf course. (209) 683-6620.

§ **Mariposa Ranger District** Information and wilderness permits. P.O. Box 366, Oakhurst, CA 93644. (209) 683-4665.

BASS LAKE • Population 500–5,000 summer; elevation 3,500 feet

From a recreational standpoint, Bass Lake is much like all the other foothills reservoirs, only with pine trees. Speedboating and water skiing are so popular that the sheriff's office has built a lookout (it looks like a prison tower) so a traffic cop can keep track of things. Erosion, caused by boat wakes, became so severe that much of the shore is now lined with rip-rap. Old summer homes are on one side of the lake, and campgrounds line the other.

Recreational Facilities

ΔΔ **Miller's Landing** 9 rustic lake-side cabins, boat dock. 37976 Road 222, Wishon, CA 93669. (209) 642-3633.

ΔΔ **The Forks Resort** Rustic store, cafe, and bar, and 10 cabins. 39150 Road 222, Bass Lake, CA 93604. (209) 642-3737.

ΔΔ **The Pines Resort** Huge complex with supermarket, restaurant, bar, marina, and 84 chalets. Boat excursions. P.O. Box X, Bass Lake, CA 93604. (209) 642-3121.

Δ **Forest Service Campgrounds** 5 campgrounds have 225 sites.

MINARETS HIGH SIERRA ACCESS

Alice Young, who works at the information center, told me that Sierra National Forest has plans to promote a series of logging roads as a scenic loop, where motorists can get a feel for the high country without having to drive on a lot of dirt roads. It's not yet a reality, but many of the roads are paved, and although twisty, lead to some pretty country. And they provide access to Yosemite's **Clark Range** and the **Ansel Adams** (formerly Minarets) **Wilderness.** The loop can be made in either direction, but the drive is more spectacular if you begin at **South Fork,** a sawmill town a half-dozen miles south of Bass Lake. Minarets Road, also called Road 8009, soon wiggles onto the upper slopes of the San Joaquin canyonside. The first fifteen miles are rather uninteresting, but as the road climbs, chaparral and manzanita give way to conifer forests. Shortly, you round **Mile High Curve,** and the reason for making the loop in this direction becomes stunningly apparent. Picnic tables have been set out at this viewpoint, one of the finest in the Sierra. Granite is ubiquitous, from Shuteye Peak behind you to Hells Half Acre below. The Sierra slabs upward here, displaying its westward tilt in an obvious manner. The spikey peaks of the Mammoth Crest and Mounts Banner and Ritter poke at the northeast skyline. In the 1980s, Southern California Edison dammed the river, forming **Mammoth Pool** (elevation 3,200 feet), reached by a paved road that drops steeply into the canyon. The reservoir is popular for boating, fishing, and water skiing.

The road continues up the canyon rim, ducking in and out of side ravines, soon passing numerous domes, the most prominent being the twin granite teats of Fuller Buttes and, across the river, Balloon Dome (which looks more like a tipi than a balloon). The pavement ends at the junction of the road to Beasore Meadows, our route back down the mountain. Seventy-five miles of twisty, mountain road—three-plus hours of treacherous mountain driving—keep most people away from **Clover Meadow** (elevation 7,000 feet). Loggers were cutting old-growth red fir when I visited the site, and so I found myself in the middle of controversy. The ranger at the Forest Service outpost told me that if he finds a single spotted owl in the vicinity, he will shut the logging down. This shy creature, one of the largest of the owl family, has become a *cause célèbre*—the symbol of a battle being fought between logger and conservationist. Birders say the owl's continued existence demands *old-growth* trees—cut them down, they argue, and the birds will inevitably become extinct. Dick Pland, a logger friend of mine, said, "Bullshit! I'll take you into the woods some day, play owl songs on my tape recorder, and show you so many birds you won't believe it." Echoing his feelings were the people running the resort at Beasore Meadows. A bumper sticker on a the pickup out front reads: "Save a Logger, Eat an Owl," and the day's menu, scrawled on a blackboard, advertises: "Dessert! Spotted Owl Wings."

Trails provide access to some of the western Sierra's finest backcountry. Dave Segobia, who works at the pack station, told me that stream fishermen prefer the remoteness of the **San Joaquin** (elevation about 4,500 feet), reached by two short but steep trails. Lake fishermen and those who just love high country head for any of the two dozen lakes of the **Granite Creek Area** (8,000–10,000 feet), part of the **Ansel Adams Wilderness. Lillian Lake** (six miles, one way) is the most popular destination. Peakbaggers test their skills on a number of beauties in the Clark Range, including **Madera Peak** (10,509 feet), **Triple Divide** (11,607 feet), and **Merced Peak** (11,726 feet). If you can believe Clarence King, **Mount Clark** (11,522 feet) is the most challenging:

> About seven feet across the open head of a *cul-de-sac* was a vertical crack riven into the granite; below it opened out into space. Summoning nerve, I knew I could make the leap, but the life and death question was whether the *débris* would give way and leave me sure to fall and be dashed to atoms. Planting my foot on the brink, I sprang. While in the air I looked down, and a picture stamped itself on my brain never to be forgotten. The *débris* crumbled and moved. I clutched both sides of the cleft, relieving all possible weight from my feet. The rocks wedged themselves again, and I was safe.

Two trails serve the southern portion of Yosemite National Park: **Fernandez Pass** (elevation 10,200 feet) leads to the Wawona area, whereas the **Isberg Pass** (10,520 feet) trail continues on to Merced Lake High Sierra Camp (Chapter 6). Clover Meadow is also the jumping-off point for the **Devil's Postpile,** less than twenty miles distant via the "Trans-Sierra Phantom Road" (Chapter 13). Other trails lead to the spectacular back side of the **Ritter Range** and, of course, to the **Minarets,** the landmark that gave this back road its original name. Even a violent storm here could not stem Muir's enthusiasm:

> Noble mountains rise close about me. A stream sings lonely. Storm, thunder, hail on water, grasses wincing. Rush of new-made cascades.

Revenues from timber sales pay for these back-country roads, so in time you will be able to make this loop entirely on pavement. Until then, the return to Bass Lake requires some dirt-road driving. Globe Rock, a granite erratic, is the principal landmark on the way to **Beasore Meadows,** a private in-holding amidst Forest Service lands.

Recreational Facilities

△ **Wagner's Mammoth Pool Resort** Grocery and RV park.

△ **Jones Beasore Meadows Resort** Cafe and grocery.

△ **Forest Service Campgrounds** 5 campgrounds, 60 mostly primitive sites.

§ **Minarets Ranger District** Information and wilderness permits. North Fork, CA 93463. (209) 877-2218. Clover Meadows Ranger Station. (209) 877-7171.

Ω **Minarets Pack Station** Cabins and meals for those going on pack trips. 23620 Robertson Boulevard, Chowchilla, CA 93610. (209) 665-3964.

The twin villages of **North Fork** and **South Fork** (population 980; elevation 2,600 feet) have no particular interest to the tourist, save for the tiny **Sierra Mono Indian Museum.** Neither does **Auberry** (population 1,100; elevation 1,995 feet), reached by narrow and twisty Road 222, which crosses the San Joaquin River in the low-foothill country. From there, proceed back up the four-lane Tollhouse Grade to the high country on the south side of the river.

SHAVER LAKE • Population 400 winter—2,000 summer; elevation 5,370 feet.

One C. B. Shaver built a millpond in a gentle swale on the ridgetop separating the San Joaquin and Kings rivers. After sawing, the lumber was floated down a forty-mile flume to Clovis. When the timber gave out, the lake was purchased by a forerunner of the Southern California Edison Co. (SCE) and, after enlargement, became a principal component of their Big Creek hydroelectric project. Therein hangs a controversy. Except in extremely wet years, the half-a-hundred reservoirs dotting the Sierra foothills have more than enough capacity to store the runoff the rivers deliver. Irrigation needs are well provided for. But the utility companies also wanted a hydroelectric component; power generated from falling water is cheap, clean, reliable, and can be put on line almost immediately. So high-altitude reservoirs were built to store the snow-melt before sending it through the turbines. That has been both good and bad. Construction roads provide access to places we otherwise might not go, and some of the reservoirs, particularly Shaver and Huntington, have become resorts. The flip side is that three beautiful high-country valleys that might otherwise have been included in the wilderness areas now lie beneath the waters of Lake Edison, Florence Lake, and Courtright Reservoir.

The town of Shaver Lake is too remote to be a Fresno bedroom community, but the climate is perfect for retirement and for summer homes, of which there are many. The place is quite pretty when the lake is kept full, but unfortunately, it hasn't been in recent years, much to the grumbling of the locals. Cross-country skiing is encouraged at the SCE campground.

Recreational Facilities

🛏 **Musick Creek Inn** Motel, P.O. Box 8, Shaver Lake, CA 93664. (209) 841-3323.

ΔΔ **Shaver Lake Lodge** Restaurant, bar, rustic cabins. 44185 Highway 168, Shaver Lake, CA 93664. (209) 841-3326.

Δ **SCE Campground** 150 reservable sites, open all year. Hookups and showers. P.O. Box 6, Shaver Lake, CA 93664. (209) 841-3444.

△ **Forest Service Campgrounds** 2 campgrounds, 80 sites.

● **The Sawmill** Popular restaurant. (209) 841-3272.

§ **Pineridge Ranger District** Information and wilderness permits. P.O. Box 300, Shaver Lake, CA 93664. (209) 841-3311.

HUNTINGTON LAKE

Highway 168 begins to probe deeper into the heart of the Sierra, crossing Sierra Summit (elevation 8,709 feet) and then dipping into the densely forested basin of Big Creek, a tributary of the San Joaquin. **Sierra Summit Ski Resort,** although not fancy, is a nice place to ski. Five lifts serve the north and east sides of Chinese Peak (8,709 feet). The resort has a respectable vertical, but the mountain, unfortunately, has an almost flat shelf halfway down. The most challenging runs are therefore short. Intermediate skiers are well served, as are those less skilled, who enjoy the four-mile-long Academy run. The on-site lodge is convenient but not particularly good.

Huntington Lake (elevation: 6,950 feet) is prettier than Shaver, and the power company does a better job keeping it full, so it is a wonderful summer resort. The winds are reliable; sailing in Lasers, Day Sailers, and Hobie Cats attract avid racers. The mountains north of the lake are now included in the small **Kaiser Wilderness,** an area capped by 10,000-foot Kaiser Peak. Several tiny lakes, reached by a good trail, nestle in the granite on the north side of the ridge.

Recreational Facilities

✔ **Huntington Lake Condos** P.O. Box 348, Lakeshore, CA 93634 (209) 893-3384.

✔ **Sierra Summit Inn** Restaurant, bar, and 50-room hotel adjacent to the ski lifts. P.O. Box 236, Lakeshore, CA 93634. (209) 893-3305.

✔ **Tamarack Lodge** 9-unit housekeeping motel. P.O. Box 175, Lakeshore, CA 93634. (209) 893-3244.

ΔΔ **Huntington Lake Resort** Cafe, marina, and cabins. P.O. Box 408, Huntington Lake, CA 93629. (209) 893-3226.

ΔΔ **Lakeshore Resort** 1922-era restaurant, store, and 28 cabins. P.O. Box, 197 Lakeshore, CA 93634. (209) 893-3193.

Δ **Forest Service Campgrounds** 5 campgrounds, 275 sites. Reservable through Mistix. (800) 283-CAMP.

§ **Sierra Summit Ski Resort** 5 lifts, 1,500 foot vertical. P.O. Box 236, Lakeshore, CA. 893-3316. (209) 893-3311.

Ω **D&F Pack Station** P.O. Box 156, Lakeshore, CA 93634. (209) 893-3220.

JOHN MUIR WILDERNESS HIGH SIERRA ACCESS

The road into the high country has been kept in a wonderfully deplorable condition: paved, but one lane, steep in spots, and slow going throughout. Once atop **Kaiser Pass** (elevation 8,800 feet), you drop into a rock-bound paradise. Spectacular views abound, especially from **White Bark,** reached by a one-mile rough road. **Mono Hot Springs** (6,600 feet), an old resort that is more or less in the middle of things, has long been the place that trail-weary backpackers head for first. Why? Hot water, piped into deliciously deep bathtubs, provides soothing salve for aching bones and is a satisfying way to dissolve a crust of trail dust. **Lake Thomas A. Edison** (7,650 feet), built in 1960, provides easy access to the northern sections of the **John Muir Trail.** The little resort, which runs a water taxi in the summer, does a thriving business catering to the needs of long-distance hikers. Their most sought-after purchase—ice cream. **Florence Lake** (7,320 feet), built in the 1920s, also has a grocery and provides water taxi service when the water is high enough. Adeline Smith, who has owned the place since 1948, told me she does a good business packing in "food caches" to Muir Tail hikers who detour slightly to her wonderful retreat at privately owned **Blayney Meadows** (7,600 feet). **Muir Trail Ranch,** an outpost of civilization in the wilderness, has a kitchen/dining room complex (hydro-powered electricity), tent and log cabins, and two pleasant hot springs. The ranch now caters to groups rather than individual vacationers.

A sizable number of long-time back-country devotees will insist that **Evolution Valley** is the most beautiful spot in the Sierra. Theodore Solomons gave the valley its name because, as he put it:

> I felt that here was a fraternity of Titans that in their naming should bear in common an august significance. And I could think of none more fitting to confer upon it that the great of evolutionists, so at one in their devotion to the sublime in Nature.

The surrounding peaks are named after Charles Darwin, Thomas Huxley, Herbert Spencer, Alfred Wallace, Ernst Haeckel, and John Fiske. William Brewer met foul weather here, but loved it nonetheless:

> The intensely clear sky, dark blue, *very* dark at this height: the light stars that lose part of their twinkle at this height; the deep stillness that reigned; the barren granite cliffs that rose sharp against the night sky, ill-defined; the brilliant shooting stars, of which we saw many; the solitude of the scene—all joined to produce a deep impression on the mind, which rose above the discomforts.

Recreational Facilities

ΔΔ **Mono Hot Springs Resort** Cafe, grocery, cabins, baths. Lakeshore, CA 93634. (209) 227-2631.

ΔΔ **Florence Lake Resort** Store, boat rentals. P.O. Box 269, Ahwahnee, CA 93601.

ΔΔ **Vermillon Valley Resort** Cabins, grocery, boat rentals, and ferry service on Lake Edison. P.O. Box 258, Lakeshore, CA 93634. (213) 697-0312.

ΔΔ **Muir Trail Ranch** P.O. Box 176, Lakeshore, CA 93634.

Δ **Forest Service Campgrounds** 6 campgrounds, 90 sites.

§ **High Sierra Ranger Station** Information and wilderness permits. (209) 877-7173.

Ω **High Sierra Pack Station** (Florence and Edison Lakes) Mono Hot Springs, CA 93642. (209) 299-8297.

Ω **Lost Valley Pack Station** (Florence Lake) P.O. Box 288, Lakeshore, CA 93634.

DINKY LAKES (Sort of) WILDERNESS

Returning to Shaver Lake, take the wide, paved road that heads southeast toward Wishon Reservoir, an area where Frank Dusy kept sheep in 1863. A grizzly got the best of his dog Dinkey, so Frank honored the area with the unfortunate mutt's name. When the Forest Service was conducting its Roadless Area Review and Evaluation (R.A.R.E.) survey in the 1970s there was a strong push to designate this area as wilderness. Four-wheel-drive clubs were outraged; the plan would have required closing a number of roads including the **Ershim-Courtright Jeep Road,** one of the Sierra's most challenging. So a compromise was reached. Today, a swath, 300 feet wide and twenty-six miles long, punches through the middle of the wilderness, effectively making a joke out of the concept "roadless area." "You need a wilderness permit to go there," Dennis Beard told me, "unless you stay inside the 300-foot strip. But if you want to fish or whatever outside that boundary, you have to get one. But in a Catch-22 way, if you are a Jeeper, the Forest Service won't give you one. Crazy, huh!" Affectionados recommend three days for the trip (covered wagons made better time) and, unless you have a very low "granny gear," you should go from north to south because it is safer to descend the infamous Chicken Rock than to go up. Rock gardens and swamps, and unbelievable grades, make it a Class C road, meaning that at least two vehicles (with great big tires) should travel together—one to pull the other out if you "lose it" going up a hill or through a swamp. Altogether, there are a hundred miles of jeep roads in the Sierra National Forest, most maintained by the Four Wheel Drive Club of Fresno. **Dinkey Creek** itself is a popular vacation area; the City of Fresno operates a large camp here. Nearby is **McKinley Grove,** a small but pleasant stand of sequoias (nice picnicking).

Wishon and Courtright Reservoirs together make up what PG&E calls its Helms Pumped Storage Project—in effect, a giant storage battery. When peak power is needed, water is sent down 2,000 feet through penstocks from Courtright to Wishon, turning massive turbines. At times of slack electrical demand, the process is reversed; the turbines become pumps, the water is sent back up to Courtright. Like Mile High Curve, noted earlier, I was hardly prepared for the sight that presented itself when I approached **Courtright Reservoir** (elevation 8,184 feet). At the top of the grade you suddenly look out over a granite domeland nearly as impressive as that on the Tioga Road. The whole basin is composed of granite; only where the elements have caused it to decompose do trees grow, and they are mostly stunted tamarack. This is one of the few places you can drive to that has a wonderful High Sierra feel. Backpackers, able to leave a shuttle car at Florence Lake, can make a nice trek to Evolution Valley by crossing the LeConte Divide at **Hell For Sure Pass** (11,300 feet). Peakbaggers make a detour south, heading up the Goddard Canyon to Martha Lake, base camp for an assault on **Mount Goddard** (13,568 feet). Legendary climber Norman Clyde said of it:

> Due to its central and somewhat isolated position at the southeastern end of Evolution Basin, it possesses one of the most extensive views that can be had in the Sierra—one commanding the main axis of the range from Mt. Whitney to Mt. Lyell. The ascent is rather easy.

Wishon Reservoir, by contrast, is down in a hole. A giant boat ramp is well used, but water skiing is not allowed on any of the four "high-country" reservoirs. Several roads (mostly bad) fan out to trailheads serving the upper reaches of **Kings Canyon National Park.** Seldom visited Tehipite Valley (elevation 4,200 feet) lies at the foot of spectacular **Tehipite Dome,** a towering monolith of Yosemite-class grandeur, hovering 2,500 feet above the flat valley of the middle fork of the Kings. It's a tough hike in, and a tougher one coming out; a 3,500-foot climb followed by a twelve-mile trek, but my friends that have been there say Tehipite Valley's splendors equal those in Yosemite, the south wall a slab of granite higher than El Capitan. A trail continues up the Middle Fork canyon, eventually connecting with the John Muir Trail at LeConte Canyon. Adventurers detouring up Goddard Creek will find themselves at **Enchanted Valley,** according to Theodore Solomons the most isolated spot in the Sierra.

Recreational Facilities

ΔΔ **Dinkey Creek Inn** Store and cabins. (209) 841-3435.

ΔΔ **Wishon Village** Store and RV campground. 54890 McKinley Grove Road, Shaver Lake, CA 93664. (209) 841-5361.

Δ **Forest Service Campgrounds** 3 campgrounds; 190 sites. Dinkey Creek is reservable through Mistix. (800) 283-CAMP.

Δ **PG&E Campgrounds:** Trapper Springs, 30 sites; Lily Pad, 16 sites.

§ **Dinkey Creek Ranger Station** Information and wilderness permits. (209) 841-3404.

Ω **Clyde Pack Outfitters** 12267 East Paul, Clovis, CA 93612 (209) 298-7397.

Adventuresome explorers can have a memorable experience by taking **Black Rock Road** to Pine Flat Reservoir. For awhile you drive on dirt, then graded gravel, and then pavement; but don't get your hopes up for an easy time of it. At one point this narrow, one-lane road traverses an area so steep that the builders resorted to hanging the roadway on a bridge jutting out from the side of a granite wall. With a thousand-foot drop only a couple of feet from your car window, driving faster than five miles an hour borders on the reckless. Those suffering from acrophobia should retreat to Shaver Lake and then take Tollhouse Road to Pine Flat Reservoir. A faster, but even less-daring way to Kings Canyon is to retreat all the way to the San Joaquin Valley, turn left at Academy, and take the farm road to Highway 180.

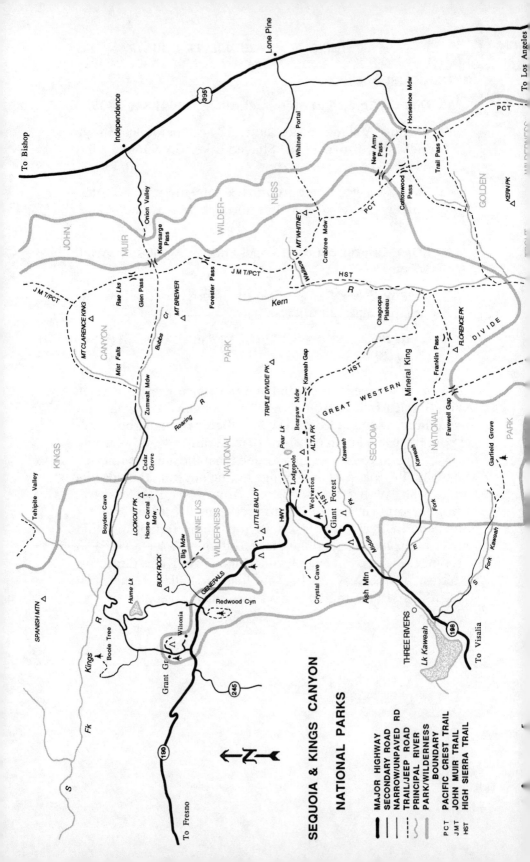

SEQUOIA & KINGS CANYON

NATIONAL PARKS

◀◀◀◀◀◀◆ 10 ◆▶▶▶▶▶▶

SEQUOIA
AND KINGS CANYON
NATIONAL PARKS

A Vast Hall Pervaded by the Deepest
Sanctities and Solemnities
That Sway Human Souls

John Muir's last solo wanderings in the Sierra (in 1879) were
among the sequoia groves south of the Kings River. Like all who
have followed, he was awe-struck by their beauty:

> When I entered this sublime wilderness the day was nearly done,
> the trees with rosy, glowing countenances seemed to be hushed
> and thoughtful, as if waiting in conscious religious dependence on
> the sun, and one naturally walked softly and awe-stricken among
> them. I wandered on, meeting nobler trees where all are noble,
> subdued in the general calm, as if in some vast hall pervaded by
> the deepest sanctities and solemnities that sway human souls.

We will visit those sanctities in the pages that follow, but we will
also explore some of the most rugged, yet sublimely beautiful
backcountry the Sierra has to offer. Begin at the northern entrance to the now-combined Kings Canyon/Sequoia National

Parks. An elaborate sign announces your arrival, but it is hardly necessary—a lone sequoia, standing alongside the road, says it more eloquently. The tree antedates Christ by 1,500 years.

GRANT GROVE

Old-growth sequoia have little commercial value, save for making shingles, grape stakes, fence posts, and pencils, but nevertheless, in the late nineteenth century, loggers began falling them at a furious pace. Mills were constructed at Converse Basin and Redwood Canyon, and at Hume Lake, where a flume was built to transport lumber fifty-four miles down to Sanger in the San Joaquin Valley. Trees were cut of such size that, had they been growing in the middle of New York's 42nd Street, would have left no room for cars. Mark Twain's friend Dan DeQuille was suitably impressed, but he apparently didn't understand the tenacity of the tree:

> Why, if one of the smallest of them should be cut down, the butt would be lying on the ground so long as to be perfectly rotten before the top got to the ground.

Perfectly sound logs lie about that fell thousands of years ago. A giant called the Centennial Tree was felled and a portion exhibited at the Centennial Exposition in Philadelphia in 1876; another was sent to the Chicago World's Fair in 1892, and a round from the Mark Twain Tree now resides in New York's Museum of Natural History. George Stewart, influential editor of the Visalia *Delta*, got mad at the carnage and campaigned to have the unlogged groves set aside as nature preserves. He is now considered the "father" of Sequoia National Park. Time heals all wounds, they say, but here healing takes centuries; you can get a sense of the waste loggers wrought (less than half the wood ever reached the mill) by taking the short **Big Stump Trail** near the park entrance.

Ranking third among the world's largest, the **General Grant Tree,** perhaps for reasons suggested by early explorer Smeaton Chase, is officially "the Nation's Christmas Tree."

> And when I reflected that on the night before the Crucifixion when Christ stood in Pilate's hall, this tree was standing much as it

stood now, lifting its arms, ancient even then, to the hushed sky, it seemed to take on in truth the character of an unconscious intercessor, a representative of the awestricken mute creation.

The fire-scarred, hollowed-out trunk of the nearby Fallen Monarch was, at times, variously used as a residence, a stable, and, improbably, a tavern.

The Grant tree is but one of many giants that cluster about a modest community of campgrounds, lodges, and an in-holding of private homes named Wilsonia. **Grant Grove Village** (elevation, 6,589 feet) serves as a nice base camp for exploring the more accessible parts of the Kings Canyon Park and the surrounding Sequoia National Forest. The park service operates a visitors' center here, and a concessioner provides food and lodging. Guests stay in rustic, thin-sided, wood stove-heated cabins that stretch out along the side of a lovely meadow. When I asked Ranger George San Miguel how one keeps warm in winter, he replied rather succinctly, "You burn lots of wood." The drive and short walk to **Panoramic Point** is rewarding, especially late in the day when the light is best. Swimming and boating activities are centered at **Hume Lake,** site of a large church camp. The nearby **Converse Basin Grove** was heavily logged prior to the creation of the park, but one giant, the **Boole Tree,** was spared. Whether Frank Boole, the logging foreman, wanted it to be his legacy, or whether he left it standing as an act of atonement for the desecration he had wrought, we do not know.

Recreational Facilities

- ✔ **Grant Grove Village** Grocery, restaurant, bar, and 60 rustic cabins. Sequoia Guest Services. P.O. Box 789, Three Rivers, CA 93271. (209) 561-3314.

- ✔ **Wilsonia Lodge** Cafe, grocery, and motel. P.O. Box 808, Kings Canyon National Park, CA 93633. (209) 335-2310.

- △ **National Park Campgrounds** 3 campgrounds, 370 sites.

- △ **Forest Service Campgrounds** 2 campgrounds near Hume Lake, 150 sites.

- § **Hume Lake** Grocery and boat rentals.

§ **Grant Grove Visitors Center** Information and wilderness permits. (209) 335-2315.

§ **Hume Lake Ranger District** Information and wilderness permits. 36273 East Kings Canyon Rd., Dunlap, CA 93621. (209) 338-2251.

Ω **Horse Corral Pack Station** P.O. Box 641, Woodlake, CA 93286. (209) 564-2709.

KINGS CANYON

Glaciers scooped out four lovely granite-walled valleys in the western Sierra. Of these, Hetch Hetchy is now full of water, Yosemite is full of people, and Tihipite is virtually inaccessible. The fourth, Kings Canyon, was inaccessible too (hikers and fishermen took the steep trail down from Horse Corral Meadow), but in 1939 a road, ten years abuilding using convict labor, opened, and now anyone willing to brave an hour's drive on a twisty, steep, and narrow highway will find himself in a hidden jewel. After driving alongside dry, chaparral-covered slopes, you enter the canyon at a spectacular portal called Kings Gate. Privately owned **Boyden Cave** is open for tours. The valley is low; the granite is pink, not gray as in Yosemite, and jumbled with brush growing from cracks. But many of the nearby peaks rise up higher than at any other place in North America. Spanish Mountain stands 7,800 feet above the river, making Kings Canyon deeper than the Grand Canyon or the Snake River gorge in Idaho. Surprisingly, the area has an almost desertlike feel; manzanita, chaparral, and that splendid Southern California plant, the Yucca, abound. William Brewer came to Cedar Grove in 1864 and waxed enthusiastic:

> Next to Yosemite this is the grandest canyon I have ever seen. A pretty valley or flat half a mile wide lies along the river, and covered with trees. On both sides rise tremendous granite precipices, of every shape, often nearly perpendicular, rising from 2,500 feet to above 4,000 feet. They did not form a continuous wall, but rose in high points, with canyons coming down here and there, and with fissures, gashes, and gorges. The whole scene was sublime.

The day was Epiphany in 1805 when Gabriel Moraga camped at the river's mouth, so he named it *Rio de los Santos Reyes*. **Cedar Grove** (elevation 4,635 feet) is the center of activities, with all the comforts of home, including a top-quality motel, grocery, and take-out food service establishment. Nearby **Roaring River Falls** is an impressive cataract, viewed from a short trail. Brewer commented:

> We camped at the head of this valley by a fine grassy meadow where the stream forked. On both sides rose grand walls of granite about three thousand feet high, while between the forks was a stupendous rock, bare and rugged, over four thousand feet high. We luxuriated on trout for the next two meals.

The trout are planted now and not as wild as when my father came here in the mid 1930s, before the road was built. He quite easily caught all the fish he could eat—a good thing since a vexatious bear ate his store-bought food. Such events have become so troublesome that the Park Service has set out about seventy food-storage lockers (bear boxes) in the more popular back-country camping areas.

An informative self-guided nature trail circles **Zumwalt Meadow**. A walk to **Mist Falls** (eight miles round trip), however, makes the perfect day hike. Giant water-worn holes in a slab of granite, catch the roiling waters of the Kings and throw it in the air, forming splendid rooster tails, which fill the canyon with wind-borne spume.

High-Country Access

I once had an oil company map of California that contained a wonderful error. The draftsman, I suspect, looked at the lines showing the Cedar Grove road and another heading west from Owens Valley and figured that since the ends were only a quarter of an inch apart, the roads must meet. So he penned in a connecting line. What the poor chap didn't know is that there is a rock wall between those two roads, and the wall is a mile high. Apparently the assumption is common, for at Grant Grove, a couple of teenagers asked me how to get to Bishop. "Go down to Fresno, drive up to Yosemite, take the Tioga Road, and then go back down the Owens Valley," I advised. "How far is that?," they asked. "A couple of hundred miles," I cautioned, "and you have to go over three major passes." "But we're out of gas and we only have $5 between us," one lamented. With that, I suggested that they would do better to head back to Los Angeles whence they had come.

Sixty hikers a day are allowed onto the forty-mile-long **Rae Lakes Loop** trail, thirty of whom can take the somewhat easier clockwise route through Paradise Valley; the other thirty have to climb steeply up Bubbs Creek. (Two-thirds of the permits are issued by mail, the rest are first-come, first-serve on the day of arrival.) The route crosses spectacular **Glenn Pass** (11,978 feet) on the **John Muir Trail.** Another sixty hikers a day come in from Owens Valley over **Kearsarge Pass** (Chapter 12). Though it sounds crowded, there is lots of country to explore, including the spectacular **Sixty Lakes Basin.** Most spend five or six days in the area. Brewer wrote:

> The whole aspect of this region is peculiar; the impression is one of grandeur, but at the same time of desolation—the dark pines, the light granite, the sharp cones behind, the absence of all sounds except the singing of the wind through the pines or the rippling of streams. During the night there is no sound. The sky is very clear and almost black; the stars scarcely twinkle, but shine with a calm, steady, silvery light from this black dome above.

Today, an hour after sunset and an hour before dawn, the black dome is also laced with the glow of artificial satellites streaking across the sky. Four nearby peaks are named for members of the Whitney survey: Gardner, Cotter, Brewer (the highest at 13,570 feet), and Clarence King (both first and last names are used to distinguish it from another peak named for Reverend Thomas Starr King).

Recreational Facilities

✔ **Cedar Grove Motel** Grocery, snack bar, and 18 rooms in a modern building overlooking the Kings River. Sequoia Guest Services. P.O. Box 789, Three Rivers, CA 93271. (209) 561-3314.

ΔΔ **Kings Canyon Lodge** Cafe and cabins on the road to Cedar Grove. (209) 335-2405.

△ **National Park Campgrounds** 3 campgrounds, 268 sites.

Ω **Cedar Grove Pack Station** P.O. Box 295, Three Rivers, CA 93271. (209) 561-4621.

THE GENERALS HIGHWAY

In 1934 a road, appropriately called the **Generals Highway,** was built to connect the General Grant and General Sherman groves. It's a pretty drive, the northern part keeping to the ridge separating the Kings and Kaweah rivers. The great declivity of Kings Canyon can be seen from a vista point near **Quail Flat.** Across the way, a rough dirt road leads to the trailhead for **Redwood Canyon,** a wonderful place to be quite alone while wandering among some giants. Two six-mile day hikes are recommended: take the upper trail to Sugar Bowl Grove, returning by the Redwood Canyon trail, and the loop trail to the Hart Tree, returning by the same Redwood Canyon trail.

On the east side of the highway, there is a fine view from the fire tower at **Buck Rock** (dirt road, short walk), where much of the Sierra crest (but not Mount Whitney) can be seen. Nearby, a nice day hike from Big Meadow leads to Weaver Lake, located in the **Jennie Lakes Wilderness.** The backroad continues to the base of Lookout Peak where, after a short hike, you are rewarded with a magnificent view of Cedar Grove, here lying directly below.

Back on the Generals Highway, my favorite walk is the two-hour excursion on the moderately steep trail to **Little Baldy,** the best place to get a sense of the principal landform of the southern Sierra. William Brewer, having struggled up the peak that now bears his name, was astounded, as Clarence King later explained:

These snow crests bounding our view at the eastward we had all along taken to be the summits of the Sierra, and Brewer had supposed himself to be climbing a dominant peak, from which he might look eastward over Owen's Valley and out upon leagues of desert. Instead of this a vast wall of mountains, lifted still higher than his peak, rose beyond a tremendous cañon which lay like a trough between the two parallel ranks of peaks.

The Whitney Survey Party had just discovered the **Great Western Divide,** a subsidiary range of sullen peaks every bit as forboding as the Sierra Crest itself. Mount Brewer, (elevation 13,570 feet) anchors the northern part of the range, Mount Florence (12,432) the southern. In between are some beauties: Triple Divide Peak (12,634), where lie the fountains of the Kings, Kaweah, and Kern rivers; Kaweah Peak (13,802); and Mount Stewart (12,205), named for the park is founder. The cañon Brewer saw was the great trench of the Kern (Chapter 11). Though disappointed at not gaining the Sierra Crest, he was awe-struck:

> Such a landscape! A hundred peaks in sight over thirteen thousand feet—many very sharp—deep canyons, cliffs in every direction almost rivaling Yosemite, sharp ridges almost inaccessible to man, on which human foot has never trod—all combined to produce a view the subliminity of which is rarely equaled, one which few are privileged to behold.

Recreational Facilities

- ✔ **Montecito-Sequoia Lodge** 42 rooms and 10 summer cabins. American-plan family resort. (209) 565-3388. Reservations: 1845 Redwood Dr., Los Altos, CA 94022. (415) 967-8612.

- ✔ **Stony Creek Lodge** Cafe, grocery, and small motel. (209) 561-3314.

- △ **Forest Service Campground** 3 campgrounds, 80 sites.

LODGEPOLE/WOLVERTON

Most Sequoia National Park visitors' facilities are being relocated near Lodgepole (elevation 6,720 feet) along the Marble Fork of the Kaweah River, because the area is less sensitive to environmental damage than the big tree forests themselves. The most popular day hike here is to **Tokopah Falls** (four miles round trip), where the rocks at the base of the cascade are home to the wonderful little Mickey Mouse-eared pika, a member of the rabbit family. The larger and more serious-minded marmot also frequent the area. Another trail leads to **Twin Lakes** (9,500 feet). Almost too popular is the overnight (fourteen-mile round trip) trek to **Pear Lake** (9,500 feet). Campsites are numbered, and a reservation is required. The Sequoia Natural History association maintains a small hut here (winter use only), built by the Civilian Conservation Corps in 1940. The trailhead is at **Wolverton** (7,350 feet), site of a small winter play area. More aggressive hikers overnight at **Mehrten Meadow** (8,800 feet), base camp for climbing **Alta Peak** (11,204 feet), one of the few west-side vistas high enough that Mount Whitney can be seen over the top of the Great Western Divide.

Recreational Facilities

ΔΔ **Pear Lake Hut** 10-person wilderness hut. Sequoia Natural History Association. Ash Mountain, Box 10, Three Rivers, CA 93271.

Δ **Park Service Campgrounds** Dorst Campground, 238 sites; Lodgepole Campground, 260 sites, reservable through Ticketron.

§ **Lodgepole Visitor Center** Information and wilderness permits. (209) 565-3341.

§ **Wolverton Ski Area** Platter and rope tows, open winter weekends. (209) 565-3381.

Ω **Wolverton Pack Station** P.O. Box 641 Woodlake, CA 93286. (209) 565-3445.

GIANT FOREST

John Muir gave the grove its name:

This part of the sequoia belt seemed to me the finest, and I then named it "the Giant Forest." It extends a magnificent growth of giants, grouped in pure temple groves, ranged in colonnades along the sides of meadows.

Muir suspected he was seeing the largest of living things on this planet, and he was right; the **General Sherman** tree currently claims that honor (no one knows what tree might be growing faster and thus could dispose the monarch). This corpulent conifer is a hundred feet around at chest level, soars 272 feet into the air, and contains two-and-a-half times as much wood as the largest coastal redwood. One branch is seven feet in diameter. The tree is gorgeous. But others here are nearly as big, including the Washington tree (second), President (fourth), Lincoln (fifth), and two others that rank in the top twelve. Most can be seen by taking the **Congress Trail** and then looping around **Circle Meadow,** a wonderfully sobering, more-or-less level jaunt that takes a couple of hours. Former park Superintendent Walter Fry said of this trail:

> At the entrance to a grove of trees the Romans would place the inscription: *Numen, inest,* "God is in this place." And when the traveler turns his back upon roads and automobiles, and directs his feet up the trail to the Congress group, it is almost inevitable that he pause when passing between the four trees that form The Cloister, feel there the spirit of the forest, mellowed by the centuries, and know, although there is no bronze or marble plaque to tell him so, that "God is in this place."

Giant Forest is unique among sequoia groves because here the trees are in perfect harmony with another Sierra wonder, the mountain meadow. A spur road leads to **Crescent Meadow,** a place that inspired John Muir to write:

> It seemed impossible that any other forest picture in the world could rival it. There lay the grassy, flowery lawn, three fourths of a mile long, smoothly outspread, basking in mellow autumn light, colored brown and yellow and purple, streaked with lines of green along the streams and ruffled here and there with patches of ledum and scarlet vaccinium. Around the margin there is first a ring of azalea and willow bushes, colored orange yellow, enlivened with vivid dashes of red cornel, as if painted. Then up spring the mighty walls of verdure three hundred feet high, the brown fluted pillars so thick and tall and strong they seem fit to uphold the sky.

A trail leads to **Tharp's Log,** a hollowed-out fallen giant, sometime home to Hale Tharp, discoverer of the Giant Forest. The meadow here was heavily grazed during Muir's time, and he was furious:

All the basin was swept by swarms of hoofed locusts, the southern part over and over again, until not a leaf within reach was left on the wettest bog, the outer edges of the thorniest chaparral beds, or even on the young conifers, which, unless under the stress of dire famine, sheep never touch.

Sheep proved to be more adaptable and therefore more profitable than cattle and were, for a while, the scourge of the Sierra. George Stewart, on a month-long outing in 1899 to Mount Whitney, fumed:

Flocks of sheep for more than thirty summers had swept the cañon bare of everything that could be eaten, nibbled, trampled or destroyed, and no young trees were growing to replace the large timber slowly disappearing from various causes.

Sheeping is now banned in most of the Sierra, partially because of Muir and Stewart's complaints and also because the diseases they brought were largely responsible for the annihilation of the native big horn. Herders were loath to obey until the park superintendent had the ingenious idea of ushering the offenders out one side of the park, their flocks out the other.

Giant Forest has some dubious attractions, the Tunnel Log (you drive through a slot cut in a prostrate tree), and the Auto Log, a fallen giant that you can drive up onto for a picture of your car perched atop a log. Better is a tour of **Crystal Cave,** operated by the nonprofit Sequoia Association. The most famous trek is to climb the 400 steps to the top of **Moro Rock,** a 300-foot-high granite dome (the downhill side is several thousand feet high) hovering over the Kaweah River. In 1932 a somewhat scary stone and concrete trail was built to replace the rickety old wooden stairway. Evening is the best time to make the climb, because the sun casts a golden palate on the Great Western Divide.

Although Benjamin Harrison signed the bill creating Sequoia Park in 1890, there was much uncertainty as to who actually owned the land. Many locals felt that the Kaweah Colony, a socialist organization, deserved title under the Swamp and Overflow and Timber and Stone acts because they had occupied much of the area and had made many improvements, including the first road, which stopped just short of Giant Grove. But the federal government threw out their claims, perhaps because the colonists insisted on calling the General Sherman Tree the Karl Marx Tree. Nevertheless, for a while Giant Forest remained a "pleasuring ground" for those with more acceptable political beliefs. Bill Rowland, whose parents built a cabin at Round Meadow, told me of spending delightful summers here, his father coming up on weekends from his job in Visalia. "That was before the Generals Highway was built," Bill said. "The road was so bad, wives worried about their husbands' safety. So they insisted the men send a postcard noting their safe arrival back in the valley. Well, Mac Loveless wrote his postcards in advance, thus saving the bother, but on one trip, he drove too fast (probably fifteen miles an hour), missed a turn and went tumbling down a cliff and into Kaweah River. Though battered and bruised, he calmly reached into his pack and pulled out a card which he handed to a companion to drop in the mail, thereby sparing his wife knowledge of the mishap till the following weekend."

Today, a store, two restaurants, some motel units, and a hundred cabins are crowded into Giant Forest. But they threaten the trees (see Sequoiadendron Gigantea, below) and so are to be demolished, the community to be removed to a site near Lodgepole. "The process has taken longer than anyone envisioned," Bill Tweed told me. "It was easy to get rid of the private inholdings like your friend's cabin, and later to relocate the government facilities. Unfortunately, though, there's a lot of paperwork and procedures we have to follow before we can remove the overnight accommodations. But unlike in Yosemite, there is no controversy. You know, people are willing to do whatever is necessary to protect *living* things."

Sequoiadendron Gigantea

Old? They were old when the world was young!
The mating song of the spring was sung
In the kindly heart of each brave old tree
When the good Christ walked on Galilee.

Almost everyone has admired their tenacity. J. Smeaton Chase observed:

The Sequoia becomes conscious of his destiny, answering the inward urge, makes for the skies in a

climbing, high-hearted fashion that is fine to behold. Their deep-rifted bark clothes them with dignity and age; the great limbs, mossed and lichened, stand out oak-like above and athwart the pines and firs. Here a thunder-bolt has ploughed a heavy furrow, and that fearful scar marks the place where a tree-like arm was torn away.

That ability to shrug off fire is particularly intriguing:

You see a thick strip of ruddy bark, only a few inches wide, yet supplying sap and new life to a heaven-reaching branch of foliage. The tree still lives; and, given protection and a few hundred or thousand years, it may heal over the ninety-five percent portion which is now blackened and dead.

Walter Fry, commissioner of Sequoia National Park, commented:

They quite literally are the nearest thing to immortality in the material universe—a link between things material and things spiritual. You must deal with these trees in terms rather of geology than of dendrology. The age limit of the Big Tree is unknown, because we have no record of one dying of old age.

Man is the biggest threat. With a shallow root system spreading out over a wide area, the tree suffers from ground compaction caused by too many human footprints. So trails are being rerouted, visitors encouraged to stay away. A good thing, for as Ralph Waldo Emerson observed: "The wonder is that we can see these trees and not wonder more."

High Sierra Access

Crescent Meadow (elevation 6,700 feet) is the southern terminus of the fifty-mile **High Sierra Trail,** the logical extension of the John Muir Trail, which it joins thirteen miles north of Mount Whitney. Yosemite's Half Dome is a 250-mile trek. Many hikers go only eleven miles to **Bearpaw Meadow** (7,700 feet), where the park concessionaire operates a small camp, similar to the High Sierra camps surrounding Tuolumne Meadows (Chapter 6). The Park Service built the camp in 1927 during construction of the High Sierra Trail, which opened in 1932. Most guests stay at least two or three nights and spend the days visiting the numerous nearby lakes. From there the trail crosses the Great Western Divide at **Kawaeh Gap** (10,810 feet) and then makes a gradual descent to the **Chapoga Plateau** before dropping steeply into the lovely canyon of the **Kern** (6,700 feet), an area Bill Tweed, who works for the Park Service, thinks is the prettiest in the park. After following the river for ten miles, the trail climbs steeply up Wallace Valley, where it meets the John Muir Trail at an elevation of 10,400 feet.

Recreational Facilities

ΔΔ **Giant Forest Accommodations** 150 cabins and motel rooms. Restaurant and bar—grocery, cafeteria, and bar nearby. Sequoia Guest Services. P.O. Box 789, Three Rivers, CA 93271. (209) 561-3314.

Δ **Bearpaw High Sierra Camp** 6 two-person furnished tents located eleven miles from nearest road. Meals. Sequoia Guest Services. P.O. Box 789, Three Rivers, CA 93271. (209) 561-3314.

ASH MOUNTAIN

The Generals Highway drops dizzily into the Middle Fork of the Kaweah River, loosing 5,000 feet in only seventeen miles. A **visitors' center** is located at the Ash Mountain entrance station (elevation 1,700 feet). There is little grandeur here, but the Kaweah River is one of the few Sierra streams in the public domain that traverses the Upper Sonoran life zone. Especially around Easter, hikers are rewarded with a dazzling display of wild flowers: California poppies, miner's lettuce, filaree, and lupin. Watch for poison oak and take mind of ticks.

Recreational Facilities

Δ **Park Service Campgrounds** 2 campgrounds along Kaweah River, 72 sites.

§ **Ash Mountain Visitors Center** (N.P.S.) Information and wilderness permits. (209) 565-3456.

MINERAL KING

The name evokes the expectations of those who, in the 1870s, groveled for silver in this high canyon. Enough metal was found to persuade investors to build the road, but fortunes were as rare as spotting a Sierra mountain lion at noontime. Nevertheless, when the park was expanded in 1926, Mineral King was excluded because of extensive private in-holdings. Then, in 1964, Walt Disney, encouraged by the Forest Service, looked about and thought ski resort. He proposed a Squaw Valley-sized complex, capable of handling 10,000 skiers a day. Several knowledgeable Sierra Clubbers had toured Mineral King in 1948 and, although they saw problems, they did not oppose development, concluding: "The terrain and snow conditions appear excellent for ski touring but the suitability as a ski resort center is questionable because of the expense of a winter road, the problem of moving people from suitable lodge sites to suitable ski slopes, the hazards of avalanche and terrain, and the problem of supply." They were right about the avalanches; the mine buildings were destroyed in the 1870s, as was a small hotel built a hundred years later. The size of Disney's project caused the club to reverse itself, taking an active opposing role, insisting: "1) The project is too big, 2) [It] was not planned with the protection of Sequoia National Park in mind, and 3) Experts warn that the cost of an improved access road might be twice as much as now estimated." With such a formidable foe, the Forest Service withdrew the permit; the area was subsequently included in the National Park, thus ensuring its relatively primitive character.

The road to Mineral King (elevation 7,800) is terrible—in places fifteen miles an hour constitutes dangerous speeding. The valley is lovely. Marmots scurry about, feasting on the water hoses of hikers' parked cars. An occasional bear glomps about, looking for carelessly stored camp food. But most come here because Mineral King is the principal access point for the upper Kern River. Trails to **Sawtooth Pass** (11,600 feet) and **Franklin Pass** (11,800 feet) lead to numerous glacial tarns located near the spine of the **Great Western Divide.** The latter provides the shortest access to the great trench of the Kern. Well-named **Farewell Gap** (10,587) leads to the remote Little Kern watershed in the **Golden Trout Wilderness,** an area also reached from Lloyds Meadows (Chapter 11). A ten-mile trail heads south from the **Artwell Grove** of giant sequoias, first dropping into the East Kaweah and then climbing to lovely **Hockett Meadows** (8,500 feet).

Recreational Facilities

ΔΔ **Silver City** Store and cabins.

Δ **Park Service Campgrounds** 2 campgrounds, 50 sites.

§ **Mineral King Ranger Station** Information and wilderness permits. (209) 565-3341 extention 812.

Ω **Mineral King Pack Station** P.O. Box 61, Three Rivers, CA 93721. (209) 561-4142.

SOUTH KAWEAH RIVER

Park Headquarters is at **Three Rivers** (population 900; elevation 800 feet), a modest low-level town near the confluence of the South, Middle, and Marble forks of the Kaweah. Adventuresome travelers should explore the seldom-visited South Fork, where a small campground is especially popular in spring. The twelve-mile road is paved for the first nine miles. Two trails leave from the oak-studded area (elevation 3,500 feet), the easier of which follows the river for a couple of miles. Those willing to tackle a 2,500-foot climb will be rewarded with the splendors of **Garfield Grove,** one of those places, like the South Calaveras Grove (Chapter 5), where the hand of man is barely visible. The trail slabs upward through the middle of this large forest. Usually, only the trunks of nearby giants capture your eye, but in spots, the regal tops of those farther down the slope are graciously revealed. Interestingly, the Sequoia National Park was originally conceived for the purpose of protecting only this grove.

Recreational Facilities

✓ **Best Western Holiday Lodge** 47 motel units. P.O. Box 192, Three Rivers, CA 93271. (209) 561-4119.

Δ **Park Service Campground** 13 sites on the South Kaweah River.

§ **Sequoia-Kings Canyon National Park** Three Rivers, CA 93271. (209) 565-3341.

◀◀◀◀◀◆ 11 ◆▶▶▶▶▶

KERN RIVER COUNTRY

A Gentle Wilderness

South of the Kings River, the Sierra's chain of high peaks splits in two, the main crest continuing unbroken while a subsidiary range pushes southwest in a series of two-mile-high peaks that form the Great Western Divide. These again split, with the relatively low Greenhorn Mountains forming the southernmost Sierra rampart. In between is the gently rolling Kern Plateau, a mile-and-a-half-high triangle roughly thirty miles on a side, which in turn is bisected by the awesome Kern River trench. Seen from outer space, the southern Sierra looks like a gigantic crab leg, with the main crest forming the wider and more powerful claw and the Greenhorns the smaller pincer. This has always been sort of the stepchild of the Sierra, the place that has received the least public attention and the fewest visitors. Two reasons account for this relative lack of interest: the scarcity of access roads and the almost total absence of those wonderful rock-bound lakes that lure people to the rest of the range. The lack of roads is surprising, considering the incredible stands of harvestable timber on the Kern Plateau. Only in the last few years have paved roads been punched into this vast forestland. The dearth of lakes may be disappointing, but that shortfall is more than compensated for by the incredible number of meadows that grace the

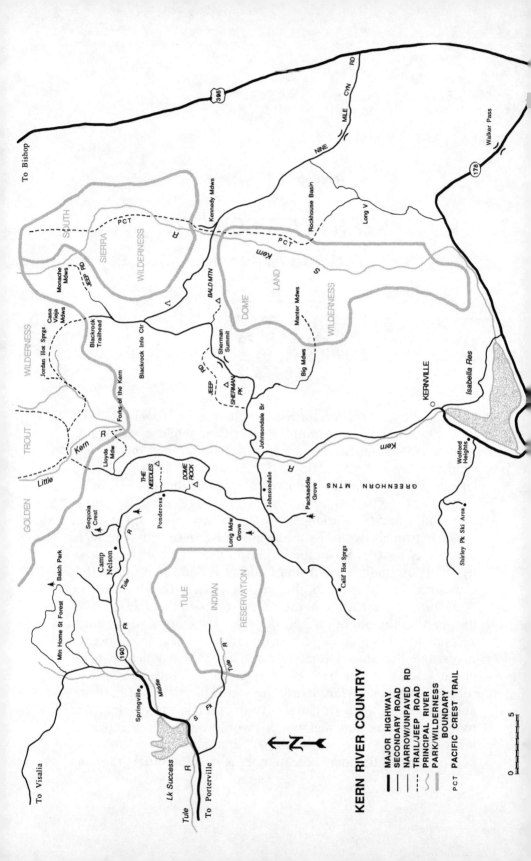

KERN RIVER COUNTRY

MAJOR HIGHWAY
SECONDARY ROAD
NARROW/UNPAVED RD
TRAIL/JEEP ROAD
PRINCIPAL RIVER
PARK/WILDERNESS BOUNDARY
PCT PACIFIC CREST TRAIL

0   5

To Bishop

395

SOUTH SIERRA WILDERNESS

GOLDEN TROUT WILDERNESS

Little Kern R

Forks of the Kern

Lloyds Mdw

Jordan Hot Sprgs

Casa Vieja Mdws

Monache Mdws

JEEP RD

Blackrock Trailhead

Blackrock Info Ctr

PCT

Kennedy Mdws

NINE MLE CYN RD

Rockhouse Basin

Long V

DOME LAND

Kern S

PCT

BALD MTN

Sherman Summit

JEEP RD

SHERMAN PK

Manter Mdws

Big Mdws

WILDERNESS

Walker Pass

178

Johnsondale Br

Kern R

KERNVILLE

Isabella Res

Wofford Heights

Shirley Pk Ski Area

Calif Hot Sprgs

Packsaddle Grove

Johnsondale

GREENHORN MTNS

DOME ROCK

THE NEEDLES

Ponderosa

Sequoia Crest

Camp Nelson

Balch Park

Mtn Home St Forest

Long Mdw Grove

TULE INDIAN RESERVATION

Tule R

Tule FK R

Middle FK Tule R

S FK Tule R

190

Springville

To Visalia

Lk Success

Tule R

To Porterville

N

landscape. My first view of the Kern Plateau was from 11,000-foot Trail Pass, located on the Sierra Crest a scant dozen miles south of Mount Whitney. Expecting to see granite, I was astounded to look out upon a sea of undulating, densely forested hills marked by sinuous ribbons, clear-running mountain streams whose quickening flow was, from time to time, interrupted by meadows, luxuriant in resplendent greenness. John Muir coined the phrase "gentle wilderness," and although his wanderings never took him to the Kern Plateau, he would certainly consider it an appropriate description of the area.

Much of the timberland was saved from the logger's axe by the creation of three wilderness areas, Golden Trout, Dome Land, and South Sierra, which now provide protection for over a half a million acres of roadless wonderland. The presence of man is not lacking, though; for years cattlemen have found these meadows ideal for summer pasturage, and their influence is still strongly felt. Ten thousand head graze in the Sequoia National Forest. Fishermen long ago discovered that the ice-cold streams were filled with lovely golden trout (the California state fish), one of only two trout indigenous to the Sierra (the other being the Lahontan cutthroat). Deer hunters too come to the area—though Bill Deisman, who works for the Forest Service, told me that of the 14,000 deer tags issued each year, only two percent ever get affixed to the horns of a buck. In recent years, river running has become the sport of choice; the untamed "killer" Kern is now one of the most popular (and dangerous) white-water adventures in the Sierra.

A caution is in order. Exploring the Greenhorns and the Kern Plateau requires driving on some treacherous mountain roads. Readers wishing to go directly to the east side of the Sierra (Chapter 12) can avoid the problem by turning east at Bakersfield and taking State Highway 184 to **Walker Pass** (elevation 5,250 feet), the southernmost and lowest of the trans-Sierra highways. (Joe Walker wanted no repeat of his 1883 High Sierra ordeal, so he returned east on this route, the first white man to do so.) Walker Pass hardly seems Sierran. Most of the route follows the South Kern River through a wide, arid valley, and although the summit is densely forested, the trees are the desert-loving, spiny, cactuslike Joshua.

TULE RIVER REDWOODS

We will begin our exploration by visiting **Mountain Home State Forest** (elevation 6,600 feet), a densely timbered tract on the short but steeply flowing North Fork of the Tule River. Two roads climb the scarp, both bad. One is narrow and twisty, the other steep and twisty. The northern Balch Park Road is lightly used, but log trucks frequent the southern Bear Creek Road, the lower portion of which is only one lane wide. Legally, you have the right of way if you are going uphill, but that's of little importance when the fellow coming at you from around a blind curve is a forty-ton truck and there is a thousand-foot cliff on your side of the road. He has no particular problem, but you do. It's best, therefore, to make the loop in a clockwise direction—the truck coming toward you is not only geared down for the uphill grind, but is not loaded. And the truck is on the scary side of the road.

Balch Park, a small section of the forest, is owned by the county of Tulare. Nearly a hundred campsites nestle beneath some of the largest redwoods found anywhere. Allen Russell, long-time park ranger, told me proudly that the tree they named after him is the fifth or sixth largest in the world, but he's wrong. According to Wendell Flint, the authority on such matters, two other trees in the state forest are larger: the Genesis on the south side of the park and the Adam near Shake Camp. No matter, all are magnificent. In the 1880s promoters got the bright idea of hollowing out one of the downed logs, mounting it on wheels, and using it for a railroad dining car. Halfway through the project they realized that the log was too big to pass through mainline tunnels. An hour-long **nature trail** leads into the state forest (purchased from private interests in 1946) where much of the hillside has recently been logged. I was surprised to read in a pamphlet that young sequoias are a valuable commercial tree. Unlike their elder brethren, they are not brittle and have wood similar to the red fir. Sequoia National Forest now plants 10,000 redwood seedlings a year.

State Highway 190 wiggles up the middle fork of the Tule River to **Camp Nelson** (elevation 4,800 feet), a place of resort since 1886, when John Milton Nelson established a High Sierra packstation. George Stewart (of Sequoia National Park fame) came through here on a trek to Mount Whitney in 1899 and wrote:

> The last night on the Middle Fork was spent like most of those preceding it, around a blazing fire. But it retains a lasting place in our memories mainly because of the serenade that drowned the "voices of the night" at the hour when slumber was due. Donkeys and mules belonging to parties unknown were grazing in the vicinity, and these added to our own made a double quartette with all parts represented. Some of these animals were inside the field that night and others shut out, and the lamentations that filled the air in consequence were doleful, loud and unforgettable.

Those who have enjoyed a Sierra pack trip know exactly what he was talking about.

Sequoias proliferate along the north-facing canyon walls. A nice trail goes upstream from the Belknap campground and leads to several groves. The biggest trees around, however, are along **Alder Creek,** on private land near the community of **Sequoia Crest.** The largest, named for football coach Amos Alonzo Stagg, is thought to be the sixth largest in the world.

Recreational Facilities

↙ **Camp Nelson Lodge** Restaurant and 8 motel units. P.O. Box 94, Camp Nelson, CA 93208. (209) 542-2461.

∆∆ **Camp Wishon Resort** Cafe, grocery, and cabins located in a side canyon. P.O. Box 652, Springville, CA 93265. (209) 542-2423.

∆ **Forest Service Campgrounds** Coffee Camp, Belknap, and Coy Flat near Camp Nelson together have 53 sites. Wishon has 36 sites.

∆ **Tulare County Campground** Balch Park, 71 campsites.

§ **Sequoia National Forest** Wilderness permits by mail. 32588 Highway 190, Porterville, CA 93257. (209) 539-2607.

Ω **Balch Park Packstations** P.O. Box 852, Springville, CA 93265. (209) 542-2816.

GREENHORN MOUNTAINS

Locals call the new road that traverses the spine of the Greenhorn Mountains, the Western Divide Highway, even though that range begins on the other side of the Little Kern River. A "Sno Park" at the little community of **Ponderosa** (elevation 7,000 feet) provides a nice place for wintertime frolicking. Snowmobiles abound. This is one of the access points for the western part of the **Golden Trout Wilderness.** A logging road, paved for the first half-dozen miles, follows the ridge northward to the boundary. Three trailheads are located at the 8,000-foot level but are lightly used because the Little Kern, the most popular destination, can be better reached from the Lloyds Meadow area (see next page). Great views of the San Joaquin Valley are to be had from **Inspiration Point,** reached by a two-mile trail. Viewpoints facing east, however, are more inspiring. One of the best, and certainly most accessible, is from **Dome Rock,** a granite monolith that hovers over the furrow of the Kern like Cerberus guarding the gates to the river Styx. A short dirt road leads to an easy walk to the top. The whole of the Kern Plateau is laid out across the river, with Olancha Peak spiking the Sierra Crest. Rock climbers find the back-side face a challenge. More adventuresome sightseers drive two miles on a terrible dirt road, walk two miles, and then climb a dizzy flight of several hundred stairs to the **Needles** (8,245 feet), a fire lookout perched atop a three-pointed spire.

Several redwood groves line the Western Divide Highway, the most interesting being at **Long Meadow,** where the newly constructed, almost level Trail of a Hundred Giants leads into the woods. Signs point out the more important natural features. The sequoias are not the only beauties, as an early traveler pointed out: "Magnificent firs stood like a hand-picked regiment, every individual tall, straight and handsome." I wanted to visit nearby **Packsaddle Grove** but became frustrated when the dirt road turned bad and I was met head-on by a giant bulldozer clearing the way for logging operations. I should have persevered; two of the largest sequoias stand within a few miles of the southern limit of where virgin redwoods grow.

The Western Divide Highway ends at a T, the road that heads west dropping to **California Hot Springs** (elevation 3,100 feet), where a 1920s resort has been refurbished and is now a great place to swim. Our highway drops into the Kern Canyon, passing through the one-time mill town of **Johnsondale** (4,720 feet). Curious about a hundred identical house trailers parked at the former mill site, I inquired of a guard what was going on. "We're developing the town into a condo resort," he replied. "That's where we house the prospective buyers we bus up from L.A. and San Diego." Trailheads near **Lloyds Meadows** (5,800 feet), reached by a paved road, provide the best access to the western half of the **Golden Trout Wilderness.** The highlight of the twenty-mile drive in is the view of the Needles, here soaring several thousand feet above the road. The trail from Lloyds Meadows drops 800 feet to the **Forks of the Kern,** a favorite put-in for white-water river runners (see below). From there it continues up the Main Kern for a dozen miles, eventually climbing to the Kern Plateau via Jordan Hot Springs. Another trail heads north, dropping into the Little Kern Basin via Fish Creek. This watershed is home to the endangered Little Kern Golden Trout, a subspecies of the California state fish. A modest recovery program is underway to rid the streams of brook trout, which are predators, and rainbow, which interbreed with the native stock. Except for the main fork of the Kern, all fishing in the Golden Trout Wilderness is restricted to using barbless hooks on artificial lures. Creel limit is five.

Recreational Facilities

ΔΔ **Ponderosa Lodge** Cafe and cabins. Route 2, Springville, CA 93265. (209) 542-2579.

Δ **Forest Service Campgrounds** Quaking Aspen and Peppermint (7,000 feet), 51 sites. Redwood Meadow, with 15 sites, is nestled in an old-growth redwood grove. Those heading into the Little Kern Basin should stay at Lower Peppermint, 17 sites.

Ω **Golden Trout Pack Station** P.O. Box 756, Springville, CA 93265. (209) 561-4142.

KERN RIVER

Vortex, Satan's Slot, Fender Bender, Slalom, Sock'-Em-Dog, Tombstone, White Maiden's Walkway, Pin Ball, and Royal

Flush—all are fanciful names that river rats have given to the rapids of the Kern. Kayakers especially seem to thrive on living on the edge of eternity. A tour operator's brochure describes one shoot as "A good play—at certain flows, nose stands are possible." Seven people drowned on a single spring weekend, a fellow in Kernville told me. Nevertheless, three sections of the river are run commercially, the most popular being the stretch downstream from the Johnsondale bridge. But the upper Kern is a favorite too—fifteen miles of frothing water in a canyon so steep there isn't even room for a stream-side trail. River runners tote their kayaks and rafts down the three-mile trail to the put-in at **Forks of the Kern** (elevation 3,740 feet). The third runable section is below Lake Isabella Dam.

Kernville (population 1,660; elevation 2,600 feet) is the place to stay if you don't want to sleep out at one of the six campgrounds along the river. Half a dozen motels and restaurants make up this almost-new town, which was removed to this site in 1953 when Lake Isabella was filled. A small **museum** relates the history of the place. A substantial retirement community has sprung up around the reservoir. **Lake Isabella** (population 3,428) has a huge shopping center; virtually every resident of the pleasant community of **Wofford Heights** (population 2,112) lives in a house trailer. Outdoor activities center primarily on fishing and boating on the warm waters of the reservoir. Snow skiers head for **Shirley Meadows,** a mom-and-pop resort with a small chairlift and a rope tow.

Recreational Facilities

- ✔ **Hi-Ho Resort Lodge** 7 housekeeping units. Rt. 1, Box 21, Kernville, CA 93238. (619) 376-2671.

- ✔ **Kern Lodge Motel** 15 units. P.O. Box 66, Kernville, CA 93238. (619) 376-2223.

- ∆∆ **Road's End Resort** Cabins, store, and restaurant. Star Route 1, Box 98, Kernville, CA 93238. (619) 376-6562.

- ∆ **Forest Service Campgrounds** 6 campgrounds along the Kern River; 285 sites.

- ∆ **Corps of Engineers Campgrounds** Isabella Lake has 6 RV campgrounds.

- **McNally's Fairview Lodge & Restaurant** Star Route Box 95, Kernville, CA 93238. (619) 376-2430.

- **Ewing's on the Kern** Restaurant and bar. (619) 376-2411.

§ **Shirley Meadows Ski Area** P.O. Box Q, Wofford Heights, CA 93285. (619) 376-4186.

§ **Kern Valley Golf Course** 9-hole short course. (619) 376-2828.

§ **Cannell Meadow Ranger District** Information and wilderness permits. P.O. Box 6, Kernville, CA 93238. (209) 376-3781.

Ω **Sierra South** River tours and raft rentals. P.O. Box Y, Kernville, CA 93238. (619) 376-3745.

Ω **Kern River Tours** P.O. Box 3444, Kernville, CA 93238. (619) 379-4616.

Ω **Mountain River Adventures** P.O. Box 858, Kernville, CA 93238. (619) 376-6553.

DOME LAND WILDERNESS

County Road M99 climbs steeply from the **Johnsondale Bridge** (elevation 3,740 feet) in one of the longest continuous grades in the Sierra—fourteen miles of two-lane, twisty highway on which you grind up the hill in second gear for forty-five minutes, struggling to reach 9,000-foot **Sherman Summit.** Then suddenly you are presented with a fine view of the Kern Plateau and the Sierra Crest. Nearby, a tough Jeep road goes around the back side of Sherman Peak, but enthusiasts advise people not to attempt it without a companion Jeep carrying a winch. There is reason to detour slightly here to visit the western portion of the **Dome Land Wilderness,** an area unique in that although relatively high (about 7,000 feet), the country is semi-arid with a decidedly Southwestern flavor. Piñon pine and sage replace the fir and Jeffery pine of the area farther north. The wilderness takes its name from a series of relatively small granite domes (they look more like bananas) that ring the upper reaches of the South Kern. If they were pink, not white, you might well feel like you were in Sedona Arizona. The most popular trail leaves from the southeast corner of **Big Meadow,** a mile-square sea of grass that is reached by taking a thirteen-mile logging road (paved half-way). Backpackers take the two-and-a-half mile 34E37 trail, which first climbs to a modest summit (8,200 feet) and then drops into **Manter Meadow.** You can make day trips from there.

You don't have to walk far, however, to get an overview of the Dome Land Wilderness. Continue on beyond Sherman Summit and take the short dirt road to **Bald Mountain Lookout.** Hardly a place in the Sierra has a better view. The Dome Land Wilderness lies directly below. Farewell Gap, which marks the boundary of Sequoia National Park, flanks the southern reaches of the Great Western Divide, which culminates in **Florence Peak** (12,432 feet). The Kern Plateau is laid out on the north, marked by **Kern Peak** (11,510 feet), which dominates the middle scene. Puncturing the eastern skyline is Olancha Peak (12,123 feet), a monadnock towering above the plateau. But it is Mount Whitney (14,495 feet) that captures your attention. From here it looks like a tiny pyramid, framed by the gray, rounded masses of Mount Hitchcock and Mount Langley.

Recreational Facilities

Δ **Forest Service Campground** Horse Meadow, 41 sites.

THE KERN PLATEAU

Blackrock Information Center, operated by the Forest Service, is the focal point of the Kern Plateau. From here a new first-class stub road goes north to the principal staging area for the eastern half of the **Golden Trout Wilderness.** The huge parking lot (fifty or more spaces) at **Blackrock Trailhead** (elevation 8,800 feet) attests to the popularity of this area. Many spend the first night at **Casa Vieja Meadows,** a little over a mile north, reached by an easy trail. But **Jordan Hot Springs** is a more special place to visit (see A Step into Yesteryear, next page).

A Step into Yesteryear

In Chapter 2 we toured a theme park, Ponderosa Ranch, which purports to be the Wild West home of the Cartwright family, heroes of the television series *Bonanza.* It's all fake, of course. But the life depicted in that series was real, and fortunately you can still get a sense of that day and age by visiting a wonderful place, Jordan Hot Springs. Jordan started life as a cow camp in 1862, and the first building still survives. (John Jordan was a visionary who dreamed of building a toll road to the Owens Valley. While scouting out a suitable crossing of the Kern he was swept away by spring floods and drowned.) The site was chosen not because the grazing was especially good (the meadow is rather small), but for the hot mineral waters that flow out of the ground. Before the road to Blackrock was built, getting there involved a twenty-five-mile trek from Kennedy Meadows, but now you can walk there in two hours (three coming back). Most everything required for the camp was hauled in by mule, including a two-ton, cast-iron, wood-fired cookstove, a relic from an abandoned sailing ship. A sawmill was constructed on site to mill the rough-hewn lumber for the house, barn, and outbuildings. Shakes, used for both walls and roofs, were split from cedar bolts cut nearby.

I had mixed feelings about making the trek; it was late in the season, the forest was dusty, and I knew the five-mile trail dropped 2,400 feet into a steep-sided canyon. The walk back would be unpleasant. But my effort was well rewarded, because the minute I passed through the giant log gate, with the word WELCOME carved on the lintel, it seemed like I was stepping into yesteryear—a world filled with saddle sheds, hitching posts, water troughs, blacksmithing paraphernalia, and all of the other accouterments of a turn-of-the-century cattle ranch. The odor of harness leather and horse manure overpowered the sweet smell of vanilla from the Jeffery pines. If Lorne Green had walked out the front door I would not have been particularly surprised. Food and drink is kept in an outdoor storage box made out of burlap stretched over a frame built of lodgepole pines.

Constantly dripping water keeps everything cool. The main house, just two rooms (the kitchen in one, everything else in the other) seems perfect for the location, with a dining table big enough to serve a crowd. A cast-iron "long-box" stove is used for heat, but the day I was there it was warm and the banging of the screen door seemed a throwback. Coleman lanterns were the only compromise with the "modern" world. Ranch guests, most of whom come in by horse, sleep in little wooden shacks, each fitted with several lumpy-mattress-covered cots. They fish (a nice day-walk leads to the Main Kern), soak in hot water piped to several bathtubs made of concrete, or just sit around and read. Backpackers use the facilities too; everyone is made welcome.

The Blackrock area is also popular for a different kind of sport, OHV (off-highway-vehicle) riding. Huge **Monache Meadows,** eight miles long and three miles wide, was kept out of the wilderness because Jeepers and motorcyclists have long made it their back-country destination (the road isn't that bad). Separate trails have been set aside for two-wheel vehicles as opposed to ATVs (all-terrain vehicles), and rules have been established for their use. OHVs must have a "green sticker"; those driven on paved roads must be "street legal." And there is to be no "joy riding" or "cruising" in the campgrounds.

Recreational Facilities

Δ **Forest Service Campgrounds** Troy Meadows and Fish Creek campgrounds have 110 sites. Backpackers can stay one night at the Blackrock trailhead.

Ω **Kennedy Meadows Pack Trains & Jordan Hot Springs Wilderness Lodge** P.O. Box 1300, Weldon, CA 93283. (619) 378-2232.

SOUTH SIERRA WILDERNESS

Our road continues, dropping into the basin of the South Kern, only a fraction the size of the Main Kern (good fishing, though).

Kennedy Meadows (elevation 6,200 feet) has an eastern Sierra flavor; long-needle pines dominate, sage is the principal ground cover. A few homesites, not one having electricity, provide wonderful isolation for their owners. The roadhead at Kennedy Meadows was the traditional southern gateway to the Golden Trout Wilderness, but today, trekkers use it mainly for access to the **Pacific Crest National Scenic Trail,** which heads north toward Mount Whitney. To the south the trail stays west of the Sierra Crest in an area called the South Sierra Wilderness. Much of the land here is administered by the Bureau of Land Management; roads seem to dart out in all directions. A graded gravel road heads south to the Walker Pass Highway. About halfway along, a dirt spur leads to **Long Valley,** gateway to an area of the Dome Land Wilderness called **Rockhouse Basin.** Ranger Lorna Olle told me that the countryside is beautiful here but the access road is bad. Our highway continues southeast, eventually crossing the Sierra Crest on an un-named pass (6,600 feet), after which it drops down Nine Mile Canyon to meet Highway 395 out in the desert.

Recreational Facilities

Δ **Forest Service Campground** Kennedy Meadows, 38 sites.

§ **Kennedy Meadows Store** Groceries and gas.

The transition is now complete. Having started in dense redwood forests, we are now ready to explore the dry valleys and the dizzying heights of the eastern Sierra.

◄◄◄◄◄◄◆ **Part Four** ◆►►►►►►

THE EAST-SIDE
SIERRA

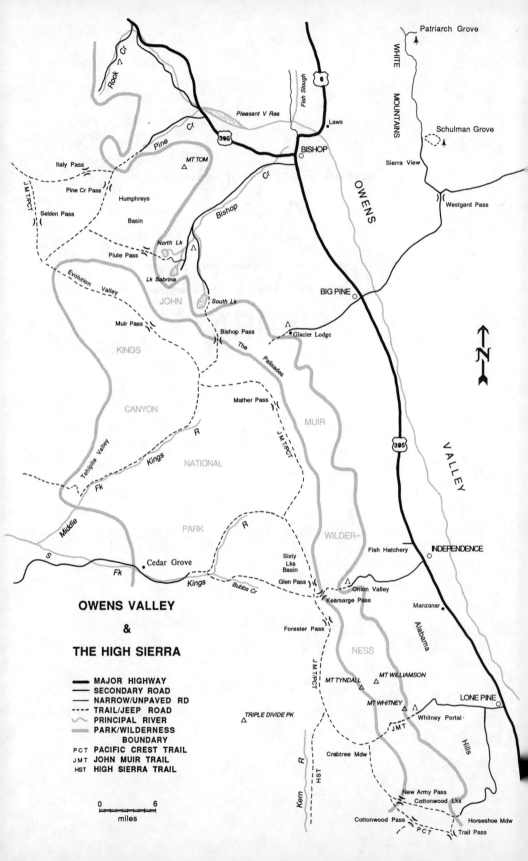

OWENS VALLEY
&
THE HIGH SIERRA

- ▬▬ MAJOR HIGHWAY
- ▬ SECONDARY ROAD
- — NARROW/UNPAVED RD
- --- TRAIL/JEEP ROAD
- 〜 PRINCIPAL RIVER
- ▬ PARK/WILDERNESS
        BOUNDARY
- PCT PACIFIC CREST TRAIL
- JMT JOHN MUIR TRAIL
- HST HIGH SIERRA TRAIL

0   6
├─┬─┬─┬─┬─┬─┤
       miles

◀◀◀◀◀◆ 12 ◆▶▶▶▶▶

OWENS VALLEY
AND THE
HIGH SIERRA

Scenes of Sublime Desolation

William Brewer, a member of the Whitney Survey Party and one of the first to set eyes on the High Sierra, stood atop Kearsarge Pass on July 27, 1864, and wrote:

> The summit is a very sharp granite ridge, with loose bowlders on both sides as steep as they will lie. It is 11,600 feet high, far above trees, barren granite mountains all around, with patches of snow,—the whole scene was one of sublime desolation.

Sublime indeed, as countless backpackers can attest, but desolate too, for most of the area is well above timberline and in places the snow lingers all year. Indians called this place Inyo, meaning "dwelling place of a great spirit." It seems fitting.

By contrast, Owens Valley (Captain Richard Owens served with Frémont), a graben the geologists tell us, is a hundred-mile-long, five-mile-wide trench that has its own sense of desolation. This is America's most extraordinary juncture of mountain and desert, a place where you may swelter in hundred-degree heat

205

while looking out at an icy glacier ten miles away, or enjoy a
winter golf match while blizzards rage on nearby peaks. "Deepest
Valley," it has been called, and for very good reason. With nary a
foothill to give presage, the Sierra soars 10,000 feet straight up,
forming the most dramatic scarp on this planet. The Swiss boast
of their four-thousanders, mountains over 4,000 meters (13,120
feet) high. Here, nearly three dozen peaks achieve that distinction. From the valley the great Sierra block looks dark and
forboding, as inviting as a gray prison wall. But there are gate-
ways: steep and narrow canyons, carved by streams too short to
qualify as rivers yet too boisterous to be ignored. Over the years,
roads have been punched into five of these canyons, and upon
entering each, you unexpectedly find yourself amid loveliness.
Owens Valley's most illustrious author, Mary Austin, said of this
domain:

> Well up from the valley, at the confluence of cañons, are delect-
> able summer meadows. Fireweed flames about them against the
> gray boulders; streams are open, go smoothly about the glacier
> slips and make deep bluish pools for trout. Pines raise statelier
> shafts and give themselves room to grow, gentians, shinleaf, and
> little grass of Parnassus in their golden checkered shadows; the
> meadow is white with violets and all outdoors keeps the clock.

Less spectacular, but just as fascinating, is the White Mountain
range on the east, which most people are surprised to learn soars
to equally lofty heights. Here, an inhospitable moonscape nur-
tures the bristlecone pine, a kind of arboreal Rip Van Winkle—
the oldest living thing on this earth. Between these ranges runs
(or ran, actually) a clear mountain river, its banks lined with
cottonwoods. With an elevation approaching 4,000 feet, Owens
Valley boasts a fine climate (rainfall at Bishop is less than six
inches a year, and at Lone Pine, considerably less) and has something Los Angelenos covet even more: deliciously clean air.

The Inyo National Forest map shows land ownership for the
Owens Valley by depicting private lands (including Indian reservations) in white, BLM (Bureau of Land Management) lands
in tan, Forest Service lands in green, and those owned by a city in
yellow. The city is Los Angeles. There is almost no white. The tan
comprises the sloping sides of the valley, great alluvial fans com-

posed of debris washed down from side canyons. It's a desolate world of boulders and sand, sage and jackrabbits. The green, of course, is the high country on both sides of the bottomland. Though not exactly timbered, it is the country that is our primary interest. Running down the center of the map is a yellow strip showing land sixty-five miles long and five miles wide, a ribbon of fertile but unwatered soil bordering the trickle of the Owens River. What happens on that land, whether it is farmed or left fallow, settled or squandered, is the exclusive province of the City of Los Angeles (see We Are Going to Turn Inyo County Dry, below). It is land that, because of that ownership, has little relationship with the Sierra, or its surroundings. Author William L. Kahrl in his insightful book, *Water and Power*, observed:

> The wholesale land and water acquisitions had created an anomalous situation whereby one public entity, the city of Los Angeles had become the virtual owner of another public entity, the county of Inyo. [It is] essentially a colonial relationship.

Today, with almost no private land to govern, the supervisors of Inyo County must often suffer attacks of acute impotency.

We Are Going to Turn Inyo County Dry

In 1859, Captain J. W. Davidson was sent to the Owens Valley to check up on some recalcitrant Piutes. What he found was a sleepy tribe living along a meandering stream fifty feet wide and from fifteen to twenty feet deep. In his report Davidson was moved to observe:

> The mountains are filled with timber, the valleys with water and meadows of luxuriant grass. Some of these meadows contain, at a moderate estimate, ten thousand acres, every foot of which can be irrigated.

His words were sagacious. But it was cattlemen who originally settled the Owens Valley, led by one Samuel Bishop, who arrived in 1861. Soon, 200,000 head were grazing along the banks of the river. The potential for farming became apparent, however, and by the turn of the century, orchards of apples, pears, peaches, and nuts began to appear. Imitating the Piutes who had

lived here for a thousand years, crude ditches were constructed to irrigate the land. And that's when the trouble started.

Employees of the newly created Reclamation Service
looked the valley over and found it perfect for the in-
vestment of federal money to build an extensive irrigation system. Unfortunately, they sent a fox to guard the
hen house. Joseph B. Lippincott, though on the federal
payroll, was in cahoots with another man who had
covetous eyes on the Owens River, William Mulholland,
director of the Los Angeles Department of Water and
Power. Lippincott's duplicity was extraordinary. Having
withheld much of the public land from homesteading,
he then assisted his friend Fred Eaton (Mulholland's
former boss) in buying up the remaining acreage (much
of it for $1.25 an acre) so that it could be withdrawn
from production, thereby freeing the water for other
uses. All the while, he was passing on confidential
Reclamation Service data to the city of Los Angeles.
Using that data, Mulholland was able to push through a
bond initiative in 1905 that set the stage for Los Angeles'
grab of Inyo's water. Eleven thousand people, five percent of those then living in Los Angeles, voted the
money that was to catapult their drowsy pueblo into
becoming the second largest city in the nation.

When L.A.'s intentions were revealed, some Owens
Valley residents were incensed. Mary Austin wrote
movingly about what she considered an outrage, a
water grab that future writers would refer to as "the
rape of Owens Valley." But Mulholland sensed a division
among the community, and he skillfully moved to ex-
ploit it. Riding a horse, he reasoned, was more
glamorous than tending a ditch; cattle ranchers looked
down on shovel-carrying dirt farmers. Only half of the
Owens' water was then being used for irrigation (much
of it wastefully), and Mulholland assured the locals that
he only wanted another twenty-five percent. Pop-
pycock, of course. In 1906 Theodore Roosevelt, acting
on the advice of Gifford Pinchot, decided who got what,
writing: "It is a hundred or thousandfold more important to state that this [water] is more valuable to the
people as a whole if used by the city than if used by the
people of the Owens Valley."

Mulholland built a 223-mile aqueduct to carry the Owens' water south. In order to justify the project, he had to build a bigger pipe than the city needed and that set off a fascinating side drama. He schemed to deliver the surplus water to land purchased by his cronies, a syndicate called the San Fernando Mission and Land Company, whose shareholders were the moguls of southern California: Henry Huntington, I. W. Hellman, Harrison Gray Otis, Harry Chandler (Otis's son-in-law), and Edgar Rice Burroughs (who named the town he founded Tarzana). Later, to get voter approval of even more money, Mulholland feigned a water shortage, a ruse that became the subject of the movie *Chinatown*. But the city grew faster than anyone expected. As late as 1928 the department was still mouthing the fiction that they "sought only to use the surplus waters of Owens River after the needs of the ranchers had been fulfilled," but in fact they were buying more and more land, gaining the rights to more and more water. By 1926 they owned ninety percent of the valley, prompting the *Sacramento Union* to fume:

The city reverted to ruthlessness, savage disregard for moral and economic equations, to chicanery and faith breaking. The municipality became a destroyer, deliberately, unconscionably, boastfully.

Local merchants, suffering as land was taken out of production, demanded reparations, but the city refused. Frustrated beyond belief, the farmers seized the Alabama gates (which control the flow into the aqueduct) and sent the water back down the river. The caper made headlines—Tom Mix, who was filming a movie nearby, sent over a brass band—but public sympathy was not enough. Two local bankers, Wilfred and Mark Watterson, organized a resistance that turned into out-and-out war. Night riders blew holes in the side of the canal. When farmers dynamited the siphon at No-Name Canyon, Mulholland retaliated by sending a trainload of guards bearing tommy guns. Other properties were attacked, and the governor threatened to send in the National Guard. But the gesture was the farmers' swan song. When the Watterson brothers' bank failed, Owens

Valley's economy collapsed; all opposition ceased. The rout was complete. For a while it didn't seem to matter, as a long-time resident commented:

The soil is so good and water so plentiful that the grass kept coming back each spring as if the farms were still there. But it got drier and drier, until the sagebrush took over.

Twenty years earlier a land-speculator had queried his friend William Mulholland about the prospects for Owens Valley. "Do not go into Inyo County," he replied, "We are going to turn that country dry." And he did.

The aorta of the Owens Valley is no longer the river but U.S. Highway 395, which works its way up the Western interior from the Mexican border to Canada. Even during the construction of the aqueduct in the early 1900s, the road was almost impassable. Caterpillar tractors broke down; mules proved more reliable. In 1910 a state bond issue was passed creating "El Camino Sierra," but the Sherwin Grade segment wasn't completed until 1916, and before the Deadman Summit section was paved, cars sank to their axles in the soft, floury pumice. But by 1931, drivers could go all the way on "the hard road." Today locals call it the "diamond necklace," because of the continuous string of head-lights, cars going to and from the Mammoth area. The first town you come to of any significance is Lone Pine.

LONE PINE • Population 1,684; elevation 3,710 feet

With the abandonment of farming in the Owens Valley, Lone Pine nearly lost its reason for existence, but providentially, the appeal of the High Sierra gave birth to a modest renaissance. Today it is a tourist town, the base camp for an assault on **Mount Whitney.** The three-block-long shopping street boasts a traffic light, one of the few between Los Angeles and Carson City. Travelers curious about which is America's loftiest peak (outside Alaska) should look due west here. The highest summit on the horizon is puny little Lone Pine Peak (elevation 12,944 feet), which seems to dominate the sky simply because it is closer.

Leading to the right, a sawtooth ridge and two rocky spires pace toward a smallish, almost symmetrical pyramid soaring 14,495 feet into the sky. From here Whitney doesn't look impressive; Mount Williamson, six miles north and only a hundred feet less lofty, seems far more spectacular, rising up from the valley in one single parapet 10,000 feet high. By all rights that gutsy mountaineer Clarence King, first director of the U.S. Geological Survey, deserved to be the one to first set foot on Whitney's summit, because he was the first to recognize its supremacy, gave it its name, and for nine years had made it his goal. He thought he had, writing in his characteristically enthusiastic way:

> I crept on hands and knees up over steep and treacherous ice crests, where a slide would have swept me over a brink of the southern precipice. Above us but thirty feet rose a crest, beyond which we saw nothing. I dared not think it the summit till we stood there, and Mount Whitney was under our feet.

Alas, when he wrote those words he was standing on the wrong mountain (Mount Langley, 14,042 feet). Two summers later, when he learned his mistake, he hurried back from the East and climbed the "new" Mount Whitney, only to discover that three men from Lone Pine, out on a fishing excursion, had been there thirty-two days before. The date was August 18, 1873. Climbing proved to be little more than a stroll, a long, tough stroll to be sure, but certainly nothing that required the daring-do of an intrepid mountaineer like King.

Inyo is unique among western National Forests in that here the slogan "Land of Many Uses" refers almost exclusively to recreation. Timber harvesting, mining, and grazing are virtually nonexistent. "We divide the forest in two," Ranger Carole Gevard told me, "the 'frontcountry,' where all the RVs are, and the 'backcountry,' where the bears are when they are not raiding the garbage cans in 'frontcountry.'" The frontcountry alone must keep them busy; employees look after seventy-five campgrounds with 1,700 drive-in campsites, most located near lakes or along creeks stocked almost weekly by the Fish and Game Department. The backcountry is wilderness, and that creates problems too. Today, although the saloons in Lone Pine are lively, the real action is at 6:00 A.M. at the **Mount Whitney Ranger Station,** because that is where the wilderness permits are handed out. During the summer, more people want to camp in the backcountry than the Forest Service thinks the land can support, so those who haven't secured their permits by mail (about half the quota) gather on the morning of departure to collect what pickings they can. (All Mount Whitney trail permits are by advance reservation only—a lottery determines who gets them.) A ranger told me that she has, at times, had to cope with fist fights among applicants. Travelers seeking general information should stop at the **Interagency Visitor Center,** located a couple of miles south of town.

Cottonwood and Lone Pine Creeks High Sierra Access

The boldly rugged, low-lying **Alabama Hills** separate Lone Pine from the high country. (The *Alabama* was a Confederate raider, subsequently sunk by the Union Army's *Kearsarge*.) House-sized scaly brown rocks, looking like gigantic baked potatoes, frame a scene that early Hollywood directors considered the quintessential "Old West" landscape. Dozens of oaters were shot along Movie Flat Road, an unpaved but perfectly satisfactory side excursion.

Most mountaineers head to Whitney Portal, and we will too in a bit. But first take the new paved road that heads south, paralleling the mountains for half a dozen miles before climbing steeply to **Horseshoe Meadows.** Of all the east-side Sierra access roads, this is the most precipitous. Switching back and forth six times, the road clings to the scarp, climbing from 5,000 to 9,000 feet in less than eight highway miles. In places, you instinctively steer to the wrong side of the road, simply to put some distance between your car and that awful precipice on your right. Near the top, a viewpoint looks out over the valley—as the crow flies, only a couple of miles away. It strains your imagination, but before the water diversions, two steamboats, the *Bessie Brady* and the *Molly Stevens,* chugged across the white alkali flat that was then Owens Lake. Now, what little water bubbles out of Dirty Sock Spring soon evaporates in the hot desert air. Driving on, you quite unexpectedly enter a different world, one unique to this tortured country. Ruggedness abruptly gives way to gentleness, bleak rocks are replaced by splendid green meadows rimmed by luxuriant pine forests. Horseshoe Meadows (elevation 10,000 feet), it happens, marks the southern boundary of the scabrous High Sierra, the place where jagged peaks and rock-bound glacial tarns are replaced by rounded mountaintops with trees rising to their summits and small creeks are bountiful with trout.

Three trail systems radiate out from the end of the road. The most popular, because it leads to the really high country, heads north to the **Cottonwood Lakes Basin** and on to **New Army Pass** (elevation 12,385 feet). (The trail was rerouted because Army Pass, lying on a north-facing slope, was often snowbound through August.) From there, it is a dozen-mile hike to lovely **Crabtree Meadow** (10,400 feet), a favorite base camp for a western assault on Mount Whitney. **Cottonwood Pass** (11,200 feet) leads to the **Big Whitney Meadow** area and the upper **Kern River,** while **Trail Pass** (10,800 feet) takes you into the **Golden Trout Wilderness** and the south part of the **Kern Plateau** (Chapter 11). These two passes are connected by the **Pacific Crest Trail,** making possible a pleasant ten-mile day hike.

Whitney Portal (elevation 8,300 feet) is a nice place to go, just to get out of the valley heat. A small trout pond is heavily stocked, picnic tables and a grocery are nearby. The challenge of bagging a trophy peak, however, brings most people. Fifty permits a day are issued. Horses and pack stock are banned. Though the summit is less than eleven trail miles away, it is 6,000 feet higher and only a well-conditioned hiker or a masochist should attempt to go up and back in one day. Most spend two or three in the effort, staying at Lone Pine Lake (9,900 feet) Outpost Camp (10,300), Trail Camp (12,000), or at the summit itself, where everyone gets up early to watch the sun come up. A stone building graces the summit, built by the Smithsonian Institution for climatological experiments. Nearby is the country's highest outhouse—actually, not a house, just out. The trail is steep; one section has a hundred switchbacks. It crosses into the Kern watershed at **Trail Crest Pass** (13,777 feet), the Sierra's highest for a maintained trail. A spur leads up a gentle slope to the summit. People of all ages have made the climb, including my friend Bill Rowland's aunt, who did it in 1899 at the age of six, and Professor Whitney's grandniece, who, when in her seventies, stood proudly on the top. The dauntless mountain man Norman

Clyde climbed it in 1914 and by his account repeated the feat fifty times, including the first ascent of the treacherous east wall. In spite of Whitney's popularity, my peakbagger friends insist that other mountains in the area (Muir and Tyndall, for example) are more fun: there are fewer people and the views are better.

Recreational Facilities

- ✔ **Best Western Frontier Motel** 56 units. 1008 South Main, Lone Pine, CA 93545. (619) 876-5571.

- ✔ **Dow Villa Motel** 39 units. 310 South Main, Lone Pine, CA 93545. (619) 876-5521.

- △ **Forest Service Campgrounds** Horseshoe Meadows, 2 campgrounds, 25 sites; Lone Pine (6,000 feet), 43 sites; Whitney Portal (8,000 feet), 44 sites.

- △ **Inyo County Campground** Diaz Lake Recreation Area, 200 RV sites.

- • **Margie's Merry Go-Round** Restaurant. (619) 876-4115.

- § **Mount Whitney Ranger District** Information and wilderness permits. P.O. Box 8, Lone Pine, CA 93545. (619) 876-5542.

- § **Arête Climbing Centre** Mountaineering school. P.O. Box 751, Lone Pine, CA 93545. (619) 876-5446.

- § **Mount Whitney Golf Course** 18 holes. (619) 786-2345.

- Ω **Cottonwood Pack Station** State Route 1, Box 81-A, Independence, CA 93526. (619) 878-2015.

- Ω **Mount Whitney Pack Trains** P.O. Box 1514, Bishop, CA 93514.

INDEPENDENCE

As you drive north on Highway 395, the loneliness of the desert is punctuated by two tiny stone buildings supporting roofs designed to look like pagodas. Once they were guard houses, but now the windows are gone, and rusty hinges are all that remain of long-disappeared doors. Tumbleweeds scud across remnants of chain-link fences. This is **Manzanar** (Spanish for apple orchard), a place most people would like to forget (see below).

Executive Order 9066

President Franklin Roosevelt signed the order: 100,000 men, women, and children of Japanese descent were to be removed from their homes along the Pacific Coast. More than 10,000 were trucked off to Manzanar. It was an act of panic. As authors Donald Pike and R. R. Olmsted put it:

Americans had spent a century learning to hate and fear the Japanese, and after the catastrophe of Pearl Harbor they lashed out—half in habit, and half in frustration—at the only available enemy.

Almost without exception, the internees were loyal; most were citizens, and many had sons serving in the American military. The army chose the site of a stillborn water colony, begun here in the 1920s. It was a bleak place, and dust was ubiquitous except when an occasional rain turned the streets to mud. Having suffered a wrenching dislocation of their personal lives, the internees were forced to live in tarpaper shacks incapable of deflecting winter gales. Nevertheless, they managed to keep their social and religious traditions alive. To provide something for them to do, irrigation water was piped in. Before long, they had turned the land into a prosperous truck farm—a disquieting reminder of what might have been in Owens Valley. In 1944, the Supreme Court ruled the order unconstitutional and Manzanar closed, but even upon returning to their homes, many still faced blatant discrimination. Merchants in my town, Auburn, posted signs in store windows reading "We Do Not Solicit Japanese Trade," or even worse, "We don't want any Japs back here, EVER."

While visiting here, I was joined by a prosperous-looking American Indian. "I stop every time I come up from L.A.," he said. "What they did to us, they did to them, so I say a little prayer for one of my Japanese buddies who was sent here. You know, they gave him only a few days to sell his possessions. He lost almost

everything." **Both Ansel Adams and Dorthea Lange came to Manzanar, and their photographs, available in book form, provide poignant reminders of the indignities the internees suffered. The museum in Independence devotes a portion of its space to this sad chapter in American history.**

Independence (Population 1,000; elevation 3,925 feet) looks as if it might dry up and blow away if it were not the county seat. But there is a special reason to pause here. The **Eastern California Museum** is one of the nicest we visit on this sojourn. Housed in a dreadful modern building, it contains the usual assortment of items no one wanted either to keep or to throw away, augmented by a wonderful collection of Piute and Shoshone art and basketry. Relations with the Indians weren't always cordial, as William Brewer pointed out:

Our camp was the scene of a fearful tragedy a year ago. The Indians attacked a party of one man, a nigger, two women, and a child. The nigger was on horseback and fought well, killing several. In attempting to cross the river the team horses were drowned. He gave his horse to the women—both of whom got on it, and they and the white man escaped to Camp Independence. The Indians caught the negro and afterward said that he was tortured for three days.

Outside, a "pioneer village" has been created out of old buildings removed to this site. Nearby is the house Mary Austin lived in when she moved here in 1896. A relic from the past is the Winnedumah Hotel, a once stately hostelry that has seen better days. The place still hosts tourists, though it is hard to see how— no brochure, no advertising, not even a business card at the front desk. The architecturally handsome, Tudor-style **Mount Whitney Fish Hatchery,** the state's second oldest, is a pleasant place to stop for a picnic.

Independence Creek High Sierra Access

John Muir remarked:

Between the Sonora Pass and the southern extremity of the High Sierra, a distance of nearly 160 miles, there are only five passes through which trails conduct from one side of the range to the other. These are barely practicable for animals; a cañon through which one may, the exercise of unlimited patience, make out to lead a mule, or a sure-footed mustang; animals that can slide or jump as well of walk.

Today's trails are well graded; pack stock need not possess acrobatic skills to negotiate the way to **Kearsarge Pass** (elevation 11,823 feet). One of the most frequented in the High Sierra, it provides the easiest (a relative term) access to the wildly picturesque **Rae Lakes** and **Sixty Lakes Basin** areas. The route makes a nice trans-Sierra crossing; as the crow flies, the roadhead at **Kings Canyon** (Chapter 10) is only a dozen miles away. The trail begins at **Onion Valley** (9,200 feet), reached by another of those zigzaggy but paved roads that scale the Sierra's eastern face. Much of the nearby **Inconsolable Range** is the home of the bighorn sheep; we of the humanoid species are unwelcome. Across the valley, a herd of rare tule elk graze along the Owens River.

Recreational Facilities

✔✔ **Winnedumah Hotel** 20 rooms. P.O. Box 24, Independence, CA 93526. (619) 878-2040.

Δ **Forest Service Campgrounds** Gray's Meadow and Oak Creek (6,000 feet), 75 sites; Onion Valley, 29 sites.

Ω **Rainbow Pack Outfit** P.O. Box 1791, Bishop, CA 93514. (619) 873-8877.

BIG PINE • Population 1,510; elevation 4,000 feet

Big Pine advertises itself as the gateway to the Ancient Bristlecone Pine Forest, but that is not all. The southernmost glaciers in the United States feed Big Pine Creek, and the area boasts the finest mountaineering challenges in the east-side Sierra. We'll explore the bristlecones first.

White Mountains/Ancient Bristlecone Pine Forest

Plan on at least four hours to visit the White Mountains—all day is better, especially if you begin before daybreak, because

halfway up the hill at a place called **Sierra View** you are rewarded with a spectacle. The rising sun, coming up over the
Whites, slowly brushes a descending pink, then golden swath
across the Sierra scarp. (Caution: start with a reasonably full tank
of gas and lots of drinking water.) Begin by taking the old Deep
Springs toll road over Westgard Pass. You start at an altitude of
4,000 feet, schadscale scrub country with soil leached of alkali,
barite, and lime. At 6,500 feet you enter a piñon pine and juniper
woodland where sagebrush flourishes. At 9,000 feet, though the
countryside seems no less dry, no less harsh, the world of the
mountain mahogany and the bristlecone pine unaccountably
begins.

Astonishingly, it turns out that the things that live the longest
on this earth do so because of adversity, not in spite of it. For
years it was believed that the giant sequoias were the oldest living
things; they certainly were big enough to claim the honor. But
Superintendent Al Noren of the Inyo National Forest suspected
otherwise. He had roamed the Whites and was intrigued by the
scraggly trees that grew here. Enlisting the aid of Dr. Edmund
Schulman, a noted dendrochronologist (tree-ring specialist) at
the University of Arizona, the two set out in the 1950s to measure
their age. Studying core samples, Schulman was astounded to
learn that these living trees predated the redwoods by 1,500
years—the oldest found to date started life 4,700 years ago, during the time of the Babylonians. Dead but still strong specimens
lying about on the ground are even older. By matching rings
between living and dead trees, scientists realized that they were
dealing in terms of geology rather than dendrology, a continuous
growth record extending back perhaps 10,000 years.

Bristlecone pine is the popular name for a tree that grows
throughout the arid West. This subspecies is called, appropriately
enough, *Pinus longaeva*. Numerous reasons have been put forth to
explain their longevity. They don't need particularly good soil
whereas potential competitors do, so they have the area pretty
much to themselves. The country is dry, and that's a good thing,
because too much water makes trees grow too fast, tall with less
dense wood—so they die at an earlier age. Spacing between trees
is wide, roots can spread out to seek what moisture is available,
forest fires can't spread. Their leaves are particularly adapted to
the dry climate, dead wood doesn't rot, and a high resin content

keeps the bugs away. Since the growing season is only four to six weeks long, they mature slowly and carefully, often confining a year's new production to one side of the tree. Annual rings are no wider than a sheet of paper is thick. Man is the biggest threat, contributing to soil erosion and sometimes even desecrating the trees by carving initials in their trunks. For this reason the identity of the oldest tree has not been made known, in the hopes that it will be left alone.

The paved road ends at the **Schulman Grove,** where the Forest Service has established a small visitors' center. Two trails radiate out; the shorter has the better view and the more battered trees. John Muir knew their beauty but misjudged their age:

> While on the roughest ledges of crumbling limestone are lowly old giants, five or six feet in diameter that have braved the storms of more than a thousand years. But whether old or young, sheltered or exposed to the wildest gales, this tree is ever found to be irrepressibly and extravagantly picturesque, offering a richer and more varied series of forms to the artist than any other species I have yet seen.

The longer trail (five miles round trip—two to three hours) leads to the **Methuselah Grove,** where you can speculate on which of the dozen or so candidates is the oldest and wisest, the Nestor of the forest.

The wildly haunting **Patriarch Grove** is a dozen miles farther up the ridge at an elevation of over 11,000 feet (a driving altitude record on this sojourn). Is the long, bumpy drive (an hour each way) worth the effort? Some people think it a magical place— naked peaks all around, tortured and dwarfed ancients puncturing an astonishingly lucid sky, tiny wildflowers, no more than three-eighths of an inch high, garnishing a stubborn soil. Others call it a moonscape—the dreariest place on earth. They're wrong.

The public road ends at a locked gate 12,000 feet above sea level. Beyond, a high-altitude research lab, operated by the University of California, is said to be the highest inhabited place in America. A seven-mile public trail leads to the summit of **White Mountain Peak** (elevation 14,246 feet), a scant 250 feet lower than Mount Whitney.

Big Pine Creek High Sierra Access

Even in August, as you look up at the mountains west of Big Pine, you see patches of white, perennial snow fields for the most part, but some are slabs of living ice, active moving glaciers. That explains why so many backpackers you see on the trails are carrying crampons and ice axes. This is the **Palisades,** a five-mile-long, 14,000-foot-high clutch of serrated pinnacles, jagged ridges, and icy-tarns that attract almost as many mountaineers into its rocky realm as do Yosemite Valley and Tuolumne Meadows. A mountaineering school offers classes in both rock and ice climbing. Students in the latter graduate when they have mastered the "V notch," a particularly devilish, almost vertical wall of ice. Climbers wear rigid plastic boots (as big and as uncomfortable as ski boots) and use two ice axes, one of the standard variety, the other with a reverse curved blade. "It doesn't come out so easily," a fellow on the trail told me, "A comforting thought when the ice slabs downward a couple of hundred feet and you're without belay."

The wide, paved road now ends at Glacier Lodge (elevation 7,800 feet) because the last two miles, which climbed another 500 feet, succumbed to a flood. A lodge of one sort or another has been here for years, but avalanches and fires have taken their toll. The present building is big but uninspiring. Both the north and south fork canyons of Big Pine Creek begin beneath impossibly steep ridges, so no trails lead over the Sierra Crest. Still, it is a popular area for both day and overnight hiking. The South Fork trail, ending five miles from the lodge at **Brainard Lake** (10,300 feet), makes a nice but strenuous day hike. The more popular trail goes up the North Fork, passing a lovely but boarded-up rock lodge built by movie actor Lon Chaney. It would make a fine *berghutte,* a base camp for climbers, but the current thinking of the powers-that-be is that such things are not appropriate in the wilderness. Too bad!

A string of seven lakes (imaginatively named First through Seventh) nestle in the rock-bound upper canyon. I walked as far as **Third Lake** (10,300 feet) and was rewarded with a fine view of the spectacular **Temple Crag.** The lakes here are green, not blue, because the inflow is laden with what scientists call "glacial flour." Unfortunately, the topography of the upper canyon is such that you can't see the Sierra's biggest and most challenging glacier until you're almost directly below it, a trek that requires more than a day to accomplish. Most climbers stay at **Sam Mack Meadow** (11,000 feet).

Recreational Facilities

✔ **Big Pine Motel** 14 units. P.O. Box 54, Big Pine, CA 93513. (619) 938-2282.

ΔΔ **Glacier Lodge** Restaurant, grocery, cottages, and 9 hotel rooms. P.O. Box 327, Big Pine, CA 93513. (619) 872-0295.

Δ **Forest Service Campgrounds** Big Pine Creek; 3 campgrounds, 85 sites; White Mountains, 1 campground (no water), 26 sites.

Δ **Inyo County Campgrounds** Four nearby campgrounds have about 200 RV sites.

Ω **Glacier Pack Train** P.O. Box 321, Big Pine, CA 93513. (619) 938-2538.

§ **Palisade School of Mountaineering** 174 Short Street, Bishop, CA 93514. (619) 873-5037.

BISHOP • Population 3,333; elevation 4,137 feet

Bishop, the commercial center for the entire eastern Sierra, is the quintessential cowtown, a place where ranching has traditionally been more important than tourism. Its most famous product: sheepherder bread, baked at Schat's Dutch Bakery. "Mule Days," held on the Memorial Day weekend, celebrates the opening of the pack season. Several days later, outfitters schedule "horse drives"; dudes can sign up to accompany the band as it is being driven from Bishop's winter pastures to the high country. You camp out and eat "chuckwagon grub" on the three- or four-day trek. Trading on the escapades of Clark Gable and Marilyn Monroe, another outfitter offers a four-day ride to observe wild mustangs in the mountains east of town. More committed horse folk can go to horseshoeing school or attend a professional packing school to learn the art of tying hitches, picketing, and how to wrangle. Curious about terminology, I asked a fellow what the difference was between a cowboy, a wrangler, and a packer. "Cowboys herd cows," he replied with almost a sneer, "and cows are stupid. Wranglers take care of horses and that's better, but being a packer is the real job, because then you have to work with mules, and mules, well mules are just more choosy." Many skills are required, as Clarence King observed:

> Besides being a faultless mule-packer, he was a rapid and success-
> ful financier, having twice enriched us by what he called "dealing
> bottom stock" in his little evening games with the honest miners.

Labor Day brings the rodeo, for which, according to the Chamber of Commerce, "over 300 cowboys and cowgirls travel to Bishop to wrestle, ride, rope and tie some of the most troublesome creatures ever to travel on four hooves." Two haberdasheries cater to a Western clientele; one features Levis, the other Wranglers. Pendleton shirts are the preferred dress-up garb. But at 6:00 A.M., the largest table at Jack's Waffle Shop is crowded with ranch hands whose mud-spattered boots, sweat-stained cowboy hats, and tattered, dust-laden, sun-faded denim jackets suggest a life on the range that is anything but glamorous.

But things are changing. Bishop now boasts two dozen motels with a total of 750 rooms, most of which are used by people driving up and down Highway 395 (it's about halfway between L.A. and the Reno/Tahoe area). The Firehouse Grill is furnished with press-back chairs and linen-covered tables sporting frosted-glass lamps—hardly a cattlemen's place. "Where do you get your clientele?," I asked my waitress as she skillfully poured a bottle of pinot noir. "The motels send people here," she replied, "Almost everyone that eats here is a transient." Not all Bishop's citizenry, I learned, are pleased with the changes. "I hate all those fast-food restaurants that have sprung up along Main Street," a long-time resident snorted. Nevertheless, the seventy-five-year-old, L.A.-style bungalows in the residential areas give the place a down-home feeling.

Four Indian reservations now dot the Owens Valley. This one, the largest, resulted from land swaps with the City of Los Angeles. Apparently it was a good deal for both sides; the Indians, who had been scattered all over the place, received superior lands and a guaranteed water supply, while the city got federal, and therefore tax-free, land in exchange. With the help of Bureau of Indian Affairs (BIA) money, the natives built the **Paiute Shoshone** (unlike in Idaho, the "e" is pronounced) **Indian Cultural Center,** which has rather slick displays showing the life and lore of two of the tribes that live here. A more interesting place, however, is the **Laws Railroad Museum and Historical Site.** Slim Princess, everybody called locomotive number 9, because she was built to steam on the three-foot tracks of the Carson and Colorado Railroad. In 1883 Darius Ogden Mills built the line to provide a way of getting Owens Valley farm products to the bonanza mines at Virginia City. Passengers complained that the train was usually late because the crew insisted on stopping along the way for a swim in Walker Lake. In later years a connection was made to the wide-gauge Southern Pacific coming up from Mojave. When the last train pulled out of the station in 1960, Laws started ghosting. The depot, however, was restored, numerous other buildings were moved here, and the place now has a real "Old West" flavor. Docents, dressed in period garb, do a nice job setting the character of that era. A fine library is housed in an old church. Bishop also has a nice park, located next to the Chamber of Commerce, a great place for a picnic. Several spots north of town are of interest to vacationers. **Pleasant Valley Reservoir** is popular for fishing. A nearby stretch of the river is open all year for "wild trout" angling. **Fish Slough,** a swamp in the middle of the desert, is the protected wildlife habitat of the endangered Owens pupfish. **Indian petroglyphs** have been carved into several rock outcroppings along Fish Slough Road.

Recreational Facilities

   ✔✔ **Chalfant House** B&B in the 1896 home of P. A. Chalfant, Inyo County's famous newspaperman. 213 Academy Street, Bishop, CA 93514. (619) 872-1790.

   ✔✔ **The Matlick House** 5-unit B&B. 1313 Rowan Lane, Bishop, CA 93514. (619) 873-3133.

   ✔ **Best Western Holiday Spa Lodge** 60-unit motel. 1025 North Main, Bishop, CA 93514. (619) 873-3543.

✔ **Best Western Westerner Motel** 54-unit motel. 150 East Elm, Bishop, CA 93514. (619) 873-3564.

✔ **High Sierra Lodge** 51-unit motel. 1005 North Main, Bishop, CA 93514. (619) 873-8426.

✔ **Vagabond Inn** 80-unit motel. 1030 North Main, Bishop, CA 93514. (619) 873-4215.

△ **Inyo County Campgrounds** Pleasant Valley, 200 sites; Millpond Recreation Area, 100 sites.

● **Firehouse Grill** Restaurant and bar. (619) 873-4888.

● **Paradise Lodge** Bar and restaurant overlooking Rock Creek, 15 miles north of town. (619) 387-2370.

● **Whisky Creek Restaurant** (619) 873-7174.

● **Erick Schat's Dutch Bakery** Lunch stop since 1938. (619) 873-7156.

§ **Bishop Country Club** 18-hole golf course. (619) 873-5828.

§ **White Mountain Ranger District** Information and wilderness permits. 798 North Main, Bishop, CA 93514. (619) 873-4207.

Ω **Pine Creek Pack Trains** P.O. Box 986, Bishop, CA 93514. (619) 387-2797.

BISHOP AND PINE CREEKS
HIGH SIERRA ACCESS

Mount Tom (elevation 13,600 feet), conical in form and virtually treeless, dominates the northwest skyline. Roads around both sides provide access to the High Country. **Bishop Creek Basin** is punctured by two large lakes, reservoirs actually, which, had the timing been different, would not exist today. Snowpack is the best reservoir (and it is free), but in 1907 the Sierra's mineral, lumber, and water resources were still being exploited. Two dams were built, **South Lake** (9,750 feet) in the South Fork canyon and **Lake Sabrina** (9,170 feet) on the Middle Fork (Sabrina Hobbs was the wife of the manager of the Nevada-California

Power Company). When the reservoirs are full, they are beautiful. When they are not, they're not. But the construction roads
are wide now, paved, and with good alignment and grade, so the
area has become a popular vacation retreat for fishermen and a
great jumping-off point for backpackers. **North Lake** (9,500
feet) is the third element in this triptych, a small grassy pond
reached by a narrow, rather scary dirt road, which struck me as
being exactly like the Tioga Pass Road before it was widened.

Lake Sabrina trails are hemmed in by peaks of the Evolution
Divide, so although the country is beautiful, backpackers go in
and come out the same way. But the other two trailheads provide
one of the best loop trips in the High Sierra, and entrepreneurs
have stepped in to make it easier by providing shuttle service
between them. Most start out at North Lake and go over **Piute
Pass** (elevation 11,423 feet) on a five-mile, well-graded trail. The
views back down the canyon are spectacular. Hikers then poke
around **Humphreys Basin,** drop down Piute Canyon to the San
Joaquin River, and then work their way back up to the haunting-
ly beautiful **Evolution Valley.** The John Muir Trail, after crossing **Muir Pass** (11,960 feet), descends into the upper reaches of
the Kings River, meeting a spur that returns to South Lake via
Bishop Pass (12,000 feet). The fifty-mile trek takes a week or
more.

The road up **Pine Creek,** on the north side of Mount Tom,
sticks to the bottom of a V-shaped canyon for awhile but then
abruptly terminates in what looks to be a solid rock wall. (A dirt
road, closed to public vehicles, actually continues on to a tung-
sten mine.) This relatively low trailhead (elevation 7,100 feet) is
the starting point for excursions to **Granite Park** (11,000 feet)
and **Italy Pass** (12,400 feet). Granite Park is lovely, mostly above
timberline, but getting there is an ordeal—you're on one of those
trails where, after toiling for three hours, you can still look down
on your car parked at the trailhead. I walked it once, never again.

Recreational Facilities

△△ **Bishop Creek Lodge** Store, cafe, and 12 cabins. South
Lake Road, Bishop, CA 93514. (619) 873-4484.

△△ **Cardinal Village** Store, cafe, and 11 cabins. Route 1, Box
A-3, Bishop, CA 93514. (619) 873-4789.

ΔΔ **Parchers Resort** Store, restaurant, and 10 cabins. P.O. Box 1658, Bishop, CA 93514. (619) 873-4177.

Δ **Forest Service Campgrounds** 10 campgrounds along Bishop Creek, 225 sites.

§ **Lake Sabrina Boat Landing** Store, cafe, boat rentals. Route 1, Box 1, Bishop, CA 93514. (619) 873-7425.

Ω **Schober Pack Station** (Lake Sabrina) Route 1, Box AA-4, Bishop, CA 93514. (619) 873-4785.

Ω **Rainbow Pack Outfit** (South Lake) P.O. Box 1791, Bishop, CA 93514. (619) 873-8877.

Ω **Pine Creek Pack Trains** P.O. Box 968, Bishop, CA 93514. (619) 387-2797.

Ω **Trailhead Shuttle Service** Route 2 Box 338, Bishop, CA 93514. (619) 387-2387.

Rock Creek also drains into the Owens River near Pine Creek, but since the entrance to the recreational part of its canyon is atop Sherwin Summit, we'll visit that lovely place in the next chapter.

◄◄◄◄◄◆ 13 ◆►►►►►

MAMMOTH LAKES

Scenes of Curiosity and Wonder

> With curiosity and wonder we scanned every shelf and niche of the last descent. It seemed quite impossible we could have come down there, and now it actually was beyond human power to get back again. But what cared we? "Sufficient unto the day———" We were bound for that still distant, though gradually nearing, summit; and we had come from a cold shadowed cliff into deliciously warm sunshine, and were jolly, shouting, singing songs, and calling out the companionship of a hundred echoes.

Clarence King and his climbing partner Dick Cotter had just negotiated a particularly difficult traverse and were about to make the final assault on what they thought was the highest peak in the Sierra. It wasn't, but that hardly mattered. They were the first to challenge the highest pinnacles of the range, and their singing of songs and calling out for the companionship of echoes expresses the elation shared by all who have come and enjoyed this alpine playland.

Driving north out of Bishop on Highway 395, you soon realize that the countryside is about to change. The Owens Valley, uninspiringly flat for over a hundred miles, seems blocked by a broad, sloping ramp stretching from one side of the ten-mile-

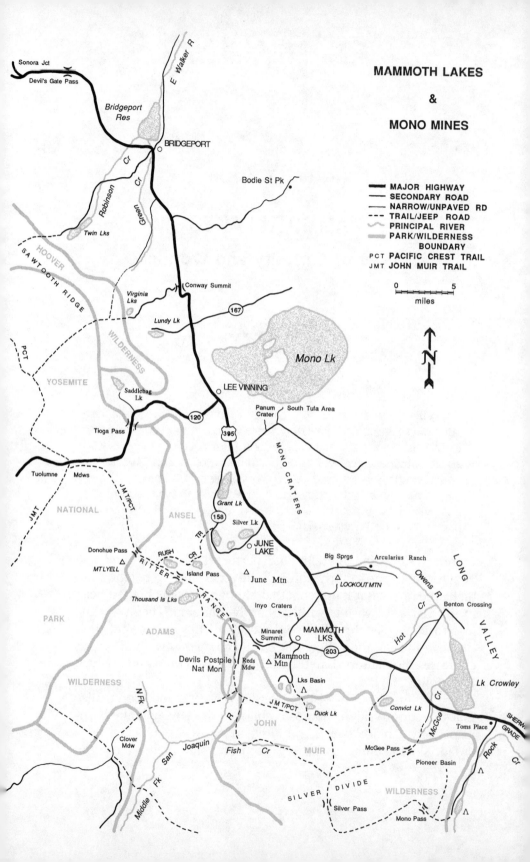

wide basin to the other. Dry and sandy, it looks like a wave of brown dirt—rather puny, until you start up its slope. For twenty minutes your eyes anxiously flit to the temperature gauge—will the groaning engine handle the toil? This is the infamous Sherwin Grade ("Vaporlock Grade," the old timers called it), the place where the desert rises up to challenge the nobility of the mountains—a 3,000-foot-high step in the drainage of the Owens River. From below it looks insignificant only because the surrounding scene is so immense; anywhere else in the country, it would be a much-talked-about landmark. Once atop the step, the land flattens out again, the river meanders through the equally barren Long Valley, but things aren't quite the same. No farms or orchards ever existed here, only summer ranges for cattle and sheep. The air seems thinner, possessing a crispness not apparent below, and it is ten degrees cooler, no matter what the time of year. In winter, sagebrush glitter with icicles, snow lies about in isolated patches along the alluvial fans. Conifer forests crowd the lower-lying hills. In places the Sierra Crest is as impressive as farther south, but elsewhere the scarp gives way to more gentle canyons, inviting both to the adventurer and the sybarite. This is "Vacationland," a thirty-mile segment of the Sierra where one can come to relax, a place with space for 1,200 tents and thousands of motel rooms. Save for Lake Tahoe, it is the largest resort area in the Sierra. To many Los Angelenos, Sherwin Grade is not an obstacle—it is quite literally the gates to Elysium.

ROCK CREEK

The Sherwin Grade is a four-lane, almost straight highway that parallels the twin penstocks of the Los Angeles Department of Power's generating plants. Adventurers should opt for the old road that works its way up the Lower Rock Creek Canyon. Seventy-five-year-old Tom's Place is the immediate destination, one of those wonderfully unpretentious roadhouses where fishermen and cowhands come to eat or whoop it up at the horseshoe-shaped bar. Highlight of the breakfast menu is "gut plugs," a stack of pancakes; for dinner, the chicken-fried steak comes with mashed potatoes, white gravy made from a powder, and canned string beans. Perfect!

The Forest Service operates an entrance station to the Upper Rock Creek Canyon. "You mean I have to ask permission to go there?" I asked the gatekeeper. "Well, not exactly," she replied, "but you know, this is the first bit of paradise you come to north of Los Angeles, and often more people want to be here than we have room for. So we keep track of campground vacancies and turn overnighters away if we're full." One of the eastern Sierra's longest and prettiest valleys, the lower campgrounds are in sage-brushy areas—cottonwoods line the trout-filled creek—but as you climb, lodgepole and hemlock begin to dominate. Man-made **Rock Creek Lake** (elevation 9,682 feet) is the focal point for the area: two small resorts and a pack station are here. Trails, ideal for day hiking, go up a south-side canyon to **Dorthy Lake** or contour around the north wall to the **Hilton Lakes Basin** (both about 10,500 feet). The road ends at **Mosquito Flat** (10,250 feet), the highest paved road in the Sierra. From there, a more or less gentle trail (before autos were banned, a short stretch was infamously known as "Crankcase Grade") works its way up into a spectacular mountain amphitheater, passing half a dozen lakes surrounded by 13,000-foot peaks. Fishermen, picnickers, and sunbathers seem to be everywhere, but the crowds in no way spoil the enchantment of this scene. In winter "snow-cats" take guests to Rock Creek Lodge, where cross-country skiers can stay or ski on to a small mountain hut at **Long Lake. Mono Pass** (elevation 12,634 feet) provides access to the upper reaches of the South Fork of the San Joaquin River. **Pioneer Basin** is a popular destination, despite its curious name (the surrounding mountains are named not for pioneers but for the four railroad barons, Stanford, Crocker, Hopkins, and Huntington). Other trails drop into **Mono Creek,** eventually joining the John Muir Trail at Lake Edison (Chapter 9). The route is popular for trans-Sierra hikers able to arrange a car shuttle.

Recreational Facilities

ΔΔ **Rock Creek Lodge** Restaurant, grocery, and 14 cabins. Route 1, Box 12, Mammoth Lakes, CA 93546. (619) 935-4452.

ΔΔ **Rock Creek Lakes Resort** Grocery and 9 cabins. P.O. Box 727, Bishop, CA 93514. (619) 935-4311.

ΔΔ **Tom's Place** Store, cafe, and 9 cabins. Rural Station, Bishop, CA 93514. (619) 935-4239.

Δ **Forest Service Campgrounds** A dozen campgrounds, 400 sites.

Ω **Rock Creek Pack Station** P.O. Box 395, Bishop, CA 93514. (619) 935-4493.

LONG VALLEY

The eastern scarp of the Sierra presents a dramatic scene as you drive north from Tom's Place. Though still barren, at times the area gets a fair amount of snow, and wildlife abounds. Although the 1878–1979 winter was bad, humor apparently prevailed, for the *Mammoth City Herald* reported rather matter-of-factly:

> As Mose Brockman was taking some snowshoe exercise on his way home to Bishop some days ago, a grizzly came down from the mountains with an apparent desire of interviewing him. The bear was without snowshoes, but made satisfactory progress between frequent rests. Never was the same space of Long Valley covered so quickly by any pedestrian. When reaching Bart McGee's his bear-ship decided to go for some cattle, which he did. Mr. Brockman says he w-w-wasn't frightened.

Tiny McGee Creek seems much too steep for a road, but a four-mile dirt track heads up to another popular trailhead (elevation, 8,100 feet). **McGee Pass** (11,900 feet) leads to the upper reaches of **Fish Creek,** the canyon appropriately presided over by Mount Isaak Walton, named for the Englishman who, in 1653, wrote *The Compleat Angler.*

Of all the glacial tarns in the Sierra, **Convict Lake** (elevation 7,580 feet) is perhaps the most dramatic, and certainly the most accessible. A two-mile paved road leads up the side of a magnificent specimen of a terminal moraine (a pile of rock debris dropped by the glacier when it began to retreat). At a narrow gap, you are suddenly confronted with a view of a mile-long, slatey-gray lake, rimmed on all sides by peaks soaring a mile straight up into the sky. It's a bleak-looking scene, hardly the kind of place a desperado would seek for refuge, but in 1871 escapees from the state prison in Carson City did just that. Twenty-nine inmates broke out, most of them fleeing south. Along the way they encountered one William Poor, a mail rider who had the misfortune to look like one of the prison guards. His killing prompted the citizens of Aurora and Benton to organize a posse, which cornered six convicts who had holed up in this box canyon. In the resulting gunfight, Robert Morrison, a Benton merchant, was killed, and though the convicts escaped, three were later captured and hanged from a tree on the outskirts of Bishop. Mt. Morrison (12,268 feet), named for the slain hero, is the highest peak in the area.

The Los Angeles Department of Water and Power giveth, and they taketh away. When the controversial aqueduct was built in the 1920s, Owens Lake dried up for lack of water (Chapter 12). Thirty years later the city began diverting water from the Mono Lake basin, primarily to harness the potential of the hydroelectric head afforded by Sherwin Grade. For storage they built **Lake Crowley** (elevation 6,781 feet), named for a popular priest who worked to ease tensions during the turbulent times of the "water wars." Fishing is the principal sport (17,000 anglers showed up on one opening day), but sailing, and water skiing are also popular. Stream-fishing enthusiasts work the Owens River near **Benton Crossing,** where early- and late-season angling is restricted to artificial lures. **Hot Creek** is one of those magical little streams, not very long, but filled with surprises. The **fish hatchery** is an interesting place to get an idea of what's going on. Downstream, the icy creek meanders through a privately owned meadow and then plunges into a two-mile-long, hundred-foot-deep gorge. This is a "wild fish" stream, meaning barbless-hook, dry-fly-fishing-only territory; the creel limit is zero. Devotees, however, crowd its banks for the chance to "match the hatch," that is, to study the insects flitting about and select a fly that might fool a streamwise trout that has already been hooked a couple of dozen times—the culminating achievement of the angler's sport. Sybarites drive a bit farther along the dirt road to the most famous **hot spring** in the Sierra, the place that gives the stream its name. In winter this might well be called the Adolph Coors Memorial Pool—skiers by the dozens come to have a beer while soaking their weary bones in the almost-too-hot water. The spring is amazing in that it bubbles out of the ground from a side lobe of the creek. Icy waters move past the right bank, hot past the left.

Bathers in the hundred-foot-diameter, four-foot-deep pool shift back and forth from one side to the other to find the perfect temperature. I lolled there one evening just as the sun was setting over Mount Morrison. The alpenglow was enthralling. Nearby bubbling pots, the color of aquamarine, even hotter fumaroles, and small geysers throb and hiss and spout and sizzle.

Recreational Facilities

ΔΔ **Convict Lake Resort** Restaurant and 12 cabins overlooking Owens Valley. Route 1, Box 204, Mammoth Lakes, CA 93546. (619) 934-3800.

ΔΔ **Hot Creek Ranch** Fly-fishing resort. Cabins. Route 1 Box 206, Mammoth Lakes, CA 93546. (619) 935-4214.

Δ **Forest Service Campgrounds** Two campgrounds, 150 sites.

Ω **Convict Lake Pack Station** Route 1, Box 204, Mammoth Lakes, CA 93546. (619) 934-3800.

Ω **McGee Creek Pack Station** Route 1, Box 162, Mammoth Lakes, CA 93546. (619) 935-4324.

MAMMOTH LAKES VILLAGE • Population 4,500; elevation 7,500 feet

Whether it was wistful thinking or a calculated attempt to wrest more "grubstake" from skeptical investors, no one knows, but in 1875 two itinerant prospectors, A. J. Wren and John Briggs, named their newly discovered quartz lode the Mammoth Mine. Whatever, it was a mammoth bust—the gold soon gave out—but the name stuck and now refers to a collection of lakes, a mountain, and the biggest town in the eastern Sierra. You come to the town first.

As late as 1965, little was here except a sort of combination post office, grocery, rooming house, and gas station that stood where the dirt road to Devil's Postpile split from the one going up to the Mammoth Lakes Basin. The site was on a gently sloping hill, almost at the exact place where the sagebrushy desert country gives way to the forests of the Sierra. Things have changed.

"Our permanent population is under 5,000," Gary Shultz at the Tourist Bureau told me, "but we have beds for 40,000. Los Angeles, a six-hour drive away, contributes ninety percent of the influx, most of whom, in winter at least, come only for the weekend." Skiing, of course, provided the impetus for the growth; first houses, then condos, mostly of handsome design, suddenly began sprouting up among the Jeffery pines and along the edges of the sage flats. When people discovered that the summer weather was absolutely delightful—dry and warm, with the scent of pine always in the air—Mammoth Lakes, the village, really took off. Mono County, which in 1960 had only 2,200 residents, suddenly found itself being wagged by the tail. Supervisors, drawn from the ranks of the ranchers and sheepmen, were hardly prepared to deal with urban growth issues. Streets were laid out on a grid and made wide, many supporting four lanes of traffic (apparently, no one thought much about where they were going to put the snow). Fast-food outlets and motels popped up strip-fashion, soon augmented by two- and three-story shopping malls, each dominated by a block-square parking lot facing the street. Though the architecture is first class, the land planning is not. With hardly a sidewalk anywhere, if you want to shop at a store in the mall across the street, you jump in your car. Mammoth Village, sadly, looks as if it had been moved here from some suburban southern California town, say, Covina. The names of many of the businesses, however, suggest a European motif: the Yodeler and Matterhorn are two restaurants; you can stay at the Jagerhof, Edelweiss, or Alpenhof Lodge, and a dozen places spell "house" kind of funny (haus). There is even a Chateau Sans Nom. Other establishments take their names from some delightful European villages, Kitzbuel, Chateux d'Oex (you're advised how to pronounce it correctly), and St. Anton. But those who have had the pleasure of staying in those charmingly compact Alpine towns can only look at this scene and grieve for what might have been. Mammoth has no gracious hotels (with the possible exception of Mammoth Inn, located up the hill at the base of the ski lift), only lobbyless motels and "lock-off condos" (a bedroom has its own bath and entrance so it can be rented separately). A "mountain" feel seems particularly lacking. One cold winter night I ate in an expensive restaurant that reflected a Polynesian theme. Waiters wore Hawaiian shirts and short pants.

The menu, I suspect, was planned in some boardroom in Los Angeles and designed to be prepared by someone quite lacking in culinary skill.

Mammoth, however, has a youthful, vibrant feel. Although there are a half-dozen videotape rental stores, and a few establishments bear names like Nails Unlimited and Suzanne Morris School of Dance and Ballet, most focus on the outdoors. Ten sporting goods stores rent skis in the winter and mountain bicycles in the summer. Joggers are everywhere. Firms offer instruction in water skiing, sailing, and wind surfing (at Crowley Lake), river tubbing, rock climbing, motorcycle touring, hot-air ballooning, and, of course, horseback riding. The gondola (cable car) to the top of Mammoth Mountain is open to sightseers and "mountain descenders" during the summer. Mountain biking is the newest rage. NORBA (National Off Road Bicycle Association) holds its championship meet here. A thousand racers compete for a $50,000 purse in events such as the hill climb, observed trials (a sort of obstacle course), dual slalom, cross country, and the sinister "kamikaze," a mad dash down from the top of the mountain. Tennis courts abound, but amazingly, the first golf course wasn't built until 1990. Nancy Meyer, a condo owner, told me, however, that most vacationers prefer the simpler summer sports—swimming, going for a walk in the woods, or merely sitting in the sun by the pool. Besides skiing (Nordic and Alpine), winter activities include dogsledding and snowmobiling but, strangely, not ice skating. Mammoth Village hosts a **Summer Festival** featuring classical, jazz, rock and roll, and folk concerts. History buffs will enjoy the **Log Cabin Museum,** housed in a 1930s building. "Does Dave McCoy (see Mammoth Mountain Ski Resort, below) contribute to the historical society?," I asked Curator Michael Brant. "Naw I don't think so," he replied, "Dave is interested in the future, not the past."

Mammoth Mountain Ski Resort

At 11,000 feet, Mammoth Mountain is rather puny for this country, considering that many of its neighbors are several thousand feet higher. But it sits out all by itself, so it looks big. Almost conical (an inactive volcano), it straddles the Sierra Crest; shoulders on the north and south droop down to 9,000 feet, creating what are the lowest passes south of Yosemite. The western side, however plunges nearly 4,000 feet into the canyon of the San Joaquin, and the east side drops nearly that far to the village of Mammoth Lakes. The low passes and the relative isolation of the mountain force winter storms to do a curious and wonderful thing here—clouds are sucked in that drop an incredible amount of snow on north- and east-facing slopes, slopes that are perfect for downhill skiing. The so-called "rain shadow," which keeps most of the east side so dry, just doesn't occur here. Nearly fifty *feet* of snow fell in the winter of 1983–1984, a number made more impressive when you consider that Bishop, less than fifty miles south, averages a half a foot a year. Skiing usually starts in early November and frequently lasts well into June.

Mammoth Mountain's logo is a cartoon of a hairy mastodon, but the name more properly refers to the immensity of the ski fields. It's the largest ski resort in the world, serving well over a million skiers a year. Twenty-five thousand once swarmed over its slopes on a single day. I have heard horror stories about forty-five-minute lift lines and horrendous traffic jams, but Pam Murphy, who works here, assured me that that is no longer true. Thirty lifts, some high-speed detachable, now lace the mountain, and runs are so broad that skiers can give each other wide berth. As with all successful ski resorts, most of the runs cater to those with intermediate skills, but there are slopes to challenge anyone. The bowls off the top are as pretty as any I have ever seen, and a west-side canyon, served by a single lift, seems almost a wilderness. Mammoth is the product of one man's dream—everything about the place reflects his way of doing business. Unlike some resort operators, Dave McCoy never tried to get into the real estate business, but instead directed his unbridled energy toward developing "his" mountain (which is leased from the Forest Service). Everyone I talked to had such praise that someday I'm sure the powers-that-be will name a mountain after him. "Dave has never taken a nickel out of this place," Dave Geirman, manager of lift operations, told me. "He's put everything back into the mountain—better and safer lifts, wind-control apparatus, better-graded slopes. Whatever I need I get. We have thirty Piston Bullies [grooming machines], our own fleet of trucks, and a fantastic ski patrol. Yet the lift prices are not unreasonable and the food is downright inexpensive." I had to agree. I was also impressed by the number of kids enrolled in the ski-racing club. The day lodge seemed to be filled with ten-year-olds, each proudly wearing his crash helmet and race number bib. McCoy's resort began with a single chairlift, located seven miles from Mammoth Village. Today, a huge day lodge and a fine hotel are a few steps away. As the place expanded, more lifts were constructed on slopes nearer town, so that nowadays more than two thirds of the patrons start their ski day elsewhere. Several lifts go all the way down to the flatlands, others to a place surrounded by condominiums that is modestly called Warming Hut II (it is five stories high and can serve 1,500 diners at one time). Buses (fee) shuttle between town and the various base lifts.

I had the pleasure of skiing Mammoth in 1948, seven years before McCoy built the first chairlift. At that time he was working as a snow surveyor for the Los Angeles Department of Water and Power and running a rope tow at nearby McGee Creek on weekends. He had agreed to host a high school ski meet, but there wasn't enough snow, so he pulled us all up to his "dream mountain" behind a surplus army weasel. The portable rope tow he had installed for the occasion broke down; we had to climb. Even then you could sense that the man had a vision. It hasn't dimmed. "Someday," patrolman Eric Diem told me, "Dave is going to have lifts running all the way to June Lake, and we will be able to handle 150,000 skiers a day." We were standing atop June Mountain at the time, and Eric showed me where the lifts might go. They looked like some of the finest slopes in North America, a series of short, steep canyons providing a variety of snow conditions. But questions remain—what effect would such a massive expansion have on deer migration, and would it ruin the habitat of the area's grouse, rabbit, marmot, eagle, prairie falcon, and pine marten populations?

Lakes Basin Area

More than a dozen lakes nestle in an amphitheater a few miles above the village. Before skiing, sportsmen considered this the region's principal attraction. Lake Mary (elevation 8,900 feet) is the largest, and some insist, the prettiest of these mountain tarns, but Twin Lakes, the lowest, was the first to be developed. **Tamarack Lodge,** a two-and-a-half-story wood-sided beauty,

was built in 1923 and has remained the focal point for the area
ever since—the only place to stay in the basin that remains open
during the winter. A huge fireplace dominates a cozy, pine-
paneled living room. The restaurant, which looks out over the
lake, has a reputation for the best food in Mammoth. A little
bridge out front spans a narrow part of the lake, providing a
quintessential Sierra view; in the early morning the still water
reflects the shapeliness of a prominent granite spire called Crystal
Crag, here framed by the sawtooth ridge of Mammoth Crest.

Mining started here in 1875 but never really amounted to
much, despite the fact that upwards of 1,500 miners once
swarmed over the countryside. The heavy winter of 1878–1979
played havoc with the land. Owens Valley historian W. A. Chalfant commented on news reports:

> The livery business has been knocked in the head since Bennett
> had to sink a double compartment shaft to locate the ridgepole of
> his stable. Twenty pairs of snowshoes, each with a man on top, left
> this morning. Some wretch or wretches stole two pairs of snow-
> shoes from Sam Argall and his little boy last night. Anybody who
> would steal snowshoes would do anything mean.

In the 1930s much of remaining activity was combined into the
Mammoth Consolidated Gold Mine, the ruins of which have
been set aside as a historical exhibit. Half a dozen buildings stand;
you can look into a mine shaft or photograph the rusty remains of
a stamp mill and air-compressing machinery. The early-morning
view of Mount Banner and Mount Ritter, seen from the upper
adit, is stunning. Nearby, a dirt road leads to the site of the Mill
City stamp mill. Nothing is left except the rusting hulk of a
fourteen-ton pelton wheel.

Lakes Basin is lightly forested and not unduly steep, so it is
popular both summer and winter. Numerous campgrounds surround several trout-filled lakes, and trails quite literally go off into
the wilderness. The most popular day hike leads up the canyon
toward **Duck Pass** (elevation 10,900 feet), skirting four lakes
along the way. Backpackers and horse riders continue on the
spectacular upper reaches of Fish Creek with its lovely, meadow-
filled **Cascade Canyon,** one of the Sierra's hidden jewels. Mammoth Basin is a cross-country skier's dream, with marked and

groomed trails circling Lake Mary, Lake George, and Horseshoe Lake. Several lake-side cafes stay open during the winter, providing hot lunches to chilly skiers.

Recreational Facilities

✔✔✔ **Mammoth Mountain Inn** Full-service hotel. P.O. Box 353, Mammoth Lakes, CA 93546. (800) 228-4947.

✔✔ **Tamarack Lodge Resort** 11-room lodge built in 1923. Restaurant, 24 cabins, boating, cross-country skiing. P.O. Box 69, Mammoth Lakes, CA 93546. (619) 934-2442.

✔ **Mammoth Lakes Resort Association** Central referral agency for about 70 motels and a few condos. P.O. Box 48, Mammoth Lakes, CA 93546. (800) 367-6572; (619) 934-2712.

✔ **Mammoth Reservation Bureau** Condo rentals. P.O. Box 8, Mammoth Lakes, CA 93546. (800) 527-6273; (619) 934-2528.

ΔΔ **Wildyrie Lodge** Cabins, boat rentals, and grocery on Lake Mamie. (619) 934-2444.

ΔΔ **Crystal Crag Lodge** Grocery, boat rentals, and 24 cabins on Lake Mamie. P.O. Box 5055, Mammoth Lakes, CA 93546. (619) 934-2436.

Δ **Forest Service Campgrounds** Three campgrounds near Mammoth Village, 225 sites; five in the basin area, 250 sites.

● **Lakefront Restaurant** At Tamarack Lodge. (619) 934-3534.

● **Roget's** Continental cuisine. (619) 934-4466.

● **Matterhorn** Swiss restaurant. (619) 934-3357.

● **O'Kelly & Dunn** Great breakfasts. (619) 934-9316.

§ **Mammoth Ski Resort** 28 lifts; 3,100 foot vertical. P.O. Box 24, Mammoth Lakes, CA 93546. (619) 934-6166.

§ **Mammoth Ranger District** Information and wilderness permits. P.O. Box 148, Mammoth Lakes, CA 93546. (619) 934-2505.

Ω **Mammoth Lakes Pack Outfit** Day rides and extended trips. P.O. Box 61, Mammoth Lakes, CA 93546. (619) 934-2434.

Ω **Greyhound Bus Lines** Service to Reno and Los Angeles. (619) 935-4975.

Ω **Alpha Air** Commuter airline service. (619) 934-2571.

DEVILS POSTPILE HIGH SIERRA ACCESS

Devils Postpile National Monument (elevation 7,600 feet), like Ireland's Giant's Causeway and Scotland's Fingal's Cave, is a rather unusual outcropping of lava that has cooled in such a way as to form hexagonal spires (called columnar-jointed basalt) several hundred feet high. The road in is paved now, and that in itself created controversy (see The Great Trans-Sierra Phantom Highway below). Bill Tweed told me that even before the improvements, the area was being overrun with automobiles, prompting the authorities to take drastic action. During the high summer season, the road beyond Minaret Summit is closed to all private vehicles except those whose drivers have a confirmed place to stay overnight. (Rangers at the entrance station keep track of campsite vacancies.) Backpackers and day hikers take shuttle buses (fee), which leave every quarter hour from the huge parking lot at the base of the Mammoth Mountain ski lifts. The plan seems to work; the resulting tranquility far outweighs the inconvenience of having to do without your car, and now one-way walks are possible because you can return by bus. Furthermore, visitors are primed with a different outlook. Rather than being just another trophy in the "famous places I have seen" collection, people ask themselves, "How can I see it best?" Taking time, they discover other delightful things as well.

The Great Trans-Sierra Phantom Highway

For years road designers cast covetous eyes on Minaret Pass. It is invitingly low (9,000 feet) and gentle

approaches, especially the one from the east, are perfect attributes for a trans-Sierra highway. It might well have happened in 1879, but the gold gave out. A movement was afoot to construct what was to be called the Fresno Flats Wagon Road, which, according to the *Mammoth City Harold,* would bring great prosperity to the region:

Madera on the Southern Pacific Railroad, being the nearest railroad point to Mammoth City, is destined at no distant day to become the entire shipping point for these places. When the Mammoth mill makes one run on pay dirt, the name of Mammoth City will be familiar to ten thousand.

Pay dirt was, as one wag put it, "As rare as finding a destitute dermatologist," so unlike Sonora, Ebbetts, and Carson passes, which owe their existence to the Mono and Washoe mines, it was not to be. Pack trains used the route for awhile, and still do, but it was never suitable for wheeled vehicles.

However, when the Forest Service, during the Nixon administration, decided to pave the road into Red's Meadow, highway planners took another look at the twenty-mile gap between Red's and the logging roads that come up from the west side and decided that the project would be extended and upgraded into a full-fledged, all-year trans-Sierra highway. Wilderness lovers were incensed. Pack outfitters, among others, appealed to Governor Ronald Reagan to have it stopped. His cowboy instincts aroused, Reagan organized a trans-Sierra trail ride, where, at an overnight campout in the wilderness, he announced the stopping of the plan. The sixty newsmen who were the governor's entourage seemed more interested in whether he had actually made the oft-quoted statement: "If you've seen one redwood tree, you've seen them all." Bob Tanner, who provided the horses and mules for the trek, told me that in spite of the theatrics, it was not really Reagan who deserved the credit, but his resource secretary, the respected conservationist Ike Livermore. Through Livermore's efforts, the route is now safely ensconced in the John Muir Wilderness—the road as phantom as ever.

Even if you are not going into the Postpile area, **Minaret Summit** is a wonderful place to drive to because the view out over the upper reaches of the San Joaquin River is grand indeed. The **John Muir** and **Ansel Adams** (formerly Minaret) wildernesses share this area. Often called the King and Queen of the Sierra, two peaks dominate the western skyline, **Banner Peak** (elevation 12,945 feet) and **Mount Ritter** (13,157 feet). Ask a long-time mountaineer which is his favorite back-country spot and likely as not the answer will be the run-together word "Banner-'n-Ritter." (Karl Ritter was Whitney's geography professor at the University of Berlin; cloud banners streaming from its summit prompted the other name.) John Muir, a man not known for his timidity, was the first to climb Ritter:

> I was suddenly brought to a dead stop, with arms outspread, clinging close to the face of the rock, unable to move hand or foot either up or down. My doom appeared fixed. I *must* fall. There would be a moment of bewilderment, and then a lifeless rumble down the one general precipice to the glacier below. When this final danger flashed upon me, I became nerve-shaken for the first time since setting foot on the mountain, and my mind seemed to fill with stifling smoke. But life blazed forth again with preternatural clearness. Then my trembling muscles became firm again, every rift and flaw in the rock was seen as through a microscope, and my limbs moved with a positiveness and precision with which I seemed to have nothing at all to do. Had I been borne aloft upon wings, my deliverance could not have been more complete. I found a way, without effort, and soon stood upon the topmost crag in the blessed light.

Except for the **Minarets**—an awesome series of basaltic *aguilles* long thought to be unclimbable—the countryside, fashioned by glaciers, is high but not unduly steep. Charles Michael was the first to challenge the needles, writing of the experience:

> With nothingness on one side and a sheer wall on the other, I had a feeling as I crossed the ledge that the wall might give me a little shove and tip me into nothingness.

The most popular segment of the John Muir Trail wends its way thirty miles from **Agnew Meadow** to Tuolumne Meadows

(Chapter 6). I walked the trail in 1951 and saw almost no one, but today, **Shadow, Garnet,** and **Thousand Island Lakes** are almost overrun with hikers, such is the beauty of the landscape. Cross-country skiers make the three- or four-day trek in winter, usually going from south to north because they can then ski out to Lee Vining and take a convenient bus back to Mammoth. Another very popular trail loops around **Lake Ediza, Iceberg Lake,** and **Lake Minaret.** The road ends at **Red's Meadow,** where a mile-and-a-half trail leads to the lovely **Rainbow Falls,** a hundred-foot cataract that breaks up the San Joaquin River into a frothing torrent. The falls are best seen at noon, when sunlight catches the droplets, forming the rainbow that gives it its name. One trail leads to lower **Fish Creek,** a canyon with vertical granite walls almost as spectacular as those in Yosemite, and another goes over the **Granite Stairway,** following the Phantom Road to **Clover Meadow** (Chapter 9).

Recreational Facilities

ΔΔ **Red's Meadow Resort** Cafe, grocery, and 6 cabins. P.O. Box 395, Mammoth Lakes, CA 93546. (619) 934-2345.

Δ **National Park Service Campground** 22 sites.

Δ **Forest Service Campgrounds** Five campgrounds, 50 sites.

Ω **Red's Meadow/Agnew Meadow Pack Stations** P.O. Box 395, Mammoth Lakes, CA 93546. (619) 934-2345.

DEADMAN SUMMIT

Geologically, the Mammoth area is still in its teens, young and active. Signs along the **Earthquake Trail** explain a bit about what's going on. In the late 1970s authorities were so worried about the high level of seismic activity here that they built a separate road to provide egress in case of disaster, calling it the **Mammoth Scenic Loop.** Nearby **Inyo Craters,** only 1,500 years old, are filled with water. Another road branches off of Highway 395 and climbs to **Lookout Mountain,** where fine views overlook the upreaches of the Owens River. Another geologic oddity, a hundred-foot-high mound of once-molten glass that gushed up out of the ground like a drinking fountain, created what is called an **obsidian dome.**

The Owens River starts life almost as big as it ever gets, gushing out of the lava and pumice with great force at **Big Springs,** near a campground located a few miles east of the highway. The road continues to the broad Long Valley, where the river winds along in peaceful convolutions, its meadows surrounded by blue-gray sage. Shortly after World War I John Arcularius, an old-timer of Greek ancestry, purchased the land, intending to go into the cattle business. He did, but quickly learned that anglers loved these cold, slowly moving waters, so he built the legendary **Arcularius Ranch.** Herbert Hoover came with his fly rod, and people of wealth have been following ever since (many land at the private airstrip). It is a catch-and-release stream now, open only to those who stay in the lovely white-boarded cabins surrounding a well-tended lawn. A clubhouse gives this isolated bit of paradise a congenial atmosphere.

We take leave of the Owens River drainage at Deadman Summit (elevation 8,036 feet), so named because a skeleton was found here, the headless [or maybe not] remains of a miner [or a sheepherder] who was murdered [or froze to death] in the awful winter of seventy-nine [or eighty-nine]—take your pick. This would be the logical place to end this chapter but for one fact—Dave McCoy purchased the June Lake Ski Resort, integrating it into the Mammoth operations. So despite what the maps show (June Lake is due east of San Francisco), we haven't yet quite left southern California.

Recreational Facilities

ΔΔ **Arcularius Ranch** Fly-fishing resort. Lodge, grocery, and 17 cabins. Route 1, Box 230, Mammoth Lakes, CA 93456. (619) 648-7807.

Δ **Forest Service Campgrounds** Four campgrounds near Deadman Summit, 125 sites.

JUNE LAKE LOOP

Signs along Highway 395 urge you to take the scenic June Lake Loop—good advice, even if you are just passing through. This sixteen-mile side road passes four lakes, each snuggled beneath soaring peaks. Although one of the oldest east-side resort areas, it has been slow to gain massive acceptance, perhaps because it is another fifteen-mile drive up the long road from Los Angeles. Yet the overall beauty is unsurpassed. **June Lake** (population 614, elevation 7,650 feet) is the only real village in the area, a small community overlooking both June and Gull Lakes. Vacation homes dot the hillsides. Focal point is the landmark June Lake Lodge, once the resort of movie stars (*Road to Utopia,* staring Bing Crosby, Bob Hope, and Dorthy Lamour, was shot here, as was *Call of the Wild,* with Clark Gable and Loretta Young). The structure, built in 1928, has a magnificent log-sided common room dominated by a massive, but ugly, stone fireplace. It is now a time-share condo called Heidelberg Inn.

If you look just at the numbers, **June Mountain Ski Area** compares favorably with Mammoth: the vertical rise is only 400 feet less and the longest run is two and a half miles. But they are totally different mountains. June, like Heavenly (Chapter 2), is an inverted mountain, with the steepest runs at the bottom. They are so steep that almost no one skis them. So for all intents and purposes, June Mountain begins at the top of the tram, 1,100 feet above the parking lot. From there, lifts (including a mile-and-three-quarters-long high-speed detachable) work their way up to two separate mountains, providing access to mostly intermediate runs. The place, well run and with a family atmosphere, is a "cruiser's" paradise. The view from the top of the tram (open in summer) is sensational—Mono Lake and Mono Craters form a deserty backdrop for an otherwise Alpine scene.

Reverse Creek, so called because it flows back toward the high mountains, drains into **Silver Lake** (elevation 7,200 feet), the prettiest of the lot. Silver Lake Resort, established in 1916, claims to be the oldest in the eastern Sierra. The **Rush Creek Tailhead** provides a short but steep access to the Banner-Ritter area of the Ansel Adams Wilderness. The trail leads to **Agnew Lake** (8,700 feet), **Gem Lake** (9,030 feet), and the much photographed **Thousand Island Lake** (9,850 feet), arguably the Sierra's prettiest. **Grant Lake,** last on the loop road, is the creation of the Los Angeles Department of Water and Power and, unless you are an avid bait fisherman, is best ignored.

Recreational Facilities

✔ **Boulder Lodge** 60 lakefront rooms and cabins, restaurant. P.O. Box 68, June Lake, CA 93529. (619) 648-7533.

✔ **Gull Lake Lodge** 16 cabins. P.O. Box 25, June Lake, CA 93529. (800) 631-9081; (619) 648-7516.

✔ **June Lake Motel** 25 motel rooms and cabins. P.O. Box 98, June Lake, CA 93529. (619) 648-7547.

✔ **Whispering Pines Motel** Who can resist staying in a motel with a name like that! 24 units. Route 3, Box 14B, June Lake, CA 93529. (619) 648-7762.

ΔΔ **Silver Lake Resort** Grocery, cafe, and 14 cabins. Boat rentals. Route 3, Box 17, June Lake, CA 93529. (619) 648-7525.

Δ **Forest Service Campgrounds** Nine campgrounds, 225 sites.

● **Carson Peak Inn** Restaurant. (619) 648-7575.

● **Mountain Rose** Bar and restaurant overlooking Silver Lake. (619) 648-7273.

§ **June Mountain Ski Area.** 7 lifts; 2,700 foot vertical. Box 146, June Lake, CA 93529. (619) 648-7733.

Ω **Frontier Pack Station** Star route 33, Box 18, June Lake, CA 93529. (619) 648-7701.

◀◀◀◀◀◆ 14 ◆▶▶▶▶▶

THE MONO MINES

Good-bye God, I'm going to Bodie

Almost no one liked the place, the arid climes beyond the Sierra. Clarence King looked eastward in 1864 and wrote:

> Reaching out to horizons faint and remote, lay plains clouded with the ashen hues of death; stark, wind-swept floors of white, and hill-ranges, rigidly formal, monotonously low, all lying under an unfeeling brilliance of light, which for all its strange, unclouded clearness, has yet a vague half-darkness, a suggestion of black and shade more truly pathetic than fading twilight.

Mark Twain referred to it as "a lifeless, treeless, hideous desert," and his friend J. Ross Browne said of Mono Lake: "Not even that wondrous sea, whose bitter waters wash the ruined sites of Sodom and Gomorrah, presents a scene of greater desolation." But it was a little girl, whose name I have been unable to determine, who said it best. Told that her parents were taking her to the Mono mines, she penned in her 1881 diary the simple lament: "Good-bye God, I'm going to Bodie." Others, like Mary Austin, however, saw the desert as an expression of energy, a timeless and colorful world of rock and lizard, sage and coyote. In *Land of Little Rain* she wrote:

Beyond the desert rise the lava flats, scoriæ strewn; sharp-cutting walls of narrow cañons; league-wide, frozen puddles of black rock, intolerable and forbidding. Beyond the lava the mouths that spewed it out, ragged-lipped, ruined craters shouldering to the cloud-line, mostly of red earth, as red as a red heifer. You get a feeling of that country when you see Little Pete feeding his sheep in the red, choked maw of an old vent,—a kind of silly pastoral gentleness that lozes over an elemental violence.

Today, most would agree with Twain and Browne—at first, anyway—but it is a strange place and, oddly, the more you get to know it, the more precious it becomes. We'll visit this land of little rain, and meet some of the characters who gave it fame. But we'll also explore a place nearby, a portion of the Hoover Wilderness lying on the Sierra's eastern scarp, a land of much rain and snow, and wildflowers and meadows too, and lakes and streams and granite plateaus and spiky peaks scraping the sky. Joseph Reddeford Walker was the first American to come this way, and we'll follow the river that bears his name, a river that, quite literally, defines the verge between mountain and desert. But first we'll visit the Mono Basin, a place many Americans are familiar with, albeit remotely, because it is one of the principal landmarks you see from the window of a jet while flying between San Francisco and the East.

MONO LAKE

Trillions of brine flies habituate the shores of Mono lake, providing food for the countless birds that nest here. The Yokut word for fly is *mono*, thus the name. Most people pronounce it improperly, which angers Marilyn Brandon, who works at the county historical society. "Mono rhymes with 'Oh-no' and it is a pretty word," she told me. "Mon'o, like mononucleosis, sounds ugly."

The dozen or so gray volcanic peaks east of Highway 395, looking a bit like a sombrero, are perhaps 9,000 years old, but eruptions have occurred within the last 600 years. The mountain building was preceded by the spewing of a fountain of light, airy pumice, which forms the bulk of the surrounding soil. Then came a series of dome-building eruptions of viscous rhyolite, which cooled and shattered, forming obsidian, the volcanic glass from which the Indians made arrow points. When you walk on obsidian, it sounds like you are walking on broken pottery, not real rock. To get a sense of this weird world, drive east a couple of miles on Highway 120 and follow the dirt road leading to **Panum Crater,** one of the youngest cinder cones in the basin.

Even more bizarre are the strange limestone columns at the **South Tufa Area,** located a few miles farther east along the shore of Mono Lake. Tufa, pronounced "toofah," is formed when springs, rich in calcium, bubble up beneath alkaline waters containing an abundance of carbonate. Here, the receding waters of the lake have exposed hundreds of slaty-white, grotesque towers of stone, ten feet or more high and looking a bit like bunches of grapes turned upside down. Some of the formations poke up out of the water; paddling among them in a canoe is said to be a great experience.

Strangely, although the Mono Craters are relatively young, Mono Lake is old, having been formed 700,000 years ago during the great ice age. Mono is different from any other lake we have seen on this trek. Having no outlet, the inflow evaporates, leaving a residue that is twice as salty as the ocean. Swimming is a delightfully buoyant experience if you can stand the alkali. But many find it as uncomfortable as did Mark Twain's dog.

> We had a valuable dog. He had raw places on him. He had more raw places on him than sound ones. He was the rawest dog I almost ever saw. He jumped overboard one day to get away from the flies. But it was bad judgement. The alkali water nipped him in all the raw places simultaneously, and he struck out for the shore with considerable interest. He yelped and barked and howled as he went—and by the time he got to the shore there was no bark to him—for he had barked the bark all out of his inside, and the alkali water had cleaned the bark all of his outside, and he probably wished he had never embarked in any such enterprise.

It is the fascinating natural events that are occurring along the shore that makes the place so unique. No fish can live in the alkali water, but brine shrimp can (they look more like worms than shrimp), and brine flies, which, despite Twain's story, are not the least bit bothersome. Together they provide food for millions of eared grebes, California gulls, and snowy plovers. The Wilson's pharalope stops here before making a 5,000-mile, nonstop journey to South America. The Yokut dried the shrimp and the flies in the sun and mixed them with acorns, berries, grass seeds, and other food stuffs, making a conglomerate called *cuchaba*, which they used as a kind of bread. Early explorers, Twain included, didn't think much of this:

> Then there is a fly [that] settles on the beach to eat the worms that wash ashore. All things have their uses and their part and proper place in Nature's economy: the ducks eat the flies—the flies eat the worms—the Indians eat all three—the wildcats eat the Indians—the white folks eat the wildcats—and thus all things are lovely.

All things *were* lovely—until 1940. That's when the City of Los Angeles started diverting the inflow south and Mono Lake became a *cause célebré* (see Water and Power, below).

Water and Power

Having successfully appropriated most of the Owens River (Chapter 13), the Los Angeles Department of Water and Power cast its eyes covetously northward for additional supplies. Mono Basin was the obvious place to look. Here, five short but reliable streams flowed into an area too barren to farm, too cold to live in. The water was, in the department's view, being wasted, disappearing into thin air through evaporation. Easy pickings. So it built Crowley Lake near Mammoth, turned tiny Grant Lake into a large reservoir, and dug a twelve-mile tunnel under the Mono Craters to take the stream water south. Mono Lake started to dry up and, to the Angelenos' surprise, some people got mad.

Los Angeles officials were unprepared for the combat. Owens River battles had been waged against farmers—the conflict centered on balancing the needs of one person against those of another. Here, the injured party was a flock of birds, specifically the California gull, which nests on Negit Island, a rookery once safe from the predations of the coyote. When diversions commenced, the level of Mono Lake, of course, started dropping, forty feet in the first three decades. Salinity doubled; a land bridge to the island formed, and the coyotes had their supper. Attempts to dynamite a channel proved only marginally beneficial. In 1978 some activists were determined not to let Mono Lake go the way of Owens Lake (which is now dry). They formed the *Mono Lake Committee* to try and halt water diversions. Joined later by the Sierra Club and Cal Trout, they waged a legal attack, lobbied both state and federal legislators, and conducted educational programs to bring their concerns before the public. Sacramento lawmakers responded, forming the Mono Lake Tufa State Reserve, and Inyo National Forest established the Mono Basin Scenic Area, sharing responsibility for preserving the lake's ecology. At this writing, further lowering of Mono's level has been stopped, but the ecologists have not won an outright victory. They have, however, succeeded in forcing the department to admit that it can't simply let the lake dry up. Ironically, Los Angeles bureaucrats have come to realize that it was easier to fight the farmers in the Owens Valley than a flock of birds in Mono Basin.

LEE VINING • Population 300; elevation 6,781 feet

As late as the 1950s, highway maps showed the name as Leevining, but cartographers, learning that the town had been named for an early prospector, LeRoy Vining, finally got it right. The view out over the lake is fine, but there is little here to interest the tourist except for the nice bookstore run by the Mono Lake Committee. Some rather ordinary motels serve Reno/Los Angeles travelers. Nearby **Lee Vining Creek** is stocked with trout. Six miles north, a paved side road leads to **Lundy Lake** (8,600 feet), a little-known but pleasant vacation spot at the base of towering peaks. Numerous mines in the area had a short-lived experience. A trail climbs up a talus slope to some lovely lakes in the Hoover Wilderness near the foot of Mount Conness, but it is seldom used because hikers can avoid a 2,000-foot climb by starting at Saddlebag Lake (Chapter 6).

Recreational Facilities

✔ **Best Western Lakeview Lodge** 44-unit motel. P.O. Box 345, Lee Vining, CA 93541. (619) 647-6543.

✔ **Gateway Motel** 12 units. P.O. Box 250, Lee Vining, CA 93541. (619) 647-6467.

✔ **Murphey's Motel** 31 units. P.O. Box 57, Lee Vining, CA 93541. (619) 647-6316.

ΔΔ **Lundy Lake Resort** Store, cabins, boat rentals, RV park. P.O. Box 265, Lee Vining, CA 93541.

Δ **Forest Service Campground** Lee Vining Creek, 17 sites.

Δ **County Campgrounds** Lee Vining Creek, 34 sites; Lundy Creek, 50 sites.

§ **Mono Lake Ranger District** Information and wilderness permits. P.O. Box 10, Lee Vining, CA 93541. (619) 647-6525.

Before leaving the Mono Basin, look over to the west and you'll see a wooden penstock skirting the steep hillside north of Lundy Canyon. It was built in 1910 by the Southern California Edison Company and now, besides fulfilling its intended purpose of generating electricity, serves, symbolically at least, as a boundary marker, delineating northern and southern California.

HOOVER WILDERNESS

The road now begins its steep ascent to **Conway Summit** (elevation 8,138 feet), the highest point on Highway 395 between Mexico and Canada. The countryside here has a decidedly alpine feel, treeless but, in the summer, green and inviting. For an easy-to-get-to taste of the high country, take the paved road that climbs steeply to **Virginia Lakes** (9,500 feet). Like most in the area, these lakes are stocked every week or so, and boat rentals are available. Because of its high elevation, this is a popular jumping-off point for the Hoover Wilderness. A trail climbs to **Summit Lake** (10,600 feet) and continues on to the northern extremes of Yosemite National Park.

Green Creek Tailhead (elevation 8,100 feet) is best reached by driving eight miles north on Highway 395 and then taking the graded-gravel Forest Service Road 142. Along the way you pass curiously named **Dynamo Lake,** which holds a place of honor in some history books. This is said to be the site of the world's first long-distance electrical power-generating system, the forerunner of giants such as TVA and Bonneville Power. Credit the Standard Consolidated Mining Company, which, on December 1, 1892, first delivered power to Bodie, thirteen miles away. The power line was built without curves or bends, so local people say—engineers feared that otherwise the electricity might jump the tracks. Offering a shining example of an unlikely metaphor, a newspaper of the day reported that the dynamo would "manufacture juice to burn." Jennifer Wilkes at the Bridgeport Ranger Station told me that Green Creek is the second most popular trailhead in the district (after Leavitt Meadows, Chapter 7). Relatively easy trails lead to **Green Lake** (8,900 feet), **East Lake** (9,500 feet), and **West Lake** (9,700 feet).

Recreational Facilities

ΔΔ **Virginia Lakes Resort** Store, rustic cafe, and 20 housekeeping cabins. H.C. Route 1, Box 1065, Bridgeport, CA 93517. (619) 872-0237.

Δ **Forest Service Campgrounds** Virginia Lakes, 47 sites, some of which are reservable through Mistix. Green Creek, 11 sites.

Ω **Virginia Lakes Pack Outfit** H.C. Route 1 Box 1076, Bridgeport, CA 93517. (619) 932-7767.

BODIE STATE PARK • Population 2; elevation 8,369 feet

In Mark Twain's day, the mining district was called Esmeralda and included Bodie, Aurora, and, so everybody thought, a place of fabulous wealth known as the Lost Cement Mine. Twain spent weeks looking for the mine, and for good reason: "Lumps of virgin gold were as thick in it as raisins in a slice of fruit cake." Alas, people are still looking. E Clampus Vitus, a rogue mining fraternity, erected a marker along Highway 395 that begs:

If while hiking in the area, you happen to come upon a ledge of pure gold please notify the nearest ECV Chapter so that we might relocate this monument to the correct site.

In sort of a backwards "Three Little Pigs" story, the once bustling city of Aurora no longer survives ("The brick houses were torn down to make fern bars in L.A.," a fellow told me), whereas Bodie, built of wood, still stands. It ranks with Bannack City, Montana, as one of the two best ghost towns in America, the quintessential "Old West" mining camp, a spot where it is not the least bit difficult to imagine Gary Cooper resolutely marching down Main Street at "high noon," guns at his side, ready to run the bad guys out of town. William Body, Bodey, Bodie (take your pick), a prospector, died in a snowstorm and, for that bit of self-sacrifice, got his name appended to the most lawless town the West had ever seen (see below). J. Ross Browne said of it:

> Some eight or nine miles from Aurora we reached the base of a conical hill, very rough, jagged, and picturesque; a capital-looking place for a den of robbers or a gold mine.

But there was gold to be had, and at one time the town population swelled to thousands.

Bad Man from Bodie with a Butcher Knife in His Boot

He had sand in his craw,
But was slow on the draw;
So we buried him 'neath the daises.

Bodie's unsavory reputation lingered, fueled largely by Mark Twain's stories of the Bad Man from Bodie. Smeaton Chase gave the bad man a weapon and the legend went on. In 1880 the exasperated editor of the *Bodie Free Press* rued:

There is a state of high carnival of crime in Bodie. Within a fortnight two men have been seriously beaten over the head with six shooters, one has been shot to death, one man and one woman have been knifed, one woman's skull crushed with a club, and she may die tonight. For these seven crimes—for these five lives jeopardized and two taken—two arrests have been made. We have constables and several de-

puties, whose sworn duty it is to enforce the law; and yet crime runs riot nightly in the criminal quarters of the town.

Not surprisingly, a vigilante committee was formed. Calling themselves the "601," they tracked down at least one desperado and hanged him on the spot. It worked, for a while, for in 1881 a paper reported: "Bodie is becoming a quiet summer resort—no one killed here last week." But three years later another editor complained: There is not a case of sickness and were it not for the numerous shooting affrays that keep up a supply of wounded, our physicians could take a rest."

Apparently some of the bad men were also bad shots:

About 2 o'clock last Monday morning, two men emptied the contents of two six-shooters at each other across the counter of the barroom with no other effect than tapping a barrel of ale. One of the men retired to the street, where he obtained a fresh supply of ammunition and, the firing was kept up until nearly daylight, putting three balls through the glass doors and shooting of a cigar in the mouth of a passing stranger, making the cigar too short to smoke. This indignity caused the smoker to lose his temper, and he woke up the constable, whereupon the firing ceased.

Estimates of the town's population vary, perhaps 8,000 at the peak. Seventeen saloons (or forty-seven, depending on which source you believe) did a thriving business, as did six restaurants, two livery stables, and a gaggle of butcher shops, bakeries, grocerys, and at least one tin shop and lumber yard. The fifteen houses of ill fame were, appropriately enough, located along Virgin Alley, Maiden Lane, and Virtue Street. One *demimonde* seemed to be always in trouble. Under the banner, "The Cyprian on the Rampage," a paper reported:

Rosa Oalaque, the same Spanish maid that slashed John Green across the face got full of fighting whiskey, donned her warpaint and started out to clean out the soiled dovecotes on Bonanza Street. The offic-

ers put her in a little bed in jail, where she remains at present.

Eleanor Dumont, the famous card shark known as Madame Moustache, settled here for a time, following her old avocation of dealing in 21 and faro. But she had lost her touch, and she committed suicide in 1879.

In spite of the many ups and downs it suffered over the years, a hundred million dollars in gold was taken from Bodie. Mining would likely have ceased after the peak year of 1880, but fifteen years later the heap leach cyanide process was invented and a renaissance occurred—for a while. Disastrous fires swept through town in 1886 and 1892 and again in 1932, causing Will Rogers to grumble: "The town's attempt to stage a comeback [is] being seriously hampered by the destruction of all liquid refreshment." During the Depression things struggled along, then ceased for good. Bodie ghosted.

Or did it? In the 1980s a Canadian firm with the wonderful name Galactic Resources Ltd. began experimental drilling on the back side of Bodie Bluff. Even if it pays (right now nobody knows) and the place comes alive, it won't be the same. Twenty-mule-team wagons won't haul the ore, no miners will crowd the post office when the stage comes in, bad men won't strut down Bonanza Street. Instead, miners will drive air-conditioned ore haulers, live in house trailers trucked to the site, and spend evenings watching TV beamed down by satellite.

The hundred or more buildings that still stand are preserved in what is best described as a state of arrested disintegration. (A trip to Bodie to photograph the tumble-down structures seems to be the *sine qua non* for budding California art students.) Tourist facilities consist of little more than a water fountain and an outhouse, but guided tours of the mill are offered in the summer. A caretaker and his wife keep an eye on the place during the winter, a lonely job when the town is snowbound and the temperature drops to forty below. The cemetery is fascinating; the area inside the iron fence is the resting place for the town's better citizens—outside is where the bad men (and bad women) lie. We'll visit another "ghost town," Virginia City, in the next chapter. Bodie is better.

The principal access road is paved to within a few miles of

town—a pity, because more people come here now. It was better when the road was bad; you got a wonderful spooky feel with nobody around. The dirt road continues on to Aurora, but people tell me it's not worth the hour's drive. Recently, I went as far as the site of the Syndicate Mine, where a five-stamp mill looks about to tumble down. A nearby house, once the toll station, has lost its roof. Not to worry: no one has paid a toll in a hundred years.

BRIDGEPORT • Population 900; elevation 6,450 feet

Aurora was the county seat, but when surveyors discovered it was in Nevada, Mono County officials had to find another place for their courthouse. Happily, they chose a spot in the middle of a rich green meadow, where they built a handsome white gingerbready building with a cupola topped by an American flag waving from a brass pole. From five miles away the building looks like a snow-goose, her goslings being the squat buildings that make up the rest of the town. Given the mountains and the cattle grazing in the meadow, Bridgeport presents the kind of image you would expect to see in Austria—Mayrhofen, for example—but the streets here are quite Western, wide, straight, and laid out on a grid. Various branches of the East Walker River meander in and around the town. The courthouse was built in 1880—a time when Bodie gold was flowing freely into the county treasury. The nearby schoolhouse is now the **Mono County Museum,** a wonderful place. Curious about the town's Basque restaurant, I asked long-time resident Marilyn Brandon about their influence here. She said that most worked the Carson Valley, not the Walker. "Here the sheepherders are Mexican, and can you believe it, they live in house trailers heated by propane." "Do they like being called 'sheepherders'," I inquired. "Why, what else would you call them?" "Shepherds," I suggested, whereupon a curious look came over her face. "Shepherds live in Palestine," she replied with an unswayable tone in her voice.

In spite of it being the county seat and having ranching all around, the town relies mostly on summer tourists for its economy. The local high school is in Coleville, thirty-five miles to the north. Sage grouse, chuckar, mountain quail, duck, and goose hunting are popular in the fall, but fishing is the big sport, centered at Bridgeport Reservoir. The dam, built in 1923, was for years quite productive—one fellow bagged a trout that weighed in at twenty-two pounds, eleven ounces—but recently downstream farmers (who live in Nevada and therefore are beyond California laws), intent on getting a third alfalfa crop, drained it nearly dry. The howl from fishermen could be heard all the way to Carson City and Sacramento.

Glacier-formed **Twin Lakes** (elevation 7,100 feet) fills four miles of the Robinson Creek canyon in a setting almost as dramatic as Convict Lake. The background is framed by **Sawtooth Ridge** and **Matterhorn Peak** (12,264 feet). Twin Lakes basin is lovely in the summer, with fine swimming and boating, but the place is subject to avalanches. "Three guys were killed in the 1960s," a fellow told me. "Their bodies were swept into the lake and never found; eaten by German browns or the crawdads, I suspect." A good trail goes up Robinson Creek, entering the **Hoover Wilderness** near **Barney Lake** (7,900 feet). One branch continues over **Rock Island Pass** (10,200 feet) into the northern reaches of Yosemite National Park.

Recreational Facilities

✔✔ **Cain House** B&B. Main Street, Bridgeport, CA 93517. (619) 932-7040.

✔ **Best Western Ruby Inn** 30-unit motel. P.O. Box 475, Bridgeport, CA 93517. (619) 932-7021.

✔ **Walker River Lodge** 36-unit motel. P.O. Box 695, Bridgeport, CA 93517. (619) 932-7021.

ΔΔ **Mono Village Resort** Cafe, grocery, cabins, boat rentals, and RV park at Twin Lakes. P.O. Box 455, Bridgeport, CA 93517. (619) 932-7071.

ΔΔ **Doc and Al's Robinson Creek Resort** 13 housekeeping cabins near Twin Lakes. P.O. Box 266, Bridgeport, CA 93517. (619) 932-7051.

Δ **Forest Service Campgrounds** Five campgrounds at Twin Lakes. 148 sites; Buckeye Creek, north of town, 65 sites. Many are reservable through Mistix. (800) 283-CAMP.

§ **Bridgeport Ranger District** Information and wilderness permits. P.O. Box 595, Bridgeport, CA 93517. (619) 932-7070.

ANTELOPE VALLEY

Highway 395 now works its way over **Devil's Gate Pass** (elevation 7,519 feet) before dropping into the upper reaches of the **West Walker River.** The Sonora Pass road (Chapter 7) terminates here. The highway then twists and turns down a narrow gorge—for a time you lose all sense of the Sierra Crest— but then the canyon opens up and you find yourself in the second of the northern Sierra's great east-side meadowlands, the wide and fertile Antelope Valley. The land here is a thousand feet lower than Bridgeport, so the grass greens up earlier in the spring and stays productive longer. **Walker** (population 500—summer 1,000; elevation 5,200 feet), the larger of the two little towns in the basin, has a couple of second-rate motels. Hammerbacker's, a wonderful old-fashioned country store-*cum*-gas station, is in **Coleville** (population 40—summer 400). A well-graded dirt road goes three miles to the derelict stamp mill of the Golden Gate Mine and then climbs *very* steeply to the **Little Antelope Pack Station** (8,100 feet). Trails lead into the **Carson Iceberg Wilderness,** an area lacking great splendor but with good fishing and plenty of solitude.

Man-made **Topaz Lake** straddles the California/Nevada border at the north end of the valley, where, not surprisingly, a casino stands ready to accept your short-term investments. If gaming is not your thing, take California Highway 89, which struggles over Monitor Pass (elevation 8,314 feet) to Markleeville (Chapter 5).

Recreational Facilities

✔ **Topaz Inn** Casino, motel, and restaurant. Topaz Lake, NV. (702) 266-3338.

△ **Forest Service Campgrounds** Two roadside campgrounds along the West Walker River, 78 sites.

Ω **Little Antelope Pack Station** P.O. Box 179, Coleville, CA 96017. (916) 495-2443.

Despite the fame of Bodie and Aurora, the real money was made in the Washoe mines, a place we will visit next.

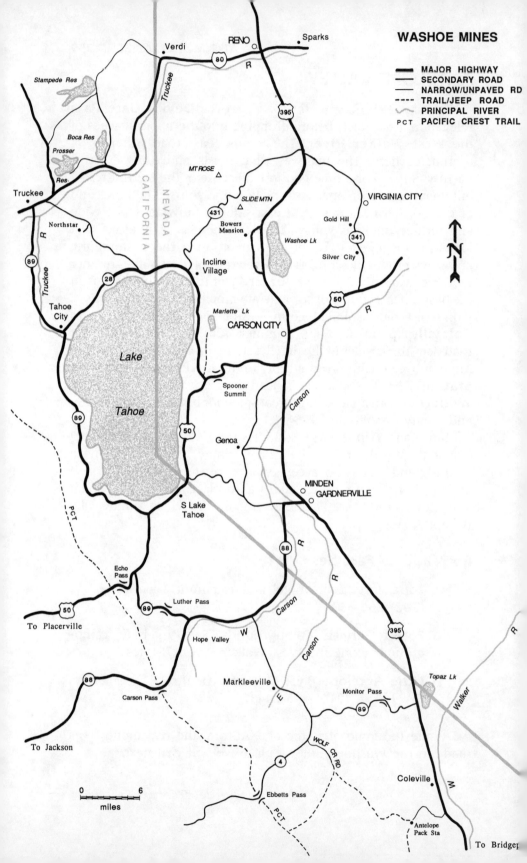

15

THE WASHOE MINES

The Big Bonanza

On his very first day in Carson City, a young would-be gold seeker named Samuel Clemens was astounded:

We were introduced to several citizens, among others, to a Mr. Harris, who was on horseback. He began to say something, but interrupted himself with the remark:

"I'll have to get you to excuse me a minute; yonder is the witness that swore I helped to rob the California coach."

Then he rode over and began to rebuke the stranger with a six-shooter, and the stranger began to explain with another. When the pistols were emptied, the stranger resumed his work [mending a whip-lash], and Mr. Harris rode by with a polite nod, homeward bound, with a bullet through one of his lungs, and several through his hips; and from them issued little rivulets of blood that coursed down the horse's sides and made the animal look quite picturesque.

Today it is the countryside that is picturesque. But the area did have its violent past, and that, of course, adds to its interest. This area was part of Utah Territory in 1860 and no doubt would have been included in the state of Utah, save for two events, one troublesome, the other fortuitous. Washington politicians, it seemed, were irked at Brigham Young's intransigence, particularly about the polygamy issue, but they coveted the recently discovered silver, which they reasoned would help pay for the Civil War. So they carved out a new state. Locals wanted to name it Washoe, which was what everybody called the place, but the name Nevada stuck, much to the consternation of the citizens of Nevada City (Chapter 17). Today Washoe is both Reno's county and the name given to a small river that drains into the Truckee. Nearly a quarter of a million people live in the area.

MINDEN/GARDNERVILLE • Population 5,400; elevation 4,721 feet

The Truckee and Carson valleys make up what was the Washoe, the latter the prettier, dominated by fertile irrigated pastures and surrounded by soaring mountains. The climate is both unusual and spectacular—unusual because of the wide daily temperature swings (often as much as forty degrees from morning to afternoon), and spectacular because summers are dry and warm and winters almost snowless. But the residents pay a price the Chamber of Commerce doesn't talk about—the winds, locally called Washoe zephyrs. Mark Twain described one as "a soaring dust-drift about the size of the United States set up edgewise." He wasn't too far off; a local fellow told me his barbecue blew away one day. "I never did find the damn thing," he said with a rather incredulous look on his face.

Sheeping has been the principal activity here since the 1890s, and as a result, about a fifth of the population is Basque. Many have prospered, including the family of former senator and governor Paul Laxalt, one of Ronald Reagan's closest friends. But the area is now becoming a retirement place and, of course, there is the gambling, which brings in hoards from California. Locals say it in one breath, Mindengardnerville, for it is really one city, and there, not surprisingly, hangs a tale. It seems that when the Virginia & Truckee Railroad decided to run a spur line down from Carson City, the people who owned the land where the depot was to be built didn't like the Gardner family. Minden, their home town in Germany, was in their view a more appropriate name. It is now the seat of Douglas County, but Gardnerville is three times as big. A new casino attracts out-of-staters, but sheepherders and cowboys hang out at Sharkey's, which features a huge collection of western saddles. I prefer the Overland Hotel, where, on Easter Sunday, I found myself in the midst of a wildly energetic bunch, none speaking English. The Picon punch the bar-lady was pouring is a Basque drink, and Easter Sunday, apparently, is the best time to enjoy it. It doesn't affect your head quite as much as it does your knees. Minden has a pleasant park, suitable for picnicking.

Nevada's oldest settlement, **Genoa** (population 145), started life as Mormon Station in 1851 and for a while achieved fame as a Pony Express station. But the town almost died, and it was Orson Hyde's fault. Hyde was the first judge of the district, then part of Utah Territory, and things were going well. But Brigham Young called the flock home to Salt Lake; settlers were forced to sell their holdings at bargain prices. When they didn't get paid, Hyde wrote the offending buyers a nasty letter, prophesying, among other things:

> You shall be visited of the Lord of Hosts with thunder and with earthquakes and with floods, with pestilence and with famine until your names are not known among men, for you have rejected the authority of God, trampled upon his laws and his ordinances, and given yourselves up to serve the god of this world; to rioting and debauchery, in abominations, drunkenness and corruption.

Whether this malediction was sufficient to induce restitution, the history books don't say.

In spite of the curse, Genoa is lovely, with an appearance only slightly altered from what James Hutchings saw in 1859:

> Its location is pleasant and romantic withal, for it stands upon a little slope at the very base of the mountains, which rise abruptly from the valley to a great elevation. It commands a view of almost the entire valley and the prospect is really beautiful, for the serpentine course of Carson river can be traced by the willows that border its either bank, while thousands of cattle may be seen scattered over its entire surface.

"Gen-OH-ah," it is called, perhaps for the same reason Neva-dans pronounce the nearby town named for the composer Guiseppi Verdi, "Ver-die." Curious, I asked long-time resident Eva Scarselli why this was and she replied: "Why not! An 'Eye-talian' friend of mine said that's the way it's pronounced in 'IT-ly.' " The four-block-square town is dominated by **Mormon Station State Park,** whose museum is housed in a log house built as a store and hotel in 1851. Summer concerts are held occasionally on the grass out back. When the county seat was moved to Minden in 1916, the outstanding, two-story brick court house was converted to a school and then later to the **Genoa Courthouse Museum.** Its highlight is a fine collection of Washoe baskets and exhibits of the sheep ranching in the area, but the exhibit that caught my eye explained the accomplish-ments of a local fellow named George Washington Ferris. Fascin-ated by how falling water could be turned into electricity, he built a twenty-eight-foot-diameter pelton wheel along the Carson Riv-er. Subsequent events took him to Chicago, where he erected a much bigger wheel for the Columbia Exposition of 1893, a twen-ty-five-story-high attraction that 2,000 people could ride at one time. The world would know it as the Ferris wheel.

Another way to capture the old-time flavor of the area is to belly up to the Genoa Bar, billed as "Nevada's Oldest Thirst Parlor." Several antique shops are nearby.

Recreational Facilities

  ✔✔ **Reid Mansion** 4-room B&B. 1431 Ezell Street, Gardner-ville, NV 89410. (702) 872-7644.

  ✔✔ **Wally's Hot Springs** Spa, restaurant, and B&B. 2001 Foothill Road Genoa, NV 89411. (702) 782-8155.

  ✔ **Carson Valley Inn** 100-room casino hotel. 1627 Highway 395, Minden, NV 89423. (702) 782-9711.

  ● **The Pink House** Victorian Genoa mansion, now a bar and restaurant. (702) 782-3939.

  ● **Overland Hotel** Basque restaurant and bar. (702) 782-2138.

  Ω **Carson Valley Country Club** Golf course. 1027 Riverview Dr., Gardnerville, NV 89410. (702) 265-3181.

CARSON CITY • Population 37,300; elevation 4,660 feet

For years Carson City was our smallest state capital, but it has grown so much that Montpelier, Vermont, now claims that dubious honor. The city, named of course for Kit Carson is famous in the world of numismatics. Even though $150 million worth of coins were minted here, those with the coveted cc sell for a dear price. The mint, built in 1869, now houses the **Nevada State Museum,** which has displays of old coinage. An interesting reproduction of a silver mine occupies the basement; the exhibits are more informative than at a real mineshaft in Virginia City. The **Nevada State Railroad Museum** houses some of Hollywood's favorite locomotives, relics from the Virginia & Truckee, which claims to have been the richest short line in the country. Tourist excursions are offered in the summer.

Carson County was formerly called Ormsby County, named for Major William M. Ormsby, dubious hero of the so-called Piute war. In 1860, attendants at Williams' Pony Express station treated some Piute women badly, probably raping them, and then locking them up in a cave. Warriors retaliated by killing the whites and burning the station. Organizing a band of volunteers, Major Ormsby promptly led them into a trap. A newspaper reported:

> Major Ormsby remained behind, calling as long as he was able, for the men to rally and cover the retreat, and save the wounded and those who were unhorsed; but all in vain! It was the most disgraceful scene that ever took place in civilized warfare. Major Ormsby remained on his horse for five or six miles, with his bridle hanging on the animal's neck. He died in his saddle, and pitched forward on his head, falling on the ground.

Twenty-five survived, eighty, including their leader, did not. Two weeks later a second expedition was launched, this time with 750 well-armed soldiers. One hundred and sixty Indians were killed in the engagement; two whites lost their lives, one of whom was Captain E. F. Storey, for whom Storey County is named. Thus ended the only Indian war in Nevada.

Recreational Facilities

✔✔✔ **Ormsby House** Casino, restaurant, bar, and 200-room hotel. 600 South Carson, Carson City, NV 89701. (702) 882-1890.

✔✔ **Winters Creek Ranch** 4-room Colonial style, modern B&B. 1201 Highway 395 North, Carson City, NV 89701. (702) 849-1020.

✔ **Best Western Trailside Inn** 67-unit motel. 1300 North Carson, Carson City, NV 89701. (702) 883-7300.

✔ **Hardman House Motor Inn** 62-unit motel. 917 North Carson, Carson City, NV 89701. (702) 882-7744.

VIRGINIA CITY

At first glance, Gold Canyon, which straggles down to the Carson Valley from the north, seems no different from any other dry desert arroyo, but a closer look reveals immense piles of yellow sand, looking like mounds left by a giant Minnesota gopher. They are but a sample of tailings from the greatest mining district in North America, the Comstock Lode. A slow drive, followed by a leisurely walk through the area, reveals a fascinating story of how this came to be. Nevada Highway 341 slabs up the hillside and enters the canyon at **Silver City** (elevation 5,000 feet), now a virtual ghost town. Here, in 1853, placer miners were having modest success finding gold, but were annoyed because a clayey muck kept fouling their sluices and rockers. Two brothers, Hosea and Ethan Allen Grosch, wrote home saying it was: "A dark gray mass [that] resembles thin sheet-lead." Their assays showed the gunk to be rich in silver, $3,000 to the ton; but capital, lots of it, would be required to get it out. Having none, they set about mining enough gold to get started. Sadly, Hosea ran a pick through his foot and died of blood poisoning. Ethan Allen, on his way to talk to San Francisco bankers, perished in a Sierra blizzard. Their find remained secret for six years. Even so, it is unlikely that the Grosch brothers would have struck it rich. Perversely, $3 million were poured into Silver City's Justice Mine, with nary a dime paid in dividends. The bonanza, it turned out, started on the other side of a prominent gap in the canyon, variously called Silver Gate or Devil's Gate.

Gold Hill (elevation 5,900 feet) saw better times, but there were ups and downs. During the good times, mines like the Belcher borrowed money from William Sharon's Bank of California. When things turned bad, he foreclosed. The Belcher subsequently made a profit of $13 million, enabling Sharon and his cohorts to gain control of more mines, all of the transportation, and most of the milling facilities of the Comstock. One wonders if President Lincoln would have granted statehood in 1864 had he known that Nevada was, at that time, virtually owned by the Bank of California. The Crown Point in the center of Gold Hill was a winner too, paying out $9 million in dividends, and the Kentuck, with only ninety-four feet along the lead, made $1 million for its owner, John Macay. But its neighbor, the Yellow Jacket, suffered a deadly fire that killed thirty-seven miners and subsequently lost several million. The most bizarre was a claim owned by Sandy Bowers, which was too narrow to work (he only had ten feet). He solved the problem by marrying Eilley Cowen, a thrice-wed washerwoman who had come into possession of the adjoining ten feet. Finding themselves suddenly rich, they built a mansion near Washoe Lake (which we'll visit in a bit) and went off to "Yoorup" to buy furnishings. Alas, slick operators bilked them of their wealth; they died penniless.

Speculation at San Francisco's mining exchanges was wild. Claims were sold by the foot, as William Brewer explained:

> Suppose a hill has a vein of metal in it; this is called a "lead." A company "takes up" a claim, of a definite number of "feet" along this vein, and the land 150 to 200 feet each side. In a mine that claims 1,000 feet, a foot sold or bought does not mean any particular foot of that mine, but one-thousandth of the whole. Thus the Ophir Mine has 1,500 feet, now worth over $4,000 per foot.

Nevada's oldest hotel, built in 1852, is at Gold Hill; remarkably, it is still in use, boasting the best restaurant in the Washoe. The highway, struggling past derelict headframes, deserted shacks, and falling-down mine houses, climbs steeply, circling around an open pit—what's left of the Imperial, Challenge, and Exchequer mines. In the mid-1970s the United Mining Company worked these rocks to little avail. "When they found the gray muck clogged their bulldozers," Reva Tawlks told me, "they up and ran, leaving us with that awful eyesore." It was at about this spot that a great event occurred in the history of the Washoe. According to authors Lucis Beebe and Charles Clegg:

> [A] tosspot and tavern valiant named James Finney [was] popularly known as "Old Virginny" from his claims to birth in aristocratic circumstances in the Old Dominion. One night, this prophetic ancient was taken in wine, and, on the way home to his shack, tripped and fell, smashing a bottle of whisky he was carrying as a precaution against the night air and altitude. Reluctant to let the liquor disappear into the elemental earth without having some good of it, he turned the catastrophe into a christening party and then and there named the tent town Virginia City.

Interestingly, **Virginia City** (population 600; elevation 6,220 feet) was incorporated by an act of the *Utah* legislature on January 16, 1861. Frank Leslie came here in 1877 and, in his *California Magazine*, wrote:

> To call a place dreary, desolate, homeless, uncomfortable, and wicked is a good deal, but to call it God-forsaken is a good deal more. We never found a place better deserving the title than Virginia City. Virginia City boasts of forty-nine gambling saloons and one church, open this day for a funeral, an event of frequent occurrence in this lawless city. The streets are mere narrow terraces built along the face of this precipice, like the vineyards along the Rhine or the steps of the Pyramids, whose arid and dusty desolation they imitate, without the grandeur and mystery.

Today, when you top the grade and look out over the town, you'll probably share his feelings. Besides being "God-forsaken," Virginia City is a tourist trap.

Virginia City would have died were it not for Beebe and Clegg, who moved here in the 1950s, bought the *Territorial Enterprise*, and began promoting its "Wild West ghost town" image. Property owners responded by opening bars (there are twenty-two at last count) with unlikely names: Longbranch Saloon (which was in Kansas) and Bonanza (which was on TV). Stores selling things only a tourist would buy opened "museums," the owners free to interpret the "Old West" any way they thought might make a buck. Gift shops selling Navaho jewelry now compete with gourmet cookie stores and restaurants featuring Cajun ribs. By nightfall the tourists, 2 million a year, have gone home; all save a couple of the bars have closed. But the tumble-down buildings with their false fronts and covered wooden sidewalks give the place a nostalgic feel, and a walk through town is a revealing experience, especially if you care about Virginia City's colorful past. Park near the Fourth Ward Schoolhouse and take a leisurely, three-mile stroll to the cemetery and back.

Twenty-three thousand lived in Virginia City at the height of the Big Bonanza, almost half the population of Nevada at that time, and they must have thought the mines would go on forever, for they spent $100,000 on a schoolhouse big enough for a thousand students. Three years later the mines began to peter out, but the **Fourth Ward School** managed to hang on for another fifty years. It is now a **museum.** The site is imposing, looking out over the mile-wide basin of the upper reaches of Six Mile Canyon.

Geologists and mining engineers quickly began to understand the nature of the lead. The Comstock turned out to be two miles long and several hundred feet wide, dipping toward the east at a forty-five-degree angle. The farther east the miners sank their shafts, the deeper they had to go to reach the ore, and the deepest of all was the mine you see across the gully, the Combination shaft, which bottomed out at 3,260 feet. The $7 million investment produced nothing but stench, country rock, and 5 million gallons of steaming hot water a day. When the pumps were shut off on October 16, 1886, all deep mining ceased on the Comstock. Mines closer to C Street (the main drag) found ore nearer the surface. The great Chollar (the "h" is silent) and Potosi produced $18 million in bullion, the Hale & Norcross $8 million, and the Savage $16 million, but in all cases the costs exceeded the revenues. The Chollar adit is open to visitors, but the shaft is short and you don't really get much sense of what life was like a half-mile underground. The superintendent's house is now a B&B.

Nearby is the **Mackay mansion,** one-time home of George and Phoebe Hearst. But a later resident, John Mackay (pronounced Mackie) played a greater roll in Virginia City's history, for by shrewdness and good judgment, he and three partners managed to break the monopoly of the Bank of California. Known as the "Bonanza Kings," Mackay and his partners, Flood, Fair, and O'Brien, became the richest men in the West—no small achievement when you consider the competition, which included Leland Stanford and his cohorts and William Sharon with his partners Billy Ralston and D. O. Mills. It is said the Bonanza Kings worked the ore for the stockholders, then reworked it for themselves, taking $17 million for the trouble. The money quite literally built the city of San Francisco. Once the Virginia & Truckee Railroad was completed, ore was freighted to the Carson Valley, where water wheels powered the mills. The line closed in 1936, but a short section of track has been reopened for summer excursions.

The hoisting works of the fabulous Gould and Curry were located just below the **Fire-house museum** between D and E streets. Mark Twain wrote of its beginnings:

> The Gould & Curry claim comprised twelve hundred feet, and it all belonged originally to the two men whose names it bears. Mr. Curry owned two-thirds of it—and he said that he sold it out for twenty-five hundred dollars in cash, and an old plug horse that ate up his market value in hay and barley in seventeen days by the watch. And he said that Gould sold out for a pair of second-hand government blankets and a bottle of whisky that killed nine men in three hours, and that an unoffending stranger that smelt the cork was disabled for life. Four years afterward the mine thus disposed of was worth in the San Francisco market seven million six hundred thousand dollars in gold coin.

Unseen, but directly below Silver Street, is the Sutro Tunnel, which, had it been built on schedule, would have saved countless dollars in mining costs. Adolf Sutro was a dreamer who proposed drilling a four-mile-long, nearly horizontal tunnel from the Carson Valley to intersect the mine shafts at the 1,600-foot level. Ore could be removed by gravity, the mines would be rid of scalding water. But the Bank of California wanted no competition spoiling their hoisting and milling business (Sharon called it Sutro's Coyote Hole), so they managed to stall the project for four years. Although it was authorized in 1865, serious drilling wasn't begun until 1869, and the tunnel was not completed until 1878. By that time the mines were almost exhausted.

Taylor Street marks the center of town, where the Bank of California and the Nevada Bank of San Francisco (forerunner of the Wells Fargo Bank) had their headquarters. Nearby is the office of the *Territorial Enterprise,* where Samuel Clemens first used the *nom de plume* Mark Twain. (Readers, it is said, quickly discovered that he wasn't disposed to let facts get in the way of a good story.) A block north of the St. Mary's Catholic and St. Paul's Episcopal churches was the hoisting works of the Consolidated Virginia, perhaps the richest mine the world has ever seen. Over a hundred million dollars in bullion was taken out of a lead only 1,310 feet long. Before the Con. Virginia was discovered in 1873, newspapers referred to the Comstock as the bonanza lode. Then it became the "Big Bonanza." Dan De Quill (Twain's friend on the *Territorial Enterprise*) inspected the various shafts, stopes, and wizens and reported:

> There are frequently found nests of pure, malleable silver in the shape of flattened wires that look as though they had been pulled in two and, in springing back after breaking, had coiled up against the pieces of ore on which they are found.

But it was Virginia City's swan song. Four years later the Con. Virginia passed its dividend and the Comstock went into a decline from which it never recovered.

Union Street marks the social center of town. **Piper Opera House** played host to the likes of Jenny Lind and Emma Nevada, but mostly, the miners liked their entertainment as raw as their whisky, preferring such extravaganzas as a battle to the death between a badger and a half a dozen bulldogs. Horace Greeley, witnessing a combat between a grizzly and a black Mexican bull, wrote about the struggle in the *New York Tribune,* and thereby gave Wall Street two of its handiest trade terms. The handsome **Storey County Courthouse** is open during business hours. The three-story Silver Dollar Hotel looks about to tumble down onto D Street. If it did, one of the more *interesting* parts of town, a place delicately referred to as "Sporting Row," would be buried under a pile of stone (see Neither Maiden, Wife, nor Widow, page 272).

Neither Maiden, Wife, nor Widow

Julia Bulette, a woman whom the newspapers of the day euphemistically called "fair but frail," lived on D between Union and Sutton streets, apparently doing a substantial business. But in 1868 an event occurred that moved the District Attorney to outrage:

On January 20th last, this community was struck dumb with horror by a deed more fiendish, more horrible than ever before perpetrated on this side of the snowy Sierra. Julia Bulette was found lying dead in her bed, foully murdered, and stiff and cold in her clotted gore. True, she was a woman of easy virtue. Yet hundreds in this city have found cause to bless her name. That woman probably had more real, warm friends in this community than any other; yet there was found at last a human being so fiendish and base as to crawl to her bedside and with violent hands, beat and strangle her to death.

Julia was of French descent, a handsome lass, judging from her portrait, which hangs behind the bar in the Bucket of Blood Saloon. The men at the fire department had named her "Queen of Engine Company 1," but the more pious of the community considered her a person who was, as they put it, "neither maiden, wife, nor widow." Whichever, the firemen gave her a lavish funeral. Their wives fumed. One John Millian was judged guilty of the crime and summarily marched to a draw near the cemetery to meet his fate. This time the wives joined the festivities. Considering him a hero for having rid Virginia City of its most famous *fille de joie*, they treated him to a sumptuous last meal. Then, while 3,000 revelers looked on, John Millian mounted the steps, passionately denied his guilt, then dropped, jerked, and dangled on the end of a six-foot rope.

Today the houses along D Street are gone; libertines have to drive almost all the way back to Carson City, to a place called Moonlight Ranch, to have their sport.

A detour up Sutton Avenue and then north on A Street takes you to the Ophir shaft, the place where it all began. Subsequent open-pit mining has obscured the site, but it's not hard to imagine what happened. As Beebe and Clegg described it:

> Four boozy and disreputable scoundrels found the world-shaking Comstock Lode. Two of them were Peter O'Reilly and Pat McLauglin who uncovered the first specimens, and a third was a blackmailer and freebooter of impressive manner and sanctimonious pretensions named Henry Comstock.

"Old Pancake," miners called Comstock, because he was too lazy to make real bread. O'Reilly and McLauglin had found the silver, but by bluff and bluster Comstock soon came to be considered not only the discoverer but the father of the lode.

More mines were worked farther north—the Mexican, Union, and Sierra Nevada—and although they produced several million in bullion, none covered expenses. Our walking tour ends at the hilltop where most of the cemeteries are located. Mark Twain was here at the time, so I guess we should take his word:

> The first twenty-six graves in the Virginia cemetery were occupied by *murdered* men. So everybody said, so everybody believed, and so they will always say and believe.

And what became of the other characters in this story? (See *Dramatis Personae*, below.)

Dramatis Personae

Henry Comstock sold his stake for $11,000, moved to Butte Montana, never lost his boastfulness, but died penniless. He did better than Pat McLauglin, who sold out for $3,500, even though his mine was producing that much in bullion in a week. Peter O'Reilly hung on longer, selling his interest for $40,000. Old Virginny, probably into his cups at the time, fell from a horse and died on the hillside above town.

Of the Bank of California bunch, William Sharon won a seat in the U.S. Senate, purchased a great estate in Menlo Park, California, and lived the good life until a

scheming woman, whom the press called the "Rose of Sharon," inveigled his money and left him penniless. His boss Billy Ralston built the most opulent hotel the West had ever seen, the Palace, but distraught over the impending failure of the Bank of California, he waded out into the chilly waters of San Francisco Bay, never to be seen again. D. O. Mills, who built the Virginia & Truckee Railroad, retired to a farm on the San Francisco Peninsula. Part of the estate became Mills Field, better known today as SFO, the San Francisco International Airport. Having made a small fortune on the Ophir, George Hearst went on to amass even greater wealth at Montana's Anaconda mine. His wife, Pheobe, provided a sizable endowment to the University of California, and their son William Randolph started the great newspaper chain.

Adolph Sutro sold the tunnel at a profit and moved to San Francisco, where he founded a great library, built a natatorium at the Cliff House called Sutro Baths, and became one of the city's most respected mayors. Mark Twain's escapades hardly need chronicling here. William O'Brien, the least influential of the Bonanza Kings, retired from the scene, dying in San Rafael in 1878. "Slippery Jim" Fair won a seat in the U.S. Senate but died before completing his mansion atop San Francisco's Nob Hill. His daughters, however, built a great hotel on the site, appropriately calling it the Fairmont, a name that has come as much to signify luxury in this country as did Caesar Ritz's name in Europe. The elegant brownstone across the street, the only surviving mansion from San Francisco's glory days, was built by his partner, James Flood. It is now the home of the exclusive Pacific Union Club. Mackay's wife spent money lavishly, becoming part of the Paris elite, while John kept always busy, building a trans-Atlantic cable and subsequently endowing much of the University of Nevada, thus returning at least a tiny bit of silver back to the state from whence it came.

Recreational Facilities

✔✔ **Chollar Mansion** B&B in a former mine superintendent's house. P.O. Box 889, Virginia City, NV 98440. (702) 847-9777.

✔✔ **Edith Palmer's Country Inn** 5-room B&B. P.O. Box 756, Virginia City, NV 98440. (702) 847-0707.

✔✔ **Gold Hill Hotel** P.O. Box 304, Virginia City, NV 98440. (702) 847-0111.

✔✔ **Hardwick House** 3-room B&B. 99 Main Street, Silver City NV 98428. (702) 847-0215.

✔✔ **House on the Hill:** New 3-room B&B. P.O. Box 625, Virginia City, NV. 98440. (702) 847-0193.

● **Crown Point Restaurant** (702) 847-0111.

§ **Moonlight Ranch** Men's sporting house. Red Rock Road, Dayton, NV 89403. (702) 246-9901.

RENO/SPARKS • Population 111,700; elevation 4,490 feet

Highway 395 climbs a low divide north of Carson City and drops into a wide valley at the foot of the Carson Range. **Washoe Lake State Park** has a nice picnic area, as does the old **Bowers Mansion,** which is open for tours in the summer. A flume once came down the mountainside, bringing Virginia City-bound lumber from the mills at Lake Tahoe. Bonanza Kings Flood and Fair once took a hair-raising ride down the track, averaging thirty miles an hour for the fifteen-mile dash. Along the way a passenger was tossed into the water, but the speeding gondola quickly caught up with the frightened fellow, and he soon found himself safely back aboard the hurtling craft. The highest peak visible from here is Slide Mountain, which recently did just that, dumping a substantial part of its mass into the Washoe Valley.

"The Biggest Little City in the World." The motto seemed appropriate in the Depression years, when Reno had a population of 18,000. It seemed big: the two blocks of Virginia Street between the railroad tracks and the Truckee River were all lit up with neon. Casino gambling was legalized in 1931, but in those days, "I'm going to Reno" was not necessarily announcing one's intention to hazard the die, but simply to say, "I'm getting a divorce." Marriages were (and still are) instant in Nevada; divorces required six weeks residency but, unlike in California, you didn't have to prove all sorts of bad things about your partner to get one. By the time other states had liberalized their conjugal laws, Reno was well on the way to becoming a gambling mecca. The Chamber of Commerce calls it a resort town, and I guess they are right, if playing the odds is a sport, but I have trouble with the moniker. Resorts are *outdoors;* Reno is *indoors.* And it is no longer little.

Union General J. L. Reno was killed at the battle of South Mountain, thus the name. From the onset, it seems to have been a place where enterprising men could extract money from the pockets of the unwary. Shortly after the railroad came this way, a Mr. Lake built a bridge across the Truckee, and in a year and a half collected $60,000 in tolls. Today, a dozen, twenty-five-story buildings rise above a town that otherwise looks like any modest Western town, such as Boise, Billings, or Spokane. But only one skyscraper is a bank; the rest are casino hotels. Six-and-a-half million people visit Reno each year, mostly for pleasure. In 1988 the Chamber of Commerce conducted a survey which revealed that the average visitor stayed a little over two nights, budgeted $128 for food, lodging, drink, and entertainment, and "spent" $179 on gaming. The word "spent," I think, means "lost." Hotel owners make it easy: you cannot register for a room, attend a show, get a meal, or buy a drink without passing through a casino. Slot machines (the player has no way of knowing the odds) are by far the most popular game, followed by blackjack, keno, and craps. Roulette, poker, baccarat, "wheel of fortune"-type games, and sports betting make up a tiny fraction of the money wagered. People seem to enjoy the betting, even though you often hear the story about the fellow who came to Reno in a $50,000 Cadillac and went home in a half-a-million-dollar Greyhound bus.

Like South Lake Tahoe and Las Vegas, Reno has top-flight entertainment. Golf is popular in the summer, but otherwise there is little to do except visit some museums, two of which were founded by casino owners. Harold Smith loved guns—his collection is at Harold Club (free)—whereas Bill Harrah was fascinated by automobiles. Many were sold when Holiday Inns bought Harrah's Club, but the cream of the collection is now housed in the new, downtown **National Automobile Museum** (fee). The **Nevada Historical Society** has a small museum on the

University of Nevada campus, where you will also find a fine mineral collection at the MacKay School of Mines. Out front is a bronze statue of a youthful John MacKay, pick in hand, ready to tackle the challenge of extracting Nevada's wealth.

Recreational Facilities

✔✔✔ **Bally's Reno** 2000-room full-service hotel and casino. 2500 East Second, Reno, NV 89585. (702) 789-2000.

✔✔✔ **Harrah's Hotel** 565-room full-service hotel and casino. P.O. Box 10, Reno, NV 89585. (702) 786-3232.

✔✔✔ **Hilton Hotel** 600-room full-service hotel and casino. P.O. Box 1291, Reno, NV 89585. (702) 322-1111.

✔ **Circus Circus** 1625-room full-service hotel and casino. P.O. Box, 5880 Reno, NV 89585. (702) 329-0711.

✔ **Fitzgeralds Hotel** 345-room full-service hotel and casino. 255 North Virginia Street, Reno, NV 89585. (702) 786-3653.

✔ **John Ascuga's Nugget Hotel** 600-room full-service hotel and casino. 1100 Nugget Avenue, Sparks, NV 89431. (702) 331-3203.

✔ **Reno Sparks Convention and Visitors Authority** Central reservations. P.O. Box 837, Reno, NV 89504. (800) FOR RENO.

✔ **The Sands Regent Hotel** 670-room full-service hotel and casino. 345 North Arlington Avenue, Reno, NV 89585. (702) 348-2200.

§ **Lake Ridge Golf Course** 18 holes. (702) 825-2200.

§ **Northgate Golf Course** 18 holes. (702) 747-8505.

§ **Washoe Golf Course** 18 holes. (702) 785-4286.

§ **Wildcreek Golf Club** 18 holes. (702) 673-3100.

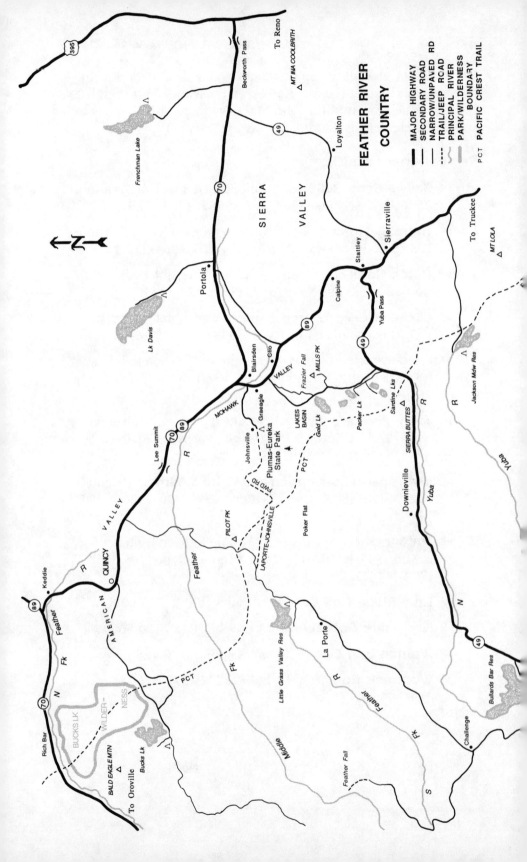

◀◀◀◀◀◀◆ **16** ◆▶▶▶▶▶▶

FEATHER RIVER COUNTRY

The Nuggets Had No Value, There Being So Many

Old Caleb Greenwood, the fellow who guided the first wagons to California, later explored the northern Sierra and had a wonderful time. But he had gotten lost during his wanderings, so he couldn't quite remember just where it was that he had found the golden lake. "The Indian children," he said, "amused themselves playing with gold nuggets; it was obvious that they had no value, there being so many." "The braves," he continued, "used the metal not only for arrowheads and ornaments but had fashioned it into beds, chairs, and other furnishings for their wigwams." Not surprisingly, men have been looking for Gold Lake ever since. We will too, but first, a visit to the lovely Sierra Valley is in order.

SIERRA VALLEY

North of Interstate 80, the apparent crest of the Sierra forms an arc, circling northwest toward the Feather River. The highest mountains include Mount Lola (elevation 9,143 feet) in the south and Spanish Peak (7,017 feet), hovering over the Feather. But the actual watershed boundary, the true Sierra Crest, continues almost due north from the town of Truckee, the rather uninteresting mountains gradually getting lower, more rounded, and much drier until the range finally dissipates at treeless **Beckwourth Pass** (5,212 feet), almost the exact elevation of Walker Pass, the Sierra's southern boundary. The great twelve-mile-wide by twenty-mile-long Sierra Valley forms a gap between these ranges. Although it looks much like the other east-side valleys we have visited (Bridgeport, Antelope, Carson), the waters here drain into the Pacific. So we find a west-side vacation land with decidedly east-side flavor: that is, cold in the winter and relatively dry, with forests dominated by the lovely Jeffery pine. Geologically, the valley is akin to the Tahoe Basin (the setting too is similar), but here the graben has been filled with alluvia. Cows graze where otherwise speedboats might roar—ranchers and timbermen predominate, not sportsmen and sybarites.

Two highways lead into Sierra Valley (elevation 5,000 feet) from the east: Highway 70, which crosses Beckworth Pass; and Highway 89, the more interesting, which crosses the Sierra divide at Truckee Summit (elevation 6,750 feet). Nearby **Jackson Meadow Reservoir** is a very popular fishing lake, reached by a wide, paved road. Highway 89 enters the Sierra Valley at **Sierraville,** a lonely village with a cafe, grocery (with a gas pump out front), and little else. Nearby **Stattley** (population 60) is even smaller. I decided to buy something, anything, at the Stately Cash Store, just to get a look inside. Wooden shelves were stocked with merchandise curiously not packaged in plastic. The oiled-wood floor seemed to weave up and down like a sea under a moderate breeze; one wall was listing fifteen degrees to starboard, a fact that caused some amount of worry for the proprietor. "We keep hoping we won't get a big blow from the west," she said with a rather anxious look about her. **Calpine,** once a mill town, now has a few scattered houses set amidst a pleasant forest.

Once, while on the way to **Loyalton** (population 1,030), I had to stop for fifteen minutes while two cowboys, driving cattle down the road, coaxed the beasts around my car. It seemed incredible that Reno, with its 150,000 people, was only forty-five minutes away. Loyalton, thanks to its sawmill, is the principal town in the southern valley.

Portola (population: 1,885), on the northern fringe of Sierra Valley in Plumas County, is a division point for the Union Pacific (*ex* Western Pacific) Railroad, a line famous for its scenic "Feather River Route." This was the last transcontinental railroad to be built, completed in 1909. A highlight for tourists is a visit to the **Portola Railroad Museum,** where dozens of locomotives are being restored. Norman Holmes told me their EMD "Centennial," a three-truck, nine-axle monster built by General Motors in 1969, is the biggest diesel ever. Several steam locomotives are fired up for summer excursions. Two nearby reservoirs, built in the 1960s, are now popular vacation spots. Surrounded by forests, **Lake Davis** (elevation 5,775 feet) and **Frenchman Lake** (5,588 feet) offer fishing, boating, and water skiing.

James Beckworth, for whom the pass is named, was a mulatto with an Indian wife, one of the earliest fur trappers, having adventured up the Missouri with Jedediah Smith and William Ashley in 1823. Illiterate, and possessing a mind incapable of distinguishing fact from fancy, he was a generous man and earned a fond spot in the hearts of the pioneers. In 1851, he rode across the Sierra carrying Ina Coolbrith, a nine-year-old Mormon lass, on his saddle. Settling in San Francisco, where she became an earlier-day Gertrude Stein, Ina joined a literary coterie that included Bret Harte, Joaquin Miller, Mark Twain, Jack London, and Ambrose Bierce, and was subsequently honored as California's first poet laureate. The most prominent peak in the area bears her name.

Recreational Facilities

  ✔✔ **Upper Feather B&B** 6 rooms in a 1910s house along the river. P.O. Box 1528, Portola, CA 96122. (916) 832-0170.

  ∆ **Forest Service Campgrounds.** 3 campgrounds at Jackson Meadow, 100 sites; 2 along Highway 89 near Sierraville, 60 sites; 3 at Lake Davis, 180 sites; 5 at Frenchman Reservoir, 200 sites.

LAKES BASIN (Gold Lake) RECREATION AREA

Highways 70 and 89 converge at Blairsden, a town we will visit in a bit. But first, take State Highway 49 over **Yuba Pass** (elevation 6,701 feet) and then turn north to the Lakes Basin area. About thirty naturally occurring lakes pock this wild landscape. Roads lead to four, and the rest are accessible by easy trails that thread among rocky outcroppings. Start by taking the side road that passes **Sand Pond** (great swimming) and terminates at the lovely **Lower Sardine Lake** (5,800 feet), where a nifty old resort stands amid a lodgepole forest. Dorthy Hunt told me she serves the best home-cooking in Sierra County, a boast that was confirmed by several other innkeepers I talked to. Lower and Upper Sardine lakes are classic glacial tarns, scooped out of the flank of the most prominent landmark in the northern mountains, **Sierra Buttes** (8,587 feet). Nearby **Packer Lake,** smaller and not quite as pretty, also has a rustic lodge. Another spur road ends at stark-looking **Salmon Lake.** The old hand-cranked telephone you're supposed to use to call the lodge on the opposite shore hasn't worked in years. Guests instead wave their arms, blow their car's horn, or flash lights to signal that they want to be picked up by the resort's water taxi. Failing that, they walk. Day hikers will enjoy the four-mile (round-trip), five-hundred-foot climb to **Deer Lake.**

Gold Lake (6,400 feet), by contrast, shares with a half a dozen other smaller ponds the wide, almost flat divide that separates the Yuba and Feather rivers. These lakes are glacial too, but more like those in Minnesota's Cambrian Shield country, rock-studded and shallow, with tamarack forests growing up to their banks. Happily, Gold Lake is full of trout, but no gold nuggets whatsoever. Numerous other lakes make fine day-hike destinations, the most popular being **Long Lake,** where a local resort rents fishing boats. To get a wonderful overview of this magnificent country, take the dirt road to the fire lookout at **Mills Peak.** Nearby **Frazier Falls** is a handsome cascade, reached by taking a short trail.

Recreational Facilities

ΔΔ **Elwell Lakes Lodge** 7 housekeeping cabins. P.O. Box 68, Blairsden, CA 96103. (916) 836-2347.

ΔΔ **Gold Lakes Lodge** Family (American-plan) resort. P.O. Box 25, Blairsden, CA 96103. (916) 836-2350.

ΔΔ **Gray Eagle Lodge & Restaurant** Family (American-plan) resort. Dinner reservations required for nonovernight guests. Cabins. P.O. Box 38, Blairsden, CA 96103. (916) 836-2511.

ΔΔ **Packer Lake Lodge** Cafe, bar, and housekeeping cabins. P.O. Box 237, Sierra City, CA 96125. (916) 862-1212.

ΔΔ **Salmon Lake Lodge** 13 housekeeping cabins. P.O. Box 121, Sierra City, CA 96125. (415) 771-0150.

ΔΔ **Sardine Lakes Resort** Restaurant, bar, and 9 housekeeping cabins. P.O. Box 216, Sierra City, CA 96125. (916) 862-1196.

Δ **Forest Service Campgrounds** The Lakes Basin Area has 6 campgrounds with 120 sites. 5 campgrounds near Yuba Pass have 75 sites.

Ω **Gold Lakes Pack Station** 1540 Chandler Road, Quincy, CA 95971. (916) 836-0940.

MOHAWK VALLEY • Population 635—summer 1,000; elevation 4,400 feet

Feather River Inn, built by the railroad, nestled in a Jeffery pine forest and surrounded by a lush golf course, was once one of the most fashionable resorts in northern California, the Western Pacific's equivalent of the Great Northern's Glacier Park Hotel. Guests, arriving on the sleek dome-liner *California Zephyr*, walked to the hotel while porters brought the luggage over in wheelbarrows. Cocktails were taken on the veranda; dining was an elegant affair. But times changed, the train stopped running when Amtrak was formed, and hotel operations ceased. For a while the building served as a college, but now it is once again a summer resort, though open only to alumni of the University of the Pacific. The life-style, however, set a pattern that has continued, and in recent years, country clubs have been built that more or less carry on that gracious tradition. The difference, however, can be summed up in one word—condominium. Vacationers live along the fairways in the well-maintained, lookalike, soft-colored buildings that modern Americans seem to prefer. Mohawk Val-

ley, which encompasses the villages of Clio, Graeagle, and Blairsden, has become the golf capital of the northern Sierra, boasting
two championship courses and two links of nine holes. The
location is perfect, high enough to escape the summer heat, yet
not so high as to get inundated with snow. Lying in the lee of the
mountains, rainfall is modest, yet streams abound, full of trout.
The valley is almost level and very pretty.

Nearby **Johnsville** (population 100, summer; elevation 5,175
feet), an old mining town, adds another dimension to the charm
of the area. Hundred-year-old buildings, some about to fall
down, reflect the wonderful gold-rush atmosphere we will find in
the following chapters. In 1872, the Sierra Buttes Mining Co.
Ltd., an English firm, began mining in a serious way, digging
seventy miles of tunnels under Eureka Peak. Mining ceased in
1943, but many of the buildings still stand and are now part of
Plumas-Eureka State Park. A small **museum,** housed in the
former bunkhouse, illustrates what went on. Rangers make the
dubious claim that the old tramway, part of which still stands,
served as the world's first ski lift. Eureka Peak still serves skiers on
a modest basis. Plumas County Ski Club runs a couple of small
lifts on Wednesdays, Saturdays, and Sundays. A county road goes
to LaPorte, but it is in such deplorable condition that four-wheel-
drive vehicles are recommended.

Recreational Facilities

- ✔✔ **White Sulphur Springs Ranch** 7 room B&B in an 1850s
  farmhouse. Pool. P.O. Box 136, Clio, CA 96106. (916)
  836-2221.

- ✔ **Graeagle Meadows Vacation Rentals** P.O. Box 344,
  Graeagle, CA 96103. (916) 836-2221.

- ∆∆ **Layman Resort** 13 riverside housekeeping cabins. P.O.
  Box 8, Blairsden CA 96103. (916) 283-2356.

- ∆∆ **Feather River Resort Park** 35 housekeeping cabins. Pool
  and nine-hole golf course. P.O. Box 37, Blairsden CA
  96103. (916) 836-2328.

- ∆∆ **River Pines Inn** Restaurant and 30-unit motel. Housekeeping cottages. P.O. Box 117, Blairsden CA 96103.
  (916) 836-2552.

△ **Forest Service Campground** Jackson Creek, 15 sites.

△ **State Park Campground** Plumas-Eureka State Park, 67 reservable sites. (916) 836-2380.

● **Olsen's Cabin** Graeagle restaurant. (916) 836-2801.

● **Iron Door** Johnsville restaurant. (916) 836-2376.

● **Mt. Tomba Inn** Feather River restaurant. (916) 836-2359.

§ **Graeagle Meadows Golf Course** 18-hole championship course. (916) 836-2323.

§ **Plumas Pines Golf Course** 18-hole championship course. (916) 836-1420.

§ **Feather River Inn** 9-hole golf course. (916) 836-2623.

QUINCY • Population (area) 4,451; elevation 3,423 feet

Ten miles west of Blairsden, near the tiny mill town of Sloat, the middle fork of the Feather plunges into a steep, virtually impassable canyon, now part of the Wild and Scenic River system. So the highway and the railroad climb slightly, cross Lee Summit (3,986 feet), and drop into the north fork. The railroad goes through a tunnel and then makes a 360-degree spiral— locomotives on long westbound freights pass underneath their own caboose. Quincy, set in broad, nearly flat **American Valley,** is surrounded by gently rising, densely forested hills. It might well be described as "Small Town U.S.A." Three-block-long Main Street is the commercial center for Plumas (Spanish for "feather") County. Two sawmills, the Forest Service, and the county government provide employment for those lucky enough to live here. The **Plumas County Museum** is adjacent to the handsome 1920s court house. Nearby **Bucks Lake** (5,153 feet), built by PG&E, is a popular fishing and water-skiing spot in the summer and a nice place for cross-country skiing in winter. Two resorts and a hundred or so homes are scattered along the shore.

Feather River Canyon

Arthur Keddie, the railroad surveyor, chose Beckworth Pass because it is 2,000 feet lower than the Southern Pacific's Donner

Pass, and therefore, has much less snow. The grade is less, one percent (half that of the S.P.), but for these benefits he paid a price. The countryside loses its gentleness as you proceed downstream, the gorge becomes very steep, and rock slides frequently damage the track. The little town of **Keddie** is interesting because it is the site of the most unique railroad wye in the country: two legs are on trestles and the third is in a tunnel. The wye forms a junction; the other track heads north to join the Burlington Northern at Bieber. The Feather River makes its big bend here and heads southwest, giving Keddie the distinction of being the northernmost town in the Sierra. Highway 89 continues north, climbing into more mountains, which, geologically at least, are different. Unlike the tilted block of the Sierra, the Cascades are primarily of volcanic origin.

Downstream from Keddie there is little to capture our attention except **Rich Bar** (elevation 2,500 feet), now nothing save for some rusting machinery and a rickety old bridge. The few people who stop come to fish or try their luck at gold panning. But Rich Bar was the two-year home of a most remarkable '49er, Louise Amelia Knapp Smith Clappe, wife of an erstwhile medical doctor. Writing under the pen name Dame Shirley, her letters provide us with a vivid picture of those turbulent days. The first day here she wrote:

> Deep in the shadowy nooks of the far down valleys, like wasted jewels dropped from the radiant sky above, lay half a dozen blue-blossomed lagoons, glittering and gleaming, and sparkling in the sunlight, as though each tiny wavelet were formed of rifted diamonds. It was worth the whole wearisome journey, danger from Indians, grizzly bears, sleeping under the stars, and all, to behold this beautiful vision. Of course, to me, the *coup d'oeuil* of Rich Bar was charmingly fresh and original.

Dame Shirley's writings greatly enrich the Gold Country chapters that follow.

Recreational Facilities

✔✔ **The Feather Bed** 7-room B&B built in 1893. P.O. Box 3200, Quincy, CA 95971. (916) 283-0102.

✔ **Spanish Creek Motel** 28 units. P.O. Box 617, Quincy, CA 95971. (916) 283-1200.

✔ **Ranchito Motel** 30-unit rustic motel. 2020 East Main, Quincy, CA 95971. (916) 283-2265.

✔ **Lariat Lodge** 20-unit motel. 2370 E. Main, Quincy, CA 95971. (916) 283-1000.

ΔΔ **Bucks Lake Lodge** Cafe, grocery, and 18 housekeeping cabins. P.O. Box 236, Quincy, CA 95971. (916) 283-2262.

ΔΔ **Lakeshore Resort** Cafe, grocery, and housekeeping cabins at Buck's Lake. P.O. Box 266, Quincy, CA 95971. (916) 283-2333.

ΔΔ **Pine-Aire Resort** Housekeeping cabins along the Feather. Twain, CA 95984. (916) 283-1730.

Δ **Forest Service Campgrounds** 4 campgrounds at Bucks Lake, 65 sites. 6 campgrounds along the Feather, 85 sites.

Δ **PG&E Campground** Haskins Valley at Bucks Lake, 65 sites.

LA PORTE

Before quitting the northern Sierra, it is fun to retreat to Quincy and then follow logging roads (mostly paved) to La Porte, the birthplace of competitive skiing in America. The road is steep in spots, and heads in the general direction of a mining camp called Poker Flat, possibly the inspiration for Bret Harte's famous story. La Porte (population, 40 winter, 400 summer; elevation 4,959 feet) seems like a place that long ago lost its *raison d être,* but there are people in California who simply want to be away from it all, so new houses are scattered here and there throughout the woods. Amazingly, the Union Hotel still stands and is open for business. Old timers insist that this was the first ski lodge in the country, hosting downhillers as early as 1863 (see Dope Is King, page 288).

Dope Is King

They came from all over, Poorman's Creek, Poker Flat, Sawpit, Port Wine, Whiskey Diggings, wherever miners were holed up, waiting for the snows to melt so they could go back to work. It was a chance to be not only a local hero, but to make some money: upwards of a hundred dollars on each race, and the competition went on for days. "Dope Is King" the poster for the 1869 meet proclaimed, and so it was. These fellows cared not a whit about style and technique. Concepts like reverse shoulder, downhill edging, and *wedeling* would have been anathema, and useless anyway, considering the equipment. Skis, which they called Norwegian snowshoes, were twelve feet long and four inches wide. The binding was a simple leather strap. A single pole, held under the armpit and wedged against the hip, served as both a brake and a rudder.

The object, of course, was to get from top to bottom quickly and, since plastic bottoms were a thing of the future, they resorted to alchemy. Dope was concocted from oil of cedar, Venice turpentine, Canada pitch, balsam of fir, Barbary tallow, camphor, castor oil, pine tar, and probably a little tobacco juice. Formulas, given fanciful names like slip easy, catch 'em quick, skedaddle, and breakneck, were cautiously passed to trusted friends, sworn to secrecy. Apparently the gunk worked: speeds of up to sixty miles an hour (faster than the trains of the day) were reported, although photographs show clouds of snow thrown up by racers who didn't quite make the finish line. Robert "Cornish Bob" Oliver, from Sawpit, won the first race. Snowshoe Thompson entered one year, but he was no match for these speed demons. And when the following year he suggested that the competition include turning and jumping, essentially a race through the forest, nobody took up his challenge.

Longboard skiing petered out in the early twentieth century and had virtually no influence on the modern sport. Nevertheless, a race was held at the Sugar Bowl in 1941 that shed some light on what it must have been like. John Redstreak, from the Plumas-Eureka Ski Club, challenged Hannes Schroll, the U.S. downhill champion, and astounded everybody by winning. Careening down

**the hill on skis twice as long as he was tall, Redstreak
was clocked at eighty-seven miles an hour.**

La Porte has seen a bit of a renaissance since **Little Grass
Valley Reservoir** was built. The shores are heavily forested and
although there are no resorts, it's a fine vacation spot.

Recreational Facilities

  ✔✔ **Union Hotel** Bar, restaurant, and 25 rooms in a gold-
rush-era hotel. P.O. Box 57, La Porte, CA 95981. (916)
675-2525.

  △ **Forest Service Campgrounds** 3 campgrounds at Little
Grass Valley Reservoir, 190 sites.

One other attraction deserves mention. **Feather Falls** plunges
640 feet into the middle fork of the Feather River, making it the
sixth highest in the nation. A seven-mile (round-trip) trail leads
to a spectacular overlook built by the Forest Service. Early spring
is the best time to visit the cataract.

◄◄◄◄◄◆ **Part Five** ◆►►►►►

THE GOLD FIELDS

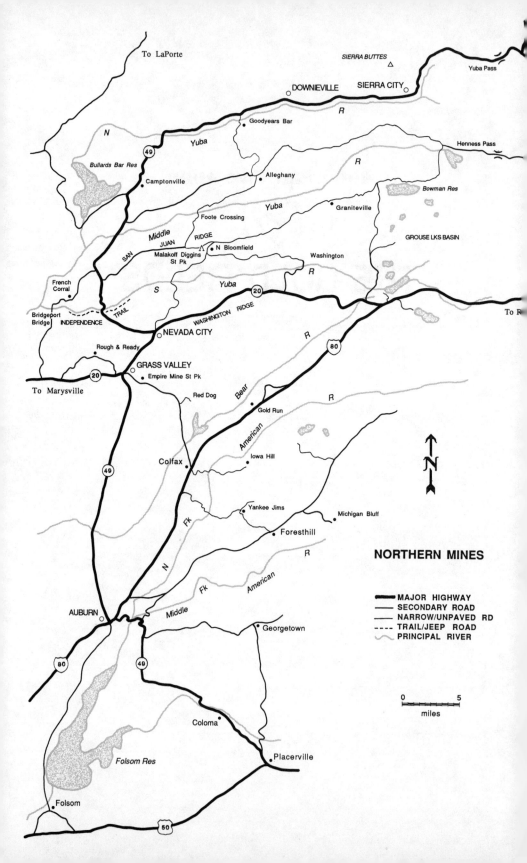

17

THE NORTHERN MINES
Gold Is Where You Find It

Once the news was out about James Marshall's discovery on the American River, the western slope of the Sierra became overrun with miners. No one knew how much gold there was; perhaps, as people were saying, thirty-pound nuggets were lying about, and if you didn't find one, someone else would. It was a time of rapacious frenzy.

> Our countrymen are the most discontented of mortals. They are always longing for "big strikes." If a "claim" is paying them a steady income, by which, if they pleased, they could lay up more in a month, than they could accumulate in a year at home, still, they are dissatisfied, and, in most cases, will wander off in search of better "diggings." There are hundreds now pursuing this foolish course.

Not surprisingly, early pickin's were easy and productive. Mother Nature had done most of the work, freeing the metal from its rocky confines and washing it down to a convenient stream bed. It was "in place" gold, what came to be called placer gold. One prospector, cooking a salmon, found gold at the bottom of his pot, and a woman, sweeping her dirt floor, discovered that her tent was literally pitched on a gold mine. Nuggets as big as a banana were found, but mostly, "color" was flakes as fine as dust. Jack London explained the panning process:

> Jealously, bit by bit, he let the black sand slip away. A golden speck, no larger than a pin point, appeared on the rim, and by his manipulation of the water it returned to the bottom of the pan. And in such fashion another speck was disclosed, and another. Great was his care of them. Like a shepherd he herded his flock of golden specks so that not one should be lost. At last, of the pan of dirt nothing remained but his golden herd.

Once the rivers had been worked over (at least superficially), prospectors looked in less obvious places: cañons, gulches, cañadas. Here they found ancient stream beds of auriferous gravel. As one miner related:

> We washed half of the day yesterday just for a commencer and obtained $40.50. We considered this the poorest dirt on the whole premises, but as "gold is where you find it" there is no telling with accuracy where the best is.

But water had to be imported, as Sarah Royce, an early settler, observed:

> Gold had been discovered in the bluffs and banks on the side of the stream, and for washing this out, a large supply of water was needed. A number of San Francisco gentlemen had organized themselves into a company to meet this want. Their plan was, to dam the river some distance above the bar, run it through a large flume, back of the diggings, and enough above them to give a sufficient fall, then sell the water to the miners, by the square inch, distributing it by means of small flumes as it was required.

Hydraulic mining required teamwork, of course; the day of the lonesome prospector, the "sniper," wandering the Sierra with pick, pan, rifle, and mule, was pretty much over.

"Where did this free gold come from?," was the obvious question, and before long, prospectors discovered that it had been formed at the same time as Mother Earth had made quartz. Find quartz and it was likely speckled with gold. But great amounts of quartz had to be pulverized; a half an ounce of gold per ton was considered pay dirt. So great mining companies were formed to dig it out.

> The gold in the rivers, the dry diggins and the ravines is accessible to any man who has the strength to use a pan or washer, a spade and pick-ax. The case will be very different with the vein-mines, which yet remain in the rock. To work them successfully will require machinery, with horse or steam power, involving an expenditure of capital in proportion to the extent of the operations.

But there was plenty of it; "lead (or lode) mining," as it was called, lasted into the 1950s, and mining for placer gold is still going on in a few places, thanks to modern earth-moving machinery, which can sift through hundreds of tons of gravel to obtain an ounce or two of color.

In the next three chapters we shall visit sites that illustrate all the ingenious ways the Argonauts found to separate the gold from its "mother lode." Highway 49 is aptly numbered, for it connects most of the fabled gold-rush towns. We'll visit mining camps with prosaic names, Grass Valley, for example, and fanciful ones too, such as Growlersburg, Rough and Ready, Fiddletown, Yankee Jims. For 230 miles, the mostly two-lane road follows cold Sierra streams, wiggles up canyon sides, and winds among bucolic oak savannahs, passing the relics and derelicts of a tumultuous age. We begin on the north fork of the Yuba.

SIERRA CITY • Population 225; elevation 4,187 feet

It seemed to me fitting that this northern entrance to the Gold Country would be defended by the specter of giants, and the brooding **Sierra Buttes** (8,500 feet) do just that, hovering over the Yuba River like Fasolt and Fafner guarding *das Rheingold*. (A steep Jeep road goes most of the way to a fire lookout.) Sierra City is a nice little town with a two-block-long business section dominated by a half a dozen ancient-era buildings. Vacationers camp alongside the river, where they fish for trout or swim in water deliciously free of the chemicals found in city pools. The Mother Lode's only still-operable stamp mill is here, now part of the **Sierra County Historical Park.** The tour wonderfully illustrates how, thanks to an invention by a local fellow, a giant stamp mill could be powered by a modest stream of water. Lester A. Pelton, a tinkerer who lived at nearby Camptonville, had as profound an effect on California mining machinery as James Watt in Scotland had on locomotives. The Sierra, of course, had an abundance of falling water. The problem was to design a turbine whereby the high-pressure water hitting the blade would not turn back on itself and interfere with the incoming jet. Pelton's solution was to direct the nozzle at the center of cupped blades, each of which looks a bit like the bottom half of a two-egg cardboard egg crate. Old-timer Jim Hutchison explained how the inspiration came about:

> [Pelton's] neighbor was out in the clover patch using a garden hose to drive a stray cow away when he observed that the stream of water hit the cow squarely on the sharp bone of its nose; the water divided as it struck, half going east and half going west with no water coming straight back.

E Clampus Vitus, one of several mining fraternities, was founded at Sierra City; Balaam Chapter, for reasons explained below, was designated as Chapter #107,402.

For the Relief of Widows and Orphans, Especially Widows

While the members solemnly sang the anthem, "We'll Take a Drink with Thee, Dear Brother," the meetings were opened by the raising of the flag (which depicted a hoop skirt and the motto: *This is the flag we fight under*), so the historians say. Others aren't quite sure because, as one member put it, "The trouble was that during the meetings none of the brothers was in condition to keep any minutes, and afterwards nobody could remember what had taken place." Apparently, E Clampus Vitus developed among those thought to be unworthy of being Masons, Odd Fellows, or Elks, so they bestowed amongst themselves exalted titles like Grand Noble (or Exalted or High Honorary or [best of all] Sublime Noble Grand) Humbug. Their official and oft-stated objective was to "Provide for the relief of the community's widows and orphans—but more particularly the widows." Other aims were equally noble, as Ezra Dane reported:

It existed principally for the purpose of taking in new members [poor blind candidates], and for the entertainment and refreshment thereby provided for the old members at the neophyte's expense. By the time he had sat in the *Expungent's Chair*, passed through the *Cave of Silence*, ridden the *Rocky Road*, endured the *Obliterating Obfuscation*, and received the *Staff of Relief*, and seen his initiation fee converted into liquid assets and consumed by the assembled Clampers, he was under no misapprehension as to what had happened to him.

As the gold gave out, so too did E. Clampus Vitus, but not forever. In 1932 Leon Whitsell, Ezra Dane, and Carl I. Wheat, became fascinated by these goings on, and set about creating its rebirth, adding, appropriately, the word *Redivivus* to the name. Carl Wheat, a noted lawyer, historian, and bibliophile (author of the definitive work, *Mapping the Trans-Mississippi West*), inducted Franklin D. Roosevelt into the ranks. In an address before the Library of Congress, Wheat explained:

It is said that the Constitution of this Ancient and Honorable Order had but two grandiose Articles: I. "All members are officers." II. "All officers are of equal indignity."

For a time during the 1960s, a penchant for red-neck rowdyism gave the organization a bad reputation (the Placerville police chief wouldn't let them in town one year), but the emphasis has returned to history. Members gather to dedicate plaques commemorating great events, some heroic, some whimsical, and many simply bizarre. As Carl Wheat put it:

Today the revived order solemnly makes annual pilgrimages to some old Sierra diggins, and, in what its enthusiasts call its "Hall of Comparative Ovations," there is celebrated the lighter side of Gold Rush life.

Recreational Facilities

✔✔ **Busch and Heringlake Country Inn** 4-room B&B in the old Wells Fargo building. P.O. Box 68, Sierra City, CA 96125. (916) 862-1501.

✔✔ **High Country Inn** 4-room country B&B. P.O. Box 7, Sierra City, CA 96125. (916) 862-1530.

✔ **Herrington's** Restaurant, bar, and 20-unit riverside motel. P.O. Box 235, Sierra City, CA 96125. (916) 862-1151.

△ **Forest Service Campgrounds** 4 campgrounds, 50 sites.

DOWNIEVILLE • Population 325; elevation 2,865 feet

Three thousand citizens live in Sierra County, most of them on the other side of Yuba Pass (Chapter 16). So it is not surprising that Downieville, the county seat, is so tiny, a toylike village. Hundred-year-old brick buildings hug the river; clapboard houses cling to the mountainside like birdcages hung on hooks. Gallows, actually used to mete out justice, stand near the courthouse, a reminder of the chaos of a tumultuous time. The act was never pretty, as Dame Shirley pointed out:

> The execution was conducted by the jury, and was performed by throwing the cord, one end of which was attached to the neck of the prisoner, across the limb of a tree standing outside of the grave-yard; when all, who felt disposed to engage in so revolting a task, lifted the poor wretch from the ground, in the most awkward manner possible. The whole affair, indeed, was a piece of cruel butchery, though *that* was not intentional, but arose from the ignorance of those who made the preparations. In truth, life was only crushed out of him, by hauling the writhing body up and down several times in succession. It is said that the crowd generally, seemed to feel the solemnity of the occasion; but many of the drunkards who form a large part of the community on these Bars, laughed and shouted, as if it were a spectacle got up for their particular amusement.

Juanita, euphemistically described as a "fandango girl," was the only female to face the hangman during that lawless time.

She was said to have run a butcher knife into the belly of one
Jack Cannon, a fellow who was either a drunken gambler or "a
man who had by his good conduct and peaceable demeanor,
made hosts of friends." Whichever, Juanita was quickly tried and
ushered to Downieville's Jersey bridge, reportedly shouting
"*Adiós Señores!*" as the drop fell.

Hanging, however, wasn't the only punishment. According to
William Swain:

> In the absence of any governmental authority, police or jail, the
> miners on each river established their own laws. On the South
> Fork there were two cases of theft. One of the men was flogged
> with 100 lashes and the other 150. The latter died.

Downieville also saw lively times when two politicians got into
a row over the moral character of a woman who had come to
town to lecture on the virtues of temperance. Robert Tevis, a
Know-Nothing candidate for district attorney, challenged Judge
Charles Lippincott to a duel with double-barreled shotguns,
loaded with ball. He shouldn't have.

Highway 49 quits the North Yuba River a dozen miles west of
Downieville and begins its long up-down wanderings along the
Sierra's western foothills. Several old mining camps now lie beneath the waters of **Bullards Bar Reservoir.** This densely forested, low-elevation (1,962 feet) lake is a nice place to camp
when the High Country is snowbound.

Recreational Facilities

ΔΔ **Sierra Shangri-La** 8 stream-side cabins. P.O. Box 285,
Downieville, CA 95936. (916) 289-3455.

Δ **Forest Service Campgrounds** 7 campgrounds along the
lower Yuba, 100 sites; 6 at Bullards Bar Reservoir, 150
sites.

BLUE LEAD MINES

Camptonville (elevation, 2,800 feet) was on the road to the
Northern Mines and therefore saw its share of "knights of the
road" "playing the coaches," as they say. Dutch Kate, from

Marysville, a woman who could swear, smoke, and gamble like the best of them, was, so far as is known, the only member of the fairer sex to join this ancient fraternity. Alas, Kate chose a stage whose strong-box was empty, and she chivalrously declined to examine a woman passenger's purse. Too bad—the lady later revealed that it was heavy with $15,000 dollars in gold. Comptonville is a sleepy place now, with only half a dozen '49er-era houses left. No mining exists.

Not so at **Alleghany** (elevation 4,400 feet), a town whose houses cling to the side of the canyon like a cluster of cliff swallows' nests. The Sixteen-to-One Mine produced a nugget that weighed nearly twelve pounds. Much of the town burned a few years ago, but Casey's Place, the saloon, survived. Heads turned with a "who's that guy?" look when I walked in. "You from around here?," the barmaid asked suspiciously, knowing full well that I wasn't. "Nah, I'm from the North Fork," I explained nonchalantly, hoping she wouldn't pursue the subject long enough to learn that I only have a vacation cabin there. A dozen miners, their boots mud splattered, were sitting at the bar; a knapsack with a shovel handle sticking out was propped up next to the door. The wooden floor looked a bit like a well-used washboard; it seemed the perfect replica of what Dame Shirley reported:

> On ball nights the bar was closed, and everything was very quiet and respectable. To be sure, there was some danger of being swept away in a flood of tobacco juice; but luckily the floor was uneven, and it lay around in puddles, which with care one could avoid, merely running the minor risk of falling prostrate upon the wet boards, in the midst of a galopade.

Given the setting, I guess I shouldn't have been surprised to hear Bing Crosby singing "White Christmas" on the juke box, even though it was late spring.

The canyons and draws around Alleghany are dotted with rusting stamp mills that haven't been used in a century, but you nevertheless see newly bulldozed roads plunging down the hillsides. A hand-lettered sign hanging from a cable across one read: "NO TRESPASSING DURING MUCKING OPERATIONS." Rob Bonner, a fellow who has roamed these canyons all his life, told me: "Red-neck gold-miner is redundant, you know. And sometimes a shot-gun welcome awaits those that get too nosy."

A dirt road (slow in spots) continues east from Alleghany, crossing the Sierra at **Henness Pass** on a route used by the '49ers. But it is the **Foote's Crossing** road to North Bloomfield that provides the best illustration of the perils of early-day travel. At one point the road, barely wide enough for a car, teeters out over a stupendous cliff on a dry-wall masonry structure. It's the perfect place to reflect on Dame Shirley's experience:

> For more than a mile we drove along the edge of a precipice, and so near, that it seemed to me, should the horses deviate a hair's breadth from their usual track, we must be dashed into eternity. Wonderful to relate, I did not oh! nor ah! nor shriek *once*, but remained crouched in the back of the wagon as silent as death. When we were again in safety, the driver exclaimed in the classic *patois* of New England, 'Wall, I guess yer the fust woman that ever rode over that are hill without hollering.' He evidently did not know that it was the intensity of my *fear* that kept me so still.

Definitely not a drive for the faint of heart.

Highway 49 crosses the Middle Yuba at Oregon Creek, site of a fine covered bridge (nice swimming and picnicking). The road then climbs to curiously named **North San Juan** (population 125; elevation 2,115 feet). The Brass Rail saloon occupies a portion of the most interesting building in town: a typical gold rush iron-shuttered, two-story brick beauty with a covered side-walk out front. Across the street is another handsome old build-ing, which upon closer inspection proves to be exactly one brick deep. The rest of the structure, including the roof, is brand new and made of tin.

The three forks of the Yuba River, as anyone can plainly see, run from east to west, joining near the valley city of Marysville. But it wasn't always so. Before the tilting of the Sierra, a tertiary river (to use the geologist's term) known as the Blue Lead ran north to south, bisecting the range at the present 3,000- to 4,000-foot level. Much of the gold found in the northern mines was dug out of that ancient river. **Malakoff Diggins State Historic Park** provides the best illustration of how that came about. Water to wash the gravel was brought down from the High

Country in flumes and then piped through monstrous hoses, which were connected to nozzles known as monitors. By this process, called "hydraulicking," whole mountains were washed down into sluice boxes where the gold was extracted. In the operation, millions of tons of "slikins" were dumped into the Yuba, where storm waters transported it to valley farms, destroying crops and laying the land to waste. A Marysville farmer named Woodruff sued the North Bloomfield Gravel and Mining Company and won. The 1884 landmark decision set down by Judge Lorenzo Sawyer not only forced the company to cease operations but helped to codify California law on actions that affect a neighbor's property. Experts speculate that $5 billion worth of gold remains locked in the gravels of The Blue Lead.

Surprisingly, the Malakoff Diggins is gorgeous, especially after a snowfall. An entire hillside, over a mile long, was exposed, leaving multicolored pinnacles, fantastic minarets, and a milk-colored lake. Pines have grown back, giving the place the look of a miniature Bryce Canyon. The miners lived in nearby **North Bloomfield** (population 9; elevation 3,306 feet), now part of the state park. Walking down the main street, you seem to be in a time warp. Graceful locusts shade a half-dozen white clapboard houses graced with freshly mowed lawns. Ostrom's Livery Stable has been restored, as has Saint Columncille's Catholic Church, and the quiet paved street is lined with mining paraphernalia, including a "Hendy Giant," the biggest monitor ever. The gazebo, built by the state, is a wonderful place for a picnic. But this isn't the way North Bloomfield looked in its mining days. As one miner put it:

> The streets are half a leg deep in filth and mud, rendering getting about awful beyond description. The city is one great cesspool of mud, offal, garbage, dead animals and that worst of nuisances consequent upon the entire absence of outhouses.

And a well-tended lawn was only a dream in homesick muckers' minds.

A hiking trail drops down to the Yuba, and another wanders six miles through mining debris to a BLM campground. A reasonably good dirt road continues on to the tiny village of **Graniteville** (elevation 4,961 feet). Ormand Show, who lives there much of the year, told me that the residents all have telephones, but they can only call around town; the lines don't connect with the rest of the world. Homes are provided with water from a ditch that serpentines down the ridge, passing each lot in its turn. (In some communities water is still sold by the "miner's inch," meaning the amount that comes out of an inch-square hole in the side of a ditch.)

Recreational mining is popular at **Washington** (elevation 2,612 feet). Some of the land is private, but on public sections of the river, all inactive mining claims were extinguished in 1969. Today's '89ers use suction pumps to rework gravels, a sport that has become so popular that seasons are now in effect and a permit to operate a dredge must be obtained from the Department of Fish and Game. Dévotees read the *California Mining Journal* and buy books explaining the difference between "coarse gold" (trapped by a 10-mesh screen), "medium" (20-mesh), and "flour" (12,000 "colors" per troy ounce). While hanging out at the Pioneer Mining Supplies store in Auburn, I learned all kinds of interesting things, such as how to set up a trummel to look for day-flood gold along a skim bar. In the old days it was hard work, as one miner reported:

> George, I tell you this mining among the mountains is a dog's life. A man has to make a jackass of himself packing loads over mountains that God never designed man to climb, a barbarian by foregoing all the comforts of civilized life, and a heathen by depriving himself of all communication with men away from his immediate circle. When I first saw the men carrying heavy stones in the sun, standing nearly waist-deep in water, and grubbing with their hands in the gravel and clay, there seemed to me little virtue in resisting the temptation to gold-digging; but when the shining particles were poured out lavishly from a tin basin, I confess there was a sudden itching in my fingers to seize the heaviest crowbar and the biggest shovel.

Another said simply:

> I can truly say, with the blacksmith's apprentice at the close of his first day's work at the anvil, that "I am sorry I learned the trade."

From Washington, a good road joins Highway 20, which continues on up Washington Ridge, eventually meeting Interstate 80 (Chapter 1). It's a pretty drive: one vista point overlooks the hydraulic workings at the Alpha and Omega Mine; another, the Sierra Buttes.

Two interesting routes go from North San Juan to Nevada City. The shorter, Highway 49, drops steeply into the V-shaped canyon of the South Yuba, where it crosses the rock-bound river on a handsome arched concrete bridge. The nearby **Independence Trail** is so named because it is one of the few places where handicapped people can enjoy the rugged outdoors. Using largely volunteer labor and private donations, a nonprofit group acquired the abandoned Excelsior Ditch and converted it into a path suitable for wheelchairs. Seven miles of canyon are now served by the trail, which twists through dense forests and soars across side canyons on what used to be flumes but are now simple board walkways. When I commented on the elaborateness of a ramp that leads down to a little stream, John Olmsted, the project director, said simply: "Well, if you're in a wheelchair and want to go fishing, this is what you've got to have." Fittingly, there is a telephone a mile down the trail, now used for emergency only. Fitting, because the world's first long-distance phone service is said to have taken place along this canal. The need was urgent; ditch tenders had to call dam tenders to regulate the flow.

An alternate route is to take the county road that goes southwest to **French Corral** (great old Wells Fargo building) and then crosses the Yuba near the **Bridgeport Bridge,** the longest still-extant covered bridge in world. The little park is nice for swimming and picnicking. Until the 1950s the Yuba Consolidated Gold Fields Company operated a dredge near **Timbuctoo.** Bill Derby, a fellow who used to run the giant machine, told me that in a good week he could mine an acre of bottomland, even though in places the gravels were as much as 120 feet deep. **Rough and Ready,** a mining town named for Zachary Taylor, is an interesting place to stop on the way back to Highway 49.

Recreational Facilities

△ **State Park Campground** 30 campsites. (916) 265-2740.

△ **BLM Campground** South Yuba, 14 sites.

△ **Forest Service Campgrounds** 2 campgrounds on Washington Ridge, 60 sites.

NEVADA CITY • Population 2,840; elevation 2,525 feet

The events that shaped Nevada City's existence occurred during the reign of Queen Victoria, and the place is much better for that bit of happenstance. A hundred or more houses from that era survive, making this town rival Washington's Port Townsend as the "Victorian Capital of the West." An early visitor wrote:

> The city is upon the hillsides, on the ridges, among the streams and over them; the muddy water rushing beneath houses, stores and hotels and through the streets, splashing and gurgling as if uttering self-congratulatory hymns for its escape from the torturing cradles, long toms and sluices.

The town began as simply Nevada and was at one time the third largest metropolis in California. Fourteen years later the word City was added when, despite local protests, the new state, carved out of Utah Territory, was named Nevada. Former mayor Bob Paine told me that a hundred years later, the editor of the local newspaper, Bob Ingram, recognizing an injustice, wrote Governor Lexalt insisting that he change the name of his state to something else. Too many people, Ingram reasoned, were getting Nevada confused with Nevada City. But in a strange way this town must share the blame, for it was here in 1859 that some grungy Washoe prospectors wandered into the assay office carrying some blue muck that proved rich in silver. The rush to the Comstock was on (Chapter 15).

Several local citizens went on to achieve world renown. Emma Wixom, born at the Alpha and Omega Mine, learned to sing, changed her name to Emma Nevada, and became a favorite coloratura singer of such luminaries as Giuseppe Verdi and Charles Gounod. Heinrich Schliemann, famed as the discoverer of ancient Troy, worked in the mines here for a while, as did Herbert Hoover.

Nevada City would be a perfect relic of early California, but Caltrans, showing great sensitivity, built a freeway through the middle of the business district. The iron-shuttered brick buildings that remain line narrow, steeply ascending streets. (Like most of the Highway 49 towns we will visit, a walking-around map describing the more interesting buildings is available from either the local museum or the chamber of commerce.) Gas lights still illuminate Nevada City's sidewalks. Tourists have discovered the place, and merchants have responded. Eight city blocks are lined with gift shops, art galleries, antique stores, and well-decorated restaurants with excellent kitchens. The theater, said to be the oldest in the state, supports amateur productions. Claiming to be the oldest continuously operating hostelry west of the Rocky Mountains, the National Hotel has a fine bar and comfortable upstairs lobby boasting a square grand piano that came around Cape Horn. A sign proclaims that two men met in room 74 and started what became the Pacific Gas and Electric Company. The hotel is a bit more upscale than what Dame Shirley reported:

> The Empire is the only two-story building in town, and absolutely has a live "up-stairs." Here you will find two or three glass windows, an unknown luxury in all the other dwellings. It is built of planks of the roughest possible description; the roof, of course, is covered with canvas, which also forms the entire front of the house. I must mention that the floor is so uneven that no article of furniture gifted with four legs pretends to stand upon but three at once, so that the chairs, tables, etc., remind you constantly of a dog with a sore foot.

Recreational Facilities

- ✔✔ **Grandmere's** 6-Room B&B in a three-story colonial-revival home with a grand porch overlooking a garden. 449 Broad Street, Nevada City, CA 95959. (916) 265-4660.

- ✔✔ **Flume's End B&B** 3 rooms. 317 South Pine Street, Nevada City, CA 95959. (916) 265-9665.

- ✔✔ **Downey House** 6-room B&B. 517 West Broad Street, Nevada City, CA 95959. (916) 265-2815.

- ✔✔ **National Hotel** Historic 44-room downtown hotel, restaurant, and bar. 211 Broad Street, Nevada City, CA 95959. (916) 265-2245.

- ✔✔ **The Parsonage** 3-room B&B. 427 Broad Street, Nevada City, CA 95959. (916) 265-9478.

✔✔ **Red Castle Inn** 8-room B&B on the hillside east of the freeway. 109 Prospect Street, Nevada City, CA 95959. (916) 265-5135.

✔ **Nevada Queen Motel** 75 units. 400 Railroad Avenue, Nevada City, CA 95959. (916) 265-5824.

✔ **Piety Hill Inn** 7-room former "auto court," now refurnished as a B&B. 523 Sacramento Street, Nevada City, CA 95959. (916) 265-2245.

● **The Country Rose** French cuisine. (916) 265-6248.

● **Michael's Garden Restaurant** (916) 265-6660.

● **Cerino's** Italian restaurant. (916) 265-2246.

GRASS VALLEY • Population 8,300; elevation 2,420 feet

Compared to Nevada City, Grass Valley is big and boisterous, a town that is enjoying phenomenal growth. The climate is nice, so retirees are moving here, and industry is too because land is cheap and there is a good labor supply. The result is that two large shopping centers have been built, one halfway to Nevada City, the other south of town. But Grass Valley has its "old town" too, and it is nice because it's not too touristy. While downing a beer at the Owl Tavern on Mill Street, the thought came to me that the historical archives of California would be greatly enriched if someone would do exhaustive, on-site research into the history of the back-bars of the Mother Lode. Many were carved in Europe and brought around the Horn in sailing ships. This would be a fine place to begin. Across the street the glass-domed Nevada County Bank building hovers over sidewalks covered with tin awnings. Sadly, the hardware store, said to be the oldest in the West, closed recently.

The handsome public library is built on the birth site of Josiah Royce, a man once described as "America's greatest thinker." Royce, one of the first graduates of the University of California, studied in Leipzig before becoming a professor of philosophy at Harvard. His mother, Sarah Royce, came across the plains in '49 and wrote about her experiences in *A Frontier Lady,* a classic. A couple of blocks south, on Mill Street, are the homes of two famous ladies, Lotta Crabtree and Lola Montez. The latter houses the Nevada County Chamber of Commerce and a small **museum.** Lotta was the successful one, but it is Lola who holds our interest (see below).

The Founder of Today's Cosmetics Industry

She shares a place in history alongside the likes of Lily Langtree and perhaps Zsa-Zsa Gabor. Born Eliza Gilbert, she took the name Lola Montez after a brief visit to Spain. Historian Joseph Henry Jackson said of her: "There was an aura of delicious scandal about her. She was graceful and she was beautiful and that was enough." With a flair for style and an Irish temper, she dazzled Europe's most illustrious intelligentsia. Alexander Dumas, Franz List, and Victor Hugo were said to have been her lovers; King Ludwig I of Bavaria rewarded her "charms" by bestowing upon her the titles Baroness Rosenthal and Countess of Landsfeldt. Whether it was her looks or her art that attracted the crowds it is difficult to say, but the enthusiasm shown by the ruffians of San Francisco when she performed her famous "spider dance" can well be imagined.

In 1853, the countess married Patrick Hull, a San Francisco newspaperman, and carted him off to Grass Valley. When Patrick shot her pet grizzly bear, she threw him out. For the next two years Lola captured Grass Valley's fancy, entertaining the more wealthy of its citizens. John Southwick, part-owner of the Empire mine, financed her lavish parties and found himself nearly penniless, prompting him to seek safer quarters at the state asylum for the insane in Stockton. When the shy, retiring editor of the *Grass Valley Telegraph* wrote a disparaging column about Lola's dancing skills, she appeared in his office with a snake whip and lashed the hapless fellow to within an inch of his life. A few weeks later he committed suicide.

But Lola also had an eye for talent, encouraging her six-year-old neighbor to accompany her to nearby Rough and Ready, where she had the young lass do a dance atop a blacksmith's anvil. Her career thus launched, Lotta Crabtree became one of the most highly paid actresses of the day and died a millionaire. (Lotta's Fountain is a San Francisco landmark). Lola's life, alas, went the other way. Tiring of Grass Valley, she attempted a terpsichorean comeback, but age had taken its toll. The Countess of Landsfeldt, née Lola Montez, née Eliza Gilbert died penniless in New York at the age of forty-three. E Clampus Vitus placed a plaque in front of her house, which reads:

In her home which occupied this site, Lola's social salons attracted men of vision whose investments in technology founded Nevada County's gold quartz mining industry. She brought culture and refinement to this rude mining camp. A mistress of international intrigue and a feminist before her time, she is one of history's most recognizable women and founder of today's cosmetic industry.

One George Knight went chasing after an errant cow. Rushing to retrieve the wandering beast, he stubbed his toe on a protruding rock. Looking closer, he saw gold imbedded in quartz, and thus hard-rock mining came into existence. At least that's what the plaque at the top of Gold Hill says. Others insist that it wasn't George at all, but Bennager Rasberry, and he didn't stub his toe, he just happened to be sitting there picking the daisies, and, in fact, he didn't even own a cow. Whichever, lead (also called lode) mining started in Grass Valley and has shaped its character ever since. The financing was American but the miners came from Cornwall, where their ancestors had been working deep tin mines for centuries. So many friends and relatives followed that they became known as "Cousin Jacks," and by 1890 the Cornish comprised eighty-five percent of Grass Valley's citizenry. They worked in legendary mines, the Idaho-Maryland, North Star, and Eureka. Gradually, these holdings were consolidated, with the survivor, appropriately enough the Empire, being one of the richest and most long-lasting in the country. The gold taken out is said to have equaled a cube seven feet on a side weighing 6 million ounces and, at today's prices, would be worth $2 billion. But the pumps were shut down in 1956 after 107 years of production, and the property was given to the State.

Most of the equipment at the **Empire Mine State Historic Park** was sold off, but a scattering of buildings houses a few relics from the glory days. Only the foundations, however, remain of the massive mill, which once had a battery of eighty stamps, each of which weighed 1700 pounds. The noise could be heard in Nevada City, seven miles away. The most visible part of the mine is no longer extant; the eight-story-high headframe was torn down because park officials in Sacramento felt that there were "potential liability concerns." Only forty feet of the underground operation is open to visitors, probably for the same reason. (The smaller Rowe mine headframe is barely visible behind a wire fence across the road.) Tunnels, *367 miles* of them, lace the underground, the deepest shaft plunging almost a mile into the earth. The three-dimensional model used by the mining engineers shows shafts, stopes, and winzes extending beneath the heart of downtown Grass Valley, several miles away. Mules employed to haul the ore lived their entire lives underground, in time becoming sightless because there was virtually nothing to see. (The story is told of an Eastern investor, noticing large expenditures for candles, who wrote to the mine superintendent instructing him to get more of his work done in the daytime.) Pride of the park is the circa-1900 "cottage" built by William Bourn, Jr. Designed by Willis Polk, this handsome English manor-style, two-story rock building is set amid a lovely garden, which the state seems more concerned with saving than the mine itself. This, incidentally, was the Bourn's summer digs, their main residence being Filoli ("fight bravely, love bravely, live bravely"), a forty-three-room mansion set on a 600-acre site on the San Francisco Peninsula.

To get a better sense of the technology used in hard-rock mining, pay a visit to the power house of the North Star Mine, which houses the **Grass Valley Mining Museum.** This nonprofit group does a fine job explaining exactly what the miners did in those horrible dank depths. The collection of photographs is especially interesting. The largest Pelton wheel ever built, thirty feet in diameter, is here. Exhibit Director Glenn Jones also showed me a still-working Cornish pump, the technological marvel imported from Great Britain that made mining at such depths possible.

Trains used to steam over the hill to Colfax, where they met the Southern Pacific main line. Officially, this was the Nevada County Narrow Gauge Railroad (N.C.N.G.), but the locals soon dubbed it the "Never Come, Never Go." In 1942 it got up and went. So did the twin towns of You Bet and Red Dog, much to the relief of Caltrans, which for many years kept having to replace a roadsign alongside Highway 40 that read:

YOU BET 5

RED DOG 6

The signs somehow kept reappearing in fraternity houses at Stanford and Cal.

Recreational Facilities

✔✔ **Murphy's Inn** Lovely 8-room B&B. 318 Neal Street, Grass Valley, CA 95945. (916) 273-6873.

✔✔ **Domike's Inn** 5-room B&B. 220 Colfax Avenue, Grass Valley, CA 95945. (916) 273-9010.

✔✔ **Annie Horan's** 4-room B&B. 415 West Main, Grass Valley, CA 95945. (916) 272-2418.

✔✔ **Golden Ore House** 8-room B&B. 446 South Auburn Street, Grass Valley, CA 95945. (916) 272-6870.

✔✔ **The Holbrooke** 18-room restored grand hotel. 212 West Main, Grass Valley, CA 95945. (916) 273-1353.

✔✔ **Swan-Levine House** 4-room B&B. 328 South Church Street, Grass Valley, CA 95945. (916) 272-1873.

✔ **Best Western Gold Country Inn** 80-unit motel. 11972 Sutton Way, Grass Valley, CA 95945. (916) 273-1393.

✔ **Holiday Lodge** 36-unit motel. 1221 East Main, Grass Valley, CA 95945. (916) 273-4406.

● **Empire House** Bar and restaurant. (916) 273-8272.

AUBURN • Population 9,000; elevation 1,255 feet

Once-sleepy little Auburn, now the largest city in the Gold Country, is rapidly becoming Sacramento's bedroom. Nevertheless, the town happily retains much of its '49er-era charm. The hilly countryside prevented orderly expansion, so two business districts developed, "upper town" or, more properly, Auburn itself, and what the locals used to call "L.A." (Lower Auburn), now "Old Town." Old Town, only a couple of blocks long, has three saloons (the Shanghai is the best, meaning the raunchiest), several restaurants trying to be quaint, and a half-dozen shops that sell antiques. The handsome court house, undergoing renovation, is scheduled to become a historical museum.

Upper town seems more real. Louie Clump's harness shop is gone, but the Auburn Drug Company still has its marble-countered soda fountain and the pool hall across the street (snooker is the preferred game) hasn't changed in sixty years. (The ghost of Elmer, the bartender, sees to it that the smell doesn't change either.) Auburn is blessed with two nice museums located at the Fair Grounds. The **Gold Country Museum** has the kind of exhibits you would expect to find at a place with that name; the **Bernhard Museum Complex** includes a Victorian house, once a hotel, and an old winery that now houses an art gallery.

Recreational Faculties

- ✔✔ **Powers Mansion Inn** 13-room downtown B&B. 164 Cleveland Avenue, Auburn, CA, 95603. (916) 885-1166.

- ✔ **Auburn Inn** 80-unit motel on I-80. 1875 Auburn Ravine Road, Auburn, CA, 95603. (916) 885-1800.

- ✔ **Best Western Golden Key Motel** 50-unit motel on I-80. 13450 Lincoln Way, Auburn, CA, 95603. (916) 885-8611.

- ✔ **Country Squire Inn** 80-unit motel on I-80. 13480 Lincoln Way, Auburn, CA, 95603. (916) 885-7025.

- • **Butterworth's Dining** Old-Auburn restaurant in a Victorian mansion. (916) 885-0249.

Though these foothills are indeed "hills," the depressions that separate them are by no means valleys, they are *canyons*. The gorge of the American River is a thousand feet deep, with walls so steep there is hardly room for a burrow track. Highway 49 wiggles its way down and then right back up again as it heads off toward Coloma, the place where the rush began.

◄◄◄◄◄◆ 18 ◆►►►►►

THE CENTRAL MINES

The New El Dorado

Henry William Bigler sat in his tent beside the American River and penned a few lines in his diary. The date was January 24, 1848; his words would prove momentous.

> This day some kind of mettle was ~~discover~~ found in the tail race ~~that~~ that that was goald first discovered by J. A. N. Martail.

Forty miles away in Sacramento City, Captain John Sutter received an employee:

> Mr. Marshall arrived at my office in the Fort, very wet. He told me then that he had some important and interesting news which he wished to communicate secretly to me, and wished me to go to a place where we would not be disturbed. He began to show me this metal which consisted of small pieces and specimens, some of them worth a few dollars. After having proved the metal with aqua fortis, which I found in my apothecary shop, likewise with other experiments and read the long article "gold" in the Encyclopedia Americana, I declared this to be gold of the finest quality, of at least 23 carats. After this Mr. M. had no more rest nor patience, and wanted me to start with him immediately for Coloma. I gave

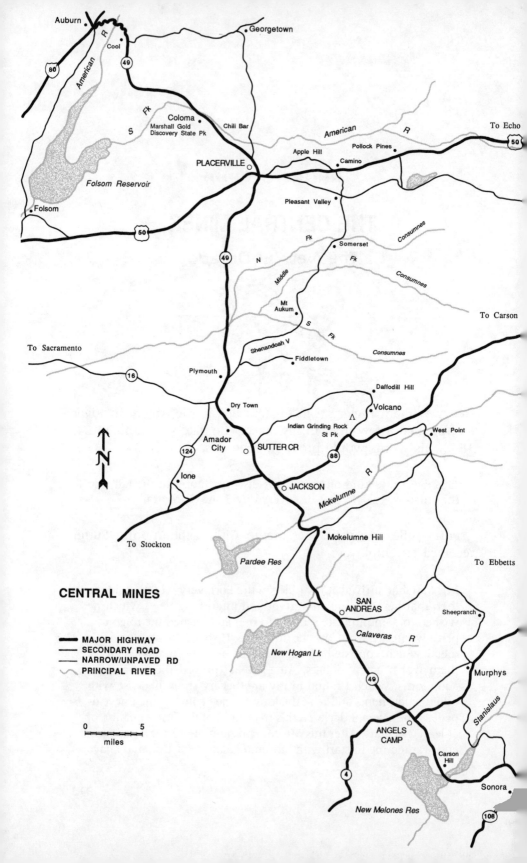

all my necessary orders and left the next morning and rode up to the new Eldorado.

Sutter's world was about to go to hell in a handbasket.

So soon as the secret was out my laborers began to leave me, in small parties first, but then all left, from the clerk to the cook, and I was in great distress.

Within days, the canyons were swarming with prospectors; within months, with the hangers on too. An observer wrote:

Sometimes a company of these wanderers will find itself upon a bar, where a few pieces of the precious metal scattered upon the surface of the ground; of course they immediately "prospect" it, which is accomplished, by "panning out" a few basins full of the soil. If it "pays," they "claim" the spot and build their shanties; the news spreads that wonderful "diggings" have been discovered at such a place,—the monte-dealers, those worse than fiends, rush vulture-like upon the scene and erect a tent, where, in gambling, drinking, swearing and fighting, the *many* reproduce Pandemonium in more than its original horror, while a *few* honestly and industriously commence digging for gold, and lo! as if a fairy's wand had been waved above the bar, a full-grown mining town hath sprung into existence.

Thousands of fairy-tale towns did grow up, and by the close of the century 2,000 tons of gold had been taken from California mines, enough to make a cube fifty-seven feet on a side. At today's prices it would fetch $22 billion. How much found its way into the monte dealers' pockets we'll never know, but of the hundreds of thousands of Argonauts who came, only a few retired rich. Most were like the "pocket miner" Mark Twain observed:

I have known one of them to hunt patiently about the hillsides every day for eight months without finding gold enough to make a snuffbox—his grocery bill running up relentlessly all the time— and then find a pocket and take out of it two thousand dollars in two dips of his shovel. I have known him to take out three thousand dollars in two hours, and go and pay up every cent of his indebtedness, and then enter on a dazzling spree that finished the last of his treasure before the night was gone. And the next day he bought his groceries on credit as usual, and shouldered his pan and shovel and went off to the hills hunting pockets again happy and content.

THE AMERICAN RIVER AND THE GEORGETOWN DIVIDE

James Marshall made his discovery at Coloma, nineteen miles south of Auburn on the American River's south fork. You can drive there in half an hour, but you'll miss some interesting country, so instead, after crossing the middle fork, turn left at the little town of Cool (one day it reported the highest temperature in the country) and head up the Georgetown Divide. Growlersburg seems more, well, more of a Gold Countryish name, and it stuck for a while because the nuggets they found here were so big they made a growling sound when washed about in the pan. But it is now **Georgetown** (population 2,000; elevation 2,654 feet), a pleasant village on the verge of the timbered Sierra. A half-dozen old brick buildings decorate the two-block-long main street. Highway 193 turns south here, crossing the South Fork of the American River at **Chili Bar,** California's most popular white-water put-in. More than forty commercial outfitters have permits to run the South Fork, because it is accessible and river flows are regulated, allowing for Class III rafting all summer. Twenty river miles are run in two segments, Chili Bar to Coloma (2.5 hours), and Coloma to Folsom Lake (6 hours), allowing either half-day, full-day, or two-day trips. You are treated to the excitement of Meatgrinder Rapids, Racehorse Bend, Triple Threat, Trouble Maker, Old Scary, and Satan's Cesspool before easing into the Recovery Room near Hospital Bar.

The American River canyon loses its abruptness near **Coloma** (population 500; elevation 750 feet). The bottomlands have a gentle feel, which is probably why John Sutter chose this site for his memorable sawmill. The State of California purchased much of the land, making it into the lovely **Marshall Gold Discovery State Historic Park,** which occupies the south bank of the river. Rusting machinery sits out front of the large and elaborate museum. Floods long ago destroyed the sawmill, but the state built a replica and a number of houses have been restored, including the one John Marshall lived in until 1879. A forty-foot-tall statue of the man, erected a hundred years ago by the Sons of the Golden West, stands atop a knoll, his finger pointing to the spot where he found the color. For the life of me I can't understand why he is held in such esteem. If Marshall hadn't, someone, perhaps a scoundrel of the worst kind, would have found the gold eventually. John Bidwell called Marshall half-crazy, harebrained, and noted that if he had built the sawmill in the right place he would never had made his discovery:

> The Mill would not run because the wheel was placed too low. It was an old-fashioned flutter wheel that propelled an upright saw. The gravelly bar below backed the water up and stopped the wheel. The remedy was to dig a channel or tail-race.

Coloma is a mellow town, a wonderful place for a picnic. Rafters paddle by; kids swim in the river when the weather is warm. I had no trouble at all imagining Henry Biegler's activities the Sunday after the great discovery. Mining hadn't yet gone high-tech with the various gadgets used to separate gold from gravel.

> That morning I said I was going over the river opposite the mill to see if I could find any, Mr. Barger said he would go with me, and over we went taking nothing but our jackknives. Indeed we knew nothing about washing it out. I believe the whole pile of mill hands were perfectly green. There were no such things thought of by us as long toms, or short toms, or rockers, or sluices. I believe there was something said about tin pans, but we had none. Our only way was to pick it up grain by grain as we found it lying on the bare rocks, or feeling after it in the seams and crevices of the exposed rocks with our knives. At night, Barger and myself between us had about ten dollars according to the way we calculated.

Folsom [population 23,000 (including 6,800 prison inmates); elevation 250 feet], a gold town located fifteen miles down river, has gone through a curious metamorphosis. Virtually every merchant along the once-sleepy three-block-long main street relocated to one of several brand-new shopping centers (this is now a Sacramento bedroom community). Artists and antique dealers, sixty in all, moved into the vacant stores. Sundays find the streets crowded with shoppers, the Sutter Street Grill jammed with city folk enjoying brunch. The Wells Fargo assay office, now the **Folsom History Museum,** has a wonderful working model of a gold dredge, and sinister **Folsom Prison** has a gift shop and museum. A paved bicycle trail goes twenty miles to Sacramento, passing **Nimbus Dam,** whose outlet is one of California's best salmon fisheries.

Recreational Facilities

✔✔ **American River Inn** 1899 boarding house, now a 20-room inn. Pool. Main and Orleans Streets, Georgetown, CA 95634. (916) 333-4499.

✔✔ **The Coloma Country Inn** 5-room B&B. P.O. Box 502, Coloma, CA 95613. (916) 622-6919.

✔✔ **The River Rock Inn** New 3-room inn at Chili Bar. P.O. Box 827, Placerville, CA 95667. (916) 622-7640.

✔✔ **The Vineyard House** Restaurant and 7-room B&B. P.O. Box, Coloma, CA 95613. (916) 622-6917.

Ω **Adventure Connection** Raft trips. P.O. Box 475, Coloma, CA 95613. (916) 622-6632.

Ω **ARTA** Raft trips. Star Route 73, Groveland, CA 95321. (209) 962-7873.

Ω **River Rat & Co.** Raft trips. 1669 Chili Bar Court, Placerville, CA 95667. (916) 622-7640.

Ω **Whitewater Connection** Raft trips. P.O. Box 270, Coloma, CA 95613. (916) 622-6446.

PLACERVILLE • Population 6,700; elevation 1,848 feet

Anybody will tell you that Placerville used to be Hangtown before it grew to such importance that the more upright citizens felt obliged to seek another name. Just who, or how many, dangled from the tree at the center of town is uncertain; some say it was two Frenchmen and a Chilean, others three members of the Owl Gang, and a few insist that it was a particularly nasty fellow named "Bloody Dick." Perhaps all of the above. Whichever, Placerville was the end of the road for thousands of pioneers who had spent months on the trail imagining what they might find when they got here:

> Hangtown gals are plump and rosy,
> Hair in ringlets, mighty cozy;
> Painted cheeks and jossy bonnets,
> Touch 'em and they'll sting like hornets!

Placerville has managed to maintain its gold-rush image in spite of U.S. Highway 50 bisecting the town. The city built a large garage, thus discouraging out-of-town malls, so shoppers enjoy old-world charm. I bought a pair of red suspenders (the kind the loggers use to hold up their jeans) at the local mercantile store. The ceiling was fifteen feet high and made of tin, the floors oiled and ancient. The clerk took out a sales book and wrote out "suspenders," giving me one copy. She made change from a wooden drawer. Placerville is not a tourist town, but visitors have a choice of several good restaurants. On special occasions, the miners ate well too, as Dame Shirley remarked:

There were oysters, which, I am sure, could not have been nicer had they just slid from their shells on the shore at Amboy; salmon, in color like the "red, red gold"; venison, with a fragrant, spicy gusto, as if it had been fed on cedar buds; beef cooked in the Spanish fashion—that is, strung on to a skewer, and roasted on the coals. Then for drinkables, we had tea, coffee and chocolate, champagne, claret and porter, with stronger spirits *for* the stronger spirits.

Oysters have endured; chefs add eggs and bacon to make a popular concoction called "Hangtown fry." Present-day diners, fortunately, enjoy a higher level of service. Shirley continued:

Last night, one of our neighbors had a dinner party. He came in to borrow a teaspoon. "Had you not better take them all?" I said. "Oh, no" was the answer, "that would be too much luxury. My guests are not used to it, and they would think that I was getting aristocratic, and putting on airs. One is enough, they can pass it round from one to the other."

On April 13, 1860, one Sam Hamilton rode into town, flung his precious packet of letters to the next rider, and allowed the adoring crowd to escort him to the Carey House for a drink. The Pony Express had arrived. We can assume that Sam met the criteria for Pony Express riders:

> Young, skinny, wiry, not over eighteen. Must be expert riders willing to risk death daily. Orphans preferred.

Philip Armour ran a butcher shop here, but he returned East to go into the meat-packing business on a grand scale. Another fellow was called "Jonny Wheelbarrow" because he made the best ones the miners could buy (one is displayed at the **El Dorado County Museum,** located at the fairgrounds). Returning to South Bend, Indiana, he joined his brothers in founding the Studebaker automobile company. The tiny downtown **Placerville Museum** is open on weekends; picnicking is nice at **Gold Bug Park,** where two mine shafts can be explored during the summer.

Foothill Wine Country

> Youthful, raspberry, blackcherry scents are intermingled with black pepper, vanillin and herbaceous notes in a complex, rather intriguing nose that leads to big and fruity sensations in the mouth.

Sonoma snobbery? Napa nabobbery? No. Sierra foothills embroidery! Wine making in this part of California has entered the big leagues. So tourism is beginning to follow. It has been a long time coming. Charles Nordhoff passed through here in 1873 and wrote:

> On our way through Tuolumne County, at Columbia, our stagecoach was stopped to water the horses. As the day was warm, some of us asked for water, whereupon a man standing at the gate of the farmhouse remarked, "If you prefer wine, there is a wine-cellar at the house." Accordingly we walked up to the house and found a cellar well stocked with wine—a red which they call claret here, but which is thin, and to my taste too strong for claret, and a very sweet angelica, almost like syrup.

The claret Nordhoff referred to is now known by its varietal name, zinfandel, the wine that made the district famous. These foothills are directly east of a gap in the Coast Range; cooling ocean breezes are sucked into the Golden Gate, dodge up through the dogleg of Carquinez Strait, and head for El Dorado and Amador counties. Lodi, which catches the winds first, has long been a jug-wine center. Up here, the soil, altitude, and topography combine to favor the premiums. "Why zinfandel?," I asked Sohung Magee at the Sobon winery. "Because it grows so easily," was her simple reply. In the 1980s white zinfandel, with its light, picnicky style, took the country by storm, but mostly it is the hard-red, robusty zin that is earning the medals. Oenophiles have discovered that these hillsides are every bit as lovely as Napa and Sonoma, and a weekend drive is even better, for there is history here too, manifested in gold rush-era buildings housing first-class restaurants and nostalgic B&Bs. City dwellers can spend a weekend living out a fantasy of turn-of-the-century country charm.

Wine making on a premium scale is a recent event. Traditionally, the foothills surrounding Placerville have seen orchards planted to pears, plums, cherries, and particularly apples. **Apple Hill,** located northeast of town, is a wonderful area with dozens of little back-country lanes (perfect for bicycling) wiggling about over hill and dale. Forty-five family ranches open fruit stands in the fall, selling apples, cider, walnuts and pears, and baked goods too: pies, turnovers, cheesecake, and tarts. And Christmas trees. So the wineries only add a new dimension to this festive scene.

Both El Dorado and Amador counties publish maps showing which wineries are open for tasting. A nice day trip is to take Carson Road out of Placerville, loop around to Pleasant Valley, and cross into Amador County on the Mt. Aukum and Shenandoah roads. Boeger Winery is open daily; Lava Cap has a nice deck overlooking the American River. Fitzpatrick is unique in that it includes a new B&B on top of a hill. The D'Agostini facility, oldest in the district, is now called Sobon Estate. A century-old fig tree, planted by Adam Uhlinger, a Swiss emigré, shades the picnic area. Monteviña has one of the largest tasting rooms and a vine-covered picnic area out back. Steiner Road leads to Amador Foothill Winery, Shenandoah Vineyards, and the Santino Winery. The latter two have art galleries on the premises.

This rolling countryside, alternately covered with fields, vine-yards, and oak savannahs, has other attractions too. The Forest Service operates its main **nursery** near Apple Hill, open to the public. Nearby is the Forest Genetics Research Center, where a short trail through the grounds provides a pleasant interlude. **Fiddletown** is one of those places that almost, but not quite died. Early settlers from Missouri played the fiddle, so the histo-rians say, but locals insist people just come here to fiddle around. Half a dozen gold rush-era buildings remain, including an old-timey general store. Back on Highway 49, **Dry Town** was named for the dry creek, not the condition of the saloon's shelves. Melodrama with oleo performances are given throughout the summer. Nearby **Amador City** is a gem, nestled in a little oak-studded draw. Two recently restored hotels, an art gallery, and two or three antique shops line the main street.

Recreational Facilities

✔✔ **Cary House** Historic 17-room downtown hotel. 300 Main, Placerville, CA 95667. (916) 622-4271.

✔✔ **Chichester House** 3-room Victorian B&B. 800 Spring Street, Placerville, CA 95667. (916) 626-1882.

✔✔ **Fitzpatrick** Winery and 4-room B&B. Plowman's lunch on weekends. 7740 Fairplay Road, Somerset, CA 95684. (209) 245-3248.

✔✔ **Fleming Jones Homestead** 6-room farmhouse B&B. 3170 Newtown Road, Placerville, CA 95667. (916) 626-5840.

✔ **Best Western Placerville Inn** 100-unit motel. U.S. 50 at Missouri Flat Road, Placerville, CA 95354. (916) 622-9100.

✔ **Gold Trail Motor Lodge** 32 units. 1970 Broadway, Placerville, CA 95667. (916) 622-2906.

● **Smokehouse Restaurant:** (916) 622-1898.

● **Zachary Jacques** Country French restaurant. (916) 626-8045.

SUTTER CREEK • Population 1,925; elevation 1,198 feet

Out-of-state tourists haven't quite discovered this lovely place, but they will, for it is the Mother Lode's version of Mendocino, with a touch of Saint Helena (Napa Valley) thrown in. Highway 49 squiggles through town, bisecting a four-block-long series of handsome hundred-year-old buildings, now almost totally devoted to the tourist trade. Sutter Creek Antiques is the biggest, but there are many more: LaBelle's, Carriage Trade, Liz Anne's, O'Neill's, Fingernail Moon, Columbia Lady, and a place called Treasures of Oro Madre. Alexanders and the Painted Lady sell fine art, the Fiber Store and the Cobweb Collection have excellent craft goods. Mother Lode Handy Works sells rag dolls; boutiques include the Clothes Mine and 32 Main Street. One store advertises "Metaphysical Books, Visionary Arts, Music Tapes, and Classes in Hypnosis." The town has a New England feel, with neat, white-clapboard homes parading up the hillsides and several little steepled country churches. I was particularly taken by the goings-on at Knight's Foundry on Eureka Street, which has been casting gray iron since 1873. Next to the green-sand foundry, thirty or so giant lathes, mills, shapers, and saws are powered by a system of pulleys and belts connected to a single turbine, powered by water brought down from a nearby hill. Owner Herman Nelson, at work in the dimly lit shop, told me they do onesies and twosies now; "Somebody else can have the big jobs." The place, modified with fire protection devices but otherwise left alone to go about its business, would make a fabulous historical museum.

Thirty-six million dollars was taken from the Eureka, but the nearby Lincoln mine has more historical value. Leland Stanford (who owned an interest as a payment for a bad debt) got discouraged and decided to sell out. His partner Robert Downs convinced him otherwise, and what would have been a $5,000 loss turned into a $400,000 gain.

The back roads here are lovely. In the spring, throngs head for **Daffodil Hill,** where a local rancher has planted a whole hillside to flowers. There isn't much to do in **Volcano** (population 250; elevation 2,050 feet), and that's part of its charm. The village is a bit off the mainstream; people who come here are trying to capture the spirit of an older day and, fortunately, the St. George Hotel is the embodiment of that bygone era. This three-story hostelry looks about to fall down, but then it has for a hundred years. Guests lounge in a large, sofa-filled living room with an immense rock fireplace and eat whatever the chef decides to serve in a turn-of-the-century dining room. Owner Chuck Inman told me that Reverend Thomas Starr King once preached here but was quick to add that the records don't reveal the names of any miners being turned from their sinful ways. Today, performances are given during the summer at tiny Cobblestone Theater. Stone facades of once-substantial buildings face one side of Main Street, a couple of gift shops and a small grocery store are on the other. Several picnic tables stand in the bottom of what was once a mine pit. Volcano lingers, dying slowly, reluctantly.

Miwoks gathered near here in the fall to celebrate the harvest and to worship their gods. A thirty-foot-diameter flat limestone outcropping serves as the focus of what is now **Indian Grinding Rock State Historic Park.** Three hundred petroglyphs and a thousand tiny basins *(chaw'se),* used to grind acorns, puncture the soft stone. The state has reconstructed a large round house *(hung-'ge)* and half a dozen bark houses *(u'macha).* A museum portrays the life of these gentle people but, in my view, the best attraction is the magnificent valley oaks that dot the meadows. Clarence King said of them:

> The oaks lock their arms and gather in groves around open slopes of natural park, and you are at home. These islands of modest, lovely verdure floating in an ocean of sunlight, thrill your blood and brain, yet leave you in peace, and not forever challenge you to combat.

It's great picnicking.

Recreational Facilities

✔✔ **The Foxes** 6-room B&B amid a lovely garden in the center of town. 77 Main, Sutter Creek, CA 95685. (209) 267-5882.

✔✔ **Botto Country Inn** 5-room Victorian B&B north of town. 11 Sutter Hill Road, Sutter Creek, CA 95685. (209) 267-5519.

✔✔ **The Gold Quartz Inn** B&B. 15 Bryson Drive, Sutter Creek, CA 95685. (209) 267-9155.

✔✔ **The Hanford House** 8-room B&B. 3 Hanford Street, Sutter Creek, CA 95685. (209) 267-0747.

✔✔ **The Heirloom** 5-room B&B. 214 Shirley Lane, Ione, CA 95640. (209) 274-4468.

✔✔ **Imperial Hotel** Restaurant, wine bar, and 6-room hotel in a renovated brick mercantile building. P.O. Box 195, Amador City, CA 95601. (209) 267-9172.

✔✔ **Mine House Inn** Keystone mine headquarters, now an 8-room B&B. P.O. Box 245, Amador City, CA 95601. (209) 267-5900.

✔✔ **Nancy and Bob's 9 Eureka Street Inn** 5-room B&B. 55 Eureka Street, Sutter Creek, CA 95685. (209) 267-0342.

✔✔ **Sutter Creek Inn** 18-room B&B in the center of town. 75 Main, Sutter Creek, CA 95685. (209) 262-5606.

✔✔ **St. George Hotel** 14 shared-bath rooms in old building. 6 motel rooms in annex. P.O. Box 9, Volcano, CA 95689. (209) 296-4458.

Δ **State Park Campground.** Indian Grinding Rock, 21 sites. (209) 795-2334.

JACKSON • Population 2,300; elevation 1,200 feet

Joseph Henry Jackson, touring the Gold Country in the late 1930s, found the town not to his liking. Writing in *Anybody's Gold,* he observed:

A parade of night-clubs, saloons and neon signs line its main street. Stucco fronts, red and blue neon, and tubular steel bar-stools do seem just a little far from the ghost-town spirit.

I think he was wrong, for in fact he was witnessing the last days of what had been a licentious mining town of the first caliber. Originally called Botilleas for all the bottles that piled up around the local watering hole, Jackson (with Watsonville) became the last town in California to close its whorehouses. A local group calling itself the Environmental Research Committee to Insure Our Natural Services (ERECTIONS) felt that this should not be forgotten. When they installed a heart-shaped plaque in a bank parking lot, the more pious of the citizenry promptly ripped it out. It read:

> Botilleas Bordello. The world's oldest profession flourished fifty yards east of this plaque for many years until this most perfect example of free enterprise was padlocked by unsympathetic politicians.

People still whoop it up in Jackson, especially on Saturday night at the National Hotel, one of California's oldest. The honky-tonk piano player, singing about a miner, '49er, and his daughter Clementine, seems rather tame though, compared to what Dame Shirley saw in 1852:

> The scene, from the description I have had of it must have been a complete illustration of the fable of Circe and her fearful transformations. Some of these bacchanals were among the most respectable and respected men upon the river. Of course, poker and euchre, whist and nine-pins, to say nothing of monte and faro, are now in constant requisition. But as a person would starve to death on *toujours des perdrix,* so a man cannot *always* be playing cards.

Today, low-ball is played in a shady-looking back-room parlor. Jackson, it seems, hasn't entirely lost its colorful reputation.

The early citizens were an intransigent lot. When Mokelumne Hill was declared the county seat (the vote count substantially exceeded the population), Jacksonites simply formed a new county, naming it after a local miner, José María Amador. In the 1970s local merchants stripped the stucco and aluminum siding off store-fronts and found gold rush-era brick. Iron shutters were repaired; the tin awnings over the sidewalks were gussied up. When merchants pulled up linoleum, they found oiled-wood floors. Antique stores soon moved into spaces vacated when the hairdresser and the druggist escaped to the outlying shopping centers. Those tubular steel barstools that Joseph Henry Jackson so detested were replaced with "period" furniture. Jackson too is a tourist town.

The hoisting gear of the Argonaut and Kennedy mines form a brooding backdrop to the city. The Kennedy (the **Amador County Museum** has a working model of its gallus frame) was the deepest in North America, plunging more than a mile straight down into the earth. Forty-seven miners died in a fire in the Argonaut in 1922. Symbolically, the nearby **Kennedy Tailing Wheels** have become the visual signature of the Mother Lode. Toxic-waste cleanup, it turns out, is not a new phenomenon. In 1912 the state legislature decreed that mines could no longer dump their tailings into creek beds, but instead must impound them at a place where they could be safely treated. To lift the debris into flumes, four giant belt-driven wooden wheels were constructed, each powered by a twenty-five-horsepower motor. When the mine closed in 1942, the buildings in which they stood were torn down, revealing the handsome sixty-foot-diameter wheels. Now owned by the city, two have fallen down, their wooden spokes littering the grassy hillside. But two still stand near Jackson Gate Road, favored by photographers seeking to capture the gold-rush image.

Recreational Facilities

✔✔ **Gate House Inn** Victorian 5-unit B&B. 1330 Jackson Gate Road, Jackson, CA 95642. (209) 223-3500.

✔✔ **Windrose Inn** 4-room Victorian farmhouse. 1407 Jackson Gate Road, Jackson, CA 95642. (209) 223-3650.

✔✔ **Ann Marie's Country Inn** 5-room B&B. 410 Stasal Street, Jackson, CA 95642. (209) 223-1452.

✔✔ **Broadway Hotel** 15-room B&B. 225 Broadway, Jackson, CA 95642. (209) 223-3503.

✔✔ **Court Street Inn** 7-room B&B. 215 Court Street, Jackson, CA 95642. (209) 223-0416.

✔✔ **The Wedgewood Inn** 6-room Victorian B&B. 11941 Narcissis Rd., Jackson, CA 95642. (209) 296-4300.

✔✔ **National Hotel** Famous old hotel, bar, and restaurant. 35 rooms, some with private bath. 2 Walker Street, Jackson, CA 95642. (209) 223-0500.

✔ **Best Western Amador Inn** Restaurant, bar, and 120-room motel. P.O. Box 758, Jackson, CA 95642. (209) 223-0970.

✔ **El Campo Cassa Resort Motel** 1930s Spanish-style auto court. 12548 Kennedy Flat Rd., Jackson, CA 95642. (209) 223-0100.

● **The Balcony** Continental restaurant. (209) 223-2855.

● **Buscaglia's** Italian restaurant and bar on Jackson Gate Road. (209) 223-9992.

● **Teresa's** Italian restaurant and bar across the street from Buscaglia's. (209) 223-1786.

MOKELUMNE HILL/SAN ANDREAS

> *Oh, what was your name in the States?*
> *Was it Thompson, or Johnson, or Bates?*
> *Did you murder your wife*
> *And then run for your life?*
> *Say, what was your name in the States?*

Jackson welcomed the *filles de joie,* but **Mokelumne Hill** (population 950; elevation 1,474 feet) had the bad guys. In a lawless time it was the most lawless town in the Mother Lode. Hinten Helper, who came here in 1855, wrote:

[I know of] no country in which there was so much corruption, villainy, outlawry, intemperance, licentiousness, and every variety of crime, folly and meanness. This abominable land of concentrated rascality can and does furnish the best bad things that are obtainable in America

Everybody got along when the pickin's were easy, but as the gold became scarcer, the Argonauts became more irascible. Racism was rampant. When some South Americans were accused of claim jumping, the so-called Chilean War broke out. Later the "French War" was fought for similar reasons. It is said that one man was killed each week for seventeen weeks, and later, five men were done in during a single week. Young men came west to find their fortune but instead met their maker. Grieving families sent money to erect monuments at places they would never see. A gravestone near San Andreas reads:

HERE REST THE REMAINS OF
WILLIAM A. SAMSON
AND
ROBERT EDES BRADSHAW
AGED 21 YEARS
BOTH OF CHARLESTOWN, MASSACHUSETTS.
THEY WERE CRUELLY MURDERED AT THE
CHILEAN GULCH, JULY 18, 1851,
BY THREE MEXICAN ASSASSINS
FOR THE SAKE OF GOLD

Ten men were strung up on the great oak at Mokelumne Hill. On at least one occasion they hanged the wrong man. Enos Christman recalled that a posse, feeling obliged to inform a young lady of her new widowhood, said rather cheerfully: "We just hanged Jim for horse-thieving, but come to find out 'twarnt him who done it, so I guess the joke's on us." There were bamboozlers too, including a bunch who thought up the bright idea of salting a worthless coyote hole with gold dust fired from a borrowed cannon. The scheme might have worked, but the cannon exploded and there weren't enough survivors to repeat the experiment.

Not all who escaped the hangman's tree went scot-free. Justice of the Peace R. C. Barry, demonstrating skills more judicial than literary, wrote:

Sentenced injun Bill to pay 32 dolars and pay for the remada and contents, in defalt to be comited to gaol 60 days and be floged 30 times on his bear back. Costs of Coort, 32 dolars, all of wich was pade by some one.

Today, Mokelumne Hill is a quiet town, with little to interest the tourist.

The old courthouse in **San Andreas** (population 2,150; elevation 1,008 feet) is now the wonderful **Calaveras County Museum,** one of the best around. Black Bart (see Knight of the Road, below) was tried and convicted of robbery in the upstairs courtroom and spent some time out back in the sinister-looking jail house. The gold rush's greatest hoax occurred here. The name Calaveras has several origins: "crazy people," dare-devils," and Spanish for "skulls," any one of which could have inspired the deed. Whether they were E Clampus Vitus brothers we do not know, but some miners stole a human skull from a dentist's office, proclaiming that they had unearthed it while working their mine. Insisting it was of Pliocene origin, this conniving bunch duped the great geologist Josiah Whitney (of Mt. Whitney fame) into certifying its authenticity. It wasn't the first time this pompous man was wrong, but it was the most embarrassing. Bret Harte kept the story alive with the poem *To the Pliocene Skull,* which begins:

> *Speak, O man, less recent! Fragmentary fossil!*
> *Primal pioneer of pliocene formation,*
> *Hid in lowest drifts below the earliest stratum*
> *Of volcanic tufa!*

> *Older than the beasts, the oldest Palæotherium;*
> *Older than the trees, the oldest Cryptogami;*
> *Older than the hills, those infantile eruptions*
> *Of earth's epidermis!*

Knight of the Road

He never fired a shot—dressed as he was, with an eyehole-pierced flower sack over his head, he was threatening enough—and he chose his locations well: the top of a hill where the horses would be at a walk. Black Bart, who signed his name P.O. 8, was the "poet laureate of outlawry," California's favorite knight of the road. Twenty-eight times he held up a stage. Twenty-eight times the gold in the strong-box was replaced with doggerel.

I rob the rich to feed the poor
Which hardly is a sin;
A widow ne'er knocked at my door
But what I let her in
So blame me not for what I've done
I don't deserve your curses
And if for any cause I'm hung
Let it be for my verses!

But he cut his hand when trying to open the box on the stage from Sonora and left behind the handkerchief he had used to succor the wound. A laundry mark led Pinkerton's men to San Francisco, where they found Charles E. Bolton living a quiet middle-class life. A Wells, Fargo & Co "Special Officers Report" said of him:

He is well informed on current topics; cool, self-contained, a sententious talker, with waggish tendencies; and since his arrest has, upon several occasions exhibited genuine wit, under most trying circumstances. He is neat and tidy in dress, highly respectable in appearance, and extremely proper and polite in behavior, chaste in language, eschews profanity, and has never been known to gamble, other than buying pools on horse races and speculating in mining stocks.

Sentenced to San Quentin, Bolton was released early on condition that he commit no more crimes, meaning, as he himself put it, he would write no more poems. I asked Ruth Matson at the Calavaras Historical Society what became of him. "Nobody knows for sure," she replied, "but Judge J. A. Smith, who sat on this bench for many years, insists he was pensioned by Wells Fargo on the condition that he rob no more stages."

Recreational Facilities

🗸🗸 **The Robin's Nest** 9-room Victorian B&B. 247 St. Charles Street, San Andreas, CA 95249. (209) 754-1076.

🗸 **Black Bart Inn** 40-room hotel and motel. 55 St. Charles Street, San Andreas, CA 95249. (209) 754-3808.

MURPHYS • Population 1,183; elevation 2,171 feet

George Hearst, father of the publisher William Randolph, got his start at **Sheep Ranch** after having walked across the country in 1850. With his partner James Ben Ali Haggin, he invested in Virginia City, amassed a great fortune, and then parlayed it into an even larger one in Montana. Today derelict autos strew the countryside around Sheep Ranch; the handsome hotel, though in good physical shape, is closed.

Murphys is a bit larger than Volcano, a town it resembles. The little park next to a stream is a nice place for a picnic, but most tourists just wander about, enjoying the special sense of ruralness this place seems to evoke. E Clampus Vitus has claimed the side of one ancient building as the "Wall of Comparative Ovations." Small plaques honor many of the heroes (and not quite heroes) we have met on this sojourn: Snowshoe Thompson, Jedediah Smith, Jim Beckworth, Emma Nevada, James Clyman, Bret Harte, Julia Bulette, and Lola Montez. A little **museum** is inside. The Murphys Hotel has gone upscale in the last decade. Though the bathrooms are still down the hall, they have been modernized and the bedroom doors now have locks, and the old-fashioned bedsteads have mattresses, not hair-filled ticks. You register at a proper lobby, not with the bartender, and a cash register has replaced the cigar box where the money used to be kept. Each room is named for a famous guest: Horatio Alger, Henry Ward Beecher, John Pierpont Morgan, Thomas Lipton, and Ulysses S. Grant (whose room is left open for inspection). Will Rogers made a movie here in 1934.

Several premium wineries have sprung up, including Stevenot, located in a little hollow. The tasting room occupies a sod-roofed miner's cabin. We're adjacent to Tuolumne County, a name that means "cave people," so it is not surprising to find limestone caves in the area. Mercer Caverns, Moaning Cavern (where you can use a rope to rappel to the bottom), and California Caverns (all charge a fee) are within a few miles of Murphys.

Recreational Facilities

✔✔ **Dunbar House** 5-room Victorian B&B. 271 Jones Street, Murphys, CA 95247. (209) 728-2897.

✔✔ **Murphys Hotel** 9 rooms in historic hotel. 20 modern rooms in adjacent motel. Bar and restaurant. P.O. Box 1375, Murphys, CA 95247. (209) 728-3444.

§ **Forest Meadows Golf Course** 18 holes. (209) 728-3446.

ANGELS CAMP • Population 3,300; elevation 1,379 feet

Mark Twain came to Angels Camp because, as legend has it, he had a difference with the San Francisco police that made it prudent to absent himself from the city until the memory of the affair grew dim. It was fortuitous; while hanging out at the Metropolitan Hotel he overheard a story about a frog. *The Celebrated Jumping Frog of Calaveras County,* originally published in a letter to Artemus Ward, established his reputation and made him rich. It also established Angels Camp's modest tourist industry. The town's Jumping Frog Jubilee, held in the spring, attracts tens of thousands. Contestants, who either bring their own frogs or rent them here, bet on how far they can jump. Rosie the Ribeter currently holds the record (twenty-one feet, five and three-quarters inches), but there were foul plans afoot. One Andy Koffman journeyed to Cameroon, West Equatorial Africa, where he discovered some giant super frogs *(Conrana goliath),* weighing more than eight pounds and able to leap thirty feet in a single bound (the competition combines three jumps). Officials complained that these hurtling carnivores (they eat mice) might jump off the thirty-five-foot stage, injuring who knows how many innocent spectators. Alas, of the three that were entered in the contest, two were disqualified and the third, a handsome brute named Jonnie Carson, placed sixty-third. "It must have been the hot weather," Koffman sputtered.

The town was named, not for the heavenly host, but for one George Angel, a fellow who mined with the Murphy brothers. A nice **museum** is located at the north end of town. At nearby **Carson Hill,** miners dug a hole about the size of the automobile you're driving, and for their efforts, walked away with $5 million in gold. One nugget was described as being too big for a mule to carry, the size of a huge crab, with legs seven inches across, weighing either ninety-five or a hundred and ninety-five pounds (or ounces), depending on what source you believe. The event might well have been the one that elicited Bayard Taylor's 1850 observation:

> Weather-beaten tars, wiry, delving Irishmen, and stalwart forest-ers from the wilds of Missouri became a race of sybarites and epicureans. It was no unusual thing to see a company of these men, who had never before had a thought of luxury beyond a good beefsteak and a glass of whiskey, drinking their champagne at ten dollars a bottle, and eating their tongue and sardines, or warming in the smoky camp-kettle their tin canisters of turtle soup and lobster salad.

Today, Carson Hill is nothing but a collection of rather junky houses.

Recreational Facilities

✔✔ **Utica Mansion Inn** Restaurant and 3 suites in an historic inn. 1090 Utica Lane, Angels Camp, CA 95222. (209) 736-4209.

✔✔ **Cooper House** 3-room B&B. 1184 Church Street, Angels Camp, CA 95222. (209) 736-2145.

✔ **Gold Country Inn** 28-unit motel. P.O. Box 188, Angels Camp, CA 95222. (209) 736-4611.

Locals claim that Mark Twain lived in a house on **Jackass Hill.** Maybe, but what is there now hardly seems believable. It's better to head straight away to Columbia (Chapter 19), which, although pushing credibility too, is a lot more fun.

◄◄◄◄◄◆ 19 ◆►►►►►

THE SOUTHERN MINES

Golden Hills

Afar the bright Sierras lie
A swaying line of snowy white,
A fringe of heaven hung in sight
Against the blue base of the sky.

I look along each gaping gorge,
I hear a thousand sounding strokes
Like giants rending giant oaks,
Or brawny Vulcan at his forge;
I see pick-axes flash and shine
And great wheels whirling in a mine.
Here winds a thick and yellow thread,
A moss'd and silver stream instead;
And trout that leap'd its rippled tide
Have turn'd upon their sides and died.

JOAQUIN MILLER

"There's gold in them thar hills" was true in 1849, but it is no longer. Today the gold is upon the hills; California, the Golden State, describes the land, not what is under it. Ironically, early on

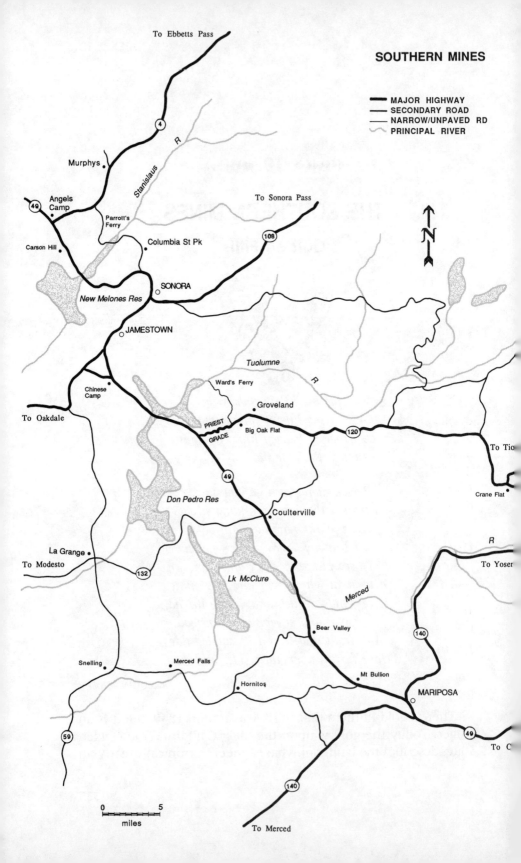

the opposite was true. The Mother Lode stayed green most of the year. But settlers brought European grasses, which have taken over; in this climate, they green-up in November and turn tawny in April. It is not the only instance when the state marches to a different drummer, but it is a spectacular one. A green California looks kind of funny—golden hills seem just right.

There is no boundary to the Southern Mines that anyone can agree on, but once you cross the Stanislaus River you're there. Columbia calls itself the "Gem of the Southern Mines," Sonora claims to be its Queen. Whether you cross at Parrott's Ferry on the back road from Murphys or at Melones on Highway 49, you can't even find the river, thanks to the Army Corps of Engineers. River runners, realizing that a precious resource was about to be inundated, got angry. When the gates to the New Melones Dam (Mexicans found nuggets as big as melon seeds, thus the name) were closed in 1978, Mark Dubois, a member of the "Save the Stan" committee, chained himself to a rock in a hidden location downstream from Parrott's Ferry. He announced that he would stay and drown rather than see this white-water paradise despoiled. His dramatic gesture saved the river for two years, but despite efforts by the Jerry Brown administration, river lovers lost. Now, at the best of times, the lake is just one more reservoir of the couple of dozen that grace the lower foothills. At the worst, during droughts, its a naked, bathtub-ringed, silt-engulfed gully. (All the low-lying reservoirs west of Highway 49 have extensive boating and RV facilities.)

COLUMBIA • Population 950; elevation 2,143 feet

A "Colonial Williamsburg" scene with a "Wild West" theme, most of the mining camp at Columbia is now **Columbia State Historic Park,** a re-creation of yesteryear, where saloons, restaurants, and shops are made to look like they did in the 1860s; where innkeepers and salespeople wear the costumes of that nostalgic age. A stagecoach, pulled by a four-mule team, rumbles up Columbia Street; children go horseback riding on nearby trails. Blacksmiths smith, fiddlers fiddle, and banjoists strum while folks belly up to the bar for a shot of red-eye at the St. Charles Saloon. There is a livery stable and a Chinese herb shop, two firehouses, a "Cheap Cash Store," and a gaslight theater.

Volunteer firemen come from all over to pump antique rigs, vintage-car enthusiasts parade their machines and compete for prizes. Children pan for "color" in a horse trough filled with gravel and salted mostly with feldspar (fool's gold). Visitors tour a "real mine" with a bearded fellow dressed like "the old prospector." On one visit I was pleased to see the streets apparently returned to dirt, but it turned out that a movie company had raided the local sawmill for wood chips to hide the pavement while they were shooting their film.

The Wells Fargo office is the most photographed building in town, a two-story beauty with windows and doors secured by somber painted iron doors. A nearby building exhibits ceremonial regalia of the Native Sons of the Golden West. Notably absent is reference to a well-known ditty:

> *The miners came in forty-nine,*
> *The whores in fifty-one.*
> *And when they got together,*
> *They produced the native son.*

The so-called miner's house the state has reconstructed here seemed to me to be a bit upscale, hardly fitting the descriptions handed down by those who lived in them. Horace Snow, a fellow who mined near Mariposa, wrote to his friend Charlie:

Our cabin is divided into two parts, inside and out. The inside being all in one room and also the out. What we lose here in one point we gain in another. Now, in America, you use wood for floors, which decays and has to be repaired, but we have a slab from Mother Earth, durable and always in its place.

Dame Shirley described her only window:

Three feet in length of a log on one side of the room is removed and glass jars inserted in its place; and the space around the necks of said jars being filled with clay.

Every single Gold Rush town burned at least once, and no wonder. Mark Twain's friend J. Ross Browne was dumbfounded:

The variety of material used in the construction of chimneys is wonderful. Stone, wood, scraps of sheet-iron, adobe-bricks, mud, whisky-barrels, nail-kegs, and even canvas, are the component parts. Think of a canvas chimney! How an Insurance Agent would stare at it!

Columbia is a great place to spend the night. Skilled craftsmen refurbished the inside of the Fallon Hotel, doing such a remarkable job that you feel like you're staying at the Ritz. The City Hotel reflects a more republican atmosphere (the bathrooms are down the hall), but the upstairs sitting room, with its velvet sofas and overstuffed chairs, is a nice place to be with friends. The bar is boisterous and the restaurant excellent. Columbia Actor's Repertory performs year-round at the **Fallon Theater.**

Recreational Facilities

✔✔ **City Hotel** Historic hotel, restaurant, and bar. 9 rooms. P.O. Box 1870, Columbia, CA 95310. (209) 532-1479.

✔✔ **Fallon Hotel** 14 rooms in refurbished historic hotel. 11175 Washington Street, Columbia, CA 95310. (209) 532-1470.

✔ **Columbia Inn Motel** 21 units. P.O. Box 298, Columbia, CA 95310. (209) 533-0446.

SONORA • Population 3,247; elevation 1,796 feet

The stage rattles you impetuously through the one long street which makes the principal part of the town. It is still the county town; and it has many signs of former importance; four churches, for instance, "but two of them don't go," explained an old resident to me; a jail—but it was empty, and, as it seemed to me, with my Eastern eyes, an endless vista of barrooms or "saloons" and restaurants; all, seemingly, like the jail, empty.

The Sonora of today is a bit more lively than what Charles Nordhoff saw in 1873, for it is the commercial center for the southern mines. The downtown, now free of Sierra-bound traffic (a bypass was built), has a wonderfully refreshing small-town-America feel, but you get a sense of the gold rush too, for many of the steep streets are lined with Victorian houses and the handsome Tuolumne County Courthouse reflects an earlier time. The jail, now a **museum,** is proud of its collection of Virgil West cowboy paintings, but I found the shop equipment of H. H. Rowell, Gunmaker, more interesting. A ditty explains why the miner considered the rifle his most useful tool:

> *Fear ye not what e'er his size,*
> *Have trust in me, I'll equalize!*

Recreational Facilities

✔✔ **La Casa Inglesa** 5 rooms in a new English tudor-style country inn. 18047 Lime Kiln Road, Sonora, CA 95370. (209) 532-5822.

✔✔ **Barretta Gardens Inn** 4-room farmhouse B&B. 700 South Barretta Street, Sonora, CA 95370. (209) 532-6039.

✔✔ **Gunn House B&B** Historic hotel. 25 rooms. 286 South Washington Street, Sonora, CA 95370. (209) 532-3421.

✔✔ **Lavender Hill B&B** 3-room Victorian B&B. 683 South Barretta Street, Sonora, CA 95370. (209) 532-9024.

✔✔ **Lulu Belle's** 4-room Victorian B&B. 85 Gold Street, Sonora, CA 95370. (209) 533-3455.

✔✔ **Oak Hill Ranch** 5-room B&B. P.O. Box 307, Tuolumne, CA 95379. (209) 828-4717.

✔✔ **The Ryan House** 4-room B&B. 153 South Shepherd Street, Sonora, CA 95370. (209) 533-3445.

✔✔ **Serenity** 4-room country B&B. P.O. Box 3484, Sonora, CA 95370. (209) 533-1441.

✔✔ **Sonora Inn** Historic Spanish-colonial downtown hotel and motel. Bar and restaurant. 160 South Washington Street, Sonora, CA 95370. (209) 532-7468.

✔✔ **Willow Springs B&B** 4-room country B&B. 20599 Kings Court, Soulsbyville, CA 95372. (209) 533-2030.

✔ **Best Western Sonora Oaks** 70-unit motel. 19551 Hess Avenue, Sonora, CA 95370. (209) 533-4400.

✔ **Sonora Towne House Motel** 112 units. 350 S. Washington Street, Sonora, CA 95370. (209) 532-2633.

● **Hemingways Cafe & Restaurant** (209) 532-4900.

● **La Tore** Italian restaurant. (209) 533-9181.

JAMESTOWN • Population 2,206; elevation 1,405 feet

Tiny Jamestown (locally, Jimtown), perhaps taking a lesson from Sutter Creek, has transformed itself into a fine tourist spot, boasting three renovated hotels, several good restaurants, and a couple of dozen antique shops. I was absorbed by the spiel of a bearded, jeans-clad huckster who was promoting his gold-panning trips with a video, set out on the sidewalk. People were signing up for two-hour lessons in gold pan, crevice hook, and suction gun operation and for special helicopter trips into remote stream bars.

High Noon, Little House on the Prairie, Petticoat Junction all featured images of a steam train puffing through the Wild West, and they were all shot here. The State of California purchased the ancient rolling stock, including it in a park called **Railtown 1897.** Steam excursions are offered on six miles of track, and the roundhouse is open for inspection.

Recreational Facilities

✔✔ **Jamestown Hotel** Historic hotel, bar, restaurant, and 8 rooms. P.O. Box 539, Jamestown, CA 95327. (209) 984-3902.

✔✔ **National Hotel** Historic hotel, bar, restaurant, and 11 rooms. P.O. Box 502, Jamestown, CA 95327. (209) 984-3446.

✔✔ **The Palm Hotel B&B** 9 rooms. 10382 Willow Street, Jamestown, CA 95327. (209) 984-5271.

✔✔ **Royal Hotel B&B** 19-room 1920s hotel. P.O. Box 209, Jamestown, CA 95327. (209) 984-5271.

§ **Railtown 1897** Steam-train excursions. Fifth Avenue, Jamestown, CA 95327. (209) 984-3953.

Ω **Gold Prospecting Expeditions** Gold-panning outfitter. P.O. Box 974, Jamestown, CA 95327. (209) 984-4653.

BIG OAK FLAT/GROVELAND

The first town south of Jamestown is **Chinese Camp** (population 175), site of one of California's worst tong wars (see That Heathen Chinee, below). It is now little more than a wide spot in the road.

That Heathen Chinee

Which I wish to remark—
And my language is plain—
That for ways that are dark
And for tricks that are vain,
The heathen Chinee is peculiar,
Which the same I would rise to explain.

Ah Sin was his name;
And I shall not deny
In regard to the same
What that name might imply,
But his smile it was pensive and child-like
As I frequently remarked to Bill Nye.

Bret Harte's famous poem spoke of the Chinese in the deprecating terms of his day. Even the state, as Mark Twain observed, was not above pure racism:

He gets a living out of old mining claims that white men have abandoned as exhausted and worthless— and then the officers come down on him once a month with an exorbitant swindle to which the legislature has given the broad, general name of "foreign mining tax," but it is usually inflicted on no foreigners but Chinamen.

The tax was $20 a month, $15 for the state and $5 for the sheriff. Despite the handicap, in 1851 one of every

ten Californian miners, 25,000 in all, were Chinese. (The 1860 census listed the names of Asians, South Americans, blacks, prostitutes—but no Indians.) Asians were called *Gum Shan Hok,* meaning "guests of the Golden Mountain," because they expected to return to their homes after they became rich. Few did. A tong war erupted in 1861 when the Sam Yaps battled the Yan Woos in a skirmish that cost four lives and produced a dozen wounded.

When the gold gave out, the Chinese hired on to build the transcontinental railroad, where they once again proved their industriousness (Chapter 1). But they remained segregated. Most eventually moved to San Francisco's Chinatown, where their progeny have slowly become part of the establishment.

As you drive south, the Sierra foothills begin to take on a pronounced escarpment, nowhere near as grand as on the east side, of course, but nevertheless quite impressive, as Clarence King observed:

> Miles of chaparral tangle in dense growth over walls and spurs, covering with kindly olive-green the starring red of riven mountainside and gashed earth.

Highway 120 climbs this scarp on the notorious Priest Grade (William Priest collected tolls in the old days), a wiggly, six-mile, narrow bit of road that Yosemite-bound motorists have learned to hate. (The Old Priest Grade, which knowledgeable drivers take, is half as long but twice as steep.) Highway 49 continues south, passing Moccasin, the principal power house for the Hetch Hetchy system.

The big oak at **Big Oak Flat** (population 500; elevation 2,800 feet), said to be thirteen feet through, toppled when miners found gold under its roots. Today, the town is remembered for having given its name to the main road into Yosemite, and for little else. For much the same reasons that Hangtown is now Placerville, residents of nearby Garotte (the "e" is pronounced) changed the name of their pleasant village to **Groveland** (population 350). The bat-wing doors of the Iron Door Saloon first swung open in

1852 and, the bartender told me, except during Prohibition it has been a boozing palace ever since. A number of other interesting buildings line the main street. There was a Second Garotte, too, which required the citizens at the other one to add First to their name. But it's mostly gone, replaced by a retirement community called **Pine Mountain Lake,** built around a reservoir bearing that rather innocuous name.

"Champagne-class white water," is what one outfitter calls the **Tuolumne River,** and most would agree. Exercising no small amount of hyperbole, another says:

> The Tuolumne thunders through a grand succession of boulder gardens and spectacular cascades. Voluptuously steep, plunging this way and that, it moves in patterns that are frolicsome, tangled and mesmerizing.

The "T," as enthusiasts call it, is the most challenging commercially run white-water river in California. The section between Meral's Pool and the Ward's Ferry bridge has been declared "Wild and Scenic," meaning that no roads will ever be built in this canyon. Outfitters grudgingly run the section in two days but recommend three, the better to capture its pristine magic.

Recreational Facilities

✔✔ **Buck Meadow Lodge** Restaurant and rooms. 7647 Highway 120, Groveland, CA 95321. (209) 962-6366.

✔✔ **Berkshire Inn** New 6 room B&B. P.O. Box 207, Groveland, CA 95321. (209) 962-6744.

§ **Pine Mountain Golf Course** 18 holes. (209) 962-7883.

Ω **OARS** Rafting outfitter. P.O. Box 67, Angels Camp, CA 95222. (209) 736-4677.

Ω **Whitewater Voyages** Rafting outfitter. P.O. 906, El Sobrante, CA 94803. (415) 222-5994.

Ω **Zephyr River Expeditions** Rafting outfitter. P.O. Box 510, Columbia, CA 95310. (209) 532-6249.

COULTERVILLE • Population 500; elevation 1,740 feet

Sonora got its name because so many of the miners came from Mexico's Sonoran Desert, but the name is appropriate for another reason. South of the Tuolumne the gold country takes on an arid character, treeless and scrubby, but not without interest. The entire business section of **Coulterville,** forty-odd buildings, is on the National Register of Historic Places. A diminutive locomotive called *Whistling Billy* has long been the town's signature, but the quiet, almost spooky, gold rush-era sidewalks seem more appropriate. The old Jeffery Hotel, sporting adobe walls three feet thick, looks quite in place, as does the former Wells Fargo office, which now houses the **Northern Mariposa County History Center.** Featured is the Studebaker wagon that Gary Cooper drove in "High Noon." Wells Fargo, of course, ran the stages, but their banking operations were equally important. A local miner explained:

> Have I told you anything about our currency here? It consists of just as many denominations as there are languages spoken. The majority of the Gold coin is American but nine-tenths of the silver is foreign. There are no cents and but very few half-dimes. Therefore the smallest piece of money is the dime. In purchasing goods, anything is sold by the bits worth—12½ cents. One dime passes for a bit and four of them will buy just as much as a half dollar. Change in some places is scarce, but as all merchants buy gold dust and weigh as small sums as a bit, there is but little trouble.

The Magnolia Saloon is the quintessential Old West watering hole, with oiled-wood floors, a carved hardwood back-bar, and smoke-stained beer signs nailed up on the walls. But you no longer can pay for your whiskey with dust. The Sun Sun Wo Co. Store, built in 1851, continued as a grocery for nearly a hundred years. As to the merchandise generally available, one observer wrote:

> The store is the most comical *olla podrida* of heterogeneous merchandise that I ever saw, though the *quality* of his goods, it must be confessed, is sometimes rather equivocal.

Prices were exorbitant, as another lamented:

The merchant, when told that men find from $16 to $100 a day, very readily concludes they can easily pay $1 for a pound of potatoes, or $2 for a pound of dried apples, as in the state of New York they can pay half a cent for the former or four cents for the latter.

Given the Mexican flavor of this area, I was not surprised to learn that the bandit Joaquín Murieta had his hideout nearby (see below).

Brigand Chief of California

They say he began his bloody career when his wife was ravished, his brother (unjustly accused of horse stealing) hanged, and he himself flogged. In 1859, the *California Police Gazette* published an article titled, "The Life of Joaquin Murieta," and the bandit became famous, the Robin Hood of the new El Dorado. Historians believe that it was mostly nonsense, that every unsolved crime in the Mother Lode was laid at his feet, and that, if anything, there were three Joaquíns about, terrorizing the land. Nevertheless, the stories of his exploits are fun, one of which made its way into the Federal Writer's Project book, *California.*

One night the desperado sat in Zumwalt Saloon, unrecognized and calmly playing cards. The talk got round to him, as it often did. Flushed with courage and Bourbon, a young miner named Jack slapped a sack of gold on the table and cried, "Here's $500 which says that I can kill that _____ Murieta, if I ever come face to face with him!" Onto the table leaped Joaquín, a pistol in each hand. "I am Murieta. Now is your chance!" No one made a move; he calmly strode out of the saloon and rode into the dark.

So terrorized did the state become that the legislature voted a $1000 bounty on the bad man's head. Captain Harry Love of Texas rode west, killed a Mexican (maybe Joaquin, maybe not), and claimed the prize. Also slain in the shootout was Joaquín's lieutenant, the notorious Manuel ("Three-Fingered Jack") Garcia, a fellow who had established a reputation for "stringing up Orientals by their queues or wrenching heads back with a deft

twist of the queue, to slit the throat." Given the side-show nature of the episode, it is not surprising than an opportunist of the day pickled their remains and put them on tour. A giant poster announced the event:

WILL BE
EXHIBITED
FOR ONE DAY ONLY

AT THE STOCKTON HOUSE
THE HEAD
OF THE RENOWNED BANDIT
JOAQUIN!
AND THE
HAND OF THREE FINGERED JACK!

Recreational Facilities

🖊🖊 **Jeffery Hotel** 1850s fandango hall now a restaurant, saloon, and 20-room hotel. 1 Main Street, Coulterville, CA 95311. (209) 878-3035.

🖊 **Yosemite American Inn** 8-unit motel. P.O. Box 265, Coulterville, CA 95311. (209) 878-3407.

MARIPOSA • Population 1,150; elevation 1,953 feet

It is ironic that anger would produce such a pretty name (the *S.S. Mariposa* was one of the most luxurious ships to sail the South Pacific), but when a swarm of pesky butterflies invaded his camp (one lodged itself in a soldier's ear, causing great discomfort), General José Joaquin Moraga testily named the place Arroyo de las Mariposas. Mariposa calls itself the "Mother of Counties," since at one time it encompassed nearly a fifth of California. Today, fewer than 15,000 people live within its borders (there are twice as many cows); there is only one public high school and not a single incorporated city. Most of the land lies within Yosemite National Park, where more people live year-around than do in Mariposa, the county seat.

Highway 49 has a time of it crossing the lower canyon of the Merced (Spanish for "mercy"). The wiggly road drops steeply to a place that early settlers called Hell's Hollow, "a cañon whose profound uninterestingness is quite beyond portrayal," according to Clarence King. It then climbs an equally steep grade to gain the rolling, pastoral country around the hamlet of **Bear Valley** (population 230; elevation 2,050 feet). John Charles Frémont had a bit of good fortune when he came into possession of *Las Mariposas*, a 44,000-acre (10-square-league) tract that more or less straddled Bear Valley. The mansion he built is gone, however, and in the nearby town there is little left save for the Simpson & Trabucco store and the Odd Fellows hall. The hamlet of **Mount Bullion** was named for Frémont's father-in-law (see below).

The Pathfinder

Looking out over the entrance to San Francisco Bay, Frémont wrote:"To this gate I gave the name of *Chrysopolæ*, or Golden Gate." It was one of his better accomplishments. His sobriquet was "Pathfinder," a nickname that historian George Stewart, in a left-handed sort of way, thought appropriate:

Frémont found no roads, no highways, not even any trails of consequence—only paths.

He earned a romantic place in the history books, even though many of his adventures were at best foolhardy and he seems to have had a knack for being on the wrong side of an issue. Most give credit for his notoriety to his wife Jessie, the beautiful, smart, and, most of all, ambitious daughter of one of the most powerful men in the country, Senator Thomas Hart ("Old Bullion") Benton.

On his first expedition to the Rockies, Frémont climbed the peak that now carries his name and, with much bravado, proclaimed it to be the loftiest in the country. It wasn't even the highest in the Wind River Range. His second expedition (1843–1844) took him to Oregon, where he brashly announced that he would proceed to California. In a misguided attempt to find the so-called Buena Ventura River, he led the party down

the wrong side of the Sierra, where they might well have perished had the weather not been mild (Chapter 4). If Frémont had bothered to read Bonneville's map or Zenas Leonard's narrative, he would have known that no such river existed. His fourth expedition to the Rockies became a debacle when he recklessly attempted a wintertime crossing of the San Juan Range. John Charles retreated, losing eleven men.

His California adventures seem to have been star-crossed too. Returning in 1846, the Mexican governor promptly kicked him out. Fleeing to southern Oregon, a band of Indians attacked his party, forcing the only battle he ever led. The result: two Frémont men were lost (both Delawares), and fourteen Klamaths were killed the following morning in retribution. When a messenger from Washington caught up with the victors, informing them of impending war with Mexico, Frémont returned to California. Recruiting a ragtag battalion from the ranks of the ruffians who had perpetrated the Bear Flag Rebellion, he marched (and sailed) up and down the state, fought no battle, but propitiously intercepted Andrés Pico's defeated army at Cahuenga Pass, where he graciously accepted Pico's surrender. Forever after, he billed himself as the "Conqueror of California." Commodore Stockton named him governor, an appointment that General Stephen Watts Kearny (who was Frémont's superior officer) countermanded six weeks later. When Frémont refused to step down, Kearny had him arrested, put in irons, and removed to Washington, but his court martial conviction was later commuted by James K. Polk.

By a rather simple maneuver, Frémont became one of the few to make a fortune in the Mother Lode (which he later lost in worthless railroad stocks). It seems that when gold was discovered on some adjacent property, he simply moved the boundaries of his land to suit. *Las Mariposis* was laughingly called "the world's only floating Mexican land grant." Thanks to his political connections, he served for a short time as a senator from California and later, carrying the standard of the newly formed Republican Party, ran against James Buchanan. He lost.

Mariposa is a bit schizophrenic these days, wanting to show off its colorful history but finding itself rather inundated with travelers heading to Yosemite. History wins for those who take the time to visit the **Mariposa Museum,** a wonderful place, crowded with things old and interesting. Mariposans are also proud of their courthouse. Built in 1854 using square nails and dowels, it is the state's oldest still in use. But it was also the scene of some shameful goings on, especially when Judge J. J. Trabucco ruled:

> Indians, mulattos, blacks, Chinese and other Mongolians are as competent to present evidence [at trials] as whites.

But only so long as they were not testifying against whites. On another occasion a fellow named Jesus (we don't know his last name), was tried on Friday and found not guilty. The town was so incensed that they tried him again on Saturday and, double jeopardy be damned, convicted the hapless fellow. Mariposa is the new home of the **California State Mining and Mineral Museum,** a rockhound's Mecca. White-water rafting on the Merced River is popular in the spring, when the water is high.

Recreational Facilities

- ✔✔ **Boulder Creek B&B** 3-room country chalet. 4572 Ben Hur Road, Mariposa, CA 95338. (209) 742-7729.

- ✔✔ **Granny's Garden** 3-room Victorian B&B. 7333 Highway 49 North, Mariposa, CA 95338. (209) 377-8342.

- ✔✔ **Meadow Creek Ranch B&B** 4 rooms. 2669 Triangle Road, Mariposa, CA 95338. (209) 966-3843.

- ✔✔ **Oak Meadows Too** B&B. 5263 Highway 140 North, Mariposa, CA 95338. (209) 742-6161.

- ✔ **Best Western Yosemite Way Station** 78-unit motel. 4999 Highway 140, Mariposa, CA 95338. (209) 966-7545.

- ✔ **Mariposa Lodge** 37-unit old-fashioned motel. P.O. Box 733, Mariposa, CA 95338. (209) 966-3607.

- • **Charles Street Dinner House** (209) 966-2366.

HORNITOS • Population 200; elevation 980 feet

Mariposa marks the southern boundary of the Mother Lode, but I wanted to explore one other mining camp a bit northwest and well off the beaten path. Located as it is in a little dale, where the summer air hangs hot, it seemed to me a shame that the miners took this country away from the rattlesnakes. The land is too rocky to plow and, except for a few weeks in spring, too dry for cattle. And now, of course, the gold is gone. So Hornitos (Spanish for "little ovens") sleeps while its adobe walls crumble.

Faded letters painted on the wall of a two-story building proclaim: "Gagliardo & Co. General Merchandise," but the iron doors are rusted shut, the wooden sidewalk on the verge of collapse. It is impossible to tell if the cast-iron hand pump could still deliver water to the horse trough: the handle is broken off. So is the one for the glass-bulbed gasoline pump across the street. A redwood water tank sits atop a sturdy wooden frame, but many of the staves have fallen out. Nearby, a buckboard stands forlornly in a field. Only the squeak of an un-oiled Airmotor pump and the barking of a chained-up cur breaks the stillness. A handsome brass plate, bolted to the remnants of an adobe wall, reminds tourists that Domingo Ghiradelli, the San Francisco chocolate king, got his start here. But oddly, the sign for the saloon, the town's only going business, is a crudely written phrase, painted on the whitewash above the door and reading "No one under 21 allowed." The names carved on marble headstones in the pretty little graveyard are now mostly too faint to read. But there will be a new one. Roy's Cafe, its windows streaked with dirt, looked like it hadn't served a meal in years and now there was a hand-lettered notice in the window announcing that Roy's memorial service was to be held at the cemetery on February 3rd. E. Clampus Vitus has claimed the town's one-room jail for a shrine and erected a sign over the door which, in fractured Latin, expresses their motto: "I believe because it is absurd." In that sense Hornitos is believable.

All this put me in a reflective mood. What was the point of it all? Why did so many '49ers cross plain and desert, or brave the Panamanian jungle, for such little reward. Reading the correspondence of Horace Snow, I think I found an answer. In an early letter he wrote:

I have no funds at my command, no inclination to *settle down*, but feel like traveling, feel as though it might improve my health, pocket and perhaps character.

Subsequent letters revealed how well he fared:

How different are our wants in this great world. Take today, for instance; some wish credit, some be extensions of payments, some wish food, some honor, some power, some love, and some, more moderate than the rest, only wish a good clear "Tom" stream of water. Yes, give some a good tom stream of water and all other things will be added.

The pan when washed, the gold dried and weighed and, Charlie, how much do you reckon I had? Only the pitiable sum of $48.50!! Wasn't I tickled!

Returning to Massachusetts, he reflected:

I placed myself beyond the annoyance of Sheriffs and proved myself worth of trust, helped my father in his old age, cheered my sister who was learning the vest-making trade [and] laid up $100.

Who could ask for more?

FURTHER READING

PERSONAL ACCOUNTS

Austin, Mary. *Land of Little Rain*. New York: 1903. Reprint, Alburquerque: University of New Mexico Press, 1976.

Belden, Josiah. *Josiah Belden, 1841 California Overland Pioneer: His Memoir and Early Letters*, edited by Doyce B. Nunis, Jr. Georgetown, CA: The Talisman Press, 1962.

Bidwell, John. *The First Emigrant Train to California*. New York: *The Century Magazine*, 1890. Reprint, Sacramento: Department of Parks & Recreation, State of California, 1987.

Bigler, Henry William. *Bigler's Chronicle of the West*, compiled and edited by Erwin G. Gudde. Berkeley & Los Angeles: University of California Press, 1962.

Brewer, William H. *Up and Down California in 1860–1864*, edited by Francis P. Farquahr. New Haven: Yale University Press, 1930. Reprint, Berkeley: University of California Press, 1949.

Bryarly, Wakeman, and Vincent Geiger. *Trail to California*. New Haven: Yale University Press, 1945.

Bunnell, Lafayette. *Discovery of the Yosemite and the Indian War of 1851*. Chicago: Fleming & Revell Co., 1880. Reprint, edited by David M. Potter, Los Angeles: G. W. Gerlicher, 1911.

Carson, Kit. *Kit Carson's Autobiography*, edited by Milo Milton Quaife. Chicago: R. R. Donnelley & Sons, 1935. Reprint, Lincoln/London: University of Nebraska Press, 1966.

Chase, J. Smeaton. *Yosemite Trails*. Boston, Houghton Mifflin, 1911. Reprint, Palo Alto: Tioga Publishing Co., 1987.

Clappe, Louise (Dame Shirley). *The Shirley Letters from the California Mines 1851–1852, Marysville Herald*, 1851–1852. Reprint, Introduction and notes by Carl I. Wheat, New York: Ballantine Books, 1949.

Hutchings, James Mason. *Scenes of Wonder & Curiosity*. Hutchings & Rosenfeldt, 1860. Portions of *Hutching's California Magazine*

(1856–1861) reproduced and edited by R. R. Olmsted, Berkeley: Howell-North, 1962.

King, Clarence. *Mountaineering in the Sierra Nevada.* Boston: James Osgood & Co., 1872. Reprint, Lincoln: University of Nebraska Press, 1970.

LeConte, Joseph. *A Journal of Ramblings Through the High Sierra of California by the University Excursion Party.* San Francisco: Frances A. Valentine, 1875. Reprint, New York: Sierra Club/Ballantine Books, 1971.

Leonard, Zenas. *The Adventures of a Mountain Man: The Narrative of Zenas Leonard.* Clearfield, PA: 1839. Reprint, Norman: University of Oklahoma Press, 1978.

Muir, John. *My First Summer in the Sierra.* Dunwoody, GA: Norman S. Berg, 1911.

———. *The Mountains of California.* New York: Century Co., 1894. Reprint, New York: Dorset Press, 1988.

———. *Our National Parks.* Boston: Houghton Mifflin Co., 1916.

———. *The Yosemite.* New York: Century Co., 1912.

Nordhoff, Charles. *California for Travellers and Settlers.* Reprint, Berkeley: Ten Speed Press, 1973.

Preuss, Charles. *Exploring with Frémont,* translated and edited by Erwin G. and Elisabeth K. Gudde. Norman: University of Oklahoma Press, 1958.

Royce, Sarah. *A Frontier Lady,* edited by Ralph H. Gabriel. New Haven: Yale University Press, 1932.

Shallenberger, Moses. *The Opening of the California Trail,* edited by George R. Stewart. Berkeley and Los Angeles: University of California Press, 1953.

Snow, Horace. *Dear Charlie Letters.* Mariposa, CA: Mariposa County Historical Society, 1979.

Taylor, Bayard. *Eldorado.* G. P. Putman & Co., 1850. Reprint, Introduction by Robert Coleland. New York: Alfred A. Knopf, 1949.

Twain, Mark. *Roughing It.* New York: Harper & Bros., 1913.

HISTORY, NATURE, AND OUTDOORS

Chalfant, W. A. *Gold, Guns, & Ghost Towns.* Palo Alto: Stanford University Press, 1947.

Dilsaver, Lary M. and William C. Tweed *Challenge of the Big Trees.* Three Rivers, California: Sequoia Natural History Association, 1990.

Engbeck, Joseph H., Jr. *The Enduring Giants*. Sacramento: California Department of Parks and Recreation, 1973.

Farquhar, Francis P. *History of the Sierra Nevada*. Berkeley: University of California Press, 1965.

Fry, Watler, and John R. White *Big Trees*. Stanford: Stanford University Press, 1930.

Glasscock, C. B. *The Big Bonanza*. New York: Grosset & Dunlap, 1931.

Hinkle, George, and Bliss Hinkle. *Sierra-Nevada Lakes*. Indianapolis: Bobbs-Merrill, 1949. Reprint, Reno: University of Nevada Press, 1987.

Holliday, J. S. *The World Rushed In: The Gold-Rush as Seen Through the Diary of William Swain*. New York: Simon and Schuster, 1981.

Huth, Hans. *Nature and the American: Three Centuries of Changing Attitudes*. Berkeley and Los Angeles: University of California Press, 1957.

Jackson, Joseph Henry. *Anybody's Gold*. New York: D. Appleton-Century Co., Inc., 1941.

Jones, Chris. *Climbing in North America*. Berkeley and Los Angeles: University of California Press, 1976.

Kahrl, William L. *Water and Power*. Berkeley and Los Angeles: University of California Press, 1982.

Kraus, George. *High Road to Promontory: Building the Central Pacific Across the High Sierra*. Palo Alto: American West Publishing Co., 1969.

Krober, Theodora. *Ishi in Two Worlds*. Berkeley and Los Angeles: University of California Press, 1961.

Krober, Theodora, and Robert F. Heizer *Almost Ancestors: The First Californians*. San Francisco: Sierra Club, 1968.

Lee, W. Storrs. *The Sierra*. New York: G. P. Putnam's Sons, 1962.

Lewis, Oscar. *The Big Four: The Story of Huntington, Stanford, Hopkins, and Crocker, and of the Building of the Central Pacific*. New York: Alfred A. Knopf, 1938.

———. *High Sierra Country*. Boston: Little, Brown & Co., 1955. Reprint, Reno: University of Nevada Press,

Matthes, François Emile. *The Incomparable Valley: A Geologic Interpretation of the Yosemite*, edited by Fritiof Fryxell. Berkeley and Los Angeles: University of California Press, 1950.

———. *Sequoia National Park: A Geological Album*, edited by Fritiof Fryxell. Berkeley and Los Angeles: University of California Press, 1960.

O'Neill, Elizabeth Stone. *Meadow in the Sky: A History of Yosemite's*

Tuolumne Meadows Region. Fresno: Panorama West Books, 1984.

Peattie, Donald Culross. *The Sierra Nevada: The Range of Light,* edited by Roderick Peattie. New York: The Vanguard Press, 1947.

Reinhardt, Richard. *Out West on the Overland Train.* Palo Alto: American West Publishing Co., 1967.

Roth, Hal. *Pathway in the Sky: The Story of the John Muir Trail.* Berkeley: Howel North Books, 1965.

Sanborn, Margaret. *Yosemite Its Discovery, Its Wonders, and Its People.* New York: Random House, 1981.

Sargent, Shirley. *Yosemite & Its Innkeepers.* Yosemite: Flying Spur Press, 1975.

Scott, E. B. *The Saga of Lake Tahoe.* Lake Tahoe: Lake Tahoe Publishing Co., 1957.

Stewart, George R. *Ordeal by Hunger.* New York: Henry Holt, 1937.

———. *The California Trail: An Epic with Many Heroes.* New York: McGraw-Hill Book Company, 1962.

Strong, Douglas H. *Tahoe: An Environmental History.* Lincoln: University of Nebraska Press, 1984.

———. *Trees or Timber? The Story of Sequoia and Kings Canyon National Parks.* Three Rivers: Sequoia Natural History Association, 1986.

Williams, John H. *Yosemite and Its High Sierra.* San Francisco: John H. Williams, 1921.

INDEX